Computer-Aided
Experimentation

Computer-Aided Experimentation:
Interfacing to Minicomputers

Jules Finkel
Director, Computer Center
Weizmann Institute of Science

A WILEY-INTERSCIENCE PUBLICATION

JOHN WILEY & SONS New York ● London ● Sydney ● Toronto

Library of Congress Cataloging in Publication Data:

Finkel, Jules, 1932-
  Computer-aided experimentation

  "A Wiley-Interscience publication."
  Bibliography: p.
  Includes index.
    1. Computer input-output equipment. 2. Miniature
computers. 3. Electronic data processing—Science.
  I. Title.

TK7887.5.F53   001.6′44′04   74-22060
ISBN 0-471-25884-9

Printed in the United States of America

10 9 8 7 6 5 4 3 2 1

To Marilyn,
Howie, Meryl, Stuie
and in
Memory of my father

Preface

This book is based on a course in computer-aided experimentation given to scientists and graduate students at the Weizmann Institute of Science. The purpose of the course and of the book is to familiarize scientists and engineers with the basic concepts and techniques needed to specify, design, and implement experiments that are computer controlled.

It is my opinion that better science results when many of the tedious, time consuming jobs in data taking and parameter adjustment and variation are under the direction of a computer. Computer aided experimentation permits the design of experiments that are either extremely difficult or impossible without a computer because of the rate of data acquisition, the numbers of data to be collected, and the need to make adjustments on line in real time as a response to the direction the experiment is taking. When properly applied, computer aided experimentation relieves the scientist from the ordinary repetitive tasks and frees him to devote more of his time to creative activities.

This book describes the various components in a computer aided experiment. Suggested criteria for the selection of system elements are analyzed. Design techniques are described with many examples of practical connections being given.

This book is designed both as a textbook and as a quick refresher on particular topics. It can be read through one chapter after the other when used as a textbook. In this way a comprehensive picture of interface design is obtained. It can also be used as a means of familiarization with a topic out of sequence, since each chapter is designed to be readable as an independent entity without the need to refer to previous chapters. In this way the scientist or practicing engineer can become familiar with a topic without reading more than the chapter of interest. To the extent possible all the major topics needed in interface specification and design are covered.

I wish to express my gratitude to the late Professor Amos de Shalit of the Weizmann Institute of Science for his encouragement and direction in setting up at the Feinberg Graduate School the course upon which the book is based. My thanks to Ruth Mauer, who suggested writing this book. I am grateful also to Miss Ronit Levy, who faithfully typed this manuscript.

JULES FINKEL

Rehovot, Israel
July 1974

Contents

Computer-Aided Experimentation

1 Introduction

An important application of minicomputers is to monitor and control experiments in real time. In these applications the minicomputer is programmed to sense what is happening in the connected experiment and to issue control signals in response to the sensed situation. Real-time computer aided experimentation involves data acquisition, data analysis, and device control directed by the minicomputer software.

Real-time minicomputer applications require an interface (Fig. 1) to connect the experimental instruments to the computer. The basic principles of interface design are similar for most real-time minicomputer applications. Signals originating in the real-time device must be conditioned to match the input requirements of the minicomputer. Similarly, computer output signals must be converted to a form that can activate the required real-time output devices. The software in the minicomputer controls the complete operation of the interface; all data transfers and control signals are under program control.

Minicomputers are a class of digital computers and require, as input, digital signals; they generate digital output signals. Very few real-time devices of interest generate digital signals; some do not even generate

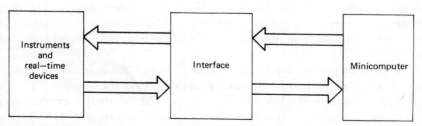

Fig. 1. An interface consists of analog and digital circuits that connect an external real-time device to a computer. Signals flow in both directions through the interface.

1

electrical signals. It is necessary, therefore, to convert non-computer-compatible signals of interest to digital computer compatible forms. In particular, the signals of interest must be in a form that is acceptable to the minicomputer to be used for the application. In general, a special interface, including hardware and software, must be designed and constructed for each new real-time minicomputer application.

PURPOSE OF THIS BOOK

The purpose of this book is to describe to scientists, programmers, laboratory technicians, experimenters, and instrumentation engineers the basic concepts and techniques needed to specify, design, and use minicomputers in a real-time environment.

The key to the success of a real-time system is the validity of the design of the interface that connects the minicomputer to the real-time device. This book describes each of the components normally encountered in the specification, design, and execution of such interfaces. The components are discussed from both performance and selection points of view. Particular emphasis is placed on connection techniques between real-time devices and computers and on the programming needed to sense and control these devices.

WHY COMPUTER AIDED EXPERIMENTATION?

"Computer aided experimentation" (CAE) means connecting experiments to the computer and then collecting data and controlling and adjusting parameters under the supervision of the computer program. Greater accuracy in data collection and a fully documented record of the experiment are obtained. Larger quantities of data at higher rates and with greater accuracy can be collected. Computer aided experimentation results in "better science" when properly applied because the scientist is relieved of tedious, repetitive jobs, thus permitting him more time for creative work.

The most important advantage obtained from CAE is in the design of new types of experiments. By taking advantage of the computer's high speed and logical-arithmetic ability, it is possible to design experiments that cannot be done effectively otherwise. The application of CAE opens new areas of experimentation to those who understand this powerful tool. This is the most compelling reason to become familiar with CAE.

It is certain that better science will be based more and more on effective utilization of this tool. Scientists and experimenters should know about CAE concepts and techniques, and problems whose solutions are best handled by CAE techniques should be recognizable.

WHERE TO BUY INTERFACES

The interface connects the real-time signal source to the computer and also transfers the resultant computer output signals to the real-time device. Interfaces are required for real-time minicomputer applications. A specially designed interface is usually needed for each specific application; very few really general-purpose interfaces exist.

Interfaces may be provided by the minicomputer manufacturer, the real-time device manufacturer, an independent engineering firm that designs and builds interfaces, or the user himself. It is usually preferable to buy the minicomputer, its interface, and the real-time device from a single vendor as a standard "off-the-shelf" package. In many cases such a package exists. This is particularly true when the package is a relatively standard item or when the interface requirements are modest and do not involve many special functions. Minicomputers users are urged to carefully consider all available standard off-the-shelf complete packages. The lowest-cost approach to system design results when an appropriate already existing interface is used.

If it is determined that a standard off-the-shelf minicomputer/interface/ real-time device package does not exist or that what exists is not suitable or cannot be made useful, then a special-purpose interface system design must be undertaken. Usually, however, the minicomputer manufacturer and the real-time device manufacturer are not interested in designing special interfaces unless a reasonable number of additional identical sales can be forecast. A one-of-a-kind design is relatively expensive in engineering and programming effort for a production oriented organization. A potential return on investment must be forecast to make new design worthwhile.

It is usually necessary either to contract for the interface with an engineering group that specializes in this type of work or to do the work in house. The make-or-buy decision is usually based on the user's budget, time scale, and available skills. Before undertaking major interface designs, a user should have the proper engineering software, management, and manufacturing skills, as well as experience. In all cases the user must specify very carefully the system he requires in order to be certain that what is delivered will conform to his specific needs. Also, he must maintain close liaison with the interface design group.

INTERFACES

This book is concerned with real-time systems in which minicomputers are connected to operational devices. The connection between the mini-computer and the real-time device is through an interface which consists of electronics and software (Fig. 2).

In addition to the hardware and software that constitute a real-time system, a human factor is involved. Most CAE systems include an experimenter who has to maintain general supervision of the overall operation. Therefore a man-machine interface must be provided that will furnish the user with the means to supervise the process. The user must be aware of the state of the experiment. It is essential that they keep the user continuously aware of the status of the system and each of its components.

WHAT IS A MINICOMPUTER?

Aside from the experiment itself, the most expensive and decisive component in a real-time CAE system is the computer. To a large extent the design of all the system components, including the interface and the soft-

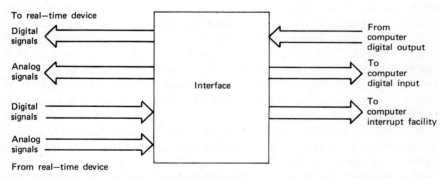

Fig. 2. The interface should accept real-time signals from the instrumentation and pass them, after appropriate conditioning, to the computer in computer compatible form. It must also perform the same functions for signals flowing in the reverse directions.

ware, is determined by the characteristics of the computer. Selection of the computer is dependent in turn on specification and analysis of the overall goals of the real-time process or experiment. An appropriate selection will greatly simplify the design and execution of the project, whereas careless or incorrect selection can greatly complicate the design job and, in the extreme case, cause the entire project to fail.

Most real-time devices that are computer controlled are connected to minicomputers. Various definitions of what falls into the minicomputer category have been proposed. The common denominator of these definitions is the relatively low cost of the computer central processor (CPU) unit. Minicomputer CPUs range in price from $1,000 to about $10,000. After sufficient storage for the application has been added and minimum input/output (I/O) devices are attached, however, minicomputer prices can greatly exceed the figures mentioned above. Many minicomputer applications require configurations that have disk drives, magnetic tape units, printers, and communication lines attached. It is not at all unusual to find real-time experiments with minicomputer systems valued at $100,000, or more.

Many real-time experiments require computers that may be defined as medium- or large-scale general-purpose computers. The principles discussed here concerning the connection of real-time devices to computers still hold. However, this book places particular emphasis on the special nature and limitations of minicomputers. Even when a large-scale computer is used to perform the real-time analysis work, a minicomputer may provide the direct connection between the large computer and the experiment. Minicomputers afford a high degree of availability that cannot be justified with a large computer. A minicomputer can be economically dedicated to a particular application; the minicomputer is always available for the experiment and for debugging, whereas a larger computer must usually be shared by a number of users to be an economically viable system. Its availability is limited to the constraints of its other applications. A minicomputer, on the other hand, can be continuously used by the real-time application. It utilizes the larger computer resources only when needed and available; at other times the minicomputer is capable of data acquisition and control on its own.

Minicomputers can be programmed (Fig. 3) to perform the same tasks as large scientific computers or commercially oriented computers. However, most minicomputer instruction sets are limited in scope and in number of different instructions in the repertoire. To perform the same job on a minicomputer requires, in comparison to a larger machine, that a much greater number of instructions be written and executed. Thus,

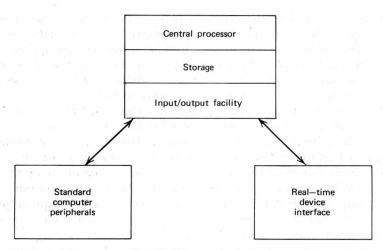

Fig. 3. Minicomputer block diagram.

although the basic speeds of a large computer and a minicomputer may be the same, the computer with a richer repertoire of instructions can performs a given task much more rapidly and efficiently.

Minicomputers generally have very short word lengths. This is one of the ways in which the cost of a minicomputer can be kept low. Also, data paths in the computer are narrower. To perform tasks comparable to those done on larger computers that have wider data paths and longer word lengths, the minicomputer must issue multiple instructions: Large computers may have word lengths and data paths as wide as 64 or 128 bits, whereas most minicomputers are designed with word sizes of 8, 12, or 16 bits.

A larger variety of standard computer I/O devices can be attached to large computers than to minicomputers. The wider the selection of peripheral devices, the simpler it is to configure a computer for a specific application. This does not imply that a dearth of minicomputer peripherals exists; indeed, the opposite is true. However, more peripherals are available for large computers. Users are usually willing and able to justify higher costs for large computer peripherals.

Minicomputers are usually serviced by the users. This is necessary in many cases because the computer is intergrated with other real-time components. Large general-purpose computers, on the other hand, are maintained by the vendor or independent maintenance firms.

The major distinction between minicomputers and general-purpose larger computers is software. Because of the limited capabilities of the minicomputer it is more difficult to provide as full a range of higher-level languages and application programs for them. A minicomputer in its basic configuration supports minimal software—generally only as assembler. Even when more extensive software is available, it works on larger configurations of the computer. Much more than the minimum primary storage and basic peripherals is required. The restriction to assembler language makes programming a more difficult task.

MINICOMPUTER CUSTOMER

Minicomputers are available from a large number of vendors. Two basic markets are serviced: the original equipment manufacturer (OEM) and the end user. The OEM offers products in which the computer is part of the overall system delivered to customers. Since computer manufacturers who sell to OEMs are interested primarily in selling large numbers of computers, it is customary to offer large discounts on volume purchases. A minimum of service—technical, interface, programming, and maintenance—is offered by the computer vendor. The OEM takes responsibility for these services as part of the product he sells. The computer, although it may be a major unit, is just another component in the system that the end user purchases. The system vendor is responsible for the complete system; the computer vendor usually has no direct contact with the user.

The computer manufacturer who intends to reach the end-user market directly encounters an entirely different customer. The end-user customer is typically interested in purchasing a single computer, or at most a few. He usually has a special application in mind that he has ascertained cannot be fulfilled by standard off-the-shelf systems. The end user is interested in the computer controlled system for his own use primarily and is not motivated by the commercial exploitation potential. He relies on the computer vendor for technical advice, programming support, and maintenance. The successful minicomputer vendor is the one most familiar with the user's application and capable of providing the necessary assistance. Although system cost is a major factor in computer selection, other considerations such as vendor support, appropriate software availability, and anticipated speed of project execution with a specific computer must be taken into account. These play an important role in assuring the overall success of the undertaking.

The minicomputer purchaser must distinguish between the types of computer manufacturers. He must know what to expect if he selects a vendor who will provide OEM support or one offering end-user support. He should expect to pay substantially more for end-user support. Some computer vendors sell to both markets, whereas others restrict themselves to one area. The computer user should define the kind of support he requires, based on his budget, skills, and project time scale. He should also make sure that the computer vendor is aware of his needs and agrees to meet them.

MINICOMPUTER SELECTION

Selecting a minicomputer for a particular application requires careful consideration. Most minicomputers can be adapted to any application for which a minicomputer is applicable. However, some minicomputers are more suitable for a particular application than others. The following discussion mentions some of the factors that should be evaluated.

The requirements of the job to be done should be compared with the specifications of the various minicomputers that are available. In most circumstances the selection criteria will not be very dependent on the general specifications unless the application is such that it requires an advanced state-of-the-art computer or utilizes a particular function at the edge of the specification range. In general, it is good practice to avoid designs that are premised on equipment working at or near the limit of its capacity. This is certainly true for computers also. A desirable feature or option that is available on one computer but not on others may be a decisive factor in favor of a particular machine. In other words, the process or experiment is such that it may be able to take advantage of an instruction or I/O feature that is peculiar to one computer.

The computer's digital input and digital output facilities should be carefully examined. This is an important consideration because the user real-time devices have direct contact with these features. Ease of interfacing can make one computer much more attractive than another.

Another important factor to be carefully weighed is software support. This includes implementation of similar applications on the computer at other locations. The most expensive single cost item in most real-time computer controlled applications is usually the program preparation work. *This necessary function is almost always underestimated in terms of the manpower and time required!* If a similar application has been implemented with a particular computer and if the software is obtainable, the same computer choice may be the most appropriate one because of the savings in cost, time, and personnel.

Another major factor to consider in evaluating software is the availability of higher-level languages and a well developed assembler. These features can greatly enhance the programming effort. Programs can be written and debugged much more rapidly when a good assembler or a higher-level language is available. It is necessary, of course, to evaluate carefully the manufacturer's claims as to software in the same way as hardware specifications are examined. In many cases the availability of a higher-level language depends on an augmented input and output peripheral configuration and much more than the minimum amount of main storage. The value of the software is greatly diminished if it is not usable on the computer configuration needed to do the specific job. It should be recognized, however, that purchase of more main memory and peripherals than are needed is justified in many cases specifically because in that way certain software can be exploited. In other words, the cost of software preparation is sufficiently high to justify hardware additions that may cut programming costs. The availability of diagnostic programs, utilities, and editors constitutes other factors to be considered.

The previous history and experience which an organization has had with minicomputers should also be considered when making a selection. If good results were obtained with a particular computer on previous occasions, the same machine should obviously be considered for future applications. Having more than one computer of the same type brings many benefits, such as lower cost because of volume purchases. In addition, the familiarity and know-how gained on one system can be used advantageously on successive applications. A single maintenance staff can handle all computers of the same type. The contacts already established with the minicomputer manufacturer's engineering and support staff can be further extended and exploited to advance the new project. Obviously, it is in an organization's interest to standardize on a particular type of computer to the extent possible.

INPUT OUTPUT DEVICES

The user has access to the computer through its digital input and digital output facilities. In addition, the computer interrupt facility, whereby external devices can gain the computer's immediate attention, may be utilized. The ease with which it is possible to interface a particular application to the computer depends to a marked degree on the arrangement of the digital input and digital output features on the computer.

Aside from the digital input and output capabilities, the conventional

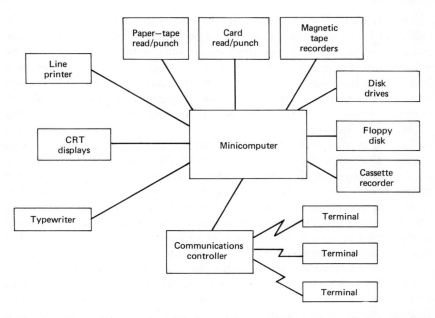

Fig. 4. A minicomputer configuration containing a variety of standard computers peripherals.

peripherals (Fig. 4) that are attachable to the computer should be considered. Availability of a disk or drum greatly increases the effective power of the computer. Operating system implementation depends to a great extent on availability of such peripherals. To store large numbers of data, magnetic tape capability may be required. Printers, card readers, paper tape readers and punches, and cathode ray tube displays are other examples of peripherals that can be effectively employed wtih a mini-computer in a real-time environment. If data are to be collected from remote locations, controllers for telephone digital communication lines may be required. These devices will be discussed in detail with respect to their applicability in a real-time environment.

SIGNAL FLOW IN REAL-TIME SYSTEMS

As indicated above, ordinary computer peripherals constitute one category of I/O devices connected to minicomputers. The other category (and the

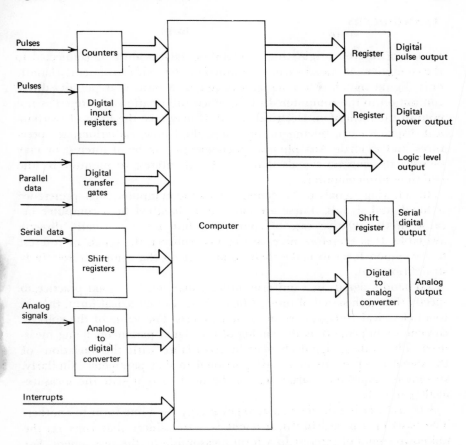

Fig. 5. Real-time signal handling components used in a minicomputer configuration.

one of major interest here) consists of the real-time signals (Fig. 5) originating in the process or experiment under investigation. Generally signals of interest in the real-time device must be converted to computer compatible input. In a like fashion, computer output signals must be converted to a form recognizable to the experiment. Various transducers and signal conditioners are used to bring the signals of interest in a common format to the analog to digital converter, which may in turn be connected to the computer digital input facility. The signal flow path and the components needed to pass the signals along are discussed in detail in the following sections.

TRANSDUCERS

Signals of interest originating in real-time devices must be connected to the computer. As stated earlier, a minicomputer can conveniently handle only digital signals. Most signals are not in a form that permits direct connection to the computer. In fact, much information of interest is not even in the form of an electrical signal. It may take the form of mechanical displacements, pneumatic pressures, fluid flow, radiations, temperatures, and so forth. Any physical phenomenon can be of interest or may be used to generate signals that may be of interest to monitor by the real-time minicomputer.

In selecting signals to be connected to the computer, first preference is for digital signals. These are most easily handled by a computer because of the relative ease of connection but are not usually directly available. It is therefore necessary to first convert all signals of interest to a common form to make their connection to the computer relatively straightforward.

To handle signals in a uniform, orderly manner, it is good practice to specify that each signal of interest be converted to electrical form, that is, to an electrical voltage, current, or impedance. The value of the voltage, current, or impedance is the analog of the signal parameter being measured. The voltage signal changes in accordance with the variations of the signal it represents and is proportional to that parameter. Similarly, current or impedance variations can be used to represent the measurement parameter.

A transducer is a device that changes energy from one form to another. The basis of a measuring instrument is a transducer that converts the unknown signal of interest to a form measurable by the instrument. For computer interface design, transducers and instruments that convert other forms of energy to electrical energy are of primary interest. A photocell is an example of a transducer that converts light energy to electrical energy. A potentiometer converts mechanical displacement to an electrical voltage or impedance. Transducer designs can be and are based on a very large number of different physical phenomena.

SIGNAL CONDITIONERS

Electrical transducers may produce currents, voltage, or impedances that are the analogs of the signals being measured. Depending on the design of the interface, it is desirable to convert all of the analog electrical signals into a common form and range. The various devices used to produce this result are usually classified as signal conditioners. The functions provided are voltage and current amplification, impedance transformation, calibration, and referencing.

The signal conditioning equpiment consists of analog electronics and reference power sources that convert the electrical analog signals to a common scale and range. Signal conditioning equipment can be quite expensive if low-level signals from high-impedance sources must be handled with great accuracy. High-level, low-accuracy signals can be handled with considerably less effort and by lower-cost devices.

ANALOG TO DIGITAL CONVERTERS

Most signals that originate in real-time devices are inherently analog in nature. Most practical transducers are analog devices. On the other hand, computers require digital signals as their input. Analog to digital converters are electronic devices that convert analog signals to digital representations. An analog to digital converter (ADC) accepts analog voltages as input and produces the digital representation of the input signal as its output.

Most real-time devices produce a great many analog signals of interest (Fig. 6). It is usually expedient to share a single ADC among a number of analog signal sources. An analog multiplexer is an electronic or electromechanical switch that perimts a number of analog signals to be connected to the ADC. Under program control, the multiplexer connects selected analog input channels to the ADC. The converter then produces as its output the digital representation of these channels.

DIGITAL INPUTS

Inputs to the computer must be in digital form. A number of different ways of implementing the digital input facilities exist. The primary distinctions among these methods are concerned with the effective data transfer, I/O loading on the computer, and the permissible response time in handling the input. As might be expected, when digital inputs requiring the fastest response at the highest data rates with the least loading or interference with the computer are specified, a high-cost system is implied. However, it is usually possible to trade off these maximum requirements for a lower-cost solution. As in all system designs, it is prudent to select

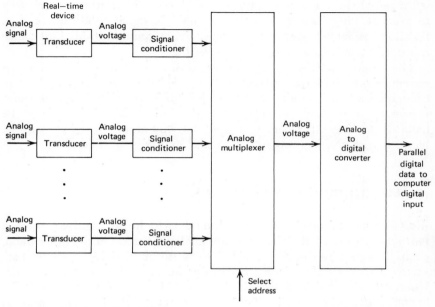

Fig. 6. Analog signal flow paths.

the best cost-performance configuration; overspecifying usually leads to a more expensive solution with unnecessary system capability.

DIGITAL OUTPUTS

The minicomputer outputs data and control signals to the real-time devices connected to it. Just as the computer accepts only digital data as inputs, it is capable of outputting only digital signals. The interface matches the digital output to the requirements of the connected devices. The interface is made up of voltage level shifters, power drivers, pulse circuits, and DACs. These circuits are matched to the computer digital output and to the drive requirements of the various connected devices.

Digital outputs may be of varying rates and in response to the requests of the connected device. Various computer techniques can be provided to obtain high data rates with low computer loading. As would be expected, the least expensive approach is limited to lower data rates.

SOFTWARE

The complete operation of the minicomputer and its connected real-time devices is controlled by the programs in the minicomputer. Depending on the process or instrumentation being controlled and the results desired, programs can be quite simple or very sophisticated. A computer configuration capable of supporting the program complexity needed must be selected. A complicated control program usually requires more extensive facilities than a very simple program. A major factor to be considered in computer selection is the ease with which the necessary computer programs can be prepared. The importance of software availability cannot be overemphasized; in most systems software is the major cost item of the total effort.

By issuing commands and sensing status via its output and input interfaces, the computer program controls the process or experiment. The program issues data acquisition commands that collect data; it also senses the status of various indicators in the real-time connected devices. These devices may also interrupt the computer when certain events occur or specific conditions exist.

The computer data acquisition program must be capable of collecting the data and responding to the real-time device interrupts and requests for service. After the collected data and status information have been analyzed by a computer program, various control actions and data outputs may be required.

Every action of the external devices is controlled by the computer programs. For the overall system to function properly, the software must be written so as to take into account every possible condition. An effective algorithm must be used to control the process or experiment.

The user can benefit a great deal from the software that is available from the computer manufacturer. In many cases an identical or similar task has been executed previously, and it may be possible to use the software directly or with very little change. When appropriate software is not available, the user must prepare his own. It cannot be repeated too often that in many cases the software is the single most costly item in a project. The difficulty and expense of software generation are usually underestimated. The high cost or unavailability of appropriate software can cause many well designed experiments to fail.

The user can benefit from the languages available on the selected computer. If the configuration of the system at hand is sufficiently large, high-level languages such as Fortran may be used to prepare the control algorithms. Higher-level languages should be used to the extent possible. Fortran programs can be prepared and debugged more quickly than programs written in low-level languages such as an assembler. A major consideration often underestimated or even overlooked is program documentation. Higher-level language statements are essentially self documenting. Only if good documentation is available is it possible to pass a program on to successive programmers for further debugging and modification. It should be pointed out, however, that most minicomputer programs must be written in assembler language because the computer configuration may not be large enough to support a higher-level language effectively.

A very useful software feature of many minicomputers consists of manufacturer supplied I/O routines for the digital input and digital output facilities. This software is very useful in program preparation. One of the more difficult programming tasks in a real-time environment is error detection and recovery. When these features are available as part of the software package, the user's job in program preparation is simplified considerably.

THE INTERFACE DESIGN TEAM

Design of an interface between the computer and the real-time device is essentially a team effort (Fig. 7). In small systems the team may consist of a single individual—the experimenter—who takes responsibility for all roles. Basically the following skills are required to design a computer real-time interface: systems analysis and design, digital hardware engineering, programming, and instrumentation engineering.

The system analysis and design function requires translating the user-experimenter requirements into a functional overall design. The designer takes into account the available instrumentation and the computer hardware and software needed to implement the required work. This function coordinates the functions of the other team members.

The instrumentation engineer is responsible for ensuring that the signals obtained from the process or experiment are sufficient to conduct it. This function must take into account signal pick-off point availability, transducer selections, signal levels, accuracies, tolerances, and transmission distances and paths. The instrumentation engineering function is responsible for delivering signals to the computer interface with an error sufficiently low to ensure accurate computation to the required tolerances. The instrumentation engineer must also specify control devices which will respond correctly to computer commands.

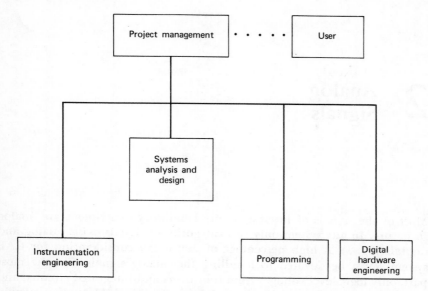

Fig. 7. A suggested table of organization needed to produce effective interfaces.

The digital hardware engineer designs the hardware interface between the computer digital input and digital output and the instrumentation. Necessary logic functions, analog to digital converters, and digital to analog converters, as well as various level shifters, are part of his responsibility.

The programming function involves designing, coding, and debugging the data acquisition and control programs. These programs control the interface input and output, acquire and store data, and sense the experiment status as well as control the experiment, in response to the computed results.

It cannot be stressed too strongly that the efforts of the team members must be closely coordinated. Close contact with the end user must be maintained at all times so that the final system will exactly match what the experimenter expects. Many experimenters take upon themselves the systems analysis and design role in order to ensure that the end result will really be what is required. The paramount consideration is that the system should do what the experimenter requires.

2 Analog Signals

Most of the signals of interest in any laboratory experiment are analog in nature. In any system only two categories of signals exist: analog and digital (Fig. 1). A high percentage of the design consideration for CAE systems must be devoted to handling the analog signals. For the most part, only logic level voltages from transistors and integrated circuits, and signals from switches and relays, are inherently digital. Most other signals, even of the digital type, start out as analog signals and are digitized by

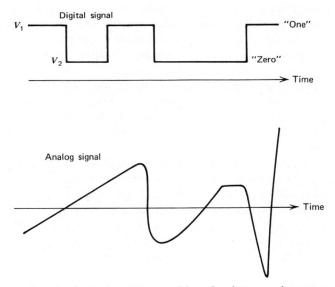

Fig. 1. An analog signal can have any possible value between the upper and lower limits of its excursion range. Digital signals can have only two values, defined as "one" and "zero."

various devices. Analog signals are usually low level and prone to disturbances from many sources. Digital signals are usually higher level and by their very nature less sensitive to external disturbances.

DEFINITION

An analog voltage varies with time and can have all possible values. In contrast, a digital voltage can have two (and only two) discrete levels or states. These are defined as "one" and "zero" or "true" and "false," or "open" and "closed," or "high" and "low." Analog signals can be represented by voltages, currents, pressures, or any other measurable physical phenomenon.

The relationship between the analog voltage and the signal source it represents may be linear, or it may have any other mathematical form. The analog signal should vary proportionally with the variable signal it represents. That signal may be time, position, or any other function.

TRANSDUCERS

Analog signals are generated by transducers (Fig. 2), which detect phenomena of interest. A transducer, as pointed out in Chapter 1, is a device

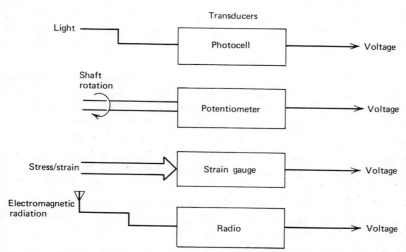

Fig. 2. A transducer is a device that converts energy from one form to another. For computer applications transducers that convert signals to electrical form are of primary interest.

that converts energy from one form to another. For instance, a thermometer converts heat energy into mercury displacement. A thermocouple, on the other hand, converts heat energy into electrical energy. One can list many different types of transducers that convert energy from one form into another. Scientists and engineers have been able to utilize many physical phenomena as sensors and transducers.

Photocells convert light energy into electrical energy. Strain gauges convert mechanical energy into electrical signals. A Bourdon tube converts pressure into mechanical energy, through the unwinding of the Bourdon helix. A potentiometer converts mechanical shaft rotation into electrical signals. Devices that produce current and voltage outputs are examples of transducers. Thus a radio receiver is a transducer that converts high-frequency electromagnetic radiation into low-frequency electrical energy and then into audio energy.

Insofar as computer applications are concerned, transducers having electrical output are preferred. It is usually most expedient to transmit signals in electrical form. When a computer (or any data acquisition system) is involved, it is desirable and often necessary to transmit all the signals to one location. This central location is usually remote from the signal sources, and it therefore becomes convenient to use transducers that produce electrical signals (Fig. 3) so that the signals of interest can be transmitted over some distance. This does not preclude, however, the use of transducers that produce other than electrical energy. For instance, many transducers modulate pneumatic energy that is transmitted along tubes over long distances. However, even a transducer of this type must eventually terminate in a device that converts the energy into an electrical analog.

The analog signals, that is, the voltages and currents that are generated by the various transducers, are proportional to the signals of interest. The relationship between the tranducer input and output signals can have any mathematical form, or can be empirically determined. For most manual operations, a linear or logarithmic relationship between the input signal and the output signal is necessary so that a human being can handle the data with relative ease. However, when computer applications are concerned, no specific relationship is required as long as it is reliable and repeatable. Thus, a computer connection allows for the implementation of nonlinear transduction devices, permitting the use of simpler transducers and less expensive devices than would otherwise be possible. One of the larger costs of an instrumentation system involves the processing of transducer signals in order to make the relationship between the measured phenomena and the signals linear or logarithmic, or at least give

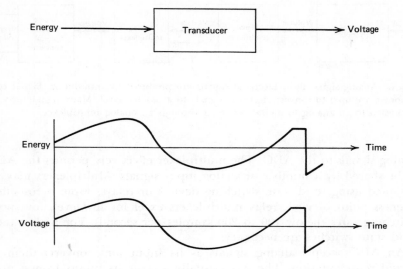

Fig. 3. A transducer converts one form of energy to another. The transducer input is converted to an electrical signal, which is an exact replica of the signal being measured.

it some regular form. If a signal is entered into a computer in its un-calibrated form, the computer can convert it into a usable form without the necessity of relatively expensive analog preprocessing circuitry.

SIGNAL PROCESSING

The number of analog signals that must be handled in an environment can be very large. In most practical systems, analog signals are not singular but occur in multiplicity. It is not uncommon to generate hundreds of analog signals from even relatively simple instrumentation. The introduction of automatic data collection equipment permits the experimenter to collect much more information than he could otherwise handle. The computer is capable, under program control, of selecting individual analog input points for entry into the computer; under pro-gram controls a command can be issued to sample a specific point, or a sequence of points can be entered into the computer.

An analog multiplexer (Fig. 4) actually executes the computer com-mands to select analog input points for connection to the computer. A multiplexer is a program controlled switching device that connects

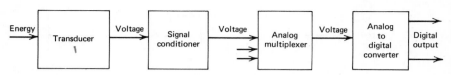

Fig. 4. Analog signal flow. Electrical signals are produced by transducers. Signal conditioners are used to convert electrical signals to a useable level. Many signals may be connected to an analog to digital converter through an analog multiplexer.

analog signals to the ADC. The multiplexer effectively permits the ADC to be shared by a number of analog input signals. Multiplexers may be designed using solid state switching devices or relays. From a cost-effectiveness point of view, relay multiplexers excel for low-level, low-speed switching rates (below 100 to 200 samples per second). For higher rates solid state switches are necessary.

An ADC accepts analog signals as its input and converts them to digital representation. The ADC usually accepts its inputs from a multiplexer, but, for certain applications it may be expedient to connect the analog signal directly to the ADC input. The ADC digitized output may be connected directly to the computer front-end or to some other data acquisition device. Usually ADC outputs are in binary form.

·INFORMATION CONTENT

Analog signals vary with respect to time or some other running parameter, such as an angle or frequency. This parameter may also be represented by an analog signal. The information in the analog signal may be represented in a relatively small number of different ways. Also, the degradations and errors introduced by the various analog signal processing circuits are common to almost any type of system, so that it is possible to generalize when discussing analog signal characteristics.

The information in an analog signal may be coded in various ways (Fig. 5). The simplest utilizes variations in the amplitude of the signal. In some cases all amplitude variations are of interest, whereas in others the desired information may be contained in the amplitude of the peaks or the area under the curve. In some cases the wave shape (Fig. 6) and the symmetry of the curve are significant. The frequency and phase relationship of the analog signal may also contain useful information. Another factor to consider is whether a signal is repetitive and, if so, its repetition rate. Some signals occur once (transients), whereas others are repetitive

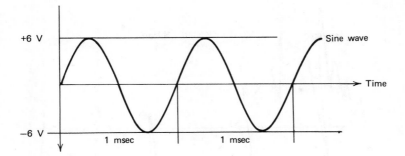

Fig. 5. An analog signal can be represented by its frequency and amplitude characteristics. The signal shown here is a sine wave of peak amplitude 6 V and repetition of 1000 times per second.

at an uncontrollable rate; some wave trains may be synchronized to occur in response to a stimulus. It is evident that the manner in which an analog signal is handled will depend, to a large extent, on how the information of interest is encoded and how its occurrence is sensed or controlled.

NOISE

All signals are degraded by noise (Fig. 7). When high-level signals are present or high accuracy is not required, the effects of noise may sometimes be neglected. Noise may be due to electromagnetic pick-up from power line and radio frequency interference and also to thermal effects. In general, noise is any unwanted signal component that is picked up along with the signals of interest. In order to recover the latter satis-

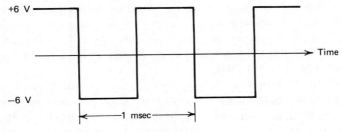

Fig. 6. A signal that is a square wave.

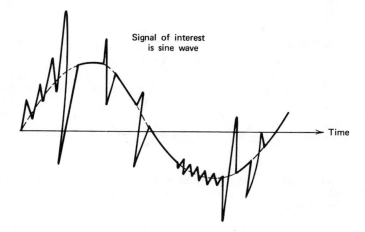

Fig. 7. An example of a waveform encountered in a normal situation. The waveform of interest is distorted by noise voltage superimposed upon it. In handling this waveform the highest-frequency component in the noise must be taken into account.

factorily, the noise content in the signals must be reduced to tolerable levels for the particular application.

A great deal of effort is usually expended in designing systems that minimize noise. Some types of noise are relatively easy to handle, whereas other noises pose extremely difficult problems. Powerline pick-up can usually be filtered out by narrow band-stop or notch filters. Noise either below or above the frequency band of interest also can be minimized by low-pass and high-pass filters. Proper filter design is usually a matter of economics rather than technology. Ordinarily it is possible to design or purchase band limiting filters to handle out-of-band noise.

Noise problems are most severe when the frequency range of the noise lies in the same band as the signals of interest. In this situation simple filtering is not feasible because the signal will be attenuated along with the noise, and other techniques must be found to reduce the noise signal itself. These techniques are usually effective in removing out-of-band noise also. It is good practice to reduce all noise. Usually it is much less expensive to minimize noise where it is generated or introduced into the system than to filter it out later.

One of the more powerful techniques in noise control is good wiring practices. Placing signal leads in locations that are not adjacent or parallel to high-voltage and high-current lines can minimize noise. Parallel lines in close proximity are closely coupled. Good grounding practices are suggested to minimize ground loop problems. A great deal of effort has gone into the area, and this subject will be discussed in greater detail later in the chapter. In conjunction with good wiring practices, proper use of wire types and components is needed for handling and processing low-level signals. It is important to use high-quality amplifiers and other active components that tend to minimize the generation of spurious signals.

Many techniques have been developed for enhancing signal-to-noise ratios. These are based on selectively improving the signal at the expense of the noise. One method involves the use of narrow band techniques, since the narrower the band, the lower the noise power. Other enhancement techniques involve time integration of the signal so as to reduce the noise components. By integrating a signal over a large number of repetitive waveforms, noise can be reduced. It is well konwn that, if a signal is examined n times, the random noise component can be reduced by a factor equal to the square root of n. In some cases cross-correlation and autocorrelation techniques are also applicable for signal-to-noise ratio enhancement.

SIGNAL QUALITY

Analog signals and analog signal processing circuitry may be characterized quantitatively by such factors as accuracy, precision, resolution, linearity, repeatability, stability, drift, gain, dynamic range, and frequency response. These factors determine the quality and fidelity of the analog signal processing circuits that handle the information. It is important to define these terms because components are bought or designed with respect to specifications defined by these terms, which also define overall system performance.

When analog signal processing specifications are set, it is important not to overspecify. This means that signal handling characteristics should be specified realistically—what is required for the particular job, and not state of the art, or beyond. To obtain or to extract a slight increase in performance in analog signal processing components, a premium price is usually required. Therefore, if a particular characteristic is not necessary, it should not be overspecified. This ensures a reasonable system cost.

ACCURACY

Accuracy is a measure of how closely the measured signal represents the actual value of the signal. Accuracy is essentially a function of the other factors described below. Usually accuracy is measured (and specified) as a percentage of full scale or a percentage of actual reading. For instance, an analog signal could be specified with an accuracy of 0.1% of full scale. Such a specification means that at any value reading the absolute error will be the same as at full scale; it follows that a signal with a value equal to 10% of full scale reading could have a permissible error of 1%. Instruments with an error specification of 1% of reading, are equal to (or exceed) 1% full scale accuracy instruments, especially for low-level signals.

Accuracy is specified as the measure of errors introduced from all sources. In other words, accuracy is a measure of overall quality and fidelity; all error contributing factors enter into the determination of accuracy. Hence accuracy is a function of resolution, linearity, repeatability, gain, stability, dynamic range, and the like.

Accuracy is generally specified as statistical or worst case. Usually accuracy is specified as the root mean square of the sum of the squares of all error contributing components. It is assumed that each error component will be statistical in nature and that all components will not simultaneously introduce additive errors in the worst case direction. Statistically, the error factors will partially cancel.

Accuracy can also be defined as a worst case condition. This assumes that each error contributing source will occur at the same time and will introduce a maximum error, and that all errors will be summed simultaneously in the worst possible direction. It is evident that a worst case error specification will be much poorer than the statistical error. It is necessary to be careful with respect to defining and specifying analog signal circuit errors.

PRECISION

"Precision" and "resolution" are two closely related terms. "Precision" usually refers to the number of significant digits to which a variable can be read; "resolution" indicates the least discernible change that is measurable by an instrument. In many cases the two terms are the same, especially in regard to digital conversion equipment. For a four-digit ADC, for example, the precision and the resolution are the same, 0.01%. As with all definitions, precision does not imply accuracy; it may be possible to discern a change of 1 part in 10,000, but that does not necessarily mean that the reading is accurate to 1 part in 10,000. Care is required in defining and interpreting specifications.

LINEARITY

Linearity (Fig. 8) is the measure of the deviation from a straight line of the response of a device or instrument when it is subjected to input signals of varying amplitude. This characteristic is extremely important in noncomputer applications because a human being has to handle the information. As was indicated previously, it is most convenient for a human operator to handle linear signals or, at the very worst, simply related mathematical functions. However, once a computer is involved, the program can be used for table look-up or linearization of signals according to various mathematical techniques.

Linearity is usually defined by drawing a best fit straight line through the curve of interest and measuring the maximum deviation of the signal of interest from the straight line. The best straight line can be specified as the best that could have been drawn through the curve, or the best with one end of the line going through the origin. Linearity is the maximum deviation of the variable from a straight line, divided by the full scale excursion of the variable under consideration. Linearity is usually expressed as a percentage.

REPEATABILITY

Repeatability is a measure of how closely one is able to obtain the same answer each time that a measurement is made, or a measure of the devia-

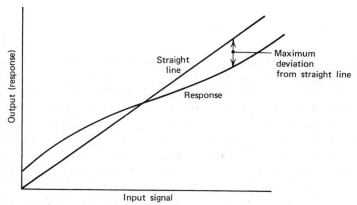

Fig. 8. Linearity is a measure of the deviation of the signal response curve from a best straight line fit through the curve.

tion of a specified number of measurements under identical sets of conditions. Repeatability is probably the most important single characteristic for analog signal processing, especially when a computer is involved. It is possible for the computer program to calibrate the signal and compute linearization and compensation corrections for drift and instabilities. What is required of instrumentation is that the same value always be generated for the same input phenomena. The computer can compensate for nonlinearities, but it cannot correct errors in the signal. It cannot be stressed too strongly that repeatability of the measured signal is the most important charactertistic to be considered in an instrumentation system.

DRIFT

Most electrical components used in signal flow paths are subject to parameter variations that are functions of environmental conditions (temperature, humidity, etc.), electric power fluctuations, component aging, and so forth. Although good design effort stresses selection of instruments that are relatively insensitive to temperature variations, it is still not possible to compensate entirely for increases or decreases in temperature. For most instruments and analog signal processing devices drift is specified— usually as microvolts per degree centigrade—as a function of temperature.

Power supply voltages should be well regulated. However, power supplies drift because of power line, load, and other factors that vary. As components age, their characteristics change. Component aging has an adverse effect on the fidelity with which signals are handled.

DYNAMIC RANGE

Another factor used to describe the characteristics of the analog signal is dynamic range (Fig. 9), that is, is the ratio of maximum to minimum signal of interest or the ratio of maximum to minimum signal that can be handled within the specified limits of the signal processing circuitry. If the minimum signal is 10 μV and the instrument also provides signals as high as 10 V, the dynamic range is 1,000,000 to 1. It should be noted that in many situations dynamic range is limited by the active circuit components rather than the signal from the transducer itself. The low limit is usually the inherent circuit noise, which for high-quality components may be on the order of a few microvolts. The maximum signal that can be handled is usually determined by the maximum nonsaturated

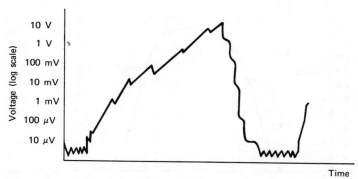

Fig. 9. The dynamic range of an analog signal is the ratio of maximum to minimum signal level that can be handled. The dynamic range shown is 10^6—the range of the signal is 10 V to 10 μV.

nonlimiting output voltage swing of the components. For most transistor devices this is a few volts.

FREQUENCY RESPONSE

The frequency characteristics of an analog signal may be determined by a detailed analysis of its time domain response. The frequency-time characteristics of a signal are important in selecting analog components and in setting sampling rates for analog to digital conversion. This topic will be discussed in greater detail. It is important to recognize that the frequency response of a transducer may be very different from the frequency response of the signal of interest, that is, the bandwidth of a particular transducer may be much wider than the actual signal range where in the information of interest is located. In many cases filters are used to eliminate or attenuate frequency components that are not of interest.

One technique for measuring the frequency response is to stimulate a transducer at discrete frequencies and to measure the resultant output amplitudes. Care must be taken to assure linearity. If nonlinearities are unavoidable, harmonic responses must be measured also. This procedure is repeated over a wide band of frequencies, and a plot of output amplitude versus frequency is made. The input stimulus frequency signals must be kept constant, or measured and appropriately compensated for when performing these amplitude computations.

The bandwidth (Fig 10) is defined as the point at which the upper and

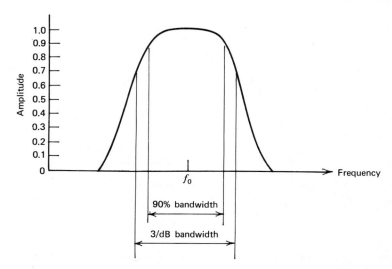

Fig. 10. The band-pass characteristics of signal flow path components. The effective bandwidth can be specified as the points where the response falls off by a preset amount from the flat portion of the curve.

lower frequencies fall off by a prescribed percentage from the average response between the two limits. The deviation from a uniform response may be specified. In some cases uniformity of response to within 95% of the average response over a particular frequency range may be used to define bandwidth. A lesser requirement may define the bandwidth as having a variation of 70%, for example. A phase response that is linear with respect to frequency is usually required.

Specifying the frequency characteristics of analog signals and analog signal processing circuits requires prudence. Overspecifying leads to excessive expense and also places a higher burden on the subsequent analog and digital elements. Wider bandwidth implies higher noise energy and higher sampling rate for the ADC, to mention just two expense-involving effects. A wider band circuit admits noise, as well as the signal of interest. If the spectrum of the signal contain sufficient power to interfere at a particular frequency band, it may be desirable to suppress that band. This cuts down the total noise as well as the band-pass requirements of the circuitry. Narrower bandwidths imply less information; therefore a lower ADC sampling rate is permissible. The computer load is also proportionally decreased.

It should be obvious, however, that underspecifying frequency band responses can lead to disastrous results by causing a loss of vital information. Worse yet, the remaining information may be erroneous or insufficient for the application. An ADC at insufficiently high rate causes the digitized signal to be "aliased," that is, when processed, the digital data will not necessarily resemble the original. Such an error can obviously be catastrophic in some circumstances.

Other techniques are also used for measuring frequency response if sweeping the transducer over the bands of interest is not practical. One method employs impulse or transient response testing. This effectively entails stimulating the transducer with a step or impulse and performing a Fourier analysis on the resultant responses. In many situations frequency response is determined through experience and the use of various empirically determined rules of thumb. In many situations, to obtain an exact value is either too complicated or not worth the effort. Nevertheless, it is necessary to have an estimate of the frequency characteristics of the signal of interest. It is also desirable to know in what portions of the spectrum useful information exists and where the information content is minimal or irrelevant for the particular experiment.

In all cases where the bandwidth of the signal of interest exceeds what is needed or used in subsequent processing, low-pass filtering should be applied to the analog signal. In addition to removing unwanted or unnecessary information, lower-bandwidth amplifiers, signal processors, lower-rate ADCs, and a less expensive (slower) computer can be used. It is almost always easier and less expensive to remove unwanted information or bandwidth by analog than by digital techniques. Simple bandpass filter methods are used.

SINGLE-ENDED SIGNALS

Analog signals may be classified as single-ended or differential floating signals. The single-ended type (Fig. 11) is referenced to ground. The signal appears on a single wire and is measured with respect to ground. Single-ended signals are usually high-level signals (a high-level signal may arbitrarily be defined as $\frac{1}{2}$ V or more). Most instrumentation devices

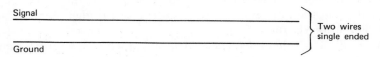

Fig. 11. A single-ended analog signal may flow over one or two wires. In two-wire systems one of the wires is at ground reference potential. The signal of interest is measured between one wire and ground.

produce differential signals. Many single-ended signals of interest are the results of previous conversion from floating differential to single-ended signals. It is very difficult to handle low-level single-ended signals because the environment contributes higher levels of noise and error than the amplitude of the signal to be measured. For this reason most low-level signals are necessarily handled as floating signals. It should be noted that the characteristics of analog signals are applicable to both single-ended and floating signal discussions.

Single-ended signals are measured with respect to ground. These signals are usually transmitted over short distances on a single wire. Over longer distances twisted pair or shielded cables are needed, one of the twisted pair leads being tied to ground. When single-ended signals are transmitted over any appreciable distance, they are handled as floating signals. A major problem with single-ended signal transmission and an important consideration in balanced (or floating) signal flow is the avoidance of ground loops and unsuspected ground current return paths. This topic is discussed in detail below. The control of ground current loops is mandatory for accurate analog signal transmission.

BALANCED SIGNALS

Differential balanced signals (Fig. 12) are transmitted over two-wire systems. The signal is not measured with respect to ground, but is the difference in potential between the voltage on the two wires. This signal is also referred to as a differential input. Most low-level transducers generate differential signals. Differential signals of interest are usually low level.

An example of a differential signal source is the familiar Wheatstone bridge, which consists of four resistance elements (or other impedance devices) connected in a bridge. An input voltage is impressed across two opposite legs of the bridge. When the bridge is balanced, as is usually the case initially, the voltage difference across the remaining opposite two legs of the bridge is zero. It should be noted, however, that the voltage with respect to ground of the two points is not and cannot be zero. Once a component of the bridge changes its characteristic, the bridge becomes unbalanced, current flows, and an output voltage difference is detected when the differential voltage on the two bridge points is measured. For instance, the bridge elements might be a strain gauge whose resistance is a function of deformation, or a temperature sensitive element which also changes resistance as a function of temperature. Other devices that produce floating signals are thermocouples and various demodulators used for handling carrier signals.

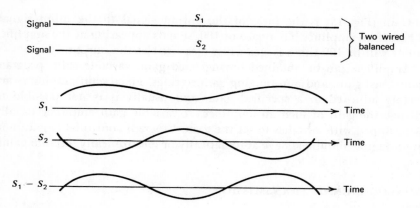

Fig. 12. A balanced or differential signal transmission system. The signal of interest is the difference in potential between the two wires. Common signals or voltages on the two wires do not interfere with measurement because only the difference is of interest.

The signal of interest is the voltage difference between the opposite points of the bridge. This is referred to as "the normal mode voltage." The bridge itself is at some voltage with respect to ground. This is the common mode voltage, and its existence introduces an error into the measurement. To minimize the error effect, circuitry having high common mode rejection ratios (CMRRs) is used.

The floating signal is measured by the difference in voltage between the differential leads. No restriction is placed on the voltage that is impressed on the floating legs, as long as it is within the safe limits of the circuitry. Since only the difference voltage is of interest, the common voltage, which can be power supplies, AC voltages, or noise, does not affect the measurement (except to the extent of the CMRR degradation). It should be noted that the difference could have been calculated after measuring the voltage of each leg with respect to ground. However, since this would have involved subtracting the difference of two almost equal values, it is far superior to handle the signals differentially.

GAIN

Most signal processing involves amplifying the signal to a level high enough to be handled by subsequent circuitry. Amplifiers have other characteristics as described above.

Gain (Fig. 13) is the ratio of the output signal to the input signal. Thus, if an amplifier has a gain of 100, signals appearing at the amplifier input will be 100 times larger when measured at the output.

Amplifiers can be obtained having fixed gain, variable gain, program controlled gain, and autoranging gain settings. Fixed gain amplifiers are factory adjusted to a specified gain, and usually it is not possible to change the gain of such an amplifier. A variable gain amplifier usually is equipped with switches to set the gain. Program controllable gain and autoranging amplifiers have automatically or electronically settable gains.

ANALOG SIGNAL TRANSMISSION

What is the maximum distance an analog signal can be transmitted? Analog signals can be transmitted over unlimited distances if suitable modulation techniques are used. By using frequency modulation, analog signals can be transmitted over voice grade phone line or radio. Of course the modulation and subsequent demodulation will introduce a certain amount of distortion and loss of information, and one must examine the acceptability of such degradation. Another technique involves pulse code modulation; the signal is digitized and transmitted as digital data. This

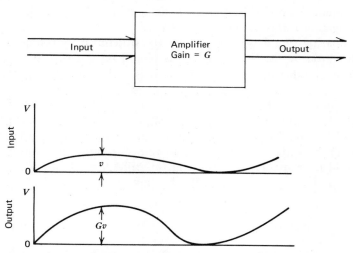

Fig. 13. The gain of an amplifier is the ratio of output signal to input signal. Fixed gain and variable gain amplifiers are available. The gain of a variable gain amplifier can be switch selected or electrically set.

technique offers the most effective means of analog signal transmission. The relative costs and merits of these transmission techniques are discussed in greater detail in Chapter 5.

For the purpose of the present discussion, "analog signal transmission" refers to hard wire connection of the analog signal source to the signal processing devices. This is undoubtedly the most economical and most common form of transmission. Analog signals, even from low-level transducers, can be transmitted reliably over several hundred meters. Precautions must be taken, however, to limit signal bandwidths; also, good wiring and cabling practices must be followed when making the connection between signal sources and destinations. With the use of voltage and/or current amplifiers distances approaching 10 km become practical. Longer distances require compromises in regard to noise specifications, dynamic range, and other parameters. High-level signals from low-impedance sources can obviously be driven over longer distances than low-level signals from high-impedance sources.

Analog signals can be transmitted over essentially unlimited distances if the proper procedures are followed and if the subsequent inevitable signal degradation is acceptable. By using more sophisticated (and, consequently, more expensive) signal transmission techniques, the effective signal transmission distance can be increased indefinitely. When pulse code modulation techniques are applied, unlimited transmission distances are attainable because straightforward digital transmission is used. Of course, bandwidth, dynamic range, and resolution will have to be traded off against the response characteristics of the digital data transmission link.

CABLES

The cable used to transmit analog signals heavily influences the reliability of transmission. It has been found that twisted shielded pairs make reliable transmission links. The newer aluminum foil shields are almost perfect, and extremely gratifying results have been obtained using this type of cable. It is important that each signal be transmitted in its own twisted shielded pair. The shields in a bundle should be insulated from one another. Cable made by Belden Cable Co. (Beldfoil) meets this description; it uses aluminized Mylar shield (with drain wire) covering individual twisted pairs. The aluminized insulated shield acts as an almost perfect shield for the twisted pair of conductors. The drain wire assures that all ground currents are returned completely to ground; ground loop current problems are thereby usually avoided.

GROUNDS

When dealing with analog signal transmission or when processing these signals, great care must be taken to prevent undesirable effects from occurring because of ground loops and ground currents. These problems are first approached by observing what are regarded as good wiring and cabling practices. Ground points are carefully selected and classed together by type, and each type is connected to a single point. This means that each category of ground connection is brought to a single point, and one point only. All cable shields are connected together, at only one end of each cable. All signal grounds are tied together, similarly, at a single point. Other ground categories include analog grounds, digital signal grounds, signal shields, cabinets, DC power supplies, primary AC power, and secondary transformer AC neutral. All the grounds should then be connected at a single point to an earth-driven ground stake.

To a significant extent grounding practices and problems (and their solutions) still constitute a "black magic" art. In practice, once all the "correct" grounding practices have been assured, the procedure involves connecting various combinations of the grounding signal points until the desired quality of signal purity is obtained.

SHIELDING

Several convenient rules can be formulated concerning signal shields and the way they should be handled. Often these rules can be violated with only minor effects. The significance of the resulting deficiency can be determined only by relating parameters such as signal level, signal-to-noise ratio requirements, and cable lengths to the resulting performance.

The rules listed below are derived from the foregoing discussion and are quite general.

1. Each separable environment (signal or power) should be enclosed in a single electrostatic enclosure.

2. The shield for each signal environment should be tied once and only once to the zero signal potential within that environment.

3. The shield tie should be arranged so that unwanted signal currents drain toward ground and do not flow in the signal conductors.

One might ask where the above rules can be violated without causing a problem. Some examples may serve to answer this question.

1. Output leads that are low impedance with respect to the zero signal return do not require shielding. Shielding is often provided just to prevent coupling to other circuits.

2. Primary power leads do not require shielding except within the confines of a transformer. The effects of leaving a power cord unshielded, for example, are usually minimum.

3. Signal leads are often treated coaxially to provide low noise or to prevent magnetic pick-up. This benefit may take precedence over attempting to provide two-wire shielded cable.

In general, common sense must prevail. The suggestions presented above are often difficult to apply because of practical considerations. It is important to realize, however, what the causes and effects are so that, if a choice is available, the best practice may be followed.

3 Instrumentation Amplifiers

This chapter describes one of the major components used in processing analog signals—in fact, the most critical component when the signals are low level. Included are all types of amplifiers, with the major emphasis on the DC type. This class of device includes instrumentation amplifiers and differential amplifiers.

The ensuing discussion places particular emphasis on design and selection criteria. Associated devices and techniques to complete the signal flow paths are also considered in this chapter. Almost all analog signals are processed by one or more of the circuits described here before entry into the digital computer.

AMPLIFIERS

Amplifiers are used to amplify analog signals. Amplification implies voltage and power gains. Since amplifiers generally have high input impedances and low output impedances, an ideal amplifier would have no loading effect on the signal source and would not be affected by loading on its output. Of course, actual circuits deviate from this ideal, as will be described below. The purpose, then, of an amplifier is to accept input signals of a particular input range and to provide as outputs reproduced replicas of these signals in amplified form. Depending on the input-to-output-impedance ratios and voltage ratios, voltage and/or power gain can be achieved. In addition to the gain and impedance transformation characteristics alluded to here, amplifiers have many other parameters that are of significance in analog signal processing before entry into a computer system.

Most signals found in laboratory applications and in the real world have frequency components of interest from DC to some upper frequency limit. Almost always, an amplifier for such applications is referred to as a DC amplifier, even though it may be required to amplify signals over a rather wide bandwidth. In other words, an amplifier is generally classed as a DC amplifier if it is required to amplify direct current, regardless of what higher frequency limit it must also amplify.

Amplifiers used for low-level signal amplification are generally required to handle differential signals. It was explained in Chapter 2 that low-level signals are generated as differential or floating signals and are more reliably transmitted in floating (differential) form. In addition to providing amplification, differential amplifiers convert low-level differential (as well as high-level differential) signals to high-level single-ended form. Most subsequent analog signal processing circuits before the ADC are more easily designed as single ended. An analog multiplexer can be designed with one DC amplifier per analog input, or the multiplexer may share, by switching, a single amplifier among a number of analog input signals. The major point, however, is that DC amplifiers appear universally in analog signal processing chains.

Direct-current amplifiers have been used for many years in various applications, particularly in analog computers, for which use they were originally very highly refined. They are variously referred to as feedback amplifiers, operational amplifiers, DC amplifiers, differential amplifiers, and instrumentation amplifiers. The basic designs are similar. The particular name implies the degree to which an amplifier has been tailored to a specific application. Feedback amplifiers include the complete family of amplifiers mentioned here. The salient feature of these components is that the gain of such amplifiers can be very precisely controlled and held at the required value through the use of feedback circuits connected between the output and the input of very high gain amplifiers. The feedback through precise passive components guarantees the required gain accuracy and stability. These are achieved relatively independently of component drift and aging, and environment fluctuations.

In the preceding discussions analog signals were described as low-level differential signals. Even single-ended high-level signals that may be presented to the computer originate, in many cases, as low-level differential signals. For the purpose of signal flow it is necessary to discuss low-level differential signals, because if these signals can be handled, high-level single-ended signals can surely be handled using the same technique but with less expensive and less precise circuits. In almost every situation, attention must be devoted to processing signals that are low level differential. High-level signals can be handled to any tolerance and precision desired, subject only to cost constraints. Low-level signal handling, on the other hand, is limited by the state of art, the components, and physical factors such as circuit noise.

To amplify low-level differential signals to a usable level, DC amplifiers of the types described below are required. It is sometimes possible to connect low-level analog signals directly to a multiplexer, but in the general case amplifiers are necessary. When an amplifier is shared by a number of input signals via a multiplexer, the amplifier characteristics are approximately the same as discussed here. A major additional factor to consider in specifying the amplifier is the higher bandwidth and faster recovery time needed because of the switching of the multiplexer between analog inputs. The ADC cycle must begin within a short time after the multiplexer switches.

DIFFERENTIAL INPUT

When discussing low-level signals, signal amplitudes as low as a few microvolts are implied. The differential nature of a signal indicates that the information of interest is the difference between the voltages on the two input signal leads. For maximum accuracy the input to the differential amplifier should have an extremely high impedance, thus ensuring that very little load is placed on the transducer signal source. The impedance with respect to ground of either input point is usually as close to open circuit as possible; a high degree of isolation from the ground reference is desirable. If single-ended signals are to be handled by such an amplifier, one input point is tied to ground. (Depending on the selected input, inversion of the output can be achieved.) From a cost point of view it is preferable to use single-ended amplifiers for this type of signal. However, for high-precision applications differential amplifiers are more easily obtained.

The differential amplifier functions to provide an output signal: $K(E_1 - E_2)$, where K is the gain of the differential amplifier and E_1 and E_2 are the voltages applied to each of the two input signal leads. As long as two input signals are applied to the inputs, the output signal is a function of the gain of the amplifier multiplied by the difference in voltage between the two signal leads. When single-ended signals are to be used with a differential amplifier, the output signal is either KE or $-KE$, depending on which of the two input legs is used for the signal. The unused leg is tied to ground.

INPUT/OUTPUT CHARACTERISTICS

The difference in impedance in either input leg of the differential amplifier is the unbalance of the differential input. Even though differential amplifiers are designed to have a high input impedance (essentially infinite), any unbalance will degrade the accuracy of the system. The design parameters are specified with an unbalance, essentially an additional impedance introduced into one of the input legs of the differential amplifier, and all measurements are made with this disturbance value included in the input circuit. Usually an amplifier is specified with an allowable unbalance of 1000 ohms, but other unbalances are, of course, permissible. If a greater unbalance is encountered, the specified accuracy will be correspondingly adversely effected. This is a contributing factor in the total common mode error.

The output of a differential amplifier is usually high level single ended from a low impedance. Full scale is usually in the range of ± 10 V with a drive capability of up to ± 10 MA. The gain of a differential amplifier may range from a fraction to several tens of thousands. Low gains are used primarily for impedance transformations. In such an application the differential amplifier accepts signals from high-input-impedance devices and converts them into low-output-impedance signals capable of high-current drive. This provides gain for driving power over long distances, for instance. Conversion from floating to single-ended signals is also accomplished at the same time.

GAIN

Instrumentation or differential amplifiers (Fig. 1) are designed around extremely high-gain DC amplifiers. Typical open loop gains are 100,000 to 10,000,000. Devices with such high gains are inherently unstable and tend to oscillate. When a very large amount of negative feedback is connected from the output to the input, however, the amplifier exhibits very

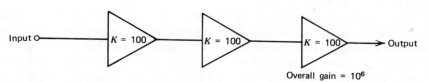

Fig. 1. A schematic of a typical basic amplifier used in instrumentation type amplifiers. This amplifier may have an open loop gain of several million.

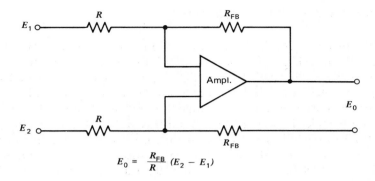

$$E_0 = \frac{R_{FB}}{R} (E_2 - E_1)$$

Fig. 2. A feedback circuit connected between the output and input of an amplifier. The gain of the amplifier is dependent on the ratio of the value of the input resistors and the feedback resistor. The gain is a function of passive components and not active elements, whose characteristics are inherently less stable.

desirable characteristics. The basic circuit (Fig. 2) is stable and relatively insensitive to parameter variations and other environmental conditions. The characteristics of the amplifier are determined mainly by the summing resistors and the feedback elements. These elements are all passive components and can be specified to any desired accuracy and precision. Hence the circuit, although built of active components connected in what is inherently an unstable connection, becomes highly stable and precisely determined through the introduction of negative feedback via passive components. The passive components determine amplifier gain and accuracy almost completely.

To provide even better stability, especially at direct current, chopper stabilization (Fig. 3) is used. This is a technique for amplifying by carrier frequency techniques the DC portion of the signal. Separate paths amplify the DC and the AC components of the signal, and the two results are summed. Chopper stabilized DC amplifiers provide extremely good stability as well as wide band frequency response from direct current to the upper frequency cut-off.

Instrumentation amplifiers are usually purchased as complete units with the feedback components and summing resistors in place. The gain of such circuits may be fixed, variable, or programmable.

Fixed gain amplifiers are designed to operate at either one fixed gain setting or a number of fixed gain settings that are switch selectable.

Variable gain amplifiers are designed so that gain precision is sacrificed in order to set the gain over a wide range of values. Gain is set in these

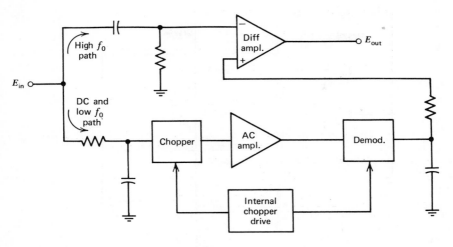

Fig. 3. A schematic of a chopper stabilized amplifier. Direct current and very low-frequency components are converted to AC form by the chopper action. These low-frequency and DC components are amplified by the AC amplifier following the chopper.

amplifiers by means of switches for overall range and a potentiometer that is used to set the exact value of gain required by the application. It should be pointed out that stability and environmental factors must be carefully considered.

In programmable gain amplifiers gain may be set remotely through voltage actuation. For digital applications, digitally controlled programmable amplifiers (Fig. 4) are important. These are essentially fixed gain amplifiers in which the gain range setting is remotely selectable by digital signal. This signal may be generated by a computer, which selects an appropriate range under program control. Alternatively, the range may be selected by circuitry connected to the amplifier output. In either case the desired gain is usually set at the point where the output is in the linear range. This assures optimum sensitivity and accuracy of the amplifier and of the subsequent analog and digital signal processing circuits. In all other respects programmable gain amplifiers possess characteristics similar to those of manual gain selectable amplifiers and fixed gain amplifiers. It should be noted that when the autoranging feature is included, that is, the capability of the amplifier to select automatically a gain that is an optimum setting, the amplifier must include an output signal that represents the self-selected gain setting. A self-programmed gain selection scheme is faster than computer programmed gain selection.

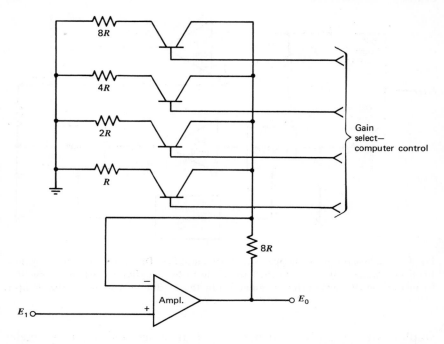

Fig. 4. A programmable gain amplifier having the capability of electrically controlled gain. By supplying additional logic, autoranging can be provided. The logic determines the optimum gain for the input range.

PRICES

Amplifiers used in applications such as those mentioned here range in price from about $5 to over $1000 each. A $10 amplifier can be a single integrated circuit, or it can be a circuit built up of individual elements. Most low-cost amplifiers are encapsulated, whereas more expensive ones are composed of replaceable components that permit maintenance. Low-cost amplifiers are based essentially on a "throw-away and replace" maintenance philosophy. Such amplifiers usually do not have either built-in feedback elements or built-in power supplies. However, complete amplifiers ready for use can be purchased for as little as $10 each. The amplifiers at the upper end of the price scale, which may cost over $1000 installed, have individual isolated, self-contained highly stable power supplies, ultrastable feedback elements, and, of course, extraordinarily good specifications.

It is difficult to make any general comments in regard to cost because price is highly dependent on the particular performance required. Obviously the tighter the specification and the higher the performance required, the greater the price that must be paid.

SPECIFICATION SHEETS

Specification sheets for typical DC amplifiers show a very wide range of characteristics. The difference in costs is approximately two orders of magnitude. If less stringent characteristics are tolerable, a large cost savings can be made. When this factor is multiplied by the number of amplifiers usually encountered even in a very simple system, the attractiveness of using the least expensive amplifier that meets the minimum requirements is self-evident.

It is recommended that the requirements of the analog signal processing be carefully examined before analog components are selected. To specify DC amplifiers the definitions and implications of their characteristics should be examined. No advantage is gained through overspecifying the amplifier characteristics; in fact, a severe penalty in terms of price and availability of suitable components is incurred by such poor engineering practices.

ERROR FACTORS

Differential amplifiers are characterized by a number of important error defining parameters. The aim in the design of every electronic component is to provide characteristics as close to the ideal as possible within the allowed cost constraints. Understanding the effect of the error producing characteristics allows one to select the most appropriate unit.

The most important parameter in the application of amplifiers in a computer environment is amplifier stability. Stability is a function of a number of different variables, such as noise, gain, temperature, component aging, and power supplies. Each of these factors affects stability in a different way; some influence short term stability (measured in seconds or less), and others alter long term characteristics (measured in weeks or months).

The gain of a DC amplifier is determined to a first approximation solely by the feedback and summing resistors. However, when high precision is required, other considerations such as open loop gain affect the gain stability and accuracy. The gain in the ideal situation is considered to be infinite, although in actual practice this is not true. To the exent that the gain is not infinite, it is affected by the instabilities of the amplifier's active components.

Another cause of concern is baseline drift, which is characterized by an apparent DC offset signal entered into the amplifier along with the signal of interest. At zero signal, a DC signal due to baseline zero drift, appears at the output. Although the amplifier may be zeroed to produce a zero output to correspond to a zero signal, input drift is inevitable and after some time the baseline will drift from the nominal zero.

The same factors, as described in the following sections, are also functions of component stability. It is well known that, with aging, components change value as a function of time. Drift is also associated with temperature variations. Regardless of how carefully components are selected to provide zero temperature coefficients, drift still is possible because of variations in ambient temperature. Similarily, variations in power supplies due to line and load regulation cause errors.

NOISE

Noise is probably the greatest factor to be taken into account. Noise components are functions of electron thermal conditions, active device self-generated noise, and induced noise due to electromagnetic interference. Some noise components may be reduced by shielding and good design practices, whereas others represent basic device limitations. Noise control techniques were discussed in the preceding sections; these include good wiring practices, shielding, guard shield techniques, and filtering to reduce information bandwidth to the range of interest, thereby attenuating noise components outside of these limits.

REFERRED TO INPUT

The error factors discussed are usually specified as equivalent error signals referred to the input (RTI). Each instability or error source, is converted, insofar as possible, to an equivalent error signal appearing at the input to the amplifier. Thus drift with respect to temperature variation would be specified as microvolts per degree centigrade.

It is convenient to refer error conditions to the amplifier input because the gain of an amplifier is normally selected by a switch on the device or under program control. As a practical matter most errors are introduced in amplifier input, and the error is thus multiplied by the gain of the amplifier. The higher the gain of the amplifier, the larger the apparent inaccuracy at the output.

ERRORS

Device errors may be measured as either statistical or worst case errors. As explained in Chapter 2, a statistical error is usually defined as the root mean square of the sum of the squares of error contributing factors. This assumes a statistical distribution of error factors. The worst case error, on the other hand, assumes that all error conditions occur simultaneously, and in the worst possible excursion for each error contributing term. Although this is usually not the case, because errors are, to an extent, self-compensating, to be absolutely safe one would have to assume a worst case condtion for certain applications. Certainly the amplifier user would prefer the more stringent worst case specification, whereas the amplifier manufacturer would describe an equivalent amplifier in terms of the more lenient statistical error conditions.

GAIN FACTOR

The gain of an instrumentation amplifier is usually selected by switching the feedback element. Many amplifiers have switch selectable gain settings that typically range from fractional values to gains of several thousand. These gain factors are voltage gains in most situations.

It should be emphasized that amplifiers typically have extremely high input impedances and very low output impedances. The amplifiers are designed to draw almost zero current from the source while being capable of furnishing a relatively large amount of current. Thus, regardless of the voltage gain, the amplifier always provides a high current and power gain. At low and at fractional gain settings, the function of the amplifier could be to provide signal transmission capabilities by taking advantage of the power gain. The low output impedance implies high drive current and power capability. Also, it is evident that low output impedance permits driving the signal over a relatively long distance.

OVERLOAD

Another factor in amplifiers specification is the overload recovery time, that is, the time required for the amplifier to recover when overloaded by an input that drives the device beyond its linear amplification range.

An instrumentation amplifier will saturate when the product of the input signal and selected gain setting reaches the maximum linear output value of the device. However, sufficient protection is usually built-in the more expensive amplifiers to permit the acceptance of signals much in excess of the saturation level without causing amplifier damage. The maximum safe overload is usually specified. When the input reaches saturation level, the amplifier overloads and takes a longer time to recover. The recovery time can be critical in certain applications and should be taken into consideration. This factor can be particularly troublesome when the amplifier follows a multiplexer. Most practical designs have overload protection diodes that prevent the amplifier from entering the saturated region.

It is important to include safety features in expensive instrumentation amplifiers. Short circuit current limiting elements assure that the amplifier will not be destroyed in the event of a short circuit overload. Similarly, input overloads can be tolerated if proper design precautions are taken.

DYNAMIC RANGE

One of the more important factors in the specification of a differential amplifier is its dynamic range. The dynamic range needed for a particular application must be calculated by the user. The dynamic signal range is the ratio of the maximum and minimum signals of interest in the system. The dynamic range of the amplifier is determined by the noise and error conditions RTI, the amplifier gain selected, and the saturation level of the output. For instance, if the noise and error factors RTI due to all causes are approximately 20 μV and the gain of the amplifier is 1000, the no-signal output will be amplified to 20 mV measured at the output. If the amplifier has a full scale output of 10 V, the dynamic range that it can handle will be 500, since the minimum output signal will be approximately 20 mV. Thus, the dynamic range is 500 to 1.

In many situations a number of analog signals, each having a limited dynamic range, must be handled. However, some signals have relatively large amplitudes, while others are low level. One way to handle such a group of signals is to provide a separate fixed gain amplifier for each signal. The gain of each amplifier is selected so that the amplified signal output will conform to a "standard" range which is compatible with the overall system configuration. For example, if the amplifiers are connected via a multiplexer to an ADC, the selected amplifier gains will be such as to match the amplifier output signal range to the ADC input range.

FREQUENCY RESPONSE

The bandwidth of a DC amplifier is the upper frequency limit with flat response. A bandwidth commensurate with the response of the input signal is required; fast response input signals require amplifiers of wider bandwidth. It should be noted that, when narrow bands are used, fewer problems with stability and noise occur. Therefore it is good practice to select an amplifier with the minimum necessary bandwidth. Even though a signal may have a very wide band charactertistic, an amplifier of narrower bandwidth may be used because much of the information at the high-frequency end of the signal may not be of interest. In this sense, a DC amplifier acts effectively to filter high-frequency components.

It is desirable to predict the frequency characteristics of an input analog signal by defining its spectrum. This knowledge simplifies processing the data. By the application of appropriate filter techniques certain low-energy or nonessential components of the signal can be deleted, thus reducing the data rate and simplifying the process.

Many high-quality instrumentation amplifiers have variable bandwidth controls that are switch selectable. This permits the user to select the bandwidth best suited to his particular on-hand application. The techniques for frequency response testing were discussed previously.

Band limiting is most expediently accomplished at the amplifier input of the signal processing chain. In many situations passive filter elements are connected into the data path at this point. With modern circuit techniques active filters that are integral to the amplifier can be used. One should be cognizant of the advantages in signal enhancement at this point and use them if applicable. Usually a simpler system results if band-limiting can be performed at the input point.

COMMON MODE REJECTION

In selecting instrumentation amplifiers, attention must be directed to common mode signals. The common mode signal is the voltage that is common to both inputs of the differential signal. As mentioned previously, the normal mode voltage, that is, the difference between the signals on the two inputs lines, is the signal of interest.

For differential amplifiers it is necessary to specify a common mode rejection ratio. This is the amount of rejection of the common mode signal as reflected by an apparent output error. Common mode rejection ratios of 10^7 are possible, although values in the range of 10^6 are more common. If the common mode rejection ratio is 10^6, for instance, a 10-V signal on both legs of the input will appear as 10-μV RTI. Common mode rejection ratios are usually specified at direct current, at power line frequency, and at 1000 Hz. When dealing with low-level signals, common mode rejection ratio figures can be significant in device selection.

4 Analog to Digital Conversion

Analog to digital converters (ADCs) are used to convert analog signals to a form that can be accepted by digital computers (Fig. 1). An ADC accepts analog voltages as inputs and produces the equivalent digital values. An ADC can usually handle a number of analog input channels, which are switched in a multiplexer.

MULTIPLEXERS

A multiplexer is sometimes used (Fig. 2) to share an ADC among a number of analog signal input channels. Multiplexers are essentially computer controlled analog signal switches that can connect selected analog inputs to a single output point. A multiplexer makes it possible for many analog inputs to share a single ADC. Many analog signals are of relatively

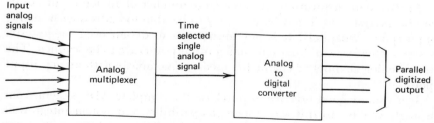

Fig. 1. A typical analog signal flow path to the computer. A number of analog signals are connected to individual inputs of an analog multiplexer. Under computer control the multiplexer selects the analog inputs and connects them to an analog to digital converter (ADC). The ADC in turn digitizes the analog signal and provides the digital equivalent as an output which is connected as an input to the computer. The ADC output is connected through the digital input facility of the computer.

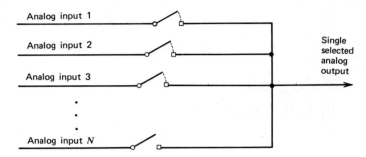

Fig. 2. An analog multiplexer is a switching device under computer control that connects multiple analog input signal points, one at a time, to a common output. A multiplexer should act as much as possible as an ideal analog switch—zero loading on the input, zero switching time, and good matching to the associated ADC.

slow speed when compared to ADC capabilities. The difference in cost between an ADC that will operate at a rate of 10,000 conversions per second and one that is capable of only 1000 conversions per second is inconsequential. These conversion rates may be in excess of those required for some of the more frequently encountered analog signals generated in the analytic laboratory. It then becomes expedient to share the ADC among a number of analog inputs, and the analog multiplexer makes this possible. The analog multiplexer under program control connects computer program addressable analog input points to the ADC. In situations where only a single analog channel is to be converted, where the ADC is just fast enough to handle one analog input channel, or where multiple ADCs (one for each input) are used, the analog signals are connected directly to the ADC.

In most data acquisition systems a large number of analog input points are of interest, and it may be necessary to be able to address each analog input point separately. It is not uncommon to design even modest size systems where several hundred analog input points are to be scanned. The term analog channel or channel is used synonomously with analog input point.

It is usually good practice to purchase the complete ADC system from a single vendor. In this way system compatibility and system integration can be assured. It is common to find vendors that produce multiplexer ADC packages. The multiplexers are usually modular and can be purchased in groups of 8 to 16 points (or channels). Analog multiplexers may be constructed using relay switches for relatively low switching rates or solid state switches for high-speed switching and for greatest compactness.

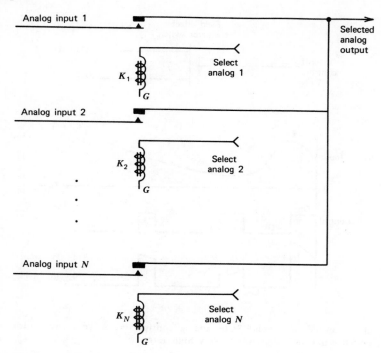

Analog input 1

Select analog 1

K_1

G

Selected analog output

Analog input 2

Select analog 2

K_2

G

Analog input N

Select analog N

K_N

G

Fig. 3. An example of a relay analog multiplexer. A separate relay is associated with each analog input point. The computer can address each relay and actuate it. When a relay is actuated, the analog input it switches is connected to the output. Multiple contact relays can be used to switch balanced signal lines.

For switching rates below approximately 200 points per second, relay multiplexers (Fig. 3) offer optimum price-performance values. Low-level differential signals can be multiplexed directly using relay multiplexers. A single instrumentation type amplifier is connected at the output of the multiplexed analog signals to bring the resultant output up to the signal level required by the ADC.

Relays are perfect switches. They have open contact resistances equal to infinity and closed contact resistances on the order of a few milliohms. The relay multiplexer can handle both high-level single-ended signals and low-level differential signals. Single-ended signals are handled by single-pole relays, whereas differential signals are handled using double-pole contacts. As long as the relay switching rate is fast enough for the particular application under consideration, the relay multiplexer is satisfactory. Relay multiplexers are reliable enough for military applications.

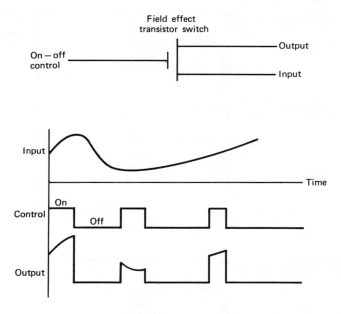

Fig. 4. An example of a solid state analog mutiplexer. A complete multichannel analog switch can switch signals at a very high rate.

Solid state multiplexers (Fig. 4) are designed using transistors or integrated circuit switching devices. The newer solid state multiplexer designs are based on the application of a field-effect transistor (FET) circuit as the switching element. A solid state multiplexer utilizes an active circuit that drives a switch (the transistor device) in series with an analog input signal, or it sets a short circuit/open circuit in parallel with the analog signal path. Solid state multiplexers can be designed to operate at rates commensurate with the highest speed ADCs. Transfer accuracy can be a problem with solid state multiplexers, especially at low signal levels. At analog inputs levels of approximately ±5 V full scale, solid state multiplexers are relatively easy to design and can be purchased as standard commercial devices. The advent of FET switches has removed even this limitation on solid state devices and permits low-level analog switching at high speeds and great accuracy. These units can have transfer accuracies that will not degrade a 14-bit (plus sign) ADC operating at rates at rates at over 200,000 conversions per second. However, at lower levels and for differential signals solid state multiplexers alone may not suffice from cost-performance considerations. It is usually necessary to use an instru-

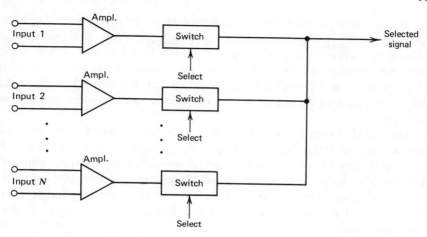

Fig. 5. In most cases where low-level, high-speed balanced analog signals are to be switched, an amplifier is needed before the multiplexer. For high-accuracy, high-speed switching, a separate instrumentation grade amplifier is required for each channel. The amplifier should handle differential signals, have a high input impedance and a single ended output. The gain should amplify the input signal range to a level satisfactory for the accuracy requirements of the appplication.

mentation grade amplifier (Fig. 5) in each analog input signal path. The amplifier provides amplification and differential floating to single-ended signal conversion. It should be noted that low-level differential switches are available. However, their cost and performance leave much to be desired. Except for specific applications, a better system can usually be designed using multiple amplifiers, one per input.

MULTIPLEXER CHARACTERISTICS

An ideal analog multiplexer should transfer any computer selected analog input signal line with absolute fidelity to the output line without disturbing the signal source. The multiplexer should be transparent to the input signal. This section discusses the factors that cause practical multiplexers to deviate from the ideal and thereby introduce errors into the signal measurement procedure.

The requirements stated above indicate that the multiplexer should present a very high input impedance to each analog signal source. When the multiplexer position for a particular analog input signal is selected, it should not change the effective load on the analog signal source. Even in the selected position, the multiplexer must present a very high impedance to the multiplexed analog signal source; ideally the multiplexer should not appear as a load on the analog signal source. Even if the multiplexer does appear as a load on the analog signal source, it must not appear as a different impedance when selected and when open. In effect, the loading on the analog signal source must remain constant at all times.

The speed of transfer of a signal across the analog multiplexer must be commensurate with the ADC being used. The multiplexer should switch the input signal in a time that is small compared to the time required for the ADC to perform a conversion. To assure that the ADC operates at its maximum rate, the multiplexer must make a connection between its input and its output in a small fraction of total analog to digital conversion time.

The settling time of the multiplexer is another factor that must be considered. This is the time required for the output to come within a specified percentage of the connected input. Since the conversion cycle of the ADC cannot begin until the switched multiplexer output is within the specified limit, fast settling time is required for accurate conversions as well as high speed.

Relay multiplexers are limited by electromechanical considerations and contact bounce. Solid state multiplexer switches are limited by electronic circuit and active device time constants.

POLARITY AND SIGNAL LEVEL

Multiplexers can be designed to handle unipolar or bipolar signals. It is somewhat less expensive to build a unipolar device. However, in view of the small difference in cost and the fact that most commercially available multiplexers are bipolar, there does not seem to be any reason to specify a unipolar converter, unless a special design for a particular application is necessary.

Relay multiplexers can handle single-ended or differential inputs over an extremely wide dynamic range, from approximately a few microvolts to tens of volts. Solid state multiplexers will normally handle signals from a few millivolts to several volts. Solid state multiplexers are sensitive to overloads and may be permanently damaged. Relay multiplexers, on the other hand, are comparatively tolerant of overloads.

RELAY MULTIPLEXERS

A relay multiplexer is conceptually simple since it is a multipole single-throw relay switch. When the relay is actuated by passing current through its coil, the input signal is connected through the closed relay contacts to the output of the multiplexer. The relay multiplexer essentially consists of high-quality relays; mercury wetted contact relays or reed relays are very satisfactory. These types have relatively little contact bounce and very low contact resistance. They can be operated reliably at speeds of approximatly 2 to 10 msec, with allowances for contact bounce time and all switching transients. Such contacts are also effective for reliably switching low-voltage, low-current circuits. Multiple contacts can be operated by the same relay coil, thereby permitting simultaneous differential (and guard) switching. In the quiescent state, the relay switch introduces very little noise into the circuit path and therefore is well suited to handle low-level differential signals. Care must be taken, however, not to sample the analog signals during the switching time of any relay device in the multiplexer because of switching transients inherently present when relays are switched. As was mentioned previously, the major limitation of a relay multiplexer is its relatively low speed switching as compared to solid state devices. Another factor, not usually of overriding consequences in laboratory data systems, is that relay switches are bulkier than solid state devices. Also, higher-power drivers and switching transient suppression are needed to control relay multiplexers.

The service life of mercury or reed relays is not a limiting factor on the life of relay multiplexers because under normal operating conditions each relay will probably not be selected at a rate close to the maximum sampling rate. Although there are usually many input points, only one point at a time is selected and therefore only one relay at a time is actuated. It should also be pointed out that, even if the system is run continuously, the lives of most relay multiplexers, especially those using mercury wetted contacts or reed contacts, are on the order of billions of cycles. At 100 switches per second, a relay rated at 10^9 operations will survive about 1 year of continuous operation. Relay multiplexers are physically large; a comparable solid state multiplexer, including all amplifiers and other components, will fit into a smaller space. Solid state multiplexers are also less susceptible to mechanical vibration. However, as indicated above, in ground based applications, especially in a laboratory environment, these are usually not major concerns.

It should be reiterated that instrumentation type amplifiers usually

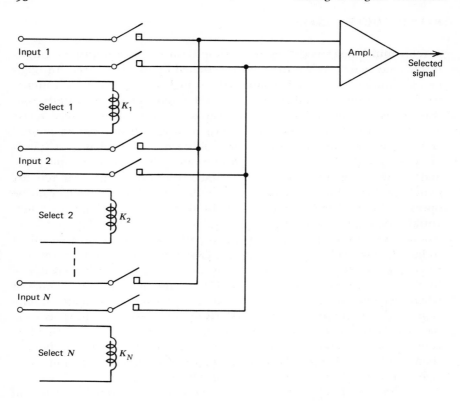

Fig. 6. A relay multiplexer schematic. The relays can be mercury wetted contact or reed contact types. These switch rapidly and have relatively little contact bounce. Multiple contacts can be provided to switch balanced signals with their signal grounds. Amplifiers can be provided for each group of relays handling signals covering the same general range. Successive stages of multiplexing following the amplifiers can be used to select the output of a particular group.

follow a relay multiplexer (Fig. 6), the output of which is connected directly to the input of an instrumentation type amplifier. The relay multiplexer can handle low-level differential signals directly. However, the following ADC usually requires a ±5 V full scale input. Thus an amplifier is needed. Relay multiplexer points are usually clustered in groups so that each group shares one amplifier. Each group then has the same full scale capabilities. Thus, for instance, all 1-mV full scale signals could share one amplifier, and all inputs with 10-mV full scale signals could share another. Cascading amplifiers in groups is also feasible. It should be stressed that specification of the amplifier characteristics must take switching times into account when bandwidth and permissible settling times are indicated.

FLYING CAPACITOR MULTIPLEXERS

An ingenious circuit technique for handling differential signals is the flying capacitor multiplexer (Fig. 7). In this circuit, double-throw, double-pole relays are used in the multiplexers. Under the normal "not selected" condition the input is connected through resistors to a large charging capacitor. The input circuit charges the capacitor to the full signal voltage. The capacitor charges only to the normal mode signal because of the way in which the differential signal is effectively connected to the charge capacitor. When a particular point is selected, the capacitor is effectively switched from the input circuit to the multiplexer output. Since the capacitor was charged through an isolation resistor, it effec-

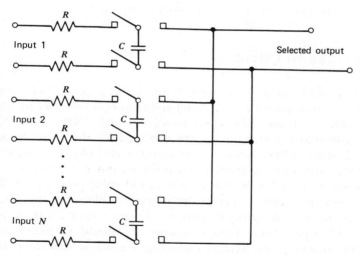

Fig. 7. A flying capacitor type multiplexer provides a relatively low cost method for handling low-level, high-accuracy differential signals. Relay multiplexers are usually used for switching. Normally the input is connected via a pair of relay contacts through resistors to a large storage capacitor. When the particular point is selected, the relay contacts are disconnected from the input and connected to the output. The voltage stored on the capacitor is then sampled. This scheme provides complete isolation between the signal source and the following analog processing circuitry.

tively represents a very small no-load condition to the input signal source. The capacitor is usually charged to a voltage that is equal to the input signal source. The fact that the input signal is never connected to the output or to the system ground within the multiplexer, keeps the ground of the input completely isolated from that of the analog to digital conversion system. The switched capacitor is the only linkage between input and output. The capacitor is connected for only a very short time to the ADC front end. It is connected through a high-input-impedance amplifier so that it has not discharged when reconnected back to the input. This type of circuit provides a very effective way of converting a differential signal to a single-ended signal and thus obviates many of the problems that occur with low-level signals.

The major limitation on the flying capacitor multiplexer is the selection rate for a particular input. The circuit works on the principle of charging a capacitor through a large resistor. This effectively is a low-pass filter. Thus the frequency response is restricted because a relatively long R-C time constant is required. It is good practice to sample at a rate no greater than one tenth the R-C time constant. This provision is not restricting, however, if low-frequency signals are under consideration, as is the case with many laboratory instruments.

SOLID STATE MULTIPLEXERS

Solid state multiplexers are most useful for high-level, high-frequency signals, as was discussed earlier. Solid state multiplexers may be designed using various types of field effect transistors and PNP and NPN transistors. Integrated circuit devices are also used for the multiplexer. The active element, either a transistor or an integrated circuit, is arranged to be a switch across the junction of two resistors. When the switch is closed, that is, when the active element is in the conducting position, an effective short circuit is connected across the junction. When the transistors are in the off, or nonconducting condition, an open circuit exists, permitting the signal to pass from input to output. It should be noted that the circuitry can also be arranged as a series connection, so that the transistors are effectively in series with the input signal. Integrated circuitry built on PNP or NPN junctions is most useful for high-level switching because offset voltages of several millivolts are inherent. Field effect transistor switches are much closer to ideal switches. Offset votlages measured in the few microvolt range are achieved.

Solid state multiplexers can be designed to operate at switching speeds

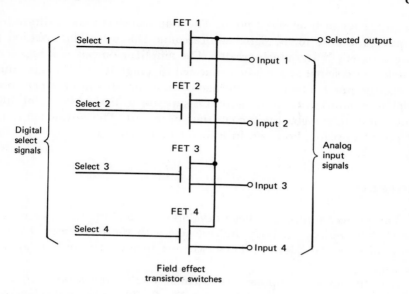

Fig. 8. An example of field effect transistor (FET) circuitry used in an analog switch. This circuit can switch a selected input to the output within 1 μsec to within 0.1% of its final value. Input signals as low as 5 μV can be handled. A signal dynamic range of 10^4 to 10^5 can be handled. The isolation between input and output is excellent; input impedance can be tens of megohms, while output impedance can be quite low.

of 250,000 to 1,000,000 operations per second with transfer accuracies to 0.01%, or better. At these rates the switch presents an extremely high input impedance to the input signal when not selected. When selected, the switch presents a series impedance to the signal of a few ohms. Solid state multiplexers that permit an ADC to operate at over 250,000 15-bit conversions per second are commercially available. These solid state multiplexers work at inputs ranging from millivolts to volts full scale. Field effect transistor based multiplexers (Fig. 8) effectively switch microvolt signals.

It is difficult to design solid state differential low-level multiplexers. Such units are on the market but are usually satisfactory only for certain specific applications. Until the advent of FET low-level switches, low-level solid state multiplexers were usually more noise sensitive and also presented varying impedance to the signal source. The impedance was a function of the individual multiplexer channel selection rate. Even though FET based multiplexers have superior charactertistics, it is usually less expensive and gives better results to have a separate differential amplifier for each low-level point. The amplifier presents a uniform high input impedance to the signal source connected to it. The isolation between signals is also much greater. The amplifier output is a high-level, single-ended signal and can be connected to a high-level solid state multiplexer terminal. The price-performance value for an amplifier per point/ high-level multiplexer combination is superior to that of low-level differential multiplexing at the present state of the art. This advantage can be expected to swing, however, in favor of FET switches.

OVERLAP

Various techniques have been developed to combine the low-cost, low-level characteristics of relay multiplexers with the high-speed characteristics of solid state devices. These schemes involve various overlap techniques.

A simple overlap approach is to connect relay and solid state multiplexer points to the same ADC input (Fig. 9). The relay multiplexers are set up in independent groups. As a practical example, assume that a relay multiplexer can select and set up a point in 10 msec, with 8 msec required to set up the relay switch and 2 msec needed for settling time and stability, and that by solid state techniques a point can be selected and converted in 50 μsec. From these figures it is evident that 40 points can be selected and converted during a 2-msec period. Thus, if many relay multiplexers are actuated simultaneously with one point from each relay group connected to a solid state multiplexer, the rate of the system can be increased considerably. The solid state multiplexer can be programmed to scan through the output of the relay groups in a very short time. Other types and combinations of overlap can also be configured, depending on the particular requirements.

MULTIPLEXER CONTROL

The multiplexer addressing scheme is determined by the computer program. Depending on the design of the multiplexer, individual points can be computer addressable or, alternatively, addressed in a sequence determined by the multiplexer control itself. Even in the latter situation, initialization is computer controlled. Various scanner sequencing schemes are possible, depending on the application.

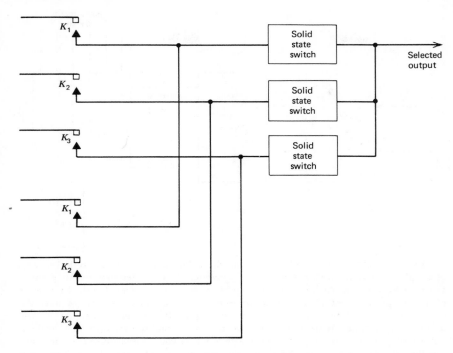

Fig. 9. An example of a combination relay and solid state analog multiplexer. Overlap is provided so that several relay multiplexer points are connected simultaneously to their respective inputs. A separate point in each relay group is selected. The output of each relay group is connected to a solid state multiplexer.

Computer selection of multiplexer addresses in three separate modes is desirable. In each mode, multiplexer selection address lines are passed from the computer to the multiplexer. The modes that may be selected are (1) single-point scan, (2) sequential scan, and (3) random scan. Depending on the computer and multiplexer hardware, one or more of these modes may be implemented (Fig. 10).

A single-point scan implies that the computer program selects one point and keeps that point continuously connected to the ADC. That input point is continuously sampled and converted. Except for very high-speed applications in which the required ADC conversion rate exceeds multiplexer switching speeds, a number of points are connected to the ADC. When a single-point high-speed signal must be connected, it is wise to consider an ADC dedicted to that input. Of course, the final decision

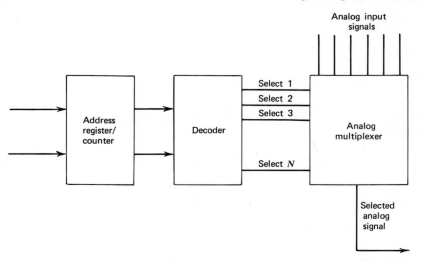

Fig. 10. An example of a multiplexer controller. The multiplexer controller consists of a register-counter, which is followed by a decoder. A single decoded output point is provided for each analog input point. The register-counter is loaded with the address of a multiplexer input by the computer program. The initiate signal connects the decoded addressed input to the multiplexer output. If the register-counter in the multiplexer controller is permitted to count after each multiplexer operation, sequential scanning of the analog input points will result. If counting is inhibited, successive samples will be taken from the same addressed input. Alternatively the computer program can load new addresses in random order after each operation.

depends on the general system considerations and multiplexing requirements.

SEQUENTIAL SCANNING

In a sequential scanning system the computer provides a starting address to the analog multiplexer and a sequential scanning mode control signal. In this mode of operation, the analog multiplexer starts scanning sequentially and continuously through the connected analog input channels from the starting address. The computer sets the sequential scan mode control in motion and keeps it actuated until the required number of analog input channels is scanned and read in. Wrap-around capability is sometimes provided, so that when the number of points exceeds the maximum analog input address, the multiplexer will recycle back to the initially selected point, or to the zero address point, and continue from there. After each analog input channel is scanned and connected for conversion to the ADC, the multiplexer address selection circuitry is automatically incremented by one, and the next sequential analog input channel is connected to the ADC.

In addition to sequencing from a starting address and sequential wrap-around scanning, other scan control sequences can be specified and designed. The simplest additional alternative technique that might be considered involves scanning from a "home" or "zero" reference each time that the computer command to scan is received; this could also be a preset address. Sequential scanning continues from that point. This approach relieves the computer of the initial address selection task since the starting address is always the same. The stop command can occur at any point in the scan sequence under program control or after a preset number of scans on the points are passed or a particular address is reached.

RANDOM SCANNING

Random scan implies that each analog point that the computer selects for scanning is an address provided by the program. If 10 points are to be scanned, for instance, 10 addresses are provided. The selected points can be in any desired sequence; the same point can even be repeated in the sequence. This feature is especially useful when signals of varying sampling rates are to be converted. In many cases it is desirable to convert each input line at an optimal rate that is different for each channel; a variable sequencing program is generated under computer control.

The sampling sequence schedule can be built up as a table of addresses in the computer memory. The computer will then output the table of selected multiplexer addresses to the analog multiplexer control unit at a rate determined by the switching circuits or controlled externally. Each analog point is selected by the multiplexer for connection to the ADC. The corresponding digital data for the converted analog input point are then accepted into the computer as input, and a table of digitized values corresponding to the analog multiplexer address table is formed in the computer memory.

DIRECT CONNECTION

In many stituations the analog input signal is connected directly to the ADC (Fig. 11). There are situations in which only one analog signal is

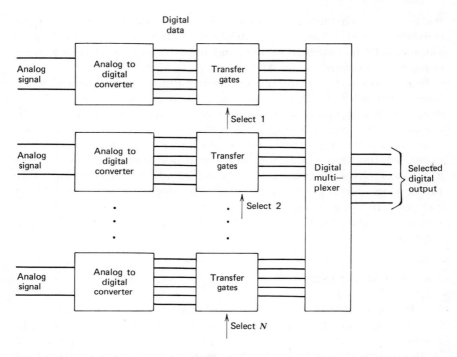

Fig. 11. An analog signal may be directly connected to the input of an ADC without preliminary multiplexing. With the advent of low-cost ADCs on a single integrated circuit chip, it is sometimes more economical to provide a separate ADC for each input signal. When multiple ADCs are used, a digital multiplexer is needed to select the desired digitized ADC output.

of interest, or the signal of interest is of such high frequency that the full ADC rate is required to satisfy the basic sampling theorem criteria. Another situation that is becoming more and more economically feasible with the advent of low-cost integrated circuit ADCs is the use of a separate ADC for each analog input channel. A complete ADC can be built on a single integrated circuit chip. The digital outputs of all the ADCs are then multiplexed onto a common digital data bus.

Another situation that makes it necessary to use a separate ADC for each signal, or a separate ADC multiplexer for each group of analog signals, occurs when the analog signals of interest originate at relatively long distances from the ADC, perhaps from instruments at relatively long distances from the central site. It may be desirable from various considerations discussed previously to transmit the signals in digital form. In such situations each instrument or group of remote signals has its own ADC. The multiplexing equipment and ADCs are located within the instrument or adjacent to it, and all the signals are transmitted in digital form from the instrument. In such cases the problem is reduced to the much simpler situation of multiplexing digital signals into the computer.

ANALOG TO DIGITAL CONVERTERS

Analog to digital converters (Fig. 12) can be purchased with conversion resolutions of at least 15 bits. This is equivalent to a resolution of 1 part in 32,768. Most ADCs are bipolar and are specified as to the number of converted bits plus a sign bit. Bipolar ADCs with 15-bit resolution can be designed to perform a maximum of approximately 250,000 independent conversions per second, considering the current state of the technology. Higher conversion rates are available but at a lower bit resolution. Analog to digital converters having conversion rates as high as 10,000,000 conversions per second but with perhaps 5-bit resolution can be obtained.

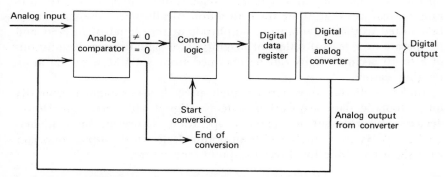

Fig. 12. A schematic diagram of an ADC. Most ADCs contain an analog signal comparator, a digital to analog converter (DAC), and logic/decision circuitry. The ADC begins its operation when it receives a "start" pulse. The analog input is assumed to have stabilized by the time the start pulse is received. The analog input is compared with the output of the DAC. The difference and its sense are used to control the DAC so as to drive its output to be equal to the analog input signal, thus causing a comparator zero error. When the ADC completes its operation, an end-of-conversion pulse is issued. This indicates that the digital data at the output of the ADC are valid and may be read by the computer. The end-of-conversion pulse can be used by the system to initiate the next cycle and to reposition the multiplexer.

Analog to digital converters are designed primarily for computer or data logging system interfacing and usually have binary electrical outputs. Since most small computers represent negative numbers in 2's complement form, it is also convenient to specify ADCs with a similar characteristic—2's complement representation of negative numbers. Although ADCs may be obtained with binary coded decimal (BCD) outputs, it is usually more convenient to handle binary codes in succeeding processing devices. Therefore, unless immediate viewing of results is mandatory, it is preferable to specify binary output ADCs.

DIGITAL VOLTMETERS

In regard to digital voltmeters (DVMs) and their relationship to ADCs, the two are, strictly speaking, actually the same device. A DVM is a relatively slow instrument designed primarily for an operator, and usually has a single analog input signal connected to it. Many older type DVMs were designed using relay logic; however, most currently designed units are solid state.

A DVM usually has a direct reading decimal display, whereas an ADC has either no display or an optional binary read-out. Digital voltmeters operate over relatively wide dynamic ranges. Most instruments have auto-ranging features that allow them to automatically select the gain range best suited to the instantaneous amplitude of the signal of interest and to operate over several orders of magnitude of signal range. Resolutions of 8 to 10 decimal digits can be obtained from a DVM with the auto-ranging feature.

Analog to digital converters are high-speed devices designed primarily for automatic data acquisition systems; digital voltmeters are slower devices with read-out for manual operation. However, most higher-quality DVMs are available with an optional electrical output connecter with signals suitable for direct computer connection.

ANALOG TO DIGITAL CONVERTER OUTPUT

An ADC expects a voltage as its input, and it converts that input voltage to a number which is proportional to the voltage. An ADC converts an input voltage at 0 V to a number equivalent to zero. A voltage equal to a full scale input is converted to +0111111 . . ., the largest number that the ADC outputs. Similarly, a number equal to minus full scale is converted to the largest negative number that can be handled by the ADC. Binary coded decimal and other codes are also available; the choice is usually dependent on the computer selected. Of course, BCD codes are less efficient insofar as data packing is concerned.

Many ADCs are designed with an overload indication capability; a separate bit is provided to indicates that the ADC input has exceeded full scale. The overflow bit is accompanied by the largest positive or negative number to show the polarity of the overflow. This is a convenient feature on an ADC and can usually be provided at little or no additional cost, if considered in the initial design.

The electrical characteristics of the ADC should be selected to match the I/O buses of the computer (Fig. 13). Thus, the "one"/"zero" voltage levels of the ADC should match the computer I/O bus specified levels. In certain cases buffers and/or voltage level shifters may be required. The major control input to the ADC is usually a "start conversion" pulse. The outputs consist of an "end of conversion" and the parallel data output signals. The "start" is received either from the multiplexer when its output has stabilized, the computer, or some external or internal clock source. When the converter completes its cycle, it issues the "end of conversion." This signals the external devices that valid data are available on the ADC output bus. Single- or double-rail output data

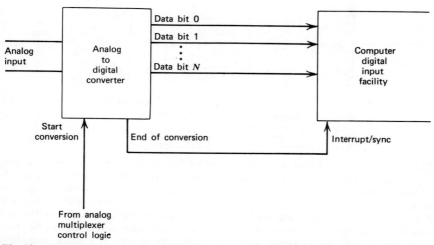

Fig. 13. A schematic showing the signal flow between an ADC and the computer. Double-rail output data buses may be provided on the ADC for convenience in interfacing.

buses can be specified. A double-rail output bus provides the output number and its complement; a single-rail bus, the number only. When the ADC/multiplexer is bought from a single vendor, the controls for these two units are synchronized by the joint control logic. This is the recommended way to buy analog conversion equipment, since the vendor can then provide the system as a single integrated package. Otherwise, some problems can be encountered in adapting the synchronization between the multiplexer of one vendor and the ADC of a second vendor. In addition, low-level analog signal connections between different equipments can create unforeseen difficulties. By specifying a complete package from a single vendor, these problems are obviated.

SAMPLE AND HOLD

For high-precision conversion a sample-and-hold amplifier (Fig. 14) is desirable at the front end of an ADC. The signal flow is from the analog source to the multiplexer to the sample-and-hold amplifier. The sample-and-hold circuit receives a control signal from the multiplexer and ADC control logic when the multiplexer has stabilized its output. Sample-and-hold control pulses are issued to the sample-and-hold amplifier and have the effect of enabling a sample timing gate of very short dura-

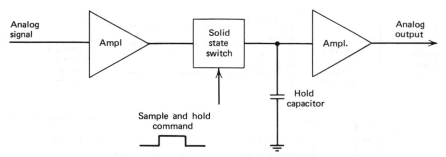

Fig. 14. A sample-and-hold amplifier is needed to handle rapidly changing analog input signals. The sample-and-hold amplifier is connected between the analog multiplexer output and the ADC input. The sample-and-hold circuit provides amplification, as well as integration and storage, and is actuated after the analog multiplexer has connected a selected analog input to its output point. The sample-and-hold circuit samples signals applied to its input. The actuate signals open a very narrow window. The input voltage on the sample-and-hold input is transferred to a charge capacitor. The charge time is less than the window aperture time, and the charge time constant is much less than the discharge time constant. The ADC converts the signal provided by the sample-and-hold output.

tion. The signal effectively opens a narrow aperture sampling gate. The voltage that exists at the instant in time when the aperture is actuated is switched over and stored on the storage capacitor within the sample-and-hold amplifier. It is this voltage that is presented to the ADC for conversion.

The sample and hold acts as an analog storage device that, under the control of ADC logic circuits, accepts a command to hold the input at a particular instant in time for a long period. The aperture time is the time during which the analog input signal is connected to the storage capacitor. Sample-and-hold times with apertures of the order of 50 nsec or less are used. Extremely short charge time constants are needed to transfer the full input signal to the storage capacitor, and relatively long discharge time constants are required to hold the signal accurately until the ADC conversion on the sample is completed.

Several advantages are gained by using the sample-and-hold technique. Extremely high precision in the timing of the analog converter can be obtained. The time of occurrence of the ADC converted signal is known precisely as the instant that the command to the sample-and-hold circuit was issued by the control logic and corresponds to the aperture actuation instant of the sample and hold. This can be precisely controlled through synchronization to external signal sources, a feature important in some data reduction algorithms.

The most important consideration is the accuracy of the converted analog signal (Fig. 15). The signal that is presented to the ADC is in the form of the held voltage on the sample-and-hold storage capacitor. It must remain constant during the whole time that the analog to digital conversion takes place. This can be accomplished by specifying that the drop or fall-off on the analog sample-and-hold circuit be very small, much less than the resolution of the ADC.

It should be noted that a 100 msec ramp changes by 0.1% in 100 μsec. If a 10-Hz ramp function were converted by a 10-bit ADC that had a 100-μsec conversion time, it would suffer at least a 1-bit error, due solely to the uncertainty in the exact value of the signal during the conversion time. Higher-resolution ADCs would be of no use in such an environment since the signal would be changing during the ADC cycle. Depending on the design of the ADC, all that is certain is that the ADC output represents some voltage that existed during the time of the conversion. No better accuracy is possible. With a sample and hold at the front end, the value and time of the signal of interest can be known more precisely. Sample-and-hold circuits with hold stabilities and timing equal to state-of-the-art ADCs are available.

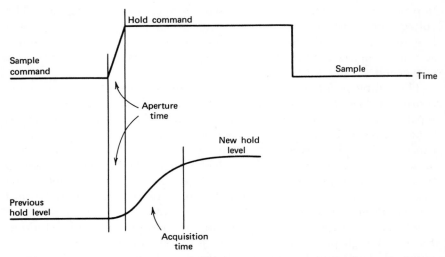

Fig. 15. The waveforms associated with the sample-and-hold amplifier circuitry.

SIMULTANEOUS SAMPLE AND HOLD

In some situations it is necessary to convert many analog signals at exactly the same instant in time. One way to do this would be to provide a separate ADC on each analog input channel and to synchronize the "start conversion" on each unit. However, this can become prohibitively expensive. A more attractive technique is to provide simultaneous sample-and-hold capability (Fig. 16), whereby a sample-and-hold circuit is connected to each analog input channel. At a particular moment in time, the sample-and-hold actuate signal is issued. The aperture on each sample-and-hold circuit is opened simultaneously, and the input signals are then sampled and held on the charge storage capacitor of each circuit. The sample-and-hold output capacitor is then connected through a succeeding multiplexer to the ADC. The signal that is converted by the ADC is the signal that was present on all the inputs at exactly the same instant.

   Simultaneous sample and hold is a relatively expensive feature to design into a system. In certain situations, however, it is necessary to be able to measure signals of interest at the exact same instant in time in order to extract time correlated data. The simultaneous sample-and-hold amplifier must have better droop and stability characteristics than the ADC associated sample-and-hold amplifiers previously described. It must be able to hold an analog voltage for a longer period of time, until the multiplexer is commanded to pick the particular point. For hybrid com-

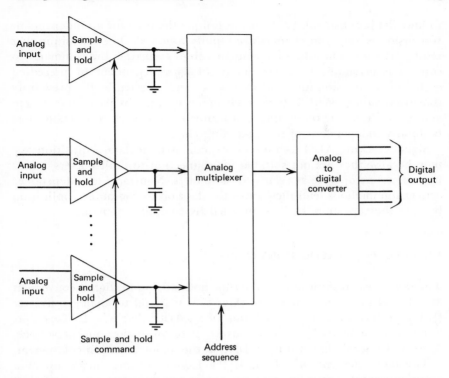

Fig. 16. In many applications the instantaneous values of many analog voltages are of interest. It may be too difficult or time consuming to perform the necessary extrapolations to determine the exact value of each voltage at a precise time. A simultaneous sample-and-hold scheme can be used. Each analog input is connected to its analog input multiplexer point via a sample-and-hold amplifier. Under computer command all the sample-and-hold amplifiers are actuated simultaneously. Thus the voltage stored on the sample-and-hold storage capacitors represents the voltage that appeared at the "command" instant in time on all the inputs. The analog multiplexer is programmed to sample the held voltages sequentially and to pass them to the ADC.

putation simultaneous sample-and-hold is mandatory because of the necessity to determine the value of a number of analog signals simultaneously.

ANALOG TO DIGITAL CONVERTER TECHNIQUES

Many circuit techniques have been developed to convert analog voltages. Some use circuitry which provides a continuous digital output that follows the input signal. With this technique the time for an independent conversion is long, but changes are rapidly followed. The technique that most ADCs use computes independent values each time the command to convert is given. Each conversion is totally independent of preceding cycles; the conversion time and accuracy are not affected by the previously converted values. With a rapidly changing output—in particular, where analog multiplexing of a number of inputs is used—each conversion must be totally independent of the preceding channel.

Signal tracking ADC techniques are not used in data acquisition systems because they are not suitable for connection to multiplexers; tracking converters operate at relatively slow rates. Nontracking independent conversion methods lend themselves to adaption to computer application because they are more easily controlled by computer demands.

DIGITAL TO ANALOG CONVERSION

The same basic techniques are used for both analog to digital conversion and digital to analog conversion (Fig. 17). A digital to analog converter (DAC) performs the inverse function of an ADC, that is, a DAC accepts a digital value as its input and converts it to an analog output voltage. Most ADCs are designed using a DAC as the major precision component.

The basic element in a DAC is the ladder network, made up of a combination of precision resistors connected together as a switched parallel network. The relationship between resistors may be in binary order or in any other convenient code. A binary ladder consists of resistors selected in a 1-2-4-8-16 weighted relationship. If a BCD ladder is required, the resistors are selected in a 1-2-4-8-10-20-40-80-100-200- . . . sequential relationship. An electronic switch is connected in series with each element of the ladder network. When a switch associated with a particular element is actuated and closed, current flows through that rung of the ladder network. The total current flow is a function of the sum of the actuated elements. A highly stable reference voltage is always required to power the ladder network. The ladder output can never be better than the precision of the reference voltage applied and the accuracy of the binary relation between the resistors making up the ladder network.

The resistors are switch selected. The switch can, of course, be electromechanical, like a relay, or electronic, like a transistor switch. When a particular switch is actuated, current flows through that resistor branch. The sum of currents flowing in each resistor branch of the ladder network is the analog equivalent of the digital input value. Each bit in the

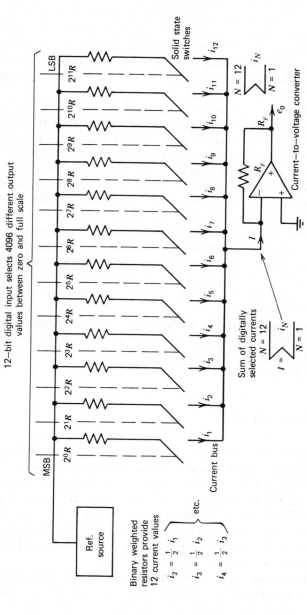

12–bit digital input selects 4096 different output values between zero and full scale

MSB · 2^0R · 2^1R · 2^2R · 2^3R · 2^4R · 2^5R · 2^6R · 2^7R · 2^8R · 2^9R · $2^{10}R$ · $2^{11}R$ · LSB

Solid state switches

i_1 · i_2 · i_3 · i_4 · i_5 · i_6 · i_7 · i_8 · i_9 · i_{10} · i_{11} · i_{12}

Current bus

Ref. source

Binary weighted resistors provide 12 current values

$$i_2 = \frac{1}{2} i_1$$
$$i_3 = \frac{1}{2} i_2$$
$$i_4 = \frac{1}{2} i_3$$ etc.

Sum of digitally selected currents

$$I = \sum_{N=1}^{N=12} i_N$$

R_F

e_0

Current–to–voltage converter

$$I = \sum_{N=1}^{N=12} i_N$$

Fig. 17. Every ADC is built around a DAC. The quality of the ADC depends to a large measure on the DAC used. The most common DAC consists of a ladder network made up of precision resistors, each of which constitutes one rung of the ladder. The values of the resistors are chosen in proportion to the code selected to make up the ADC. For binary code each successive resistor is exactly twice its predecessor. Each resistor is in series with an electronic switch that makes up a ladder rung along with the resistor. When an electronic switch is actuated, current flows through the precision resistor associated with that switch element. The currents flowing through all the actuated resistors are summed in the DAC amplifier. The output voltage of this amplifier is the analog of the digital number entered into the ladder network. As the control signals that actuate the electronic switches in the ladder change, the output analog voltage follows and changes its value proportionally.

75

digital input word to the ladder network is connected to a particular switchable resistor whose value is weighted in accordance with that bit's digital value. When a bit is set to "one," the associated switch will conduct current, thus adding its component to the total current flow. A "zero" bit inhibits current flow in that rung of the ladder because its associated switch is "open" and nonconducting. By actuating particular resistors, any binary number or BCD number equivalent analog current or voltage can be generated.

The resistor switches are activated via signals derived from a digital data register, which contains the binary or BCD digital number. The total current that flows is proportional to the binary number. The time required to select an output voltage is essentially a function of the switch enable time and the line loading capacity. Transistor and solid state switches can be set in well under a microsecond, whereas relay switches are settable in a few milliseconds. For most applications solid state switches are preferable and, of course are very much faster.

By their very nature ladder networks must be designed as high-impedance devices. This is due to the necessarily wide range of resistors needed to make the network. To provide reasonable speed and drive capability from the ladder network, a DC amplifier is used. The amplifier acts as an impedance converter and driver and also isolates the ladder from the externally connected devices.

Fourteen-bit bipolar DACs capable of following 1,000,000 inputs per second are commercially available. Lower-resolution devices can be designed to operate even faster. Digital to analog converters can be specified to be unipolar or bipolar.

COUNTING TYPE CONVERTER

The simplest ADC is the counting type converter (Fig. 18). The basis of this converter is a counter, a DAC, and a voltage comparator circuit. A reference voltage is required for the DAC ladder. A clock signal from an oscillator passes through a flip-flop controlled AND gate. When the flip-flop is in the set condition, oscillator clock pulses can pass; these pulses are directed to the counter and are counted. The counter may be binary or BCD, depending on the desired output code. The associated DAC ladder network resistors are correspondingly weighted.

The number in the counter is used to control a DAC. Thus the number in the counter is continuously converted to a corresponding analog voltage by the DAC, which must be designed to operate at the same rate

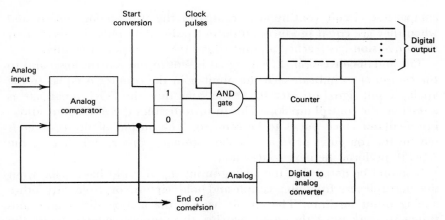

Fig. 18. A schematic of a counting type ADC. This unit consists of an electronic counter, a DAC, an analog comparator, and associated logic circuitry. The ADC begins its operation at a count of zero. The output of the counter controls the DAC. The counter accepts pulses from the pulse source and counts them. The DAC output voltage follows the count accumulated in the counter. The output voltage waveform of the DAC is in the form of a staircase voltage. Each counter input pulse increments the accumulated count; the DAC output voltage follows in turn by adding another voltage step to the staircase output. The analog comparator continuously compares the staircase voltage with the analog input voltage. As long as the analog input is less than the staircase voltage, the pulses are permitted to pass to the counter so as to increase the staircase voltage. When the staircase voltage and the analog input are equal, the control logic inhibits the input pulse source. The count in the counter at that point is equal to the analog input voltage and is its digitized value.

at which the counter can count. The limitation is the conversion rate of the DAC rather than the counter rate. The voltage at the output of the DAC represents the number in the counter and in this case is a "staircase" voltage. In other words, the analog output voltage increases in a staircase manner, one voltage resolution increment at a time, in synchronism with the count.

The output of the DAC (voltage) is entered into one input of the comparator circuit, a two-input analog circuit that compares two voltages. When the two voltages are equal, the comparator produces an output signal. The comparator consists essentially of a differential amplifier connected so that the leads are of opposite polarity. Since the amplifier can be designed to have a very high gain, the circuit can produce a very sharp equality signal.

The analog input that requires conversion is one of the inputs to the comparator, and the output of the DAC forms the other input. The comparator circuit continuously compares the two analog signals and when they are equal produces an output pulse. The pulse indicates that the conversion has reached a point where the two inputs are equal.

The end-of-conversion (EOC) signal is sent to the control logic and to the computer to indicate that the number in the counter is equal to the analog input signal of interest. At the same time the EOC signal acts as a reset on the control flip-flop. This in turn disables the AND gate, allowing oscillator clock pulses to be counted. The output of the counter is sent to the computer or to a secondary storage register, thus freeing the ADC to perform the next conversion.

It should be noted that the analog input signal could have come from the multiplexer, from the sample-and-hold circuit, or from any other analog input medium. The circuit accepts the analog signal and continues to work until the input matches the number counted to by the counter.

The counting ADC converts an analog signal in a variable time period (Fig. 19) depending on the amplitude of the analog signal. The counter is started at some value, say zero or full scale negative or positive. It is then incremented or decremented until it reaches the count equal to the analog input signal. The time required to equal the analog input is determined by the value of the analog input signal to be measured. If the ADC is a 10-bit device with a clock of 1,000,000 pulses per second, the ADC will require a maximum of 1000 μsec for a conversion. If the analog input signal is of lower amplitude, less time will be needed to reach the value.

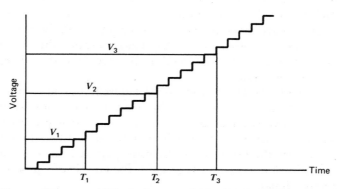

Fig. 19. The counting type ADC requires a variable time interval to perform the conversion The time to convert is a function of the analog input value. Shown are several analog input voltages and the relative time required to perform conversion for each.

This type of ADC was one of the first ones designed and is no longer used in most data acquisition applications because more satisfactory types are available. However, in one application the counting converter is excellent and is almost universally used; that is for nuclear data acquisition systems. In particular, for multichannel pulse height analyzers this type of converter is ideal because of the extremely good differential linearity that can be achieved. Hence the counting ADC is used in most applications in nuclear pulse height analysis work. Analog to digital converters with clock count rates of 40 to 100 MHz are available commercially.

SUCCESSIVE APPROXIMATION

Analog to digital converters that convert an analog input signal in a fixed time interval, independently of the amplitude of the input analog signal, are available. These converters can operate at relatively high rates that are dependent on the number of bits and not the signal amplitude. A 10-bit converter requires 10 cycles independently of the input. Similarly, if 13 bits were required, 13 cycles would be needed. Usually, some fixed time interval must be added to each conversion in order to take into account logic set-up and settling time of the analog amplifiers.

The most common type of ADC is the successive approximation converter (Fig. 20), which accepts analog input signals directly from the source, from a sample and hold, or from a multiplexer. Within a fixed number of cycles it produces the digitized output. The basic components of this ADC are the comparator, DAC, and control logic. As in any ADC, a reference voltage is required for the DAC ladder network. As its first logical operation the ADC logic sets the DAC register to half-full scale. The logic sets the highest-order bit in the DAC register to "one," and this in turn is converted by the DAC to a voltage equal to half-full scale. This voltage is compared to the analog input in the comparator, which can produce output signals equivalent to "less than" or "greater than," depending on the relationship between the DAC generated voltage and the input analog signal. If the result is "greater than" the ADC control logic sets the bit to "zero"; if "less than," the bit is retained as a "one." The converter logic sets the next lower significant bit to "one" and examines the comparator condition—"less than"/"greater than." This cycle is repeated for each bit of ADC resolution.

The speed of conversion for each bit is dependent on the DAC rate and comparator decision time. The speeds of conversion for all bits are

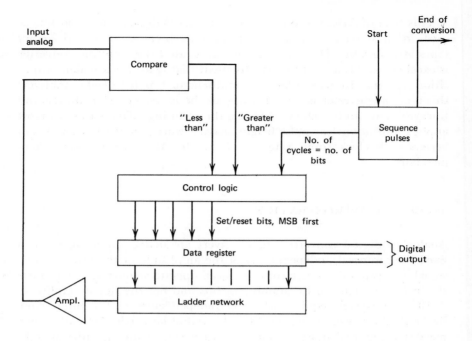

Fig. 20. The successive approximation ADC is the most commonly used type. It consists of an analog comparator, a DAC, an output register, and associated logic circuitry. The time required to perform a conversion is the same for any analog input value and is a function of the number of bits to be converted. A single ADC clock cycle is needed for each bit in the ADC digitized output. The DAC output is compared to the analog input by the comparator. The comparator output signals either "greater than" or "less than." These signals control the setting of the register bits. The conversion process begins with the most significant bit, which is set to "one." The resultant DAC analog output is compared to the analog input signal. If the comparator signals "less than," the "one" remains in the register bit position. A "more than" indication causes the bit under examination to be set to "zero." This process continues until each bit in the register is similarly examined. The number of cycles for successive approximation is equal to the number of bits in the converted digital output word.

essentially equal. The control logic time is small compared to these values. Accuracy is a function of the DAC, the comparator sensitivity, and the reference voltage for the ladder network. Present technology converters are capable of 500,000 15-bit-plus-sign operations per second. Most of these converters use the successive approximation techniques.

INTEGRATING ANALOG TO DIGITAL CONVERTERS

The integrating ADC (Fig. 21) is used in applications where the integrated value of the input analog signal is desired. The outputs of such ADCs present the integral of the input voltage during the time of conversion. Although analog integration techniques and standard ADCs could be used, it is usually more desirable to employ an integrating converter that can accept an analog input and convert it directly into integral form. The overall effective system performance is improved by using this technique; greater accuracy and a smaller load on the computer and ADC are obtained simultaneously.

A voltage controlled oscillator (VCO), which is essentially a frequency modulation oscillator, is used as the basis of the integrating ADC. The VCO output frequency is a function of its input voltage; its amplitude is

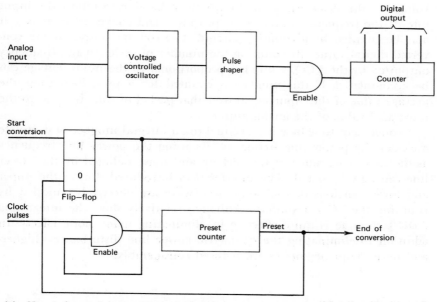

Fig. 21. A form of integrating ADC. The analog voltage is the input to a voltage controlled oscillator (VCO). The VCO output is connected to a counter, which is permitted to count for a specified time interval. The accumulated count is proportional to the average input voltage during the counting interval. A convenient time base for the time interval is a full cycle of the power line frequency. In this way pick-up and noise that result from power supply disturbances can effectively be attenuated.

constant independent of frequency. The VCO is designed so that when the input is at 0 V the frequency of the VCO is at the nominal center frequency. When the voltage goes to minimum (full scale) negative voltage, the VCO output oscillates at its minimum frequency, or maximum frequency excursion, depending on the design. Similarly, full scale positive voltage causes the VCO to oscillate at the other frequency extreme. Thus the frequency at which the VCO oscillates is linearly proportional to the input voltage applied.

This technique is the basis of frequency modulation (FM) radio transmission. Analog FM tape recording represents another application of VCOs. Output frequency is a function of input voltage in these examples. When the input voltage rises, the output frequency changes. When the input decreases, the output frequency follows. The deviation of a VCO is a function of the design of the unit. Frequency deviations of various designs are from $\pm 7\frac{1}{2}$ to $\pm 40\%$ of nominal frequency for full scale.

The instantaneous frequency of oscillation is a function of the input voltage to the VCO, which, of course, must be able to follow the input rate. If the frequency waveform is processed and converted to pulses, it may be counted by a counting circuit. The counter output is the converted digital value. By counting the number of cycles in the frequency outputted by the VCO, a number proportional to the input voltage can be accumulated. If this number is counted for a prescribed time, the average value of the input signal over that period of time is equal to the integrated value of the analog input.

A convenient time base is one equal to an integral number of complete cycles of the power line frequency. By using the power line frequency as the time base, much of the pick-up and noise radiated by the power line can be eliminated. The interferences introduced during the upper and lower portions of the power line wave are effectively canceled by counting the VCO deviations. Although relatively slow, the integrating ADC technique is quite effective in eliminating many noise effects. In addition to eliminating the symmetric power line disturbances, higher- and lower-frequency noises are reduced considerably.

SAMPLING RATE

Sampling rate is a major topic that must be considered when specifying ADCs. According to the fundamental theorem of sampling, by sampling at a rate equal to twice the maximum frequency component of the wave signal of interest, and through the application of Fourier transforms, all

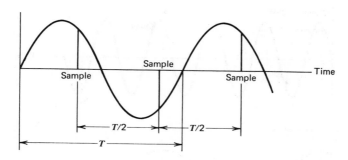

Fig. 22. The sampling rate needed for correct sampling in an ADC must be at least twice the rate of the frequency of the highest signal component in the signal being measured. For the sine wave shown here, two samples per cycle of the wave would be sufficient. These samples would enable a program invoking Fourier techniques to recover all the information in the waveform.

the information content in the input signal can be recovered. As a practical matter, sampling rates (Fig. 22) in excess of twice the maximum frequency component of the waveform are used in order to simplify the subsequent signal processing. Higher sampling rates impose less stringent requirements on the necessary computer processing. However, it would be possible, if sufficient computer time were available to extract all the information by working at rates that were only twice the maximum frequency component. It is usual to sample at rates of 5 to 10 times the maximum frequency component to simplify processing.

If the sample rates are not sufficiently high, that is, are less than twice the maximum frequency component, it is not possible under any circumstances to recover the information in the waveform (Fig. 23). Attempts to reconstruct the waveform either empirically or mathematically result in a false or "alias" signal. It is highly likely that totally misleading, erroneous, results will occur because of aliasing effects. A signal is aliased when the reconstructed waveform bears no recognizable relationship to the original. For example, it should be evident that if one sample for every n repititions of a waveform was made, any relationship between the original waveform and the waveform reconstructed from the samples would be purely coincidental. No useful results should be expected from such a process.

Intuitively it can be perceived that the more samples taken, the closer the approximation will be to the waveform of interest (Fig. 24). By taking enough samples the exact waveform can be recreated. However, sim-

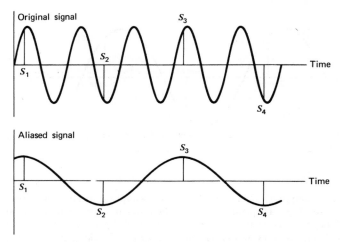

Fig. 23. If the sampling rate is less than twice the frequency of the highest component in the input waveform, it is not possible to recover the information in the waveform. In fact, erroneous information will be extracted. The reconstructed waveform shown here bears no relationship to the sampled input waveform. This is an "aliased" waveform.

ple linear interpolation between points is usually sufficient. If better fidelity is required, it is usually possible to use more sophisticated curve fitting techniques.

An important consideration in selecting sampling rates is that an excessively high rate aggravates the problem of data reduction because a high sampling rate implies high input data volumes and data rates. High data rates require the computer to spend a large percentage of its time doing input/output of essentially redundant information. When the data rate is too high, successive samples are too close to each other and represent essentially the same information. The computer therefore spends an inordinate amount of time on I/O and data reduction and is prevented from doing useful computations. High data rates usually require large amounts of memory to be devoted to buffers. It cannot be stressed too strongly that overspecifying sampling rates can lead to excessive equipment costs and also to poor computer utilization.

A typical sampling rate selection criterion may be considered in regard to strip chart recording. These recordings are characterized by many peaks rising from a baseline. By selecting a sampling rate that allows about 10 samples during the narrowest peak, one is able to recover all

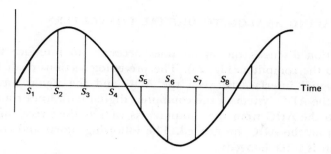

Fig. 24. As a practical matter, sampling rates of 5 to 10 times the highest frequency component are used. As shown here, higher sampling rates permit a better reconstruction of the input waveform. Less computer time is needed to fill in points between samples. Prudence should be exercised, however, in specifying excessively high sampling rates; high rates require larger amounts of computer attention to process data arriving at a high input rate. In addition, extra storage area is required to store the data words.

the information contained in the waveform. Such an approach to sample rate selection is usually adequate. Complicated waveforms are more difficult to analyze in order to select an appropriate rate.

The maximum frequency component of a waveform may be obtained by doing a Fourier analysis on the waveform. This means determining the frequency spectrum. From this information the necessary sampling rate can be determined.

In many cases high-frequency components are introduced into the wave as noise and other extraneous signals. These must be taken into account when determining the maximum frequency components and the sampling rate. In some cases very little energy is contained in the very high frequency components; in others, the high-frequency component is noise rather than signal. In these cases it is reasonable to use analog filtering techniques to eliminate the high-frequency components. It is preferable to use filters and other analog techniques to band-limit the waveform. This limits the high-frequency components, both noise and signal, and permits lower sampling rates. It is always easier and more economical to filter signals by analog techniques than by digital processing.

One advantage of randomly sequencing the analog multiplexer can be deduced from the foregoing discussions. Each input channel can be sampled under program control at a rate that is commensurate with its frequency response. Thus high-frequency channels should be sampled more frequently than slow channels.

INTERFACING ANALOG TO DIGITAL CONVERTERS

This section discusses the signal lines necessary to interface the ADC system to the computer (Fig. 25). The preceding sections dealt with the analog signal interface between the ADC and the signal sources. To connect the ADC system to the computer, digital data lines transmitting signals to the ADC from the computer as well as lines receiving digital signals from the ADC are needed. The following signal and control information is interchanged:

Multiplexer address.
Sequence selection.
Start conversion.
Digital data.
Overflow and polarity.
End of conversion.
Synchronization signals.

The first function of the computer is to start the multiplexer and to specify the various options. The program does this by issuing an appropriate I/O instruction. The computer transmits a multiplexer address that selects a particular input analog point. The start-of-conversion sig-

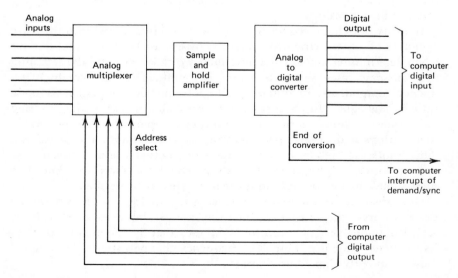

Fig. 25. The signal and data flow paths between an ADC subsystem and a computer.

nal will also be generated as soon as the multiplexer channel has had time to stabilize. If external synchronization was not specified by the I/O instruction, the front-end sequence logic will wait until the multiplexer stabilizes and will then issue the start conversion signal to the ADC. If external synchronization was used, the ADC will wait until the external synchronization signal occurs before beginning the conversion cycle.

After the ADC completes its conversion cycle, it issues the end-of-conversion signal to the computer to alert it that valid data have been prepared for transfer to the computer. The digitized data appear in parallel form on the ADC/computer I/O bus. The EOC signal indicates to the computer that the digitized data are available for transfer. In certain computers the EOC signal is used to interrupt the CPU to indicate the presence of valid digitized data on the ADC bus connection. If data channel operation is specified, the EOC pulse activates the cycle-steal mechanism. In every case, transfer of data to the computer is indicated when the ADC issues the EOC signal.

The end-of-conversion signal also has the effect of priming the ADC/multiplexer to begin the next cycle. If sequential scanning was specified by the I/O instruction, the multiplexer will advance to the next sequential address. Random scanning is effected by outputting the next computer stored analog multiplexer addresses. These can be brought out under program control or data channel control, depending on the capability of the computer.

5 Telemetry: Remote Sensing

It is desirable to locate data reduction and analysis equipment as close as possible to the data sources because the quality of a signal is highest at its source. A signal sent over a long path is subject to greater interference, more attenuation, and more distortion than a comparable signal over a shorter circuit path. The difficulties encountered with a data acquisition or computer control system are eased when the computer system and the data source are in close physical proximity. A signal that must be transmitted from its source over any distance must be protected against electrical and magnetic interferences, crosstalk from other signals, noise, transmission losses, and various other degradations. To overcome these effects, special signal conditioning circuitry, amplifiers, modulators, and high-grade transmission links are needed. In addition, other complications are introduced when installation and maintenance must be done in remote, multiple locations. In such cases the logistics of these operations obviously present greater difficulties than when all the components are in one location.

Unfortunately, however, it is not always feasible to locate the computer and data sources in close proximity. This is obviously the case when the signal sources are distributed over a large physical area or when multiple experiments or processes are to be connected to a single computer. In some cases the signal source is mobile and/or small and cannot support an on-board data system, as is true of missiles or biological specimens, for instance.

The purpose of this chapter is to introduce the basic concepts and techniques of remote signal sensing—telemetry (Fig. 1). The techniques used to enter such data into the computer are also described. Generally "telemetry" refers to a one-way data link—from the data source to a remote data receiving station. The medium for data transmission can be

Fig. 1. A typical telemetry system consists of data acquisition equipment located remotely from the central computer. A number of different remote sites may be connected to the central facility. The transmission media may be telephone lines or radio links; the type of connection depends on distances and physical conditions at the remote site.

either a hard wire connection or a radio link. Three major forms of telemetry are in common use:

Frequency modulation/frequency modulation (FM/FM).
Pulse amplitude modulation/frequency modulation (PAM/FM).
Pulse code modulation/frequency modulation (PCM/FM).

The first term in each pair refers to the data encoding technique, and the second indicates the data transmission method. Many other techniques have been developed and are also in use, but these are the most common. It is to be noted that FM data transmission is most often used. The characteristics and applications of the various types are discussed below.

INTER-RANGE INSTRUMENTATION GROUP

Standards for all forms of telemetry were established by The Inter-range Instrumentation Group (IRIG), White Sands, New Mexico. This group has produced and continuously revises standards for telemetry signals and equipment. Transmit and receive signal specifications have been published and are continuously updated to reflect changes in technology and requirements.

The importance of these standards is that many manufacturers have designed and offer for sale telemetry equipment that conforms to IRIG specifications. Equipment from a number of different vendors can be integrated to form a single system when equipment conforming to IRIG standards is specified. It is desirable to select equipment conforming to IRIG specifications whenever such a choice is possible; the advantages of using standardized signals and hardware are many and self evident. Also, since equipment conforming to IRIG specifications has been developed over a number of years by many manufacturers, the quality and reliability of the resultant hardware are excellent and it is competitively priced. This equipment was designed for aerospace and military applications requiring a high degree of reliability and minituarization and is capable of operating under difficult environmental conditions—high temperature, high altitude, vibration, radiation, and so forth.

FREQUENCY MODULATION

Frequency modulation (FM) is a method of encoding information so that it is contained in the instantaneous frequency of the carrier. In frequency modulation, the frequency of a carrier signal is made to deviate from the center reference frequency by the information signal. The deviation as a percentage of maximum frequency deviation is adjusted to be proportional to the information signal. The information signal thereby frequency-modulates (Fig. 2) the carrier center frequency.

As an example, a carrier or reference frequency may be selected at 1 MHz with a deviation ratio or index of modulation of 0.1 or 10%. The input information bearing signal would frequency-modulate the carrier signal from 950,000 to 1,050,000 Hz for the maximum excursions of the input. Signals that are less than the maximum permissible value at the input cause the carrier frequency to deviate proportionally less. Generally, for small values of index of modulation, the frequency bandwidth of the modulated signal is equal to the deviation.

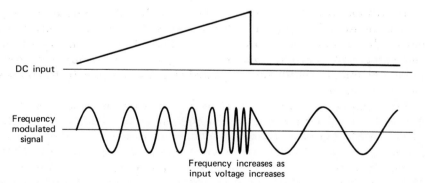

Fig. 2. An example of frequency modulation. The input signal is a slowly varying waveform. The frequency modulator provides an output frequency whose instantaneous frequency of oscillation is proportional to the input voltage.

As stated previously, the information of the frequency modulated carrier is contained in the instantaneous value of the carrier frequency; the amplitude of the carrier frequency does not convey information. In contrast, amplitude modulation signals carry all their information in the amplitude of the carrier. Therefore, to extract the information from a frequency modulated carrier, one need be concerned only with the frequency content. This factor is what makes frequency modulation attractive for signal transmission and information encoding. Frequency modulation is much less sensitive to such signal degradation effects as attenuation, fading, and noise than most other transmission and encoding techniques. In fact, before detection, a frequency modulation signal is usually amplified to saturation and clipped, thereby removing all amplitude variations.

Frequency modulation is frequently used in telemetry for both information encoding and transmission. A major application area that usually uses frequency modulation signal processing effectively is the encoding of DC and low-frequency signals when the normal intended signal flow paths do not have adequate low-frequency response characteristics. For instance, recording on magnetic tape using direct recording techniques inherently restricts low-frequency recording. Instrumentation recorders overcome this limitation by providing an FM recording mode. Direct current and low-frequency signals frequency-modulate a carrier signal, which in turn is recorded. Similarly analog transmitted over telephone lines are usually transmitted as frequency modulated tones because the telephone network does not normally provide DC response.

FREQUENCY MODULATION/FREQUENCY MODULATION TELEMETRY

Frequency modulation/frequency modulation telemetry (Fig. 3) entails a double set of frequency modulators. The data to be transmitted are used to frequency-modulate a subcarrier. A number of different subcarrier frequencies may be used in one system. Each data source independently frequency-modulates a separate subcarrier frequency. The only requirement is that each subcarrier be set at a different frequency and that sufficient separation between frequencies be provided so that there will be no interference between channels at maximum deviation.

Standard subcarrier frequencies are specified by IRIG specification 160-60 and are shown in Fig. 4. Two groups of subcarriers channels are specified: a relatively narrow band set with deviations of $\pm 7\frac{1}{2}\%$, and

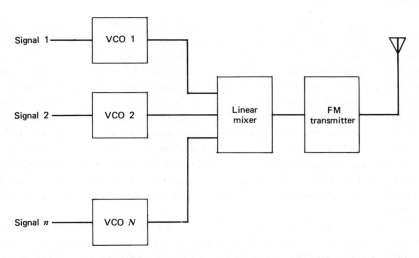

Fig. 3. An FM/FM telemetry system. A number of subcarrier oscillators are connected to a common FM transmitter. Each subcarrier oscillator is an independent frequency modulator, producing an output frequency proportional to the input signal connected to it.

wider band subcarrier channels with deviations of ±15%. The maximum permissible information frequency signal that can be handled by each channel is specified. Specifications are conservative to prevent overmodulation and interference between channels. In fact, the center frequency of each channel is also selected so as to ensure that inadvertently generated harmonics will tend to fall outside the bands of higher-frequency channels, thus minimizing interference. It should be borne in mind that a large number of subcarrier channels are ordinarily used in a single system, and chaos would result if careful attention were not focused on this point in the system design.

As an example of a frequency modulation system, consider three transducer outputs that modulate three separate subcarrier channels. Channel 1 is centered at 400 Hz, and the applied data signal produces a peak deviation of ±30 Hz; channel 2 is centered at 560 Hz, and its peak deviation is ±42 Hz; and channel 3 deviates ±55 Hz around a center frequency of 730 Hz. The three channels can be mixed together and placed on a common transmission medium. They cover a frequency band ranging from 370 to 785 Hz. Not only is there no overlapping between channels, but also an unused "guard" band lies between them to ensure separation and thereby decrease the effects of interference that would

IRIG Channel Number	Channel Center Frequency, kc	Deviation, %	Data Cutoff Frequency, Hz
1	0.40	±7.5	6.0
2	0.56	±7.5	8.4
3	0.73	±7.5	11.0
4	0.96	±7.5	14.0
5	1.30	±7.5	20.0
6	1.70	±7.5	25.0
7	2.30	±7.5	35.0
8	3.00	±7.5	45.0
9	3.90	±7.5	59.0
10	5.40	±7.5	81.0
11	7.35	±7.5	110.0
12	10.5	±7.5	160.0
13	14.5	±7.5	220.0
14	22.0	±7.5	330.0
15	30.0	±7.5	450.0
16	40.0	±7.5	600.0
17	52.5	±7.5	790.0
18	70.0	±7.5	1050.0
19	93.0	±7.5	1395.0
20	124.0	±7.5	1860.0
21	165.0	±7.5	2475.0
A	22.0	±15	660.0
B	30.0	±15	900.0
C	40.0	±15	1200.0
D	52.5	±15	1600.0
E	70.0	±15	2100.0
F	93.0	±15	2790.0
G	124.0	±15	3720.0
H	165.0	±15	4950.0

Fig. 4. Standard subcarrier frequencies specified by IRIG specifications 106-60.

adversely affect data recovery. At the reciving end of the system, band-pass filters separate the channels, sending them to individual discriminators for demodulation and recovery of the original signal. The output of each discriminator goes to a suitable display device or recorder to provide a quantitative reading of the parameter being measured.

The combined outputs from a number of frequency modulated sub-carrier channels are often used to frequency-modulate a radio transmitter. This is known as an FM/FM system because two steps of frequency modulation are involved. The first "FM" indicates the type of subcarrier modulation, and the second the type of radio frequency modulation. An FM/PM system is one in which frequency modulated subcarriers phase-modulate the transmitter. Inter-range Instrumentation Group standards specify the frequency ranges for telemetry radio data transmission in the VHF and microwave bands.

VOLTAGE CONTROLLED OSCILLATORS

Voltage controlled oscillators (VCOs) are usually used to frequency-modulate subcarrier channels. A VCO (Fig. 5) is a variable frequency oscillator whose instantaneous output frequency is proportional to the instantaneous value of the VCO input voltage. In practice any transducer capable of producing an output voltage can be used as the input to a VCO.

Voltage controlled oscillators having sensitivities of ±50 mV full scale to ±3 V are available, as well as VCOs for each IRIG specified subcarrier channel. The frequency response permissible for each channel is specified by the IRIG standard. One IRIG subcarrier VCO channel is allotted to each transducer output to be encoded. The frequency responses of the transducers are matched as far as possible to the VCO permissible frequency responses. Each VCO must be selected to operate at a different subcarrier frequency. Thus, although all the VCOs operate concurrently, each occupies a separate portion of the available frequency spectrum. Each VCO continuously follows its input signal. At any time that the VCO output frequency is sampled, the correct encoded value of the input is available.

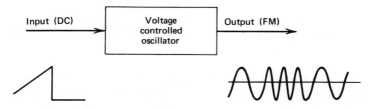

Fig. 5. A voltage controlled oscillator. The VCO can receive an input in the form of a voltage applied to its input or by mechanically varying one of its frequency sensitive elements.

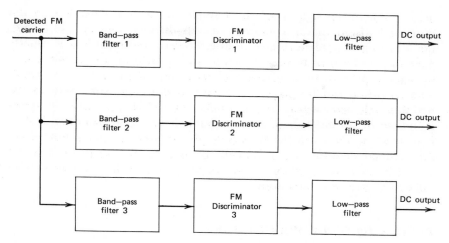

Fig. 6. A linearly combined set of VCO signals is detected by the telemetry receivers. The mixed signal is passed through channel band-pass filters to separate the individual subcarriers. Each subcarrier is then detected by a discriminator tuned to the subcarrier frequency range. A low-pass filter is used to remove high-frequency components.

The outputs of the various VCOs (Fig. 6) are linearly mixed together to form the input to a FM transmitter. The resultant FM signal is transmitted and is detected at the receiving end by the use of standard FM discrimination techniques. This signal represents the linear combination of all the mixed VCOs. The various subcarrier signals are separated by passing the combined signal through a number of band-pass filters, a separate filter being needed for each subcarrier in the group. An FM discriminator detects the signal information encoded in each channel. The output of the discriminator is a close approximation of the signal that was inputted to the VCO.

Overall accuracies of about 0.1% are achieved using high-grade components and a low-noise communications link. Frequency modulation telemetry should be used for sensing signals requiring accuracies of between 1 and 2%. To achieve higher accuracies reliably, PCM telemetry is usually specified.

PREDETECTION RECORDING

In some cases it is desirable and necessary to record the combined FM signal on magnetic tape. The point to select the signal to be recorded may be where the signals are on a single line before detection by the individual discriminators connected to each channel. This type of recording is known as predetection recording. Predetection recording is usually done in parallel with regular detection, thus providing a convenient way to make a permanent single-channel recording of the telemetry signal. The recording can be played back and used in the same way as the real-time telemetry signal. If the number of FM channel discriminators is limited or the number of output channels or signal handling devices is insufficient, the extra signals can be played back at a later time when the channel detectors are realigned. By having the predetected signal available, various signal processing techniques may be used to extract difficult signals at a later time.

PULSE AMPLITUDE MODULATION

All channels of a pulse amplitude modulation (PAM/FM) system use the same portion of the frequency spectrum, but not at the same time (Fig. 7). The signal in each channel is sampled in regular sequence by a commutator. When all channels have been sampled, the sequence repeats, beginning with the first channel. In this way samples from a particular channel are interleaved in time between samples from all the other channels.

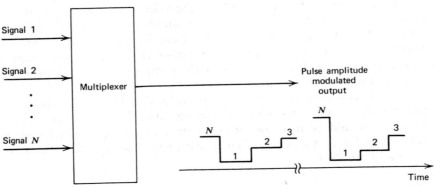

Fig. 7. A pulse amplitude modulation (PAM) signal may be obtained from a commutating sampler or an analog multiplexer. The inputs to the commutator are a number of analog input signals. The output is a pulse train; in each pulse interval a different input channel is connected to the output. The pulse train is used to frequency-modulate a carrier frequency.

Since no channel is monitored continuously in a PAM system, the sampling must be rapid enough so that the signal amplitude in a particular channel does not change too much between sampling intervals. Theoretical studies based on an idealized case show that no information is lost if the sampling rate is at least twice the highest-frequency component in the sampled signal. This sampling rate, however, is based on "perfect" filter characteristics, which cannot in actuality be attained. Practical telemetry systems use much higher sampling rates in order to preserve all the information in the original signal without unnecessarily complex circuitry. The sampling rate in a typical telemetry system is about five times the highest-frequency component in the sampled signal. For example, if the highest-frequency component in a particular channel is 40 Hz, the channel is sampled about 200 times per second. If there are eight such channels in a system, the commutator must take at least 1600 samples per second.

At the receiving end of the system, a decommutator operating at exactly the same frequency as the commutator distributes the parts of the multiplexed signal to the proper output channels. Since a time-division system is based on precise timing, it is important that the decommutator be synchronized exactly with the commutator. Otherwise, information on fluid flow, for example, might be misinterpreted as temperature information.

The commutator output signal is a pulse amplitude modulated pulse train, that is, the height of each pulse represents the instantaneous am-

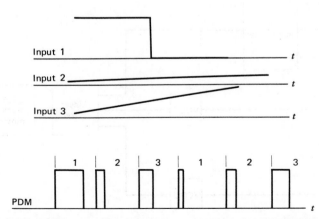

Fig. 8. Pulse duration modulation (PDM) is a variation of PAM. The width of each pulse conveys the information; each pulse width is proportional to the amplitude of the sampled waveform for the sample interval in question.

plitude of the sampled waveform. A smooth curve drawn through the tops of the pulses would reconstruct the original waveform. Pulse amplitude modulation is the simplest modulation technique and is effective are not very stringent.

A disadvantage of PAM is that any noise "riding" on the signal changes the pulse height, thereby introducing distortion. One solution to this problem is to use pulse duration modulation (PDM), in which the PAM signal goes to a keyer that produces new pulses of uniform height but varying length (Fig. 8). The information is then carried by the pulse length, or duration, rather than by the pulse height as in PAM. Although PDM is somewhat less susceptible to noise than PAM, any distortion of the pulse shape may change the apparent pulse duration, thereby producing a distorted output signal.

Pulse amplitude modulation and PDM signals are used to modulate FM transmitters. The signal is transmitted by the same technique as was described for FM/FM telemetry.

Combinations such as PAM/FM/FM are also possible and are used (Fig. 9). In effect a subcarrier FM channel is connected to the PAM output. Thus the pulse trains representing the amplitudes of the sequentially sampled inputs are used to control the frequency of a subcarrier channel. Care must be exercised that the PAM frequency bandwidth

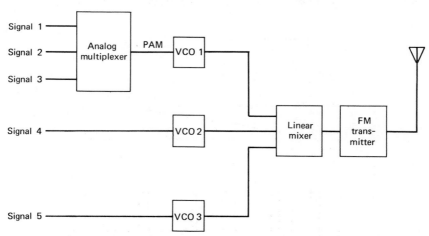

Fig. 9. A fully developed telemetry system. A number of FM subcarrier channels are mixed together. In addition, some of the FM subcarrier channels are modulated by the output of a PAM commutator.

matches the response specified for the subcarrier channel. Several PAM/ FM combinations can be provided. The PAM/FM signal is mixed linearly with other PAM/FM signals and with VCO FM signals before modulating the FM transmitter.

PULSE CODE MODULATION

The most sophisticated form of telemetry is pulse code modulation (PCM). The data are converted immediately by the telemetry data acquisition system to digital form and transmitted in that form. A large number of channels at a high degree of accuracy can be encoded. Pulse code modulation requires considerable receiver equipment for separating channels, recognizing frame synchronization words, and remaining in synchronism with the data source. All the problems inherent in digital communications exist in a PCM system, but the obvious advantages mentioned above make PCM the most flexible form of telemetry and the most useful one for computer work. Standard PCM telemetry receivers are designed to interface to computers directly.

Frequency modulation/frequency modulation telemetry receivers require ADCs to convert analog discriminator signals to digital form for computer entry. The FM encoding and decoding processes are analog; only the last step in the process involves a digital technique. Pulse amplitude modulation/frequency modulation is also basically an analog technique. An ADC is used to convert the received analog pulse train to digital form for computer entry.

For all intents and purposes, discussion concerning analog to digital conversion applies equally to PCM telemetry (Fig. 10). In these cases a number of analog signals are sequentially connected through an analog multiplexer to an ADC. When the multiplexer/ADC is directly under the control of a local computer, the identify of each sample is selected and known by the computer control program. Furthermore, the computer multiplexer/ADC connection is made over a parallel data path. On the other hand, in a telemetry environment the telemetry multiplexer/ADC combination operates independently and out of synchronization with the remote receiving station where the computer is located. In almost all cases a single link exists between the telemetry source and the receiver; hence it is necessary to serialize the ADC output. In addition, signals other than converted analog data may be inserted in the transmitted pulse train. Frame and word synchronization pulse trains are also interspersed with the data. Thus the problem of separating the data from

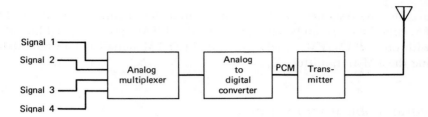

Fig. 10. A pulse code modulation (PCM) transmission system. A number of analog input channels are connected through an analog multiplexer to an ADC. The resultant digitized signal is serialized and applied to the FM transmitter.

the synchronization signals at the receiving station is complicated. In addition, the receiver must be capable of separating the serial data pulse train into individual data words and of identifying the source of each data word.

THE BASIS OF PULSE CODE MODULATION

Various types of pulse modulation have long been used for data transmission because they are closely allied with time-division multiplexing, a technique that permits a number of separate data channels to share a single transmission medium by allotting a particular time interval to each channel. The channels are sampled in a regular sequence, and the samples from the various channels are interleaved in time to form a single pulse train (Fig. 11).

Many types of pulse modulation are used in telemetry. In pulse amplitude modulation, for example, the height of an individual pulse represents the magnitude of the original signal at a given sampling instant.

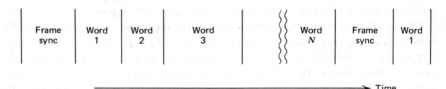

Fig. 11. A typical PCM frame. Each frame is divided into subframes with individual frame and subframe synchronization patterns. Each word consists of a serially digitized sample.

Pulse length represents the signal magnitude in pulse duration modulation. In both cases, the intelligence is carried in analog form. If the pulses were received exactly as transmitted, and if the receiving equipment accurately determined the appropriate characteristics of the received pulses, the original waveform could be reconstructed to any desired degree of accuracy. Because of noise and distortion, however, the received pulses are degraded versions of the transmitted pulses. As a pulse accumulates noise, its boundaries become uncertain, causing difficulty in reconstructing the received signal. Errors are cumulative and tend to get worse as the transmission distance increases.

Considerable immunity to noise and other transmission difficulties can be achieved if the multiplexed signal is coded as a series of identical pulses and spaces. Then the receiving equipment need only make a simple "one"/"zero" decision as to the presence or absence of a pulse at a particular time. Before being coded for transmission, the original signal is sampled, just as in other forms of pulse modulation. The range of possible pulse heights, from zero to full scale, is then divided into discrete steps so that each step can be represented by a particular arrangement of binary pulses. This coded arrangement of binary pulses is the pulse code modulation signal.

Since the PCM signal is an approximation of the original signal to the nearest discrete level at each sampling instant, the waveform reconstructed at the receiving end of the system is distorted. It is a quantized approximation of the original signal. The disparity between the original waveform and the quantized digital representation is termed quantizing noise. It results from the signal amplitude represented by the nearest quantizing level code at each sampling instant.

The series of pulses which represents a single sample from a single channel is called a word. One complete sampling cycle, including a word from each channel, is termed a frame. Each pulse or space in the word is a bit. The total number of bits in each word determines the resolution—the number of different discrete signal levels that can be identified and coded.

In binary systems, the number of quantizing levels possible in any given code is 2^n, where n is the number of digits in the code. Thus, in a 3-bit code, there are 2^3, or 8, discrete codes. This allows the system to assume seven amplitude levels above zero. In an 8-bit code, which is frequently used in telemetry, 256 discrete codes are possible. In a 10-bit system 1024 numbers are possible, allowing the decimal numbers from 0 through 1023 to be presented. As an example of relative resolution, if a 10-bit system is used to encode a signal having a peak-to-peak amplitude of 5 V, the quantizing levels are 0.005 V apart. The quantizing error is then less than ±0.0025 V, ±0.05%. The ratio

$$2 \exp \frac{\text{full scale analog magnitude}}{\text{number of bits in the code}}$$

describes the relative resolution of the encoded samples.

Another factor that affects the fidelity of the reconstructed wave is the rate at which the original signal is sampled. Theoretically, no information is lost if the sampling rate is at least twice the highest frequency in the sampled signal. However, this is based on certain idealized assumptions, and therefore practical PCM telemetry systems usually sample at about five times the highest data frequency. However, higher sampling rates produce data at higher rates and consequently require transmission links of greater bandwidth.

A PCM signal is always an approximation of the original signal—how good an approximation is primarily a matter of economics. When the quantization is made as fine as that possible with a 10-bit code, the resolution of the PCM system exceeds that of many laboratory instruments and is considerably above the level attained in most analog data transmission systems.

PULSE CODE MODULATION/FREQUENCY MODULATION TRANSMISSION

A typical PCM/FM telemetry system consists of the following components: analog multiplexer, analog to digital converter, digital multiplexer, parallel to serial converter, controller, and FM transmitter.

The analog signals are connected to the analog multiplexer through appropriate signal conditioning components, which consist of amplifiers and filter circuits necessary to match the analog signals to the input requirements of the telemetry system. Low-level signals must be amplified. Signals that have components outside the sampling rate capabilities of the ADC are eliminated by passing the signal to the multiplexer via a low-pass filter.

The analog multiplexer transfers the analog signals in turn to the ADC. Each time a connection is made, after allowing sufficient time for switching transients to settle, the ADC is actuated and a conversion takes place. The output of the ADC is a sequence of digital words corresponding to the digitized value of the converter analog inputs.

The digital multiplexer accepts digital inputs from the ADC output, the digital devices, and the controller. The sequence of accepting signals for further transmission is determined by the controller. Control signals to the digital multiplexer determine from which data source a word is to be accepted at every instant. Words from the ADC consist of digitized analog values; words from the digital data sources consist of digital signals that arise directly and do not need conversion. Data from the controller consists of frame and word synchronization information. These are inserted directly in the data stream and are used by the telemetry receiving equipment.

The parallel to serial converter accepts parallel words from the digital multiplexer and outputs a single serial data stream to the FM transmitter, which in turn is modulated by the PCM serial data stream. The type of modulation circuitry in the transmitter depends on the transmission medium. This could be a wire or radio link.

The PCM/FM telemetry transmitter is under full control of the controller. All the timing and synchronization signal sequences needed to assure reliable and recoverable data transmission are produced by the controller.

PULSE CODE MODULATION/FREQUENCY MODULATION RECEIVERS

A PCM/FM telemetry receiver (Fig. 12) must be a very sophisticated package if reliable, error-free reception of telemetry information is desired. A typical receiver system consists of an FM receiver, bit rate synchronizer, frame and word synchronizer, serial to parallel converter, and programmed controller.

Standard high-quality FM reception techniques are used to detect the FM signal. With radio frequency transmission, the signal is detected by various receiver techniques. In many cases the signal is highly distorted and suffers from transmission degradations. Bit rate synchronizers are used to maintain the receiver bit rate clock in step with the transmitted clock rate. The output of the FM receiver and bit rate synchronizer is a serial clocked data pulse train. The clock is derived from the bit rate synchronizer and is used to sample the received data.

The frame synchronizer extracts the frame synchronization pattern from the serial data pulse train. Pulse code modulation data are transmitted serially with a frame synchronization sequence inserted periodically to

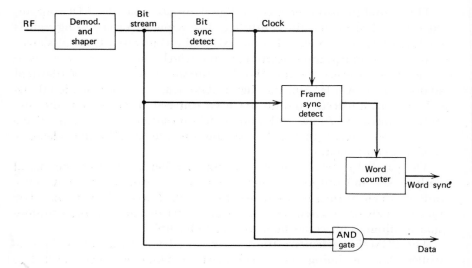

Fig. 12. A PCM receiver. The bit rate synchronizer extracts the bit stream in a clock synchronized form from the information received. The frame synchronizer provides frame synchronization information to extract channel data. The word counter separates the data in words.

denote the beginning of a frame. A frame synchronization pattern consisting of a 33-bit code might be inserted every 1024 bits. Each frame in turn consists of a number of data words. The number of bits in each data word need not be the same. The frame synchronization circuitry recognizes and strips the frame synchronization pattern from the serial data stream.

The word synchronization circuitry operates under the supervision of the programmed controller. Each time that a number of bits equal to the word currently being received arrives, the received data word is passed on to the connected computer. The process involves serial to parallel conversion of the serial data stream and transfer to the associated computer. The word identifier in the word synchronizer is used by the computer to recognize the sequence in the frame of the individual words.

PULSE CODE MODULATION SUMMARIZED

From this description it is evident that PCM telemetry involves a much more sophisticated technology than any other form of telemetry. Pulse code modulation telemetry can provide any desired accuracy. For poor quality transmission links PCM is superior to any other encoding technique.

Pulse code modulation telemetry is the type best suited to a computer environment, since the essentially digital nature of PCM telemetry makes it directly connectable to an on-line computer. Further processing is required to prepare PAM, PDM, or FM for computer entry.

6 Position Encoding

Most real-time digital data systems require shaft position measurements. In fact, these measurements are usually primary inputs concerning the status of the external environment. Position measurements in regard to both linear displacement and angular position are usual requirements. The linear position of a rod and the angle of a shaft are commonplace examples. It is more convenient and usually easier to measure angular position rather than linear displacement, because most instruments available for position measurement are designed to measure angular displacement. A lead screw coupled to a rack and pinion is a simple example of a device that converts linear to angular displacement. Dimensions can range from microinches to many feet. Although transducers capable of converting linear displacement to electrical signals are available, most of the ensuing discussion will be centered on angular displacement transducers. Linear displacements can be easily and accurately converted to rotation values.

Three basic electromechanical devices are commonly used to transduce rotational displacement to an electrical equivalent: (1) potentiometers, (2) synchros, (3) shaft encoders. These devices are useful in computer applications because the electrical outputs either are in digital form or can be converted to digital equivalents with readily available ADCs. As in all component selections, accuracy, number of devices, speed, and overall cost objectives must be taken into account. The greatest accuracies are attainable with either shaft encorders or coupled synchros. Lowest cost is achieved through the use of potentiometers, particularly when the positions of a large number of shafts are to be digitized. To digitize the instantaneous angular position of a high-speed rotating shaft, certain types of shaft encoders are more suitable than others. In some systems, such as a radar system where a rotating antenna is involved, synchros are almost universally used to repeat remotely instantaneous antenna pointing angles. Synchros are also used to drive cathode ray tube display yokes. It is most convenient to use electronic synchro to digital converters in such situations because to adapt to the existing equipment standards is easier than to specify costly and difficult modifications.

In many situations, in particular where equipment exists, regardless of what the ideal solution may be, it is necessary to obtain signals representing angular position from what the original designer included in the instrument. Many instruments were designed at a time when connection to a computer was not contemplated. However, to connect these to a computer requires adapting and modifying them mechanically to install an appropriate transducer and electrically to create a suitable signal for indicating parameters of interest.

POTENTIOMETERS

A potentiometer, that is, a fixed resistance element with a movable wiper arm (Fig. 1), can be coupled to a shaft so that the wiper arm voltage is proportional to the angular position of the drive shaft. The wiper arm is moved along the surface of a fixed resistance element and makes electrical contact with the element, across which a fixed voltage is applied. The

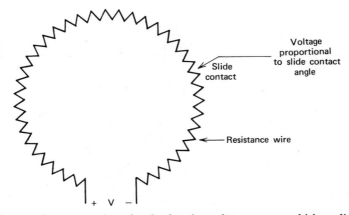

Fig. 1. A potentiometer consists of a fixed resistor element upon which a slider contact can be positioned. The slider contact can be moved to any position along the resistor. A fixed voltage is impressed across the full resistor length. The voltage measured on the contacting slider is proportional to its angular position along the resistor.

voltage measured at the movable wiper arm represents the displacement of the arm along the length of the fixed element.

Potentiometers with linearities of 0.01% are available commercially. Linearity is the deviation of the measured voltage as a function of angular position from the theoretically correct voltage if the potentiometer were a perfect device. Relatively expensive potentiometers have linearities of 0.01%; readily available, less expensive ones have linearities of 0.05%. On the assumption of a tight mechanical linkage that prevents gear backlash and other mechanical errors, a maximum resolution of digitized shaft position of 1 part in 2000 is reasonably possible.

Nonlinear potentiometers are also available. Readily available types include sine-cosine devices. In this case, instead of obtaining a voltage proportional to angular displacement, the potentiometer output will be a voltage proportional to the sine and consine of the shaft angle, for example.

STRIP CHART RECORDER

A useful form of potentiometer is the retransmitting slide wire, a readily available accessory on strip chart recorders (Fig. 2). Most strip chart recorders have slide wires upon which rides a wiper arm to sense the voltage along the slide wire. Attached to the same wiper arm mechanism

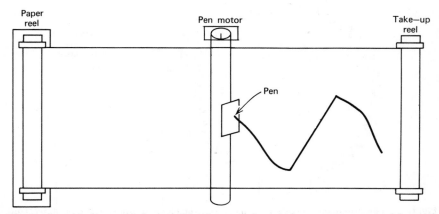

Fig. 2. A strip chart recorder consists of two major moving parts: a paper drive and a pen motor. The paper drive imparts a constant motion along the length of the paper. The pen motor drives the pen to a position corresponding to the instantaneous input voltage, and the pen traces on the paper a curve representing the input voltage.

is the pen carriage. Thus the voltage sensed by the wiper arm is proportional to the position on the slide wire and also to the position of the pen, which is linked to the wiper arm and is positioned across the width of the strip chart paper. The wiper arm voltage is compared electronically with the input voltage to the recorder amplifiers. The difference between the input voltage and the wiper arm voltage is proportional to the error in where the pen should be with respect to the value of the input signal. The amplified difference or ˙error voltage controls the pen carriage motor (Fig 3) and drives the pen carriage to a position where the difference between the wiper arm voltage and the input voltage is minimum. As the motor drives the pen carriage, the pen path is drawn on the moving strip chart recorder paper, which is driven by a synchronous motor and runs at a constant rate. The paper motion represents the time axis.

This example is cited because one of the most common ways to interface an instrument to a computer is through the addition of a retransmitting slide wire to its strip chart recorder. Most older instruments relied on strip chart recorders as the primary output media. An accessory kit for installing a retransmitting slide wire is available from the instrument manufacturer or strip chart manufacturer. Thus one of the simplest ways of connecting an older instrument to a computer is to tap the

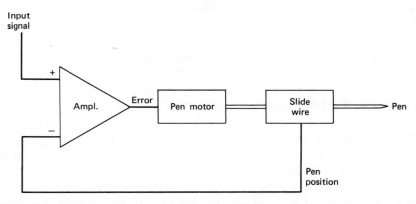

Fig. 3. The pen motor is part of a servosystem. The pen motor drives the pen and a slide wire potentiometer. The slide wire voltage is proportional to the pen motor position. The pen position voltage is compared with the input voltage signal in the servoamplifier, and the difference is amplified and applied as a drive voltage to the pen motor. The motor drives the pen position so as to provide a minimum error signal.

retransmitting slide wire on the strip chart recorder and connect it to the computer ADC.

It should be mentioned that strip chart recorders are available for electrical and nonelectrical signal inputs. In the case of nonelectrical signal input strip chart recorders, such as those that are actuated by hydraulic or pneumatic signals, the retransmitting slide wire output acts a transducer that converts the input signal to an electric output. In electrically activated strip chart recorders, the signal output on the retransmitting slide wire is electrically isolated from the input source. In addition, the output signal is amplified. It should be evident that, when the electrical signal input is from a low-impedance source, it may be preferable to connect the signal directly to the multiplexer. Where feasible, it is desirable to bypass the strip chart recorder, thereby eliminating any error that may be introduced by this instrument.

The accuracy of a strip chart recorder is no better than 0.1% in most cases. However, most instruments that were designed for read-out using strip chart recorders are not capable of accuracies higher than the recorder accuracy. For this reason, using the retransmitting slide wire as a relatively easy means of obtaining electrical output is justified. It has the further advantage that filtering of noise and operations with low-level signals are obviated because the strip chart electronics performs the amplification and filtering functions.

The accuracy and bandwidth of the signals obtained through the retransmitting slide wire may not be adequate for computer applications. However, as a start this technique is usually the most expedient and is certainly recommended where feasible because it provides a simple and economical method for connecting an instrument to a computer.

POTENTIOMETER SIGNAL CONVERSION

A potentiometer output is a voltage proportional to the angular position of the shaft (Fig. 4) with reference to the potentiometer resistance element. The accuracy of the wiper arm voltage is a function of the stability of the power supply applied across the extremities of the potentiometer. A stable DC voltage of about 5 V may be applied to a potentiometer. The relatively high voltage also overcomes many low-level signal processing problems, particularly at small angles.

To digitize the wiper arm voltage, ordinary analog to digital conversion techniques are used. The wiper arm voltage is connected to an input point on an ADC. When a number of potentiometers are to be digitized,

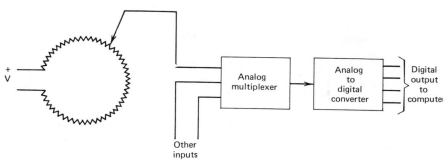

Fig. 4. A convenient way to input angular position to a computer is to couple a shaft to a potentiometer. The potentiometer slider output voltage is connected to the computer ADC via a multiplexer input point. The digitized voltage representing shaft position is entered into the computer.

a multiplexer is used, each potentiometer shaft analog voltage being connected to a separate port on the multiplexer.

The chief advantages of using potentiometers for digitizing shaft or angular position are the relative simplicity and low cost, especially when a number of shafts are involved. Accuracy and resolution are limited and can, of course, be no better than those of the potentiometer itself. By relying on mechanical contact between the wiper arm and the resistance element, potentiometers can be used only for relatively low-speed applications. Another factor to consider is the limited life of potentiometers, especially when higher speeds are involved.

SHAFT ENCODERS

A large variety of shaft encoders with a wide range of accuracies, speeds, and costs are available commercially. High-accuracy, high-speed, and resultant high-cost shaft encoders are on the market, as well as low-speed, low-accuracy, and low-cost types. Shaft encoders are available as absolute encoders and incremental types. They can be constructed using brush contacts, or with optical or magnetic sensing. Various codes have been devised to overcome ambiguity problems. Binary encoding and decimal encoding are available.

The output signals from shaft encoders can be connected directly as inputs to a digital computer. No interface is needed between the encoder and the computer in these cases. Modern encoders are quite compact. They are usually coupled to their input drive shafts directly or via gear trains when multiple-turn arrangements are used.

There are two broad categories of shaft encoder read-out methods, contacting and noncontacting. The contacting type utilizes pick-off brushes that touch the code surface. The noncontacting type employs sensors and code surfaces that do not touch each other. The choice of encoder for a particular application depends on many factors, such as resolution, total counts required, life, operating rpm, environment, reliability, and cost. Contact read-out is used for slower rotations and is less expensive to implement than the noncontact variety. The noncontact types have much longer life because there is no contact between moving parts.

CONTACTING ENCODERS

Chronologically, contacting encoders were developed first because materials for the code disk and brushes were readily available and construction techniques were adequate for the initial performance requirements. The first brush encoders were merely counting devices. Rotational velocities were very low. The brushholders were made by molding precious metal brush wire into a plastic block or by soldering the wire onto a brushholder. Then the brush wire was bent to some established dimension to result in a force when placed on a code disk. The first code disks were constructed by an etch and fill or a plating process.

Systems application of these encoders required them to digitize under dynamic conditions, that is, to perform nonambiguously while the input shaft was rotating. At this point, various problems appeared. The most severe of these concerned noise. Noise caused by brushes appeared at the "make" and "break" portions of the output signal. Also there was noise during the logical "one" and "zero" intervals of the output; this was contact noise. Both types of noise interfered with the fidelity of the output data because the noise was large. The output data were ambiguous and erroneous. These initial noise problems were solved by such techniques as increasing the size of the brushes contacting the code disk and/or increasing the brush force.

OPERATION

The most common means of translating a shaft angle into a digital code is to use an arrangement of coded disks (Fig. 5) consisting of electric conducting and nonconducting segments (or an analogous disk of transparent

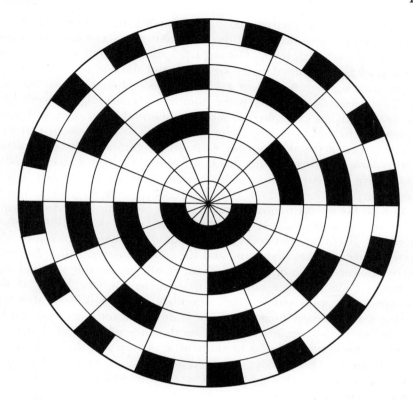

Fig. 5. An example of a code disk for a shaft encoder. The outermost concentric circle consists of alternate conducting and nonconducting segments. This is the least significant bit. The innermost concentric circle consists of one conducting segment and one nonconducting segment; it represents the most significant bit. Brushes riding along each track make contact with the surface and read out the angular position.

and opaque optical segments, or magnetic and nonmagnetic segments) with a shaft driven set of brushes making electrical contact (or optical or magnetic sensing) of position with respect to the disk. The disk has concentric tracks, each track representing a binary digit. The least significant digit track is at the furthest diameter of the disk, the more significant digit tracks being placed toward the center. The most significant digit is represented by the innermost track. The number of binary digits to be represented by one rotation of the shaft is equal to the number of tracks.

Each track is divided into a number of segments, which provide alternate stretches of conducting and nonconducting areas upon which the brush associated with the track rides and makes contact. A separate brush is associated with each track. The angular span of an individual segment of the track is determined by the significance of the digit.

The least significant digit in a binary encoder has segments that are $360/2^N$ (in degrees), where N is the number of binary digits encoded by the device. An an example, the most significant binary digit will have segment spans that equal $360/2^1$, or 180 degrees. It can be seen that successive tracks in the direction of decreasing significance have segments half as long as the preceding track segments. A 10-bit binary encoder would have segment spans of $360/2^{10}$, or 0.35 degree in the least significant binary track.

An 8-bit binary shaft encoder would consist of an encoding disk having eight concentric tracks. The innermost track would normally be etched to encode the most significant bit. It would be divided into two 180 degree segments, one conducting and the other nonconducting. Depending on the convention of the manufacturer, the conducting segment can be binary "one" and the nonconducting segment binary "zero." If the encoder uses optical sensors, the concentric tracks will have alternate opaque and transparent segments. The least significant binary bit will be encoded on the outermost track because the circumference of that track will be longer, permitting allocation of a greater length for each bit segment. In the 8-bit encoder described here the least significant bit will have 256 segments, each 1.4 degrees; 128 segments will be conducting and 128 nonconducting.

ENCODER AMBIGUITY

Consider ideal sliding brushes of zero width placed along a radial line, one for each track of a shaft encoder, together with a common brush. As described above, the disk contains concentric bands consisting of alternate conducting and nonconducting segments. A brush that contacts a conducting segment has electrical continuity with the brush common through the conducting segment; a brush that contacts a nonconducting segment is insulated from the brush common. Each brush gives an output depending on the conducting (or nonconducting) state of the segment with which it is in contact at any time. The combined output of the total number of brushes is a binary representation of disk position.

A number of practical considerations make the "ideal" arrangement less than ideal. The following deficiencies are listed in order of decreasing importance:

1. Finite widths of contact brushes.
2. Inaccuracies in disk pattern.
3. Nonalignment of brushes during encoder life.
4. Concentricity errors between disk and shaft.
5. Bearing inaccuracies.

These inaccuracies may cause a fundamental problem of output ambiguity at the transition points between digits. In the natural binary code, for example, it frequently happens that more than one binary digit will change when going from one number to the next. Since all the brushes cannot change over from one segment to the next at the same time, there occur narrow intervals of partial transition where some, but not all, of the brushes have made the next contact. As a result, and also because the numbers corresponding to these conditions do not necessarily interpolate between the pair of numbers before and after the transitions, a random output may occur.

There are two solutions to this problem: the development of special binary codes which change only one digit at a time, such as the Gray code, or the addition of extra brushes, selected by logic circuitry to avoid ambiguity. The principal disadvantage of the Gray code is the necessity to reconvert to natural binary or some other convenient code before use in digital equipment.

The second solution is known as "V-scanning" because of the V-nature of the brush arrangement, calling for two brushes per track on all tracks except the least significant. One brush of each pair is selected by external logic circuitry, depending on the direction of rotation of the encoder and the reading of the less significant bits. The logic circuitry must examine each brush pair in turn, starting with the least significant bit. The resulting output, after being operated upon by the logic circuitry, is the selection of one output from each brush pair. The resultant binary conversion accuracy is obtained within a quantizing error of $\pm\frac{1}{2}$ LSD value.

GRAY CODE (CYCLIC BINARY)

The pattern of this code, changes the state of the least significant disk only once in every two counts instead of once per count as in natural binary code, permits substantial reduction in encoder size. Examples of binary code and Gray type code for the numbers 0 to 16 are shown in Fig. 6. Note that for binary code all the bits can change from "one" to "zero" between successive numbers, whereas Gray code permits only a single bit to change from "zero" to "one" or vice versa. Many Gray code variations are used.

Decimal	Binary	Gray Type
0	00000	00000
1	00001	00001
2	00010	00011
3	00011	00010
4	00100	00110
5	00101	00111
6	00110	00101
7	00111	00100
8	01000	01100
9	01001	01101
10	01010	01111
11	01011	01110
12	01100	01010
13	01101	01011
14	01110	01001
15	01111	01000
16	10000	11000
17	10001	11001

Fig. 6. Gray code binary code. Note that each successive Gray code differs from its predecessor by only a single-bit change. In contrast, successive binary codes can differ in each bit position.

Since only one digit changes at a time in Gray code, reading errors of more than one count are impossible, even with a single brush per digit. For this reason, no external antiambiguity circuitry is necessary. The code cannot be used for computation, however, without first translating it into natural binary. However, reading Gray code directly into a computer is quite practical because with the aid of a simple program the Gray to natural binary code conversion can be effected. Connecting the shaft encoder output to the computer is straightforward. In most cases the logic levels are compatible. The most that may be needed are logic level shifters to match the encoder voltage to the computer input.

INCREMENTAL ENCODERS

The incremental encoder (Fig. 7) is by far the simplest encoder since the only requirement is to generate a single pulse for each equal increment of input shaft angle. The encoder may also contain a zero reference marker. The direction of shaft rotation can be readily detected through

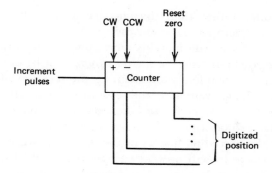

Fig. 7. An incremental encoder system consists of a pulser that provides a pulse each time the shaft advances by a preset angle. The pulses are counted by an up-down counter. By sensing the direction of rotation, the counter is set to count up for clockwise shaft rotation and down for counterclockwise shaft rotation. To provide for absolute encoding and take into account errors and dropped pulses, a zero or "home" angle setting is required. Each time the shaft passes this point, the counter is reset to zero.

one additional sensor. Circuitry is simple and power requirements are modest. High resolutions with minimal size units are possible, particularly with optical types. The associated electronic circuitry consists only of an up-down counter. For each increment in the clockwise direction a one is added to the count; each increment in the counterclockwise direction causes one to be subtracted.

The advantages of the simplicity of the encoder are obvious; so are its weaknesses. If for any reason power is interrupted to the encoder or a transmission or reception failure occurs, counts will be lost. If the encoder has no zero marker, this loss is permanent and results in an error that will persist until the counter is reset to zero. In units with zero reference, the error will persist until the zero reference has been sensed. In addition, some means must be provided for accumulating the output of the encoder. The required counter may be either external or internal. It should be noted that in systems using a number of encoders time sharing is not possible; every encoder must be equipped with its own counter. This requirement can lead to a considerable increase in cost and bulk and to lower reliability.

Nevertheless, in many applications, the incremental encoder represents a nearly ideal solution to the encoding problem. For example, incremental encoders without zero markers are used in many X-Y plotters. In this application, the encoder is used in the "floating zero" mode because the counter rather than the encoder defines the zero point by being cleared and zero set on command.

Absolute encoders are considerably more complex in construction, since the encoder delivers not only the smallest increment or bit of shaft angle rotation but also a complete word defining the location of the least bit sensed. The principal advantage of the absolute encoder is that it is in effect its own counter, since it sums and simultaneously displays the total number of bits from the zero position. The second important advantage is the lack of concern for the preceding history of the unit. A power failure or error condition, for example, will prevent encoder output during the malfunction, but when power is restored the encoder will again immediately provide the absolute shaft position read-out.

It would be difficult to overstate the importance of this ability to present absolute shaft angle position at any time and' without the necessity of knowing the prior history of the encoder. The absolute encoder is an "on-demand" component and needs no attention from the system until its information is required—a capability that gives the designer a powerful tool for reducing complexity. Shaft position can be determined at any time by sensing the encoded output.

MAGNETIC ENCODERS

Magnetic encoders utilize the magnetic core saturation principle for converting shaft position into digital information.

The code pattern is magnetically imprinted on a barium ferrite disk attached to the encoder shaft. During manufacture this code disk has had its constituent particles of barium ferrite aligned in a direction parallel to the axis of the disk. This results in a material having a preferred sense of magnetization. When a disk of this type is coded by "writing" on its surface with a suitable magnetic paint, the disk becomes magnetized at the areas on which the writing has been done. Because of the axial alignment of the ferrite crystals, this writing will exist in depth through the disk but only slightly laterally across the disk surface, thereby yielding sharply edged patterns.

Toroids are positioned directly over each code track on the barium ferrite code disk in the same positions that brushes for contacting encoders would normally occupy. The core is mounted in close proximity to the disk. If the core rests over a nonmagnetized area of the disk, an output will appear in the secondary winding, as explained above. If, however, the core is positioned above a magnetic area of the disk, the flux lines from the area will link with the core, aiding saturation in one half of the toroid.

Magnetic encoder resolution is determined by the diameter of the case in which the encoder disk is to be housed. A maximum resolution of about 8 bits can be generated on a simple disk. To obtain greater resolution from a magnetic encoder several disks are coupled through appropriate gear trains. (The same gearing technique is also used for coupling contact and optical type devices.)

Despite the modest resolution capabilities of most magnetic encoders, they have certain features that make their choice attractive in a number of applications. First, they are without question the most rugged encoders available today. This ruggedness is due not only to the magnetic principle employed, but also to the care with which the encoder design has been accomplished and the materials chosen for the construction of the unit. Magnetic encoders have been run totally submerged in boiling water, with the water having full entrance to the interior of the units. They have been operated successfully from below $-55°C$ to well above $100°C$, and tests have indicated their potential usefulness to almost $200°C$. They are capable of operation at from 0 to 10,000 rpm. Units have performed during 115 g shock without degradation of performance.

No contacting or optical encoder has approached the endurance capabilities of the magnetic unit. Magnetic units are a logical choice, therefore, where the worst environmental conditions are encountered.

In addition to their ruggedness, these units derive their ultimate reliability from the fact that, unlike contacting encoders, there are no brushes or disks to wear out and, unlike optical encoders, no lamps to replace. In a magnetic encoder, only the bearings wear, and these have been tested through many hundreds of millions of revolutions.

OPTICAL ENCODERS

Optical encoders range from relatively simple devices having very low resolution and primitive operational characteristics to enormously large, costly, and delicate devices capable of counts beyond 19 binary digits per turn and operable only under the most restricted environmental conditions.

The increasing use of optical encoders, particularly of the incremental variety, is due to the advances made in lengthening the life and increasing the reliability of tungsten lamps and to the introduction of solid state light emitters such as the gallium arsenide source. In addition, the availability of low-cost silicon transistors has considerably enhanced the reliability and environmental capability of the associated electronics.

7 Analog Recording

In many laboratory automation systems the signals of interest are recorded on magnetic tapes. For a number of reasons it is not only expedient but also necessary to record the analog signals on magnetic tape in analog form rather than perform data analysis and digitization. Analog recorders are quite different in design and performance from digital recorders. The methods of recording, mechanical tape transport characteristics, and data handling electronics are all quite different.

Analog recorders are used to record analog signals that may range in frequency response from DC to several megahertz. In some situations the signals occur only once or are very difficutl to obtain again; therefore it is necessary to preserve them. These may be signals that require extensive processing before digitization and information extraction, or signals that are relatively unknown and cannot be processed in a pre-determined fashion, so that a trial and error multiple-processing approach is appropriate. Such signals must be preserved in their analog form. In other cases, signals are retained in analog form because large quantities of data must be stored and analog recording inherently requires less space than digital techniques.

Analog tape recorders must be more carefully designed, both elec-tronically and mechanically, than digital recorders. A high-quality analog recorder is more expensive than a digital recorder of comparable quality. The characteristics and applications of analog recording technology in laboratory automation systems are discussed in the subsequent sections.

BANDWIDTH

The current commercial state of the art of digital tape recording permits data packing densities of 6250 bits per inch (bpi), using phase encoding techniques. A total of 12,500 flux changes per inch are recorded. The

120

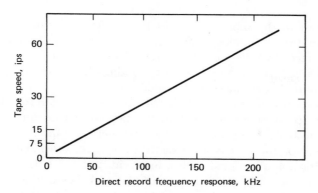

Fig. 1. Response of analog tape recorder as a function of tape speed. High-frequency response is approximately a function of tape speed, low-frequency response is limited by tape head gap and the rate of change of record flux.

bandwidth of an analog recorder is primarily a function of the relative speeds of the tape and record head (Fig. 1). As a rule of thumb, which varies greatly between manufacturers and specialized techniques, a bandwidth of 2 to 5 kHz per inch per second of tape to head motion can be expected.

A major application of analog recording involves situations where the bandwidth of the analog signal of interest is beyond the capacity of the digital system. A very high speed digital recording mechanism will permit digital transfer rates of as much as 1 to 2 megabytes. This assumes recording on disk or drum, or reading data into main memory for a limited recording interval. Such devices have limited storage capacity and fill up very rapidly; therefore they can accept data for only short durations before additional relatively slow actions, such as repositioning heads or head switching, can be completed. The data transfer rate of approximately 1 to 2 megabytes based on the fundamental theorem of sampling theory, would indicate that analog signals having at most a bandwidth of about 1 MHz could be handled. In practice, however, analog signals with bandwidths of about 100KHz can be accommodated with these data transfer rates.

In cases where any action must be taken on the incoming data, the effective maximum equivalent analog bandwidth is considerably reduced. A high-speed minicomputer can execute about 1 million instructions per second. Even a program requiring the execution of a few instructions per data point will slow the maximum effective analog data rate to no more than 100 kHz. A short burst of much higher bandwidth could be accommodated but only for a very short interval.

In contrast to the shortcomings in handling such high data rates in digital form directly, analog recording offers advantages. Analog recorders capable of recording signals with bandwidths to 10 MHz or even more can be obtained. Thus high-frequency analog signal recording presents no insurmountable technological problem.

An important characteristic designed into an analog recording system is multiple speed capability, that is, the tape unit can, under operator control, run at different speeds. The ratio between speeds and the absolute values of the speeds are exactly controlled and closely matched. Thus a recording of a signal with a bandwidth of 500 kHz at a speed of 120 inches per second (ips) will appear as a 62.5-kHz signal at 15-ips playback, and as a 31.25-kHz signal at 7.5-ips playback. By playing back an analog tape at a slower speed, the bandwidth of each signal recorded on the tape is reduced by an amount equal to the ratio of tape speeds. The slowed down signal can be conveniently handled by ordinary signal processing techniques, because the bandwidth of the analog signal that must be handled is reduced in proportion to the reduction in speed. This illustration demonstrates a primary reason for resorting to analog recording: high-frequency signals that cannot be handled by ordinary signal processing equipment can be slowed down to a frequency range that lends itself to straight forward manipulation. It is apparent that along with the slow-down in speed comes a longer time for playing back the tape; a 1-hr recording made at 120 ips would be played back in 4 hr at 30 ips. Real time is slowed down.

It should be noted that the reverse capability is also useful: slowly varying signals can be recoded on magnetic tape at a very slow speed. The tape is then played back at a faster speed, thereby decreasing the time needed to process the data. In one case real time is slowed, whereas in the second example it is speeded up.

MULTIPLE PASSES

In many situations it is not possible to determine the appropriate or best signal processing algorithm until after a major portion of the signal of interest has been examined. When the signal is recorded on analog tape, the signal can be played many times to determine the best processing strategy. This can be more convenient than digitizing the signal and subsequent processing because in many cases the analog to digital conversion technique is a factor in determining optimum signal processing strategy. Thus by recording the signal on analog tape the experimenter can replay the signal many times and try various approaches.

Raw data can be preserved in analog form for future processing. In some situations the value range of the data may not be known, or the data may have been created on a previous occasion that may not even be related to the present situation. Preservation of data in their original analog format permits future processing of the same data many times, even for information that may not have been considered beforehand.

DATA RELIABILITY

It is evident that less equipment is needed to record a signal on analog tape than to digitize the signal, preprocess it, and record it on digital tape. If a major factor is the importance of capturing and preserving signals, a reliable technique is to record the signals using analog recording. The amount of electronics between the signal source and the tape is less in an analog system.

Satellite data and biological data are examples of cases in which it is important to save the raw source information. Obtaining satellite data is extremely expensive, and repeating an experiment may be beyond any reasonable budget limit. In the second example, the subject may not be available to perform the experiment again. In both cases only one-time data acquisition is feasible and the conditions are difficult to repeat or beyond the experimenter's control to reproduce. In situations of this type it is imperative to have permanent records that can be subsequently reprocessed to reveal information not extracted on previous runs, or perhaps lost because of a mulfunction in subsequent processing.

Another factor to consider is the value of the raw data. Analog recording is less susceptible to equipment failure because of the fewer number of components. Availability of the raw analog data also permits the user to handle the data entirely differently at some later time. The preprocessing techniques normally used to convert analog data to digital form can remove information content that may be useful in later experiments. By having the source data recorded on analog tape, additional opportunities for meaningful data manipulation can be exploited.

SPACE SAVINGS

Analog data can be stored at much higher densities than digital data, as is evident from the examination of bandwidth capabilities given previously. A 2400-ft reel of $\frac{1}{2}$-in-wide digital tape can store approximately

400×10^6 bits when nine data tracks are recorded at 1600 bpi. A comparable analog recorded tape can store the equivalent analog data of all nine tracks on one track. A single analog tape channel would need over two full digital tapes for storing its data in digitized form. In addition, the number of analog channels on a given tape width is comparable to the number of permissible channels. When large quantities of data are to be stored, far less space is needed to store them in analog form.

LIMITATIONS OF ANALOG RECORDING

The foregoing sections may give the inaccurate impression that analog recording is a superior mode of recording data. For certain applications and under the specific conditions discussed here, analog recording may be preferable. However, as in all engineering decision making, a trade-off analysis must be carried out, weighing both the advantages and the limitations of analog versus digital recording for the particular application. Analog recorders introduce errors into the recorded (and played-back) signal because of mechanical eccentricities of the tape transport. The signal itself is degraded by the record and playback electronics through the introduction of distortions and nonlinearities. In addition, the dynamic range of the signal is limited by the signal-to-noise ratio of the electronics, the magnetic tape, and the record head.

These are some of the major factors that limit the applicability of analog tape recorders. As is true of most systems, good design practice coupled with precision parts can overcome some of these limitations. Thus, if one or more of the limiting factors in the utilization of analog recording are to be overcome, a considerable increase in system component costs must be acceptable.

INSTRUMENTATION RECORDERS

Recorders capable of recording analog signals can be categorized as audio, video, and instrumentation recorders. Although the basic recording principles are the same for the three types, the design criteria are quite different.

Audio tape recorders of a high professional quality have many of the characteristics of an instrumentation recorder. Although not specifically designed for instrumentation recording, many audio recorders are used where instrumentation recorder quality is not absolutely essential. Aside from precise control of certain specifications in the design and manufacture, audio recorders very much resemble instrumentation recorders. The most evident difference in specification is implicit in the term audio tape recorders: these recorders are designed to operate primarily in the audio frequency range from less than 10 to 20,000 or 30,000 Hz. Signals of interest in many true instrumentation recorder applications range from DC to well beyond the audio range and into the megahertz range. Audio recorders usually have built-in pre-emphasis networks that shape the frequency response characteristic to compensate for loudspeaker system characteristics and the response of the human ear. The resultant response as a function of frequency is decidedly not flat. A major design effort is devoted to compensation networks. At the high and low ends of the frequency range, instrumentation grade analog tape recorders have frequency response fall-offs that are precisely controlled in their characteristics. In addition, the amplitude response in the center portion of the response curve is designed to be as uniform as possible with a linear phase response characteristic. It is the careful attention to these characteristics that distinguish between audio and instrumentation recorders.

If an analog recording application can be satisfied through the use of an audio recorder, that solution should be seriously considered. Highest-quality professional grade audio recorders are considerably less expensive that medium or even minimum specification instrumentation recorders.

Video recorders are extremely wide band analog recorders designed specifically to record TV video signals. Full TV bandwidths of 8 MHz can be recorded using video recorders. Tape speed, however, is relatively slow, between 7.5 and 30 ips, so that a full 1-hr TV show can be recorded on a 14-in diameter reel of 1-inch-wide magnetic tape. Video recorders with bandwidths capable of recording both black and white and color are standard. To achieve the high bandwidth in spite of the relatively slow tape speed a rapidly rotating record/playback head is used. The high-speed rotating head effectively creates a high tape speed relative to the record head. The gap on the record head is in the form of a helix around the record head circumference. Thus, as the head rotates, a series of parallel bands across the width of the tape is recorded. It is evident that a gap can exist in the data from the points where one end of the helix leaves an edge of the tape and the other end of the helix makes contact with the opposite tape edge. This is not a deficiency for video recording, however, because the horizontal and vertical synchronization (sync) signals act as periodic interruptions in the data stream. The rotating helical head is servo-locked to the sync signals so that the head crosses the transition between tape edges during the sync interval.

The periodic gaps in the data recorded using video recorders make their use difficult except for TV-like signals. Most data situations are continuous and cannot accept such interruptions to the data flow.

Analog recording requires precise control over the speed of recording to assure time stability as well as meaningful data recovery. By its very nature the instantaneous speed of the rotating record head is difficult to maintain exactly. In addition, the frequency response characteristics are designed to conform to TV signal standards. Thus, for example, in the design particular attention must be paid to frequency response and the characteristics of the signal voice and color components. These are of no particular interest in an instrumentation recorder application. For these reasons, video tape recorders do not find wide application in instrumentation.

Video recorders provide extremely attractive price-to-bandwidth ratios, especially when compared to ordinary instrumentation recorders. Although it is difficult to use viedo recorders for instrumentation recording, in specific cases the possibility may well be investigated. The market for standard broadcast quality video recorders is extremely competitive, and therefore they are comparatively reasonably priced. With the introduction of low-cost video recorders for closed circuit TV, the attractiveness of these recorders is further enhanced.

Instrumentation recorders are essentially very high quality devices that have been specifically designed to record and play back analog signals with the highest possible fidelity. The tape transport mechanism is designed to have extremely low wow and flutter. Tape motion is uniform, and its speed is carefully and precisely controlled. The tape handling

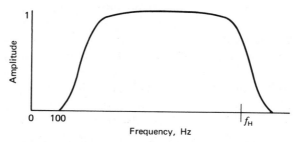

Fig. 2. The characteristics of direct recording. Frequency response is very broad. Low-frequency and DC response is not possible with direct recording. The signal-to-noise ratio of direct recording is less than that of other techniques, thereby reducing the effective dynamic range. Direct recording is the simplest and lowest-cost recording technique.

mechanism is very gentle with tape; mechanical contact with the tape magnetic coating is avoided as far as possible.

Recording on tape may be done through direct (Fig. 2) or FM recording. Direct recording permits the recording of the highest frequency attainable at the selected tape speed. Low-frequency response is inherently limited to several hertz, at best; FM recording is necessary to obtain DC response. In addition, the dynamic range is limited when direct recording is used because of the limited signal-to-noise ratio. Frequency modulation recording is more expensive in equipment (and price) than direct recording. With FM recording high-frequency response is sacrificed at the expense of wider dynamic range and DC response.

DIRECT RECORD/REPRODUCE

A record head is similar to a transformer with a single winding. Signal current flows in the winding, producing a magnetic flux in the core material. To perform as a record head, the core is made in the form of a closed ring, but, unlike a transformer core, the ring has a short non-magnetic gap in it. When the nonmagnetic gap is bridged by magnetic tape, the flux detours around the gap through the tape, completing the magnetic path through the core material. Magnetic tape is a ribbon of plastic (Mylar) on which tiny particles of magnetic material have been uniformly deposited. When the tape is moved across the record head gap, the magnetic material, or oxide, is subjected to a flux pattern that is proportional to the signal current in the head winding. As each tiny particle leaves the head gap, it retains the state of magnetization that was last imposed on it by the recording flux. The actual recording takes place at the trailing edge of the record head gap.

To reproduce a signal, the magnetic pattern on the tape is moved across a reproduce head. Again a small nonmagnetic gap in the head core is bridged by the magnetic oxide of the tape. Magnetic lines of flux are shunted through the core and are proportional to the magnetic gradient of the pattern on the tape which is spanned by the gap. The induced voltage in the head winding follows the law of electromagnetic induction: $e = N(d\phi/dt)$. It is important to note that the reproduced voltage is proportional not to the magnitude of the flux, but to its rate of change.

Several factors combine to limit the high-frequency response of tape recorders, but before these are considered the meanings of "recorded wavelength," "resolution," and "packing density" should be discussed. If a sine wave signal is recorded, the magnetic intensity of the recorded track will vary sinudoidally. The distance along the tape required to record a complete cycle, called the recorded wavelength, is directly proportional to tape speed and inversely proportional to signal frequency. For example, a particular recorder quotes 1.2-MHz response at 120 ips. There are several other ways to describe this response. Dividing 1.2 MHz by 120 in. shows that the machine is capable of a packing density of 10,000 cycles per inch. Such a signal has a wavelength of $\frac{1}{10}$ mil (0.0001 in.), which is the limit of the machine's resolution. Both packing density and resolution can be used to describe a recorder's response independently of tape speed, and thus are more definitive of recorder capability than just a frequency specification at a given speed.

Five factors contribute to the high-frequency limitation of tape recorders: (1) gap effect, (2) recording demagnetization, (3) self-demagnetization, (4) penetration losses, and (5) head losses. The reproduce head output increases with frequency up to a point and then decrease rapidly to zero. The decrease is primarily the result of gap effect and occurs as the recorded wavelength becomes shorter and shorter until it eventually equals the reproduce head gap dimension itself. At this point no magnetic gradient is spanned by the gap and thus there is no output voltage. This is the most serious single restriction on the high-frequency response of a tape recorder.

The linear range of the transfer characteristic gradually becomes nonlinear as magnetization approaches saturation. This gives the recording process what is described as "graceful" limiting; in other words, increasing the recording level above normal will gradually increase distortion before hard limiting caused by magnetic saturation occurs. To define the maximum signal level that can be recorded, it is thus necessary to state the maximum distortion which can be tolerated. In practice, the specified maximum signal level is usually tied to a 1% total harmonic distortion (THD) specification.

Dynamic range or signal-to-noise ratio is quoted in decibels and is the ratio of the maximum signal (for a given THD) to the minimum signal being determined by the noise level of the entire system over the bandwidth of interest.

High-quality instrumentation recorders should not favor any particular portion of their recorded bandwidth because of the nature of the signals they must accommodate. Their low-frequency response is usually quoted at about 400 Hz in the direct record mode so that the added noise contribution below that point can be eliminated. Of course the added noise from the higher-frequency response does increase the cumulative noise and reduce the S/N value. Also, in striving for the higher-frequency response, very narrow gaps are used in the reproduce heads with a corresponding reduction in signal voltage. The definition of maximum record level (i.e., the level which produces 1% THD) also works against the instrumentation machine.

FREQUENCY MODULATION RECORD/REPRODUCE

Data recording using a frequency modulated carrier is accomplished by deviating the carrier frequency in response to the amplitude of a data signal and recording it (Fig. 3). A signal of one polarity increases the carrier frequency, and the opposite polarity decreases it. A signal alternating in polarity will increase and decrease the carrier above and below its center frequency at a rate equal to the data signal frequency and in proportion to the instantaneous signal amplitude. In the reproduce process, the carrier's amplitude is increased to the limit and the data signal is reconstructed by detecting zero crossings, using standard FM demodulation techniques. Residual carrier signal and out-of-band noise are removed by a low-pass filter. Frequency modulation has a signal band-pass from DC to the upper frequency response of the FM process. Frequency modulation recording is extremely sensitive to tape speed fluctuations (wow and flutter) in either the record or the reproduce mode because tape speed variations produce unwanted FM of the carrier. An erratic tape speed or a change in tape speed manifests itself in playback as a spurious FM and as a noise superimposed on the signal of interest. The increased noise level in the reproduced signal and the corresponding reduction in dynamic range constitute a first-order effect of flutter. A second-order effect is the actual time base variation of the data signal. This is the same for the direct recording process.

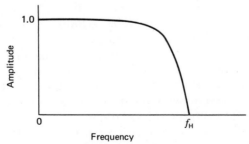

Fig. 3. Characteristics of FM record/playback electronics, which provides low-frequency and DC response.

A detailed technical description of FM theory can be found in many electronics and communications textbooks, but a few of the more pertinent factors will be discussed briefly to facilitate a cursory understanding of the FM recording process.

First, a few definitions are helpful:

f_c = carrier center frequency
Δf = carrier deviation from f_c
f' = data signal frequency
f'_{max} = highest data signal frequency
$\dfrac{\Delta f}{f'_{max}}$ = deviation ratio, or modulation index
$100\,\dfrac{\Delta f}{f_c}$ = percentage deviation

Deviation ratio is one of the most important factors in any FM process. Basically, the higher the deviation ratio, the more immunity the system will have to noise. In FM recording, there are practical limits to deviation ratios, since Δf is restricted by recorder bandwidth limitations and f'_{max} must be kept high to accommodate the data signals. Common deviation ratios in use today range from 5 in telemetry FM subcarriers to 0.675 in wide band FM recording. Frequency modulation broadcasting, which enjoys excellent noise immunity, uses a deviation ratio of 5 ($\Delta f = 75$ kHz, $f'_{max} = 15$ kHz).

A well-designed FM carrier recording system will give reasonably good amplitude accuracy, DC response, good DC linearity, and low distortion. The price paid for this improvement over direct record performance is greatly reduced frequency response for a given tape speed, added complexity and cost in the record/reproduce electronics, and a much greater need for constant tape speed (low flutter).

There are many applications for FM recording. The obvious advantages, of course, are the DC response and stability. It also is a very handy tool for time expansion and compression techniques. For example, 20-kHz data recorded at 60 ips on a 108-kHz carrier can be reproduced at $1\frac{7}{8}$ ips with the data frequency spectrum reduced by a factor of 32. Combinations of changing tape speeds and rerecording can provide time base change and frequency shift factors of well over 200. Data reduction, spectrum analysis, and other laboratory chores can be simplified with such expansion and compression techniques.

As long as recorder response was limited to about 100 kHz at 60 ips, there were fairly well defined standards for FM recording. Tape speeds of $1\frac{7}{8}$ to 60 ips were assigned FM carrier frequencies of 1688 Hz to 54 kHz, all harmonically related, that is, double the tape speed and double the FM carrier frequency. Percentage deviation was established as ±40%, and a deviation ratio of approximately 2 was selected. This provides DC to 10-kHz data response at 60 ips, 5-kHz response to 30 ips, and so on.

The majority of the systems in use today record the carrier to saturation on the tape without bias, using FM electronics provided by the recorder manufacturer. In this manner, the maximum possible voltage is obtained from the reproduce head. Direct recording (with AC bias) may also be used with voltage controlled oscillators and discriminators external to the recorder.

Carrier frequencies are proportional to tape speed and have been selected near the middle of the recorder response to keep distortion products above the passband of the head/amplifier combination. Frequency modulation record amplifiers can usually be "tuned" to any of the standard carrier frequencies by selection of the proper plug-in or switchable tuning unit. Similarly, the FM reproduce amplifier is set for a specific carrier by selection of the proper frequency determining element and low-pass filter.

Single-carrier FM recording uses ±40% deviation with a deviation ratio of approximately 2. Performance will usually equal or exceed the following values:

Frequency response: ±0.5 to 1.0 dB over the specified band.
RMS signal-to-noise: 40 to 45 dB if full deviation is used and flutter specification is 0.25 to 0.3% peak to peak.
DC drift: less than 1% of full deviation over 24-hr period.
DC linearity: within ± 1% of a zero based straight line.

If electronic flutter compensation is used, the first-order effects of flutter or flutter induced noise can be reduced to a point where other noise contributors set the noise level. At best, a signal-to-noise ratio of about 55 dB may be obtained at tape speeds of 60 or 120 ips.

INTER-RANGE INSTRUMENTATION GROUP STANDARDS

The Inter-range Instrumentation Group (IRIG) has developed over the years a set of standards for telemetry equipment, including a full set of standards concerning analog tape recording. Adherence to these standards ensures that tapes can be interchanged between transports of different manufacturers (Fig. 4). Tapes that have been recorded in accordance

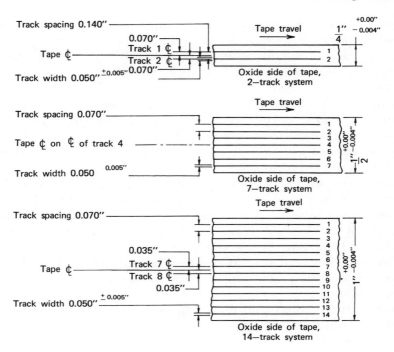

Fig. 4. The arrangement of data record/reproduce tracks on magnetic tape of various widths in accordance with IRIG specifications Following IRIG specifications ensures that data recorded on one machine can be played back interchangeably on another without adjustment or alignment. This is a major factor that makes adherence to IRIG specifications very desirable.

with IRIG standards can be played back on any recorder designed to conform to IRIG specifications. The value in producing tapes that are interchangeable among recorders is self-evident. Analog tape recording equipment should be selected to conform with IRIG standards. Most manufacturers who produce analog tape recorders make them in accordance with IRIG recommendations, which specify tape widths, head locations and spacing on the tape, and the physical parameters of the tape and the record/playback head; this assuring mechanical interchangeability. In addition, for FM recording the center frequencies are specified. The deviation ratios are also determined in accordance with the IRIG documents. By recording in accordance with IRIG recommendations electrical interchangeability is also assured.

FORMATS

A completely independent analog signal is recorded on a single track. Most analog recorders provide multitrack capacity because in most situations a number of analog signals are recorded simultaneously. Each recorded track is independent and has no bearing on the data recorded on any other track, except for time synchronization. The same time portion of the tape on each track passes under the record head simultaneously. The number of tracks on the tape is dependent on the tape width used; 4 tracks fit on $\frac{1}{4}$-in.-wide tape, 7 tracks on $\frac{1}{2}$-in.-wide tape, and 14 tracks on 1-in.-wide tape. The spacing and location of each head are specified by IRIG standards.

Provision for tracks at the tape edge are made for recording voice and other types of signals. The operator may wish to record verbally comments concerning the progress of the experiment.

TIME OF DAY

At least one track may be reserved for recording the time of day. The importance of knowing real time when reducing the data is self evident. A crude technique is to have the operator record time verbally; time tones from WWV or some other station can also be recorded. Upon playback the operator listens for these signals and enters into the computer manually via switches or an interrupt the time signal that he hears.

To make use of recorded data the time of occurrence of the events is required. In many cases the recorded data must be correlated with other data taken in different places and/or with different recorders and various other types of recording mechanisms. Frequently the reason the signals were recorded on analog tape was that the bandwidth of the signals of interest was too great to be handled in real time. The data are then played back at a slower tape speed than originally recorded. In addition, data may be reduced from one track at a time, or several tracks at a time, but not from all the tracks. It is necessary to have accurate time correlation between tracks of the tape recorder and other devices.

Standardized time-of-day codes have been designed by a number different organizations engaged in telemetry and data acquisition. These codes have been designed specifically for recording on a single track of a multitrack analog tape recorder. The codes are generated in a serial fashion and represent time of day and day of year. Time of day to the nearest

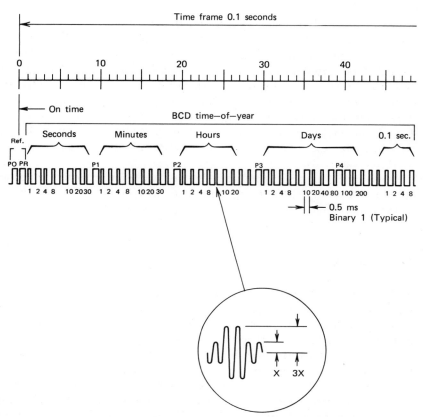

Typical modulated carrier (10000 Hz)

hundredth of a second may be recorded. Additional signals are recorded that make it feasible to determine time to a resolution of 1 msec on certain codes. Selection of the particular code to be recorded is determined by the time resolution required and the equipment on hand. It is advisable to select a code from among those that have been standardized at the various missile test ranges. Commercial equipment capable of generating these codes is available from a number of vendors at competitive prices. Changing codes is relatively easy on most of the models offered. Usually a single switch will select a number of different codes. Thus the same equipment can be used to generate a variety of useful codes.

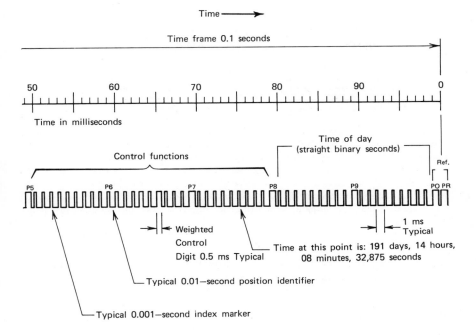

Time ⟶

Time frame 0.1 seconds

50   60   70   80   90   0

Time in milliseconds

Time of day
(straight binary seconds)

Control functions

Ref.

P5   P6   P7   P8   P9   PO PR

⟶| |← Weighted
Control
Digit 0.5 ms Typical

1 ms
Typical

Time at this point is: 191 days, 14 hours,
08 minutes, 32,875 seconds

Typical 0.01—second position identifier

Typical 0.001—second index marker

   A time code translator reads the time-of-day codes from the analog
tape at playback. In its simplest form the time code translator displays on
lamps or on a digital display the time-of-day code as read. This unit
operates on the data received from the time track at any tape playback
speed and displays the time-of-day code corresponding to the instantaneous time recorded on the tape.
   Commercial time code translators can be obtained with tape search
and control features (Fig. 5). With these additions a starting time-of-day
code and a stopping time-of-day code are entered into the equipment.
These times are usually set up by thumb wheel switches. The analog tape
is played back until the selected time-of-day code is read from the tape.
The start and stop times can also be computer selected. At the appropriate instant a signal is generated that indicates that the time-of-day
code requested has passed over the playback head. The data from the
other tracks are then processed by the data system until a second signal
indicates that the stop time setting has been passed. Some tape recorders
are capable of operating in a high-speed search mode, in which tape
search and control units are used to locate the areas of interest. When

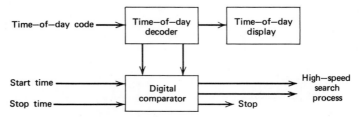

Fig. 5. Time-of-day playback and search equipment permit rapid convenient access and processing of recorded data. The start processing time and stop processing time are set on the playback equipment. The tape is run at high speed until the area of the desired start time is reached on the tape. Normal playback speed then begins to permit processing the information that was recorded during the time interval of interest. As the data are being processed, the recorded time-of-day code is decoded and passed on to the data handling circuits. When the end time is reached on the tape, processing of the data stops.

the selected data area is found, the tape is stopped, backed up, and restarted at the normal playback speed.

DATA RECORDING

Signals that have components of interest at DC or wide dynamic range must be recorded using FM techniques. If the dynamic range is much wider than can be accommodated by a single FM channel, several channels can be used to record the signal. Since each tape channel is set to a different gain level, each channel in use records a portion of the required dynamic range. Upon playback the signal from the channel whose instantaneous signal level is in the linear range is selected for processing. If the frequency response required is very high, direct recording is the only possible method.

Most tape recorders accept input signals of ±1 V full scale. Record amplifiers raise the signal to the required level for recording. Upon playback the signal delivered at the output of the playback amplifier is usually set to produce a nominal output of ±1 V full scale. Special-purpose analog recorders such as those used for medical recording have built-in amplifiers for extremely low level signals. For general-purpose applications, however, ±1-V signal levels are standard.

The responsibility of the experimenter includes signal conditioning and amplification to match the input requirements of the tape recorder. The problems of connecting analog signals to the tape recorder are similar to those involved in handling analog signals generally.

PLAYBACK

Signals played back on an anolog tape recorder will match the recorded signals except for the distortions and noise introduced by the recorder itself. As was explained previously, the tape transport introduces mechanical distortions due to the wow and fluttter of the transport and deformation of the tape itself. The higher the quality of the transport, the better the control and diminution of these effects.

The output of analog playback channels can be routed in the same way as the input signals. The advantages of tape speed reduction can be used when handling high-frequency signals or many simultaneous fast channels. In cases where wide dynamic range signals are split among a number of channels, the playback logic must be designed to select the channel carrying the instantaneous linear signal portion.

Upon playback, the reproduced analog signal from each data track is routed to a separate input channel on an analog multiplexer. The selected multiplexer output is in turn connected to an ADC. There is essentially no difference in the data flow path in the analog tape recorder playback signals as compared to the processing path of the original signals. The difference is that the actual signal must be processed in real time while it occurs, whereas in the case of the analog recorded signal the processing is done at a later time; various data reduction algorithms can be applied to handle optimally the particular signals. Techniques such as bandwidth reduction, using slow playback and prefiltering of signals, can be used. In every case, however, the basic principles of sampling theory must be observed.

8 Interface Logic Design

In order to connect a minicomputer to an instrument or an experiment, an interface must be designed and fabricated. The interface provides the circuits and the logic needed to connect the two devices (Fig. 1). The interface may be provided by the computer manufacturer or the instrument manufacturer. The availability of such an interface depends to a large extent on system marketability, and in many cases the user must provide his own interface because what is available is not suitable or, more often, nothing at all is on the market. This chapter describes the components needed to design and produce digital logic interfaces between computers and real-time systems.

INTERFACE COMPONENTS

An interface consists of a design and the components needed to implement the design. The interface design is the logic interconnection needed to suit the minicomputer input/output structure to the devices to be connected. The logic consists of various gates, flip-flops, and timing circuits, which are connected to perform the necessary control.

The physical components needed to implement the interface consist of various printed circuit modules plugged into a rack or cage that holds a number of modules. The module sockets in turn are wired together to perform the required logic functions. Cables are needed to connect the interface logic to the computer I/O bus and to the external devices.

Interfaces may be designed in a number of ways, starting with an original mechanical design complete with the necessary logic. However, an original mechanical design is very difficult and costly; it is not recommended unless existing hardware cannot under any circumstance be tailored to suit the application. Almost all interface design requirements

138

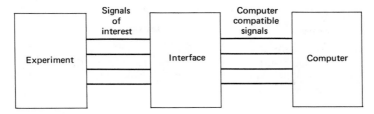

Fig. 1. Computer-instrument interface: instruments and experiments are connected to the computer via interface logic. This consists of the circuitry needed to condition experiment originating signals to digital computer input requirements and to convert computer output signals to what is needed by the experiment.

can be satisfied using standard commercially available mechanical structures and hardware.

The most practical way to produce an interface is to select the logic hardware from a particular vendor. A number of companies produce a complete line of mechanical hardware and plug-in modules that can be used to design an almost unlimited variety of interfaces. The plug-in modules and hardware are fully compatible and are designed to function together. Mechanical problems such as good contact between module pins and receptacles have been investigated and overcome. Provision for ventilation to assure adequate heat dissipation is made in the mechanical design. Usually prewired power supply lines are available. It cannot be stressed too strongly that problems arising from a poor mechanical design can defeat the best logical and electronic design. Every effort should be made to find an already available mechanical and hardware system that is suitable for the application in question.

Computer manufacturers and a number of independent producers provide a full line of logic modules and hardware. The first source of such equipment that should be assessed is the computer manufacturer. In fact, a sound criterion for the selection of one computer in preference to another is the availability of a matching logic system suitable for interface design. Such availability will simplify the interface design because the computer vendor probably has standard modules that perform many necessary functions. It is entirely feasible to purchase the interface modules from a vendor other than the computer manufacturer. In fact, in many cases it is best to buy the logic modules from an independent vendor because of the appropriateness of the available modules for the particular application.

LOGIC DESIGN

An interface performs the logic functions needed to connect the mini-computer to the external devices. The logic is implemented using a small number of basic logic modules. By interconnecting these modules, unlimited logic and control combinations are possible.

LOGIC CIRCUITS

The logic circuits used in the design of interfaces between computers and external devices are made up of three basic circuits: AND, OR, NOT (Fig. 2). Other digital logic can also be constructed using these basic circuits. Digital logic is almost universally built up of integrated circuits, which are available with these configurations in various connections that also provide functional units.

TRANSISTOR/TRANSISTOR LOGIC INTEGRATED CIRCUITS

The integrated circuits most commonly used in logic design are based on transistor/transistor logic (TTL), which may be regarded as the industry standard for general-purpose logic circuit design (Fig. 3). A number of compatible families of TTL exist; each family is designed to optimize a particular circuit characteristic. Thus, in addition to the

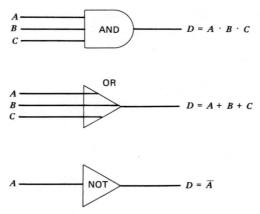

Fig. 2. Examples of AND, OR, and NOT logic elements. From these basic components all other logic elements can be constructed.

"standard" general-purpose family of TTL, a low-power dissipation family exists, as well as high-speed and ultra-high-speed families. The general-purpose standard TTL family is useful for almost all digital logic applications and can be employed reliably when switching delays of about 6 nsec per logic stage are tolerable. When low power dissipation is a necessary design goal, the appropriate low-power-dissipation TTL family should be specified. The high-speed TTL family has units equivalent to standard family members. The newly developed Schottky TTL integrated circuit family provides for ultra-high-speed switching in the vicinity of 2 nsec per logic stage. Power dissipation is highest in this family.

Transistor/transistor logic families have compatible "fan-ins" and "fan-outs," so that a system can be composed of members from the various families. Most manufacturers introduced members of the standard family first and maintain the broadest line in this family. Because of the wide acceptance of TTL, exact replacements by alternative suppliers of equivalent lines of TTL are available from a number of vendors. For these reasons it is good practice to use the standard family line of TTL in

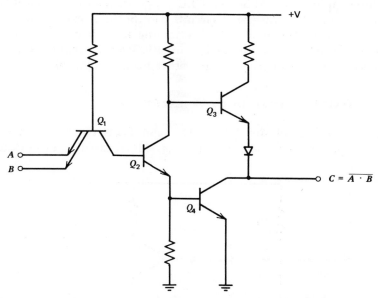

Fig. 3. Transistor/transistor logic: circuit diagram of basic element. Because of the large number of different family elements available in standard circuits and LSI, TTL is the most widely used logic family and is recommended wherever it is applicable.

digital logic design. The widest variety of readily available integrated circuits is assured. Simple, basic gates, as well as very complicated large-scale integrated (LSI) circuits and memory circuits, are available in the TTL configuration.

DIODE/TRANSISTOR LOGIC AND EMITTER COUPLED LOGIC CIRCUITS

It should be stressed that other families of integrated circuits exist and are used in large quantity, in addition to TTL. The first available integrated circuits were based on resistor/transistor logic (RTL). These were soon followed by diode/transistor logic (DTL) (Fig. 4), which still finds wide acceptance in many equipment designs. Although both DTL and TTL have characteristics that make them attractive, the larger development effort and investment in TTL and the very wide variety of TTL circuits available have made DTL less attractive. Either can be used for similar jobs.

Emitter coupled logic (ECL) has gained acceptance for ultra-high-speed switching applications. Although TTL has overtaken the original ECL in speed, current ECL integrated circuits are the highest-speed integrated circuits available. Where ultra-high switching speed is needed, as in computer central processor units, ECL is usually selected. Its high-speed performance cannot be matched by any other logic configuration.

METAL OXIDE SEMICONDUCTOR CIRCUITS

Integrated circuits of the TTL, ECL, and DTL types are all of the bipolar type. Metal oxide semiconductor (MOS) circuits use a different

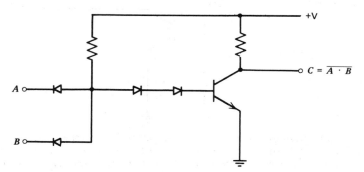

Fig. 4. Diode/Transistor logic: DTL element. DTL and TTL are essentially compatible general-purpose logic families.

type of construction technique which permits more circuits to be grown on the same chip size. Although MOS technology permits more complex circuits, they are slower than bipolar logic, and most MOS is restricted to special-purpose applications, such as desk calculator circuitry and memory devices. Bipolar logic circuits are available in larger numbers of general-purpose types and from many vendors. Most logic designs used to interface computers to peripheral devices and special-purpose systems do not employ MOS circuitry. When MOS circuity is used, logic level converters can serve to convert the negative logic level voltages of MOS to the positive logic level voltages needed for bipolar circuit operation. Many MOS circuits are designed with logic level converters as integral parts of the MOS chip to assure bipolar compatibility.

LOGIC LEVELS

Because of the almost universal application of bipolar logic, voltage levels encountered in interface design are relatively standard at 0 V and +3 to +5 V. Either voltage may be designated as the "one" or "zero" level. Each output can drive a number of compatible inputs. The loading and drive capabilities of each circuit are specified by the integrated circuit vendor.

The output drive of an integrated circuit is from a collector and is measured by the circuit "fan-out." Fan-out is defined by each device vendor and is a measure of the output drive capability. Fan-out is a number which indicates how many normalized inputs that a particular output can drive. Thus a logic element with a fan-out of 5, for example, can drive normalized input logic elements with a "fan-in" of 5, This can be 5 units or any combination that does not exceed the fan-out. The values for fan-out and fan-in should be based on the manufacturer's worst case analysis of the circuits under consideration. In other words, if all circuit parameters were to vary simultaneously, each to an allowable extreme, causing the most difficult set of conditions, and environmental and voltage conditions were at their allowable extremes, switching would still surely occur. Circuits designed in accordance with worst case design analysis help to assure reliable operation. A circuit loaded with inputs having a total fan-in equal to the driver fan-out will surely switch from the "one" to the "zero" state (and vice versa) even when the one and zero states (and vice versa) voltage levels are at their extreme values.

Insofar as the experimenter is concerned, the actual logic voltage levels are of very little import. What should concern him is the fan-out and fan-in values. Integrated circuits bought from a single vendor are specified with these values and are the basis of all logic circuit design. It is highly unlikely that the experimenter will become involved with the determination of these parameters from the integrated circuit parameter characteristics. The user should select a family of general-purpose logic modules. In this way the actual logic level voltages are not of immediate concern except in unusual cases where special circuits are necessary and cannot be made up from the logic module standard family.

Another factor to consider in the selection of integrated circuits is their sensitivity to noise. Every electronic circuit is susceptible to some degree to noise, and electronic equipment generally generates noise. Sensitivity to noise can be diminished by good circuit design and correct component layout and wiring practices. Electronically generated noise can be minimized by following good design practices and by shielding and filtering power and signal lines. Again the experimenter need not become involved in the selection of integrated circuits to achieve minimum noise condition or to shield noisy equipment. In general, the vendor of the logic module family will have taken these factors into consideration in the design of his modules; he will have selected integrated circuits with good noise immunity characteristics. High-noise-immunity integrated circuit families are available and should be used when noise spikes of several volts are present.

NOT CIRCUIT

A NOT circuit (Fig. 5) performs the inversion of an input signal. Thus, if the input to a NOT circuit is high, the output will be low; conversely a low input will cause the output of a NOT circuit to be high. A NOT circuit in its simplest form is a single transistor or integrated circuit. The collector signal of a transistor amplifier reverses the phase of the input signal and is, in effect, a NOT circuit. The basic TTL circuit performs an inversion of the input and hence the NOT function. The NOT function is defined as

$$\text{Output} = \overline{\text{Input}}$$

The basic TTL logic element can be designed with almost equal ease to have multiple inputs. The major limitation on the number of inputs is the number of pins that can be mounted on the integrated circuit package. The exact internal connections in the integrated circuit itself do not greatly influence the cost of the circuit or the difficulty in forming it. This point is important in considering the AND and OR circuit configurations.

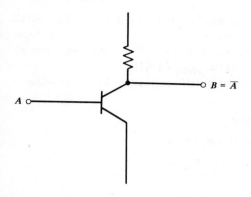

Fig. 5. NOT Circuit: a NOT circuit is the basic logic element in all logic families. It consists of an inverter circuit and performs a not-logic function:

Output $= \overline{\text{input}}$

NAND AND NOR FUNCTIONS

Multiple inputs connected to the NOT circuit previously discussed can provide the AND or OR and the NAND or NOR (Fig. 6) functions.

Consider the NOT circuit with the inputs causing the circuit to be nonconducting. When the circuit is nonconducting, the output is high, that is, the output is at the collector supply voltage level. The ouput will remain high as long as all the inputs remain low. As soon as any input becomes high, the circuit will begin conducting. Once current flows through the output collector, the output becomes low. If additional input legs go high, the state of the output will not be affected. Thus, if one or more of the inputs is high, the output will be low. If all the inputs are low, the output will be high.

From the preceding discussion it is apparent that, for a system of logic levels where the "true" or "one" state is represented by the "high" logic

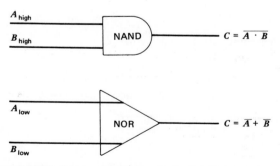

Fig. 6. NAND and NOR circuits: The same basic circuit can be used to perform the NAND and NOR functions. These circuits are based on the NOR basic circuit.

level and the "false" or "zero" state by the "low" logic level, the circuit under consideration performs the NOR function. If the reverse logic levels are used, the NAND function is executed. Thus the same circuit can provide both basic functions: NOR and NAND.

When applied as a NOR configuration the following logic equation is satisfied:

$$\text{Output} = \overline{A} + \overline{B}$$

The NAND configuration satisfies the equation

$$\text{Output} = \overline{AB}$$

GATES

Practical digital logic circuit systems are made up of a number of basic building block elements. The general-purpose one from which all other basic elements can be constructed is the gate. Gates of the NAND/NOR variety (Fig. 7) provide the basis of most digital logic systems; these gates consist of integrated circuit elements. For the reasons specified previously, TTL is almost universally used. The number of gates on an integrated circuit chip is determined mainly by the number of pins on the case.

A number of TTL units are mounted on a printed circuit card. The number of TTL integrated circuits that can be mounted on a card is physically limited by the dimensions of the printed circuit card and the number of contact pins that make connection to the card. In almost all cases the limiting factor is the number of contact pins. Multilayer cards are usually used to effect high packing density of integrated circuits on a card.

Common TTL based gate configurations are two-input and multiple-

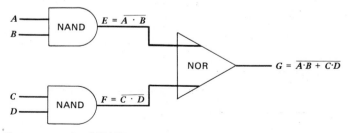

Fig. 7. Gates: example of NAND, NOR, and NOT circuits interconnected to perform logical functions.

input gates. Each gate section performs the NOR or NAND function. In many situations it is convenient to provide a clocked or transfer control common to a group of gates. This facility permits configurations of circuits that provide for simultaneous transfer of a number of bits based on a clock pulse or an enable signal from some external source.

Multiple-input gates with three, four, and eight inputs are commonly available. Transistor/transistor logic circuits are available with separate expandable inputs, permitting an almost unlimited number of inputs to be included in the gating function.

FLIP-FLOPS

The basic memory element in every system of digital logic is the flip-flop (Fig. 8). Flip-flop circuits have two stable states. Once set to a particular

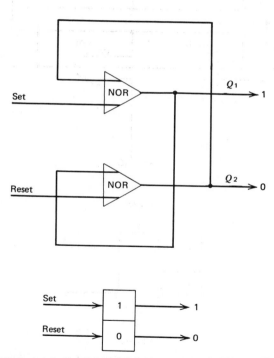

Fig. 8. The flip-flop circuit is the basic 1-bit memory element used in all logic and control systems. Shown here is the RS flip-flop configuration, which will remain in a particular state until set to the alternative one.

state, the flip-flop will remain in that status until purposely set to the other state. In other words, it will remember the state to which it has been set until reset.

The simplest flip-flop is made up of two two-input NOR gates connected together. When input A is made true, output Q_1 becomes false. Output Q_1 is connected to the second input leg on gate 2 and therefore makes output Q_2 true. Thus, at the time the true input is applied to

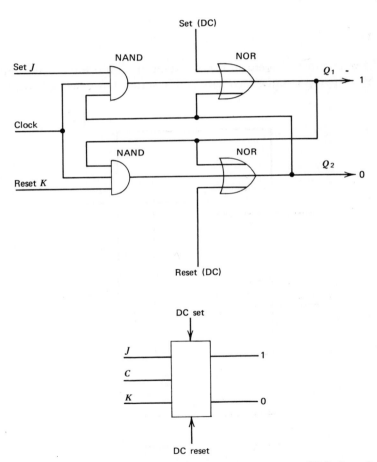

Fig. 9. J-K flip-flop is the most versatile flip-flop configuration. All logic and counting functions can be performed with this circuit. A major advantage is that no indeterminate states can exist with this circuit connection.

input A, both input legs of Q_1 are true. When input A is removed, the status of Q_1 is not affected because the second input leg of gate 1 keeps the status of Q_1 false. The status will remain until a true condition is applied to input B. Then the condition of the flip-flop will reverse, and Q_1 will become true and Q_2 false. This is the simplest flip-flop and is referred to as the reset-set (RS) type.

Flip-flops with more sophisticated gates capable of pulsed and DC response are also available. In particular, the complementary flip-flop configuration, which has a single pulsed input, is of interest. Each pulse reverses the previous status of the flip-flop circuit. Complementary flip-flop circuit configurations are the basis of counter devices.

Almost all flip-flops can be configured with DC set and reset inputs. These are auxiliary inputs that can be used to set a flip-flop to an initial condition.

Special double flip-flops known as J-K flip-flops (Fig. 9) are interconnected and available as a single TTL element. If both inputs of the RS flip-flop are made true simultaneously, an indeterminate output condition will result, and it is not possible to predict what the status of Q_1 and Q_2 will be. Flip-flops of the J-K type operate in conjunction with a clock pulse. A J-K flip-flop will respond only if the J or K input is actuated, if both inputs are actuated, the J-K flip-flop will complement. J-K flip-flops are general purpose elements and can be used for almost any application requiring a flip-flop. The J-K is the preferred general-purpose TTL flip-flop element.

FLIP-FLOP FUNCTIONS

Many functional TTL circuits are made up of variously configured combinations of flip-flops. A list of applications would be almost endless; the most important are the following:

1. Control elements (Fig. 10).
2. Counters (Fig. 11).
3. Shift registers (Fig. 12).
4. Memory elements (Fig. 13).

ONE-SHOT CIRCUITS

A one-shot circuit (Fig. 14) provides a single output pulse of fixed duration each time the input receives a voltage step. One-shot circuits can

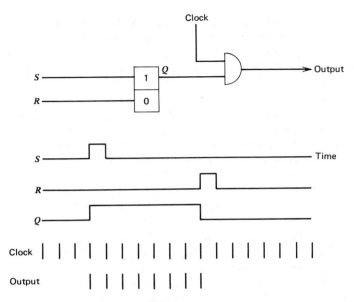

Fig. 10. Control element: flip-flop connection shown as control element. When flip-flop is in set state, control gate allows pulse train to pass; in reset state, pulse train is inhibited from passing through gate.

respond to negative or positive steps and can be designed with very short or very long firing durations. A pulse of almost any desired duration can be produced by varying the one-shot timing components, which consist of a simple resistor-capacitor combination. Timings from nanoseconds to tens of seconds are achievable with the same circuit.

The primary purpose served by one-shot circuits in a digital logic system is to provide pulses of standard width and fixed delays between events. A one-shot circuit will convert a positive or negative going edge to a pulse of standard duration. The length of the input pulse or its shape does not matter; only the change of state triggers the one-shot circuit. The trailing edge of a one-shot circuit obviously occurs a fixed time interval after the trigger.

CLOCKS

Synchronous systems require a fixed clock source. Logic actions occur simultaneously with the clock pulse. An oscillator with appropriate

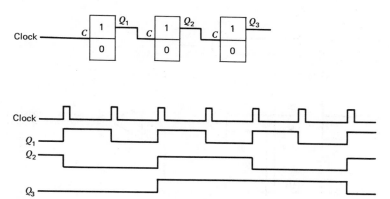

Fig. 11. Binary counter connection of flip-flops. Each pulse complements the first flip-flop stage. The first flip-flop propagates a trigger to complement the second flip-flop stage on alternate pulse inputs. The second flip-flop triggers the third flip-flop on every fourth input pulse.

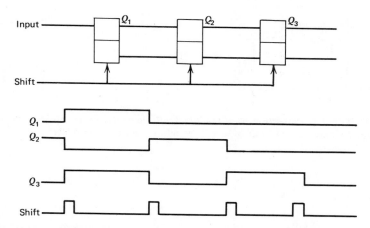

Fig. 12. Shift register connection of flip-flop elements. Serial pulse train is shifted into shift register 1 bit at a time in synchronism with input shift clock. Parallel data output is available by taking outputs from each shift register flip-flop stage.

pulse shaping circuits makes an effective clock pulse generator. To ensure accurate timing, crystal controlled oscillators should be specified. Free-running multibrators or other electronic oscillators can be used when extreme precision is not mandatory.

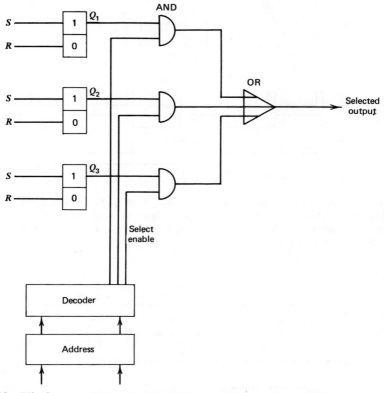

Fig. 13. Flip-flop connection as a random access memory. Each flip-flop stores 1 bit of data. To enter or read out information, address must be provided.

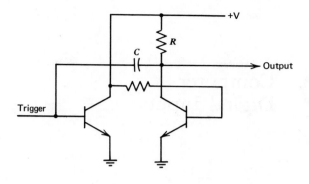

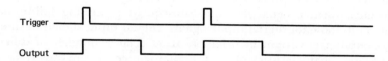

Fig. 14. Flip-flop connection as a one-shot circuit. Each time a trigger is received, the one-shot circuit fires and generates a pulse of fixed duration. The pulse duration is a function of one-shot RC time constant; practical one-shot circuits having pulses of durations ranging from nanoseconds to seconds can be obtained with a single circuit.

9 Computer Digital Inputs

Computer data input may be in digital or analog form. Analog signal characteristics and the techniques used to convert these signals to digital form were discussed previously. Once the analog to digital conversion is performed, further signal flow and subsequent processing follow paths identical to those for digital input signals. Digital input signals of interest in a computer environment originate from a large number of different sources; the characteristics of these signal sources are discussed in this chapter. It should be emphasized that signals of this type may be extracted from most types of equipment.

DIGITAL DATA SOURCES

These are as follows:

1. On-off switches.
2. Relays
3. Multiple-position switches.
4. Thumb wheel switches.
5. Logic circuits.
6. Communications terminals.
7. Analog to digital converters.
8. Shaft encoders.
9. Light sensitive transducers.
10. Frequency converters.
11. Other computers.
12. Digital instrumentation.
13. Pulse code modulation telemetry receivers.

14. Synchro to digital converters.
15. Time encoders.
16. Computer peripheral devices.
17. Counters
18. Pulse sources.
19. Elapsed time indicators.
20. Shift registers.

DATA SIGNAL CHARACTERISTICS

Although the number of digital signal source devices is quite large, the characteristics of the signals produced by these devices that must be considered for entry into a computer are relatively few. These characteristics may be grouped into hardware compatibility and software processing requirements. The hardware considerations concern the electronic compatibility of the signal sources with the computer input specifications. Under program control, the input signals are entered into the computer and are interpreted by the computer programs. As in any such input situation, trade-offs are always possible between hardware and software; that is, preprocessing the input signals via logic circuits can simplify the programming effort and speed up program execution times. The cost-performance compromises between additional special-purpose logic and additional programming effort must be evaluated. No hard rules can be established; each case and each installation must be considered in terms of the application, budgetary restrictions, and personnel capabilities in project execution. For example, if hardware-knowledgeable personnel are available who can be assigned to a project, hardware signal processing via logic circuitry will be selected for an installation in preference to programming.

The following are some of the characteristics that define digital signal sources:

1. Binary voltage levels.
2. Signal timing and synchronization.
3. Data rate.
4. Word length.
5. Format of data.
6. Parallel data.
7. Serial data.
8. Multiplexing of data.

BINARY VOLTAGE LEVELS

The first requirement is that the computer's internal voltage levels be matched by the external device that is to be connected. Most computers employed in laboratory automation are based on designs that use bipolar integrated circuit logic. Even in cases where large scale integration (LSI) is used, bipolar technology prevails. Although MOS technology is used in some computer circuits, particularly the memory, very few MOS interfaces external to the computer are implemented. Most external interfaces are bipolar logic level compatible. The nominal binary signal levels are 0 V and +3 to +5 V (Fig. 1). The definition of the "one" and "zero" levels is arbitrary and depends on the particular computer and the way in which the manufacturer specifies these levels. It is usually safer to assign the 0-V level to the "one" or "true" state. This assures that an open circuit will not be mistaken for a true condition.

For most computer applications the "one"/"zero" definition is not critical because a simple complement instruction can usually perform the necessary inversion before further processing. However, if speed of response is a major factor, it may be advisable to provide external logic level inverters.

The computer input usually assigns levels to logical "ones" and "zeros," and as long as these levels are maintained no particular problems are encountered in recognizing the levels. In most systems using integrated circuits, the problem of matching voltages is comparatively simple because of the relatively standard levels of integrated circuitry. Integrated circuit driving and loading rules are relatively straightforward. Most integrated circuits, especially those used as output stages, have good drive capability and can easily drive inputs normally encountered as computer digital inputs.

The output drive capability of a circuit, as discussed in Chapter 8, is designated as its "fan-out." This is a number that represents the number of unit loads that the circuit can drive. Ordinary DTL or TTL circuits have fan-outs of between 5 and 10 (Fig. 2). Low-level or high-speed circuits have lower fan-outs, but to be useful the value of the fan-out must

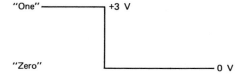

Fig. 1. Binary voltage levels: in most integrated circuit logic, binary signal levels of 0 V +3 to +5 V are standard.

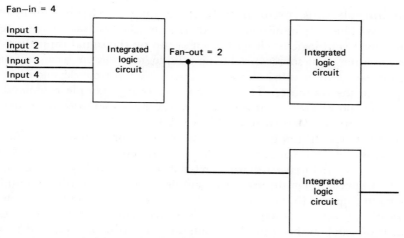

Fig. 2. Transistor/transistor logic showing fan-in = 4 and fan-out = 2. Most practical TTL circuits have larger fan-ins and fan-outs. Loading rules published by integrated circuit manufacturers should be followed to ensure reliable switching at rated speeds and noise tolerance levels. Violation of loading rules can lead to unpredictable results and unreliable operation.

be more than 1. Power circuits or integrated circuits with open collectors (therefore needing external collector resistors) can have fan-outs of between 30 and 100. A circuit having a fan-out of 10 is capable of driving 10 circuits each with a fan-in of 1.

Insofar as levels and drive capability are concerned, any series of integrated circuits can be used. High-speed families of integrated circuits may be utilized in the interface and computer hardware to minimize delays if very fast response is required. However, for most computer applications the delays encountered with the standard families of integrated circuits will be much less than most computer I/O data handling capabilities.

SIGNAL TIMING AND SYNCHRONIZATION

The timing and clock rate of the signal to be input to the computer digital input must be carefully considered. The simplest type of input signal is a signal that can be sampled at any time the computer issues an input-sample command. These signal sources provide a steady state output all the time, and such a signal can therefore be read in at any time. Signals originating from slow-speed devices, especially switches and status indicating elements, are in this category. Many logic circuits also fit into this class. The only requirement is that, when the program issues a read command, valid logic levels have been set up on the signal input lines to the computer. Data sources producing valid logic level signals continuously are the easiest to handle because the signals are not time dependent with respect to the computer. The program can issue a sample command at any time and be assured of a valid data input. No additional testing or synchronization is needed to establish validity.

Another type of input, of a more complicated form insofar as the computer data source is concerned, is the demand-response mode (Fig. 3). In this case an interactive situation exists because sampling cannot occur at any time the program issues the sample instruction. Rather, sampling occurs in response to the request of the external device. The input signal is read only when the external signal source indicates to the computer that it demands to be read. The computer may issue a command to the external device that the program wishes to read the particular input. However, the actual data transfer does not take place until the external signal source indicates by issuing a demand signal to the computer that it is ready to transfer information. The computer normally initiates the operation by issuing the sequence of instructions that actuates the device, or at least notifies it through the digital output facility that the

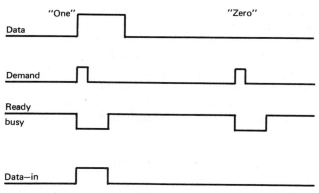

Fig. 3. Data synchronization sequence: data arrive in binary form. A "demand-clock" accompanies each data bit. This clock signals the computer that valid data exist on the computer input bus. If the computer is "ready," it can accept data. It will signal the external device that data have been received by dropping the "ready" line to "busy" status. When the computer has completed its input sequence, it will change from busy to ready status, indicating that it is free to accept the next demand-clock signal.

computer is "ready" and is in a state to accept data. A separate "ready"-"busy" line is usually brought out to provide this function.

When operating under external transfer control, transfer of data from the external digital data source takes place in synchronism with the external clock or synchronization signal. Each time this sync signal occurs, the external device essentially indicates that a valid data word is ready for transfer and the external device "demands" service from the computer. In effect, the external digital data source indicates its availability or readiness to transfer information to the computer by raising its "demand," or sync signal line. A demand-response sequence ensues in the transfer operation. The computer indicates to the external digital data source that the demand for service has been acted upon and that the data have been accepted by momentarily changing the status of the computer ready line. When the demand signal is recognized by the computer, the ready signal drops, indicating that the input digital data source is being serviced. As soon as the input data have been accepted, the ready signal is restored, indicating that the computer is prepared to accept the next demand for service. While the ready signal is down, the digital input channel is inhibited from recognizing additional "demands" for service. The ready-down state indicates that the channel is "busy" and cannot accept additional service demands.

In the preceding discussion no mention was made of a time limit between the demand signal and the response of the computer. The easiest situation to handle is one in which the input signal source remains available and valid continuously after the demand is issued. In such situations the data source notifies the computer via the demand line that it has valid data to transfer. The data are held in the device or an auxiliary register until the computer is ready to accept the information. It then responds via the "ready"-"busy" interchange. This environment is the easiest for the program to handle because it is able to effect the data transfer at its convenience. The computer can sample the input demand lines at regular intervals under program control. When the demand line is set, the program branches to data transfer operations; otherwise the main program stream continues. This data transfer is also referred to as direct program control operation.

Digital data may be accepted into the computer under interrupt control or under data channel operation. Although the non-time-dependent transfers described in the preceding paragraph can be conveniently handled through interrupt or data channel control, time dependent information transfer must almost always operate in these modes. Time dependent signals are those that remain valid for a limited time after the demand line is up or for very high data rates. In both cases the signal transfer must be effected within a short interval after the demand signal in order to ensure its capture.

A demand for service should be honored by the computer as soon as possible after its receipt. In the best case it can be honored when the computer cycle is completed. Thus, depending on the computer architecture, the delay between the "demand" for service and the actual transfer will be the time needed to complete the in-progress computer memory transfer operation or instruction. Interrupt control operates with delays that are much longer than those of data channel operation because an interrupt service program must be executed in order to effect the transfer. When the system maximum transfer rate is approached, the demand requests must be closely synchronized with the basic computer memory cycle. The system is normally responsive to demand-for-service requests before completion of the current cycle. If the requests are delayed slightly, the computer logic assigns the next cycle. Thus the timing becomes critical at the maximum rates. In many systems alternate cycles are automatically allocated to the central processing unit in order to prevent high-speed I/O from locking out the CPU completely. Of course, this type of design represents a system architecture decision and depends on the system application.

Interrupt controlled data transfers are particularly useful when handling infrequently occurring requests for transfer. It is more efficient in these cases to have the external device demand service through an interrupt than to have the program frequently test the device to determine whether it "demands" service. Because the external device immediately notifies the computer when it desires service, the actual beginning of the service routine can be much closer to the time of availability of the data. Interrupt requests can be serviced sooner than program controlled sensing of external device "ready" status.

DATA RATE

The data rate of the digital input facility may be determined by the computer program or by the external data source. The techniques for establishing the rate and the synchronization between the computer and data source were covered in detail in the preceding section.

As long as the data rate is below the memory cycle time of the host computer, it is usually possible to design a system to accept the data.

Problems will occur, however, when the external data rate approaches the memory cycle time. Careful timing of the demand service requests with respect to the computer clock must be observed to ensure synchronous operation. If synchronous operation is not achieved, the maximum data transfer rate will be halved at least. The computer can accept data at a rate equal to its clock rate, or memory cycle time. One word can be transferred corresponding to each memory cycle. If data are not ready for transfer at the start of a particular memory cycle, the computer logic immediately assigns the cycle to another computer resource, such as the CPU, or another I/O channel. In fact, most computers are designed so that the memory I/O service request must be posted before the end of the current cycle. Thus, if the external device does not signal soon enough, the transfer request must wait a full cycle before it can be recognized by the computer logic.

Another factor to consider when operating at a high I/O transfer rate is the increased sensitivity of the system to noise and other interference. At low data rates low-pass filters can be inserted in the data paths to enhance noise attenuation. As the data rate increases, however, simple filter circuits are no longer adequate. The signals are of inherently large bandwidth and cannot be filtered simply. Filters of special designs to match the interference are required. In addition, precautions to check the validity of the data become more stringent.

In many computers, the basic design prevents successive memory cycles from being assigned to a particular I/O channel. This design philosophy ensures that the memory services other I/O channels and the CPU. Otherwise, if a particular I/O device operated at a synchronous rate equal to the computer's memory rate, the I/O device could lock out the CPU and prevent simultaneous CPU-I/O operations, or I/O operations on any other channel.

WORD LENGTH

The optimum number of parallel bits that can be transferred on each digital input operation is a full computer word (Fig. 4). This is evident from an examination of computer operation. If less than a full word is transferred, less than optimum transfer efficiency is achieved since the computer inherently is able to transfer a full word. As was described, the computer registers and memory are arranged with data path widths equal to the computer word size. If more than a full word is transferred on one cycle, a buffer is needed to hold the transferred data. Auxiliary

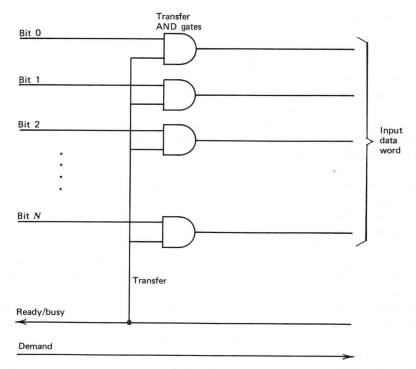

Fig. 4. Computer data entry of full word in parallel: each transfer pulse received from the connected external device effects the transfer of a full word in parallel to the computer digital input facility.

circuitry must be used to segment the data into computer word sizes and then to transfer the data one word at a time to the computer. However, no delays are encountered during the transfer operation because the word segments stored in the buffer are always ready and available for transfer to the computer.

The input data can be read into the computer in any word length equal to or less than one full computer word. Each input data transfer instruction affects the transfer of the data at the input bus to the computer. If the number of significant bits to be transferred is less than one full computer word, it is up to the user to provide appropriate software to handle the data. The information can be handled exactly as received by the program, or it may be assembled into full words. Several input transfers can be combined by the software to assemble a full computer word for subsequent storage and processing.

When transfer of data consisting of less than a full computer word is required, the transfer efficiency can be considerably improved by providing a word assembly buffer, in which a number of partial digital input words are accepted and stored. When a full word has been assembled, the contents of the buffer are transferred as a full word to the computer. As in the case of multiple word transfers, buffer storage and control logic are needed to perform these operations. As in most computer decisions, hardware/software trade-offs are made to determine whether nonstandard computer length transfers are to be handled via word assembly or disassembly buffers or via direct read-in and program controlled assembly.

Digital data inputs are handled most conveniently as full computer words. In many cases, however, data sources provide digital signals that are naturally less than or more than a full word in length. Although most minicomputers utilize 16-bit word lengths, for instance, an analog to digital converter may provide a 14-bit word as its output. It would not be useful to attempt to pack such data words; the data would be handled as 14-bit words. Nevertheless there are a number of relatively common formats of less than full word length. This is particularly true when transferring alphanumeric data; most codes handle alphanumerics as either 6-bit or 8-bit codes. In this situation, when the computer in question is a 16-bit word machine, it is usually expedient to pack words with two codes per computer word. The actual input/output may take the form of two character codes packed in each word transferred. One character at a time can be transferred when the computer program or external hardware performs the necessary manipulations to convert between packed computer word format and unpacked I/O code groups, one code at a time.

The multiple-code situation is encountered when dealing with interfaces to other computers and when multiple-word output devices are used. Computers which utilize 24-, 32-, 36-, 48-, 60-, or 64-bit words are sometimes interfaced to minicomputers. These computers have I/O data paths that are equal to these respective word lengths. The longer words are held in a buffer and accepted one minicomputer word at a time into the digital input facility.

FORMAT OF DATA

The format of the digital data input word is of major significance to the programmer because the computer program must be able to decipher the data. In some cases where preprocessing logic circuitry is involved in the data transfer paths, information contained within the transferred data may be used. However, in most situations the information is transferred directly to the computer without the intervening logic examining the information. Depending on the location and timing of the word transfers, the program ascribes various attributes to the signals. Thus the first word in each transfer sequence may indicate the type of transfer. Alternatively, a specific bit in each word may be set aside to distinguish between data and command signals. In still other systems, separate data paths are built to handle data and control signals. By defining the identifying characteristics of each transfer, the program can decipher the data. As was explained previously, the only difference between data and commands is the way the program and the hardware distinguish between them. The same signal lines and codes are useful for both. The necessity for careful, unambiguous specification is self evident.

Since it is important to ensure that the data being transferred have been transmitted correctly, the computer transfer facility should compute a check parity bit for each data word transferred. The computed parity is checked against the previously computed parity bit, which is usually carried with the information along the same data paths. If there is a discrepancy, an error flag is activated. The parity bit could be computed using software techniques; however, this is slow and rarely done. Other techniques for detecting and correcting errors in data transmission were described previously.

Many different data formats are encountered in data transfers in a real-time computer aided experimentation environment. Most of the ordinary computer codes, including binary, BCD, American Standard Code for Information Interchange (ASCII), and Extended Binary Coded Decimal Information Code (EBCDIC), are encountered when transferring data. Other nonstandard codes are also used to represent status and commands.

Binary coding is the most common form of data representation. It is certainly the most efficient code for representing specific information with the least number of bits. In most cases, especially where computer compatible I/O devices are specified, it is desirable that the external hardware operate in binary mode with 2's complement binary representation of negative numbers, which simplifies computer arithmetic algorithm implementation because most minicomputers use this representation. Commands and status information must be transmitted in binary form. The coding depends on the type of devices involved, the number of bits needed to represent the information to be transmitted, and the significance attached to each bit. Binary data transfers are normally full word transfers, that is, the number of bits in each transfer is equal to the number of bits in the basic computer word.

In systems where manual data presentation is needed or slow data rates are inherent, BCD coding is desirable. From a human engineering standpoint decimal displays and decimal representation of numeric information are preferred; BCD codes are used to represent decimal information. Alphanumeric information is also transferred by means of various different codes; these codes have either 6- or 8-bit. Eight-bit codes are usually referred to as bytes; two bytes can be packed by the hardware or software into a single 16-bit computer word. Since two 4-bit BCD digits can be packed into a byte, four BCD digits can be stored in a single 16-bit word (Fig. 5). Two 6-bit codes are usually packed into a 16-bit word. The additional 4 bits are then packed with zeroes.

PARALLEL DATA

Data transfer may be in either parallel or serial form. Parallel data format is simpler to implement on most minicomputers because of the nature of their design and organization. Also, most digital data sources provide parallel data outputs in preference to serial outputs.

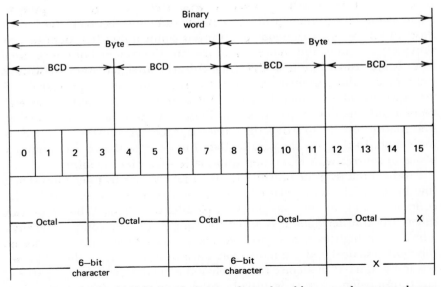

Fig. 5. Data packing in 16-bit word: data word may be a binary word or some character representation such as 8-bit bytes or 4-bit BCD digits.

Parallel data transfers require wide data paths, that is, several bits are transferred simultaneously with a separate signal line provided for each bit. The data path width may contain any number of bits; the exact number is usually determined by the word size of the data source. In addition, logical data paths equal in width to BCD digits (4 bits), characters (6 bits), or ASCII codes (8 bits) are common. Regardless of the number of bits that constitute the data transfer path, all the bits are required to be present and valid simultaneously. The control associated with the parallel data signals pertain to all the bits in the data transfer path.

Special signal lines are associated with the bits in the parallel data stream. These signal lines indicate when the parallel data are valid and ready to be read into the computer. The information may be steady state and capable of being read at any time the computer issues a sense command, or it may be transient or rapidly changing, in which case it can be read by the computer only at the specific instant when it is stable. A signal providing clock or synchronization pulses indicating that valid data are available and ready to be read must be provided when non-steady-state data are being inputted. The data are read into the computer upon receipt of this synchronization or clock pulse.

Even when the data are at their steady state, it is necessary in some cases to provide a "data-not-valid" indication when the data change state. In this way read-in will be avoided while status change is in process. As an example, a counter provides a steady state output except for a very short instant while it responds to an input count pulse. It is desirable to provide a data-not-valid indication to prevent the contents of the counter from being read while it is changing. Additional signal lines indicating the type of information on the parallel data lines can be provided and are especially useful when the parallel data lines are transmitting several types of information. Separate signal lines may indicate that the current information on the parallel data lines is data, an address, or a status indication. In this way the parallel data lines can be shared by a number of signal sources with maximum information transfer flexibility.

Parallel data transfer provides for the highest data transfer rates. Each line in the data transfer path can transfer data at a rate limited by the equipment and the line capability. A parallel data path N bits wide can inherently transfer data at N times the rate of a single comparable line. Thus, when high data rates are necessary, parallel data transfer may be the most practical and the most economical way to achieve them. Transmission of data at moderate rates (below the maximum rate of a particular transmission circuit) is usually most economical using serial data transfer techniques. The added costs of serializing and deserializing the data are usually less than the costs of N parallel transmission paths, where N is the number of bits to be transmitted in parallel. In addition, parallel transmission at high rate is affected by different delays in each data path, and compensation must be provided for each path. A single serial long distance path, on the other hand, is subject to a single delay for all bits. Over short distances, parallel transfers are the simplest and most economical. For long distances, serial transmission should be considered.

SERIAL DATA

Most practical data sources are parallel in nature, that is, a full digital input word is available on each of a number of lines equal to the number of bits of data generated by the particular source. Digital data sources are converted to serial form in order to conserve signal lines or because system or equipment considerations make serial data more convenient.

A serial data source provides information on a single data line (or signal line pair). The information is transmitted in serial form 1 bit at a time in timed sequence. A 16-bit word will appear on a single line (or line pair if balanced signal transmission is required), 1 bit at a time sequenced in 16-bit times (Fig. 6). The 16 data bits will occur in a strict time sequenced manner. An alternative technique is to provide the data serially on one line and a clock train exactly synchronized to the data on a second line. The clock pulse train is at a fixed rate and is precisely synchronized with each transmitted data bit. Thus 16 serial data bits will appear on one line synchronized to the other line of 16 clock pulses. The clock pulses usually occur at the beginning of each data pulse and always have a fixed time relationship to the data. Valid data appear on the data line whenever a clock pulse occurs.

In many designs the clock and data share the same line. The fact that each data-clock pair must somehow appear as two pulses almost always involves doubling the bandwidth of the signal circuit needed to transmit

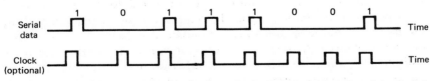

Fig. 6. Serial data stream: data arrive over a single line, each bit followed in time by the next succeeding bit.

the data. Alternatively, the timing of the data may be precisely controlled. In this case a local precision oscillator is used as the strobe source. The receiving oscillator is set to be identical in frequency with the data originating signal, and the local receiving oscillator is effectively locked in phase with the signal source serial data train. Thus each pulse from the locked-in-phase local oscillator may be used to strobe the input data line. The timing relationship between the local oscillator and the serial data is fixed. The receiving circuitry ensures that the oscillators remain in a locked arrangement during transmission.

Various phase locking techniques have been devised. The simplest is to transmit a start signal on a separate line. This signal precisely indicates the start of a sequence and is used to resynchronize the transmit and receive signal circuits. Alternatively, a composite signal may be sent, the synchronization being a special signal within the serial train. A special data sequence, a specific bit, a reversal in polarity, and a frequency burst at a preset frequency are examples of commonly used synchronization signals. The exact technique selected depends on the particular system.

Although a number of different techniques are used for transmitting information serially, the two most common involve either start/stop asynchronous or synchronous coding. These techniques are covered in detail in Chapter 15.

MULTIPLEXING DATA

Most practical digital systems generate a relatively large number of digital signals. Each input may have a different number of data bits. The data sources are usually all of the parallel type. To select a particular digital data source the computer program must identify the desired input source. The function of the digital input hardware is to select and switch many input sources onto a single digital input channel. The techniques for accomplishing this are described in this section.

A large number of digital inputs, some of the same type and others from varying sources, must be connected to the computer. Since signals from a number of separate sources are connected to a common single input port, it is incumbent upon the computer logic or the external signal logic to combine or multiplex a number of individual signal sources onto a single input channel. Larger computers may justify the expense of additional digital ports. However, in this case also a number of signal sources may be multiplexed into each input channel. Thus, in general, multiple digital input sources are multiplexed into a smaller number

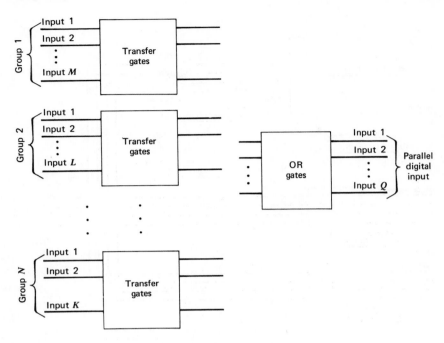

Fig. 7. Digital multiplexer: many parallel input groups are connected to the computer. Each parallel group can be selected independently for connection to the computer via the digital input facility.

(usually one) of digital input channel facilities. It will be shown later in this section how the signal from a particular source is selected by proper addressing and subsequent routing. The design of these details constitutes the computer's digital input facility. Some computers provide the addressing and multiplexing as part of the digital input facility, and in this case multiple input connections are provided. Less expensive computers are available with a single port, along with select lines implemented through the digital output facility. It is up to the interface logic to decode the address and output control signals and provide the necessary multiplexing.

Digital multiplexing is the technique used to connect a number of individual parallel digital inputs to a single digital input facility on the computer (Fig. 7). A digital multiplexer is essentially a multiple-pole, multiple-throw switch. The number of poles of the switch is equal to the data word path of the computer, and this in turn is equal to the number

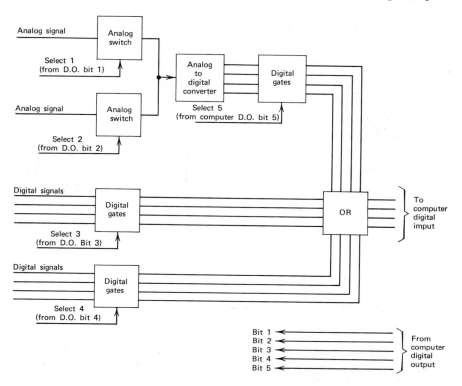

Fig. 8. The computer output facility is used to control a multiplexer facility. This can be a digital or analog multiplexer, depending on the circuitry used. The logic is the same for both—the computer "on" bit determines which input is selected and passes to the output.

of bits in the computer word. The number of throws or positions of the switching circuits is equal to the number of different digital input groups. These are usually open-ended facilities permitting easy expansion of the number of input sources. The switch position is under program control. The address presented to the switch determines which digital input is to be connected to the computer (Fig. 8).

The multiplexer may be relay operated or solid state. For all intents and purposes integrated circuits form the basis of all digital multiplexers. To a large extent this function has been taken over by LSI circuits. Relays are used for special applications only and are rarely included in new designs where digital multiplexing is involved.

The digital multiplexer is under the control of the computer program. Three modes of operation are usually selectable by the computer: random, sequential, and single channel. These modes are identical to ADC analog multiplexer modes. Random mode requires that the computer output a continuous stream of addresses. For each address the corresponding instantaneous digital input word is transferred. Any sequence or repetition of specific addresses is permissible. Sequential scan requires that the computer provide a single starting digital multiplexer address. The multiplexer begins by providing the digital input associated with the multiplexer address. The address is then advanced by one count, and the digital input corresponding to that address is transferred. Single-channel operation also requires that the computer provide a single digital multiplexer address. The digital input associated is continuously transferred as long as the computer program does not change the selection.

A very useful multiplexing technique is effected by combination of the digital input and digital output facilities. All the necessary points to be sampled are connected in parallel to the digital input facility. However, none of the devices connected to the digital inputs is powered; each group receives power from a single digital output bit. To select a particular digital input group, the single digital output bit that provides power to the group is activated under program control. The digital input group is then read in via the common digital input facility. This type of arrangement is somewhat slower than the previously described facility, where each digital input group is individually addressed. Here an output bit must be actuated before sampling. The savings in switching circuits and wiring however, more than compensate for the loss in speed for most applications where a relatively large number of digital input groups are needed.

As in all data transfers, the transfer rate may be determined by the external devices connected to the computer or the computer itself. When external device rate selection is desired, the data transfer is determined by the clock rate of the connected device. Data transfers occur each time the external device requests a transfer. When the computer controls the data transfer rate, data are transferred each time a computer data transfer instruction is issued. The maximum data transfer rate may approach the computer memory cycle rate when data channel operation is provided.

ON-OFF SWITCHES

The on-off switch (Fig. 9) is the simplest type of binary device and can be in either the "on" or the "off" condition. The "on" condition is the

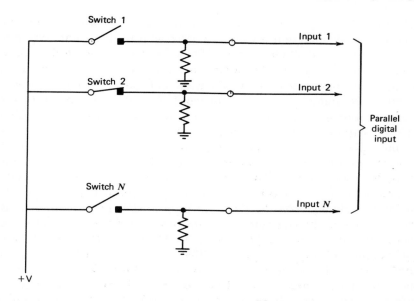

Fig. 9. On-off switches used to input parallel binary word into computer. Each switch is connected to a bit on the digital input facility.

closed or conducting position, and the "off" is open or nonconducting. On-off switches are manually operated; the experimenter or computer operator puts the switch in the desired position. On-off switches are available in a large number of configurations. A particular type is usually selected on the basis of convenience of operation and esthetic appearance because switches occupy prominent front panel space.

The most common types of switch configurations are toggle, push-button, and rotary. Push-button switches may have a pair of buttons, one for "on" and one for "off," or a single button with alternate action, each depression of the button switching the previous condition of the device. Rotary on-off switches have two positions; rotation of the switch knob in one direction turns the device on, and rotation in the reverse direction turns it off. Switches can be designed to have two stable positions so that when a particular position is set it remains set until switched again, or they can be momentary contact types that remain closed as long as the user physically holds the switch actuated. As soon as the user releases the switch actuator, the switch springs back to the normal position.

On-off switches are available with built-in lamps. Either via a separate computer controlled circuit or through direct switch actuation, the built-in lamp is lit when a particular switch position is set.

When an on-off switch is in the "on" position, the two switch terminals are connected together and a short circuit is created. In the "off" position an open circuit exists. The digital input to the computer cannot sense the presence of an open circuit or a short circuit; it can only sense two discrete voltage levels, one defined as binary "zero" and the other as binary "one." Although it is possible to design circuits that can distinguish between an open and a short circuit, most digital circuits are not designed to sense this condtion. The computer or data source must provide a current path with a suitable voltage drop through the switch. It is good practice to use switches with contacts that are electrically isolated from the device upon which they are mounted; the switch contacts should be, where practical, powered by a voltage derived from the computer rather than the device. The sense voltage must be ground referenced to the computer. If not provided from the computer, the sense voltage must be provided in the equipment to power the switch circuit. The important consideration is that the status of a dry circuit cannot be sensed; voltage must be switched. It is good practice to sense binary "one" and "zero" voltages that are referenced to the computer ground plane and are electrically isolated from the external unit.

RELAYS

In many devices the status of various relays and electromechanical switches must be sensed. A relay has two states, "on" and "off." A relay can actuate one or more sets of contacts. Each set of contacts is isolated. The most convenient method of sensing the status of a computer relay is to dedicate one set of contacts for this purpose. The same considerations relating to on-off switch sensing apply to relay status sensing. A voltage must be applied to the contacts that are to be used for sensing the relay status.

MULTIPLE-POSITION SWITCHES

Switches having many positions in addition to the two discussed above are available and used. The simplest configuration is a bank of independent switches in which each switch is set individually. The bank may consist of a number of on-off toggle or push-button switches. Each switch is handled as a separate binary bit (Fig. 10). Each computer digital input sensing operation brings in a full word width of switch sensing. In the most common arrangements, for instance, 16 switches will be sensed simultaneously if the computer has a 16-bit word structure. Any number of bits can be "on" in this configuration.

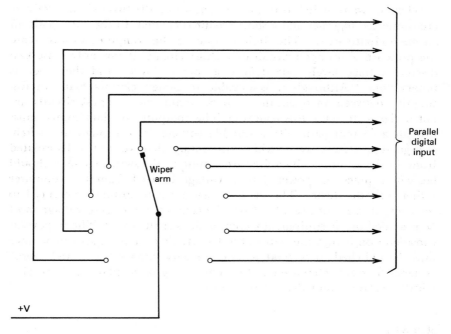

Fig. 10. Connection of multiple-position switch as parallel input facility. Each switch position is connected as an input bit on the digital input facility.

   Multiple-position switches can also be arranged so that only one position at a time can be actuated. Such switches can be, rotary or interlocked push-button types. In the rotary type only one of a number of positions can be selected each time. The interlocked push-button variety is mechanically constructed so that when a particular push button is actuated it is locked into position and the previously selected switch is released. Each position of a multiple-position switch is connected to a separate sense input bit on the computer digital input. The circuit to the selected position will be made through the wiper arm or the common bus; all other positions will be open circuited. Voltage must be applied to the wiper arm or common bus so that two voltage levels can be sensed for the open switch positions and the selected switch position. The number of bits that must be sensed simultaneously is equal to the number of permissible switch positions. Many of these switches are available with multiple electrically isolated decks. It is good practice to dedicate a separate deck for computer sensing.

   Multiple-position rotary switches are usually of the manually set variety, but rotary electromechanically actuated switches are also available. Stepping switch relays constitute another commonly used multiple-position, electrically actuated switching device. They are handled in exactly the same way as the switches described above.

THUMB WHEEL SWITCHES

Thumb wheel switches represent a special case of multiple-position switches, singled out for individual treatment because of their usefulness and convenience in data entry to computers. Each thumb wheel switch has 10 positions if decimal information is to be represented. Thumb wheel switches for octal (8), hexadecimal (16), and alphabetic information are also available. These switches can be stacked side by side so that many digits can be represented compactly, taking only a small amount of front panel area. Each individual thumb wheel switch digit is clearly apparent to the user, so that visual verification of the settings can be made quickly. Thumb wheel switches are set via lever action or push button on each digit switch. A single lever or push-button depression advances the switch setting one digit. To advance four digits, for example, would require four actuations. It should be apparent that multiple-position rotary switches can be used wherever thumb wheel switches are suitable. The major advantages of the thumb wheel switches are the compact stacking of many digits on a small front panel area and the rapid visual verification of the digit setting. The step-at-a-time lever action actuator, however, makes digit action relatively slow compared to the rapid setting possible with a knob actuated rotary switch.

A useful feature that has been developed using thumb wheel switches is data encoding. In order to make thumb wheel switches compact, the switch wafers are printed circuit elements. The wiper arm makes contact with the printed circuit pattern. The simplest type of thumb wheel switch has a single wiper arm with an output for each digit. Thumb wheel switches with various data encoded outputs are readily available; BCD and various other codes are commonly supplied configurations. This arrangement constitutes a convenient and efficient way to enter encoded data into the computer digital input. Four data sense lines are needed for each decimal digit.

Data from thumb wheel switches must be in voltage level form to be sensed by a computer digital input facility. Each bit must be represented as either of two discrete voltage levels. The voltage should be isolated from the host equipment. The ground level may then be referenced to the computer ground.

LOGIC CIRCUITS

A major digital input source consists of logic circuits of various types. Mechanical switches of the type described previously are examples of logic circuits that output two discrete voltage levels. The switching is by mechanical means. However, many of the signals in a data acquisition environment originate in various transistor and integrated circuit devices. These are logic circuits that operate at two discrete voltage levels, defined as logical "true" or binary "one" and as "false" or binary "zero."

The selection of the logic level voltages is determined by the physical and electrical characteristics of the electronic components selected by the device designers. Almost all bipolar integrated circuits (TTL or DTL) operate at positive logic level voltages between 0 V and +3 to +5 V. Metal oxide semiconductor integrated circuits use negative logic level voltages. The exact values using MOS depend to a large extent on the system design considerations because MOS circuits can be operated over a wide voltage range. For discrete logic systems based on PNP transistors, negative logic level designs are more convenient, whereas NPN transistor logic systems are more conveniently designed with positive logic levels. Because of the wide acceptance of bipolar TTL and DTL integrated circuits for most digital logic, system designs with positive logic voltage levels are almost universally used. For this reason even inherently negative logic devices such as MOS integrated circuit units are available with separate or built-in interface circuits that convert MOS logic voltage levels to bipolar integrated circuit compatible positive levels.

The types of logic circuits that may be encountered for connection to computer digital input facilities may include all possible logic devices, such as AND, OR, FLIP FLOP, and LINE DRIVERS. Most interconnections are usually via isolation devices such as inverters (NOT) or line drivers. The addition of the inverter or line driver ensures sufficient drive capability and also prevents loading of the device's internal logic circuits. When the drive distance is modest (less than about 100 ft), inverter drivers are usually adequate. For longer distances it is advisable to use cable line drivers.

Most computer digital inputs demand "0" V and +3 to +5 V as their inputs. One of these two levels is arbitrarily specified as binary "one" and the other as binary "zero." When data rates are modest, the computer program can easily complement the input if it is more convenient to provide inverted level inputs. If necessary, the user can insert an inverter stage between the signal source and the computer input to provide the specified "one" and "zero" logic levels. Logic level voltage shifters can be used to convert nonstandard logic levels to the computer specified levels. Metal oxide semiconductor to bipolar and bipolar to MOS logic level converter units perform this function effectively. It is always good practice to include a buffer or inverter stage between the data source and the computer.

COMMUNICATIONS INTERFACES

The output signal from communications devices can be directly connected to a digital input word group of the computer digital input facility. A communications interface accepts encoded serial data from a transmission line, detects and strips away the synchronization information, and converts the serial data to parallel format for entry into the computer (Fig. 11). The serial data bit stream transmitted on the communications media is assembled into parallel data words.

The input to the communications terminal is a stream of bits in either synchronous or start/stop form. The information may be DC or encoded via a suitable modulation technique for transmission over the telephone network. Synchronous communications networks involve continuous transmission of bits with no apparent distinction between synchronization and data bits. Synchronous communications links rely on establishing synchronization between the transmitter and the receiver at the start of the transmission. Synchronization is then maintained for the duration of the message transmission by precise matched clocks at both ends of the network. Alternatively, the receiver can be designed to "track" the clock rate of the transmitter. Nonsynchronous or start/stop communications are typified by a separate synchronization sequence for each transmitted

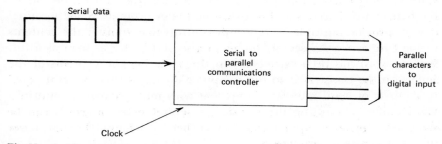

Fig. 11. Serial communications data are converted to parallel word form and transferred one word or byte at a time to the computer digital input facility synchronized to the data word clock.

character. Thus the receiver resynchronizes for each transmitted character. Synchronous communications networks can transmit more information per unit time than nonsynchronous networks because once synchronization is established continuous information can be sent. High-speed communications utilize synchronous techniques. Circuitry for implementing a synchronous communications network is more costly than start/stop circuits.

Communications terminal devices assemble serial line information into parallel words or bytes. The terminal device recognizes the synchronization bit or bit pattern and discards it. Parity checking and other verification operations are performed within the terminal device. In addition, certain characters are searched for by the input device.

The communications terminal equipment provides several signals of interest to the computer besides the data byte or word. These include a data-ready signal each time a word has been assembled and is ready for transfer to the computer. The data-ready signal may be used as an interrupt to the computer or for data channel operation. Alternatively, the data-ready signal may set a flag whose status is sampled periodically by the computer. In all cases the objective is to indicate to the computer that a full word or byte has been assembled and is ready for transfer.

It is important for the computer to respond quickly to the data-ready signal and to read in the waiting data. The communications line rate is controlled by the transmitting end and may send information at any rate up to the maximum. If the waiting information is not sensed before the word content is disturbed by the next word, an error will result. Receive devices may have single-byte or single-word or multiple-byte or multiple-word buffers. A single-byte or single-word buffer is part of the serial to parallel converter of the data receiver. The data-ready signal is issued as a complete byte or word has been assembled. The data in the buffer are valid for only one bit interval; after that the first data bit of the following byte or word arrives and disturbs the buffer contents. Some terminal devices provide multiple buffers with controls that transfer the contents of the byte or word assembly buffer to a second buffer as soon as a full byte or word has been assembled. In this situation the contents of the buffer can be transferred to the computer during a time interval equal to the byte or word interval. Equipment with multiple-byte or multiple-word buffers permitting the transfer of several bytes or words can be designed. Greater computer efficiency is thereby achieved because fewer data transfer cycles are needed.

Synchronization and/or terminal reception in progress are convenient signals to inform the computer of the status of the lines. When the line indicates a break or when data have not been received for a specific interval, the terminal issues a line-break or time-out signal. This indicator can be used by the computer to disconnect from the particular line and also to show a line malfunction. Parity error indicators may also be included in the communications terminal; such an indicator goes on when a parity error is detected in the received information.

An important feature that greatly improves the efficiency of the receiver is the capability of the hardware to recognize certain character codes. This capability is generally restricted to such control characters as end of line and carriage return.

ANALOG TO DIGITAL CONVERTERS

Analog to digital converters generate parallel data words that represent the digital equivalent of the analog signal presented at the input terminal of the ADC. Each parallel data word is accompanied by an end-of-conversion signal (Fig. 12). This signal indicates that the ADC has completed its conversion cycle and that valid data are present on the ADC data output lines. These lines may be directly connected to the computer digital facility. The EOC signal is used to indicate the read-in via the interrupt, data channel, or program controlled sense and read facilities.

The permissible delay between the EOC signal generated by the ADC and read-in of the converted data to the computer depends on the ADC mode of operation. ADCs will maintain their digital output information in valid condition until the start of the next conversion cycle. Some converters are designed with a double output buffer; one buffer is used in the actual conversion process, whereas the second holds the converted result. In this situation the data from a conversion cycle remain valid until the end of conversion of the current cycle. The ADC may derive its start

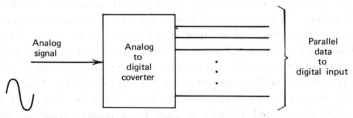

Fig. 12. Analog signal is digitized by ADC data word is transferred in parallel to computer digital input facility upon receipt of end-of-conversion signal from ADC.

conversion signal from the computer or an external source, or it may be self generated. When an analog multiplexer is used, the start conversion signal is derived via the multiplexer to assure complete switching and stabilization of the analog multiplexer channel before the start of the conversion cycle. When the start conversion is under computer control, the time of transfer of the previous conversion is not critical. However, under external rate control or when free running the computer must be able to transfer the converted digital data before the start of the next possible cycle.

Analog to digital converters are available with conversion resolutions varying from a few bits to about 15 bits plus sign, for a total of 16 bits. Subsequent processing of the converted information is considerably simplified when a single conversion is stored in one computer word. It is difficult to interface to a converter with more significant bits than the word size of the computer to which it is to be connected. If the converter has greater resolution than the capacity of the computer word, least significant bits are ignored. If the computer word is longer than the converter output, zeros are inserted in the extra positions.

SHAFT ENCODERS

Shaft encoders are electromechanical transducers that convert shaft position to a digital value. Shaft encoders are available that provide output in binary code, Gray code, BCD, and sine-cosine. Gray code or logic circuits on binary codes are used to overcome the problems associated with erroneous readings due to ambiguities when the shaft encoder is sensed at a point where a transition between two numbers occurs.

Shaft encoders for manual read-out and for many data acquisition systems can be quite expensive because much circuitry is required to translate cyclic check codes to BCD if Gray code is used. Similarly, complex circuits are needed to implement logical checks to prevent ambiguous readings. Shaft encoders may be quite simply connected to the digital input facility of a computer without cyclic code conversion circuitry or any intermediate logic. The only requirement is to assure compatible logic levels. Translation of codes or ambiguity checks can be performed using a computer program. Each shaft encoder bit position is connected to a separate bit of the computer digital input facility. Shaft encoders are available with resolutions ranging from a few bits to 19 or 20 bits. To handle long word lengths it may be necessary to read the shaft encoded data into two computer words.

Shaft encoder data are usually read under computer program control. The rate at which a shaft encoder can be read depends on the computer capability and the implementation technique of the encoder. Shaft encoders can usually be interrogated by the program at any time, and valid data can be expected. The only time that the shaft encoder data may not be valid is when the encoder is at a point where the encoded data are changing value. The validity of the sensed data can be easily checked by multiple readings and by the "reasonableness" of the sensed information. Many shaft encoders provide a signal when their output may not be read. This flag can be sensed by the computer program before issuing the shaft encoder data sense command. Alternatively, the sense command pulse and return information can be delayed by the shaft encoder read-out circuitry until the output data are valid.

Shaft encoders can be easily and effectively used as input devices to computers. Very little interface hardware is required; only logic level shifters are needed.

LIGHT SENSITIVE TRANSDUCERS

Light sensitive transducers consist of devices based on photodiodes, phototransistors, and photoresistors. These transducers change certain parameters when their sensitive areas are exposed to light. Although some devices using them are designed to take advantage of their linear characteristics, only devices based on the exploitation of nonlinear functions are of interest here. This class of devices produces binary signals: they are full on or full off, depending on the light level they are meant to discriminate.

Light sensitive transducers can sense the positions of various mechanisms without requiring physical contact. This attribute is useful for sensing when a limit is approached by some moving member. Light may also be employed to transmit information from high-speed devices or from places which are difficult to access. Light signal transmission is particularly useful when sensing signals on a device that is at a high voltage potential.

Each light transducer output is connected to a separate bit on the computer digital input facility. The major necessity is to match the voltage levels of the light transducer output to the voltage requirements of the digital input facility. These signal sources generally provide a steady state output signal and switch state only when the sensed light passes through the "one"/"zero" threshhold. The computer program can sense the light transducer signals at any time.

FREQUENCY COUNTER

A frequency counter measures the average frequency of an input signal. The number of cycles of the measured frequency is counted for a preset time interval.

A frequency counter (Fig. 13) consists of two counters, a precise time base, and gate logic. One counter receives as its input the precise time base pulse train, and the other counts the number of the unknown frequency cycles. A squaring circuit is used to shape the unknown frequency to standard pulses before their application to the second counter. The frequency counter begins its operation when it receives a start pulse. The two counters are reset to their initial values. The precise time base counter is preset to a count that will time out the desired averaging interval. This is equal to the product of the number of pre-

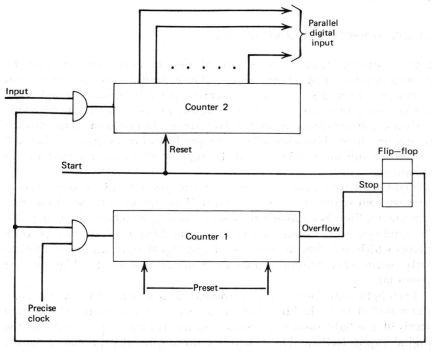

Fig. 13. Frequency counter: counter 1 and counter 2 begin to count at the same time. When counter 1 reaches the preset count, a predetermined time interval has elapsed and counter input is disabled. The count accumulated in counter 2 represents the number of unknown frequency cycles that occurred during the preset time interval. The number in counter 2 is transferred in parallel form to the computer digital input.

cise clock pulses and the time interval between clock pulses. The second counter is set to zero. The two counters begin counting their respective input pulse trains. When the timer counter reaches the preset count, a stop pulse is issued. Gates controlling the passage of pulses to the two counters are turned off, thereby inhibiting the two pulse trains. The stop signal indicates to the computer that the data stored by the second counter are valid and represent the average frequency of the input signal during the measured time interval.

The output of this counter is directly connected to the digital input facility. If the number of counter bits exceeds the word size of the computer, several input reads may be needed to accept the data. The program issues commands to read the information in response to the stop signal sent by the frequency converter. The computer may issue the read command at any time after receipt of the "stop." Most such devices receive their start signal from the computer; thus the read command can be issued at any time that is convenient. If the frequency counter is externally synchronized or free running, the read command must be issued before the next start cycle pulse.

OTHER COMPUTERS

By connecting the digital output of one computer to the digital input facility of another, one can achieve communication between the two computers. To synchronize the computers, a separate bit on the transmitting computer may be used to indicate that valid data exist on its digital output lines. The receiving computer uses this indication as an interrupt or data channel signal or data-ready sense status flag to effect the data transfer. Depending on the configuration, the receiving computer may provide an indication that the data transfer has been completed. At that time the transmitting computer prepares the next word. The receiving and transmitting computers may reverse roles by providing a second pair of reversed input and output words.

TRANSIENT ANALYZERS

Various new instrument designs are based on digital techniques. In addition, older designs have been modernized through the addition of digital displays and outputs. These include various types of transient analyzers, which consist of ADCs, digital memories, and simple arithmetic circuits. When a transient occurs, or at a preset selectable time with respect to the occurrence of the transient, an analog gate is actuated, connecting the signal of interest to the analyzer ADC. The input analog signal line is then sampled at a predetermined rate, and each sample is converted to its digital equivalent. Each digitized value is forwarded to the analyzer memory store, and successive values are stored in sequential addresses. The sampling, conversion, and storage sequence repeats until the memory has been filled with time successive digitized samples of the analog input signal. The memory then holds the digitized equivalent of the input analog transient.

The analyzer memory can be read out repetitively. The digital readouts can be passed through a DAC for display on an oscilloscope or for recording on an X-Y recorder. The experimenter can then analyze the transient waveform on a steady display.

Another variation of this analyzer provides addition circuitry. Repetitive transient signals are received. Each time an appropriate trigger is received, the cycle repeats. The input analog signal is connecting to the analyzer ADC, and sampling and conversion begin. The corresponding previously stored contents of the memory are successively fetched from the memory in synchronism with the conversion rate of the ADC. The currently converted output is added to the accumulated sum of the previously stored signals in the analyzer memory. Each converted signal point in the input signal is added to the accumulated sum of values for that point in time. This process, which can be repeated for several thousand occurrences of the transient, creates a synthetic signal. The noise in the resultant signal has been reduced, while the signal itself has been enhanced. Noise will tend to cancel after combining many samples, whereas the signal of interest will reinforce itself. The signal output is viewed by the user on an oscilloscope via a DAC.

These analyzer instruments may be readily connected to the digital input of a computer by connecting the analyzer memory output to the computer. The analyzer memory output rate can be controlled by an internal clock or by external synchronization. The output rate can thus be selected over a very wide range of values. The synchronization signal, either internally or externally supplied, is used to provide data channel pulses or interrupts to the computer. Each pulse initiates a data word read-in cycle.

PULSE CODE MODULATION TELEMETRY RECEIVERS

Pulse code modulation telemetry receivers provide synchronized digital data words to the computer digital input facility. For all intents and purposes, from the computer input port, PCM telemetry receiver data are identical to data received from any other communications channel. The PCM telemetry receiver detects the PCM telemetry clock signal, recognizes the received frame synchronization pattern, and assembles parallel word data samples. Each time a data sample has been assembled, an indicator signal is issued. This signal can be used as an interrupt or data channel transfer pulse to effect the read-in of digital data. The receiver output is connected directly to the computer digital input facility.

The telemetry receiver also provides the computer with frame synchronization and fading indicators. These show when the receiver is unable to handle the incoming bit stream because of timing problems or insufficient received signal strength due to fading and other link factors.

SYNCHRO TO DIGITAL CONVERTERS

Several different devices are used for remotely indicating shaft position. Synchros are almost universally employed in radar systems to remotely indicate the instantaneous pointing angle of the radar antenna. Synchros have been used for a long time and have proved to be reliable and capable of accurately following the rotation of relatively high-speed shafts.

Until very recently potentiometers and shaft encoders coupled to the output of synchro follower servos were used to provide computer compatible synchro positional signals. The shaft encoder served as a direct digital input; the potentiometer output voltage was passed through an ADC to the computer digital input. Solid state synchro to digital converters are now available as standard off-the-shelf components. The inputs to these units are ordinary synchro three-phase data signals and a reference voltage. The output is a digital value corresponding to the position of the remote synchro. The synchro to digital converter output may be connected directly to the computer digital input facility.

TIME ENCODERS

When data are recorded on magnetic tape, it is usually necessary to record a signal representing time along with the information. The reasons are obvious when one considers the need for correlating the data recorded on several tracks played back separately, as well as correlating these data with others taken independently or at different sites and with different recorders. Various standard time codes have been specified and are in general use; the most prevalent ones are those recommended by the IRIG. Special devices are available that handle several of the standard codes. A tape playback unit usually has thumb wheel switches, which set up a desired start time and stop time. When the recorded time code is between these time limits, the signals recorded on the magnetic tape are inspected. The tape playback unit also provides the digitized time data in parallel form. This may be connected directly to the computer digital input facility. Sensing of time is under direct program control.

COMPUTER PERIPHERAL DEVICES

It is usually expedient to design special controllers that interface between a computer and the peripheral devices attached to it. A great deal of the signal handling that would require complex program and precise time sequencing can be accomplished by simple circuits in the controller. However, in many cases it is entirely feasible to rely on the computer digital input, digital output, and interrupt facilities to handle peripheral devices. These features make it possible to attach various special-purpose peripheral devices for which the design of a special controller may not be worthwhile. In many cases, in fact, the minicomputer function is that of a programmable controller. The variety of devices that are attachable is large.

COUNTERS

A counter consists of a group of flip-flop circuits that have been connected to accumulate a count equal to the number of pulses received. Counters may be arranged to add to the existing count or to subtract from it. Counters can be connected to accumulate binary representations, BCD, or almost any other code.

The counter output may be connected directly to the computer digital input facility. The accumulated count is read into the computer under direct program control. On-the-fly read-in or static read-in is possible. Static read-in is easier because this mode implies that the counter has completed its operation and has stopped. The program can read the contents of the counter at any time. On-the-fly read-in requires that the transfer of information from the counter to the computer take place beween counter input pulses. Each pulse is accumulated by the counter. However, a finite time is required by the counter to propagate a pulse through all the stages of the counter so as to switch all the necessary stages. In certain cases fast-setting counters are required. Various logic circuit configurations are available to permit the counter to propagate the carry and to settle the counter very rapidly. Care must be taken to sample the count after the counter has completed its pulse propagation and has stabilized. A counter designed for computer interfacing can be provided with a data-valid indicator to show when the count pulse has completed propagating and the counter is stable. The computer may provide the reset, enable, and disable commands.

PULSE SOURCES

Auxiliary circuits are usually required for the computer to sense pulse sources. To be sensed by the digital input facility, a pulse must be present at exactly the instant that the computer program issues the appropriate sense command. This is obviously not feasible.

Various techniques are employed to enable the computer to sense pulses; counters and interrupts are two useful methods. In the first case the count is increased in a counter connected to the computer. In the second instance the pulse initiates a unique interrupt that permits the computer to become aware of the pulse. Both are examples of pulse storage techniques. In one case the counter provides the storage medium, and in the second the interrupt flip-flop serves this function.

In the general case some form of storage is needed to hold the pulse. A set of flip-flop circuits connected to the computer digital input facility meets this requirement. When a pulse occurs on a particular line, the associated flip-flop is set. The computer under program control senses the status of the flip-flops to determine upon which line the pulse occurred. The program also resets the flip-flop after sensing. It is not possible to determine whether more than one pulse was received on a particular line because the flip-flop is set by the first pulse and remains set until reset under program control. Additional pulses do not affect the set state of the flip-flop.

In some cases where interrupts from a number of different sources are expected, all the interrupt signals are connected together through a multi-input OR circuit. Thus, when an interrupt pulse occurs from any source, a computer interrupt is formed. The computer interrupt servicing program then issues a command to sense the status of all the interrupt flip-flops to determine which interrupt source was active and caused the pulse. The flip-flops are reset after being sensed.

SHIFT REGISTERS

Shift registers (Fig. 14) may be used as storage devices that convert serial data to parallel form and parallel data to serial form. Data entered into a computer should preferably be in parallel form in order to achieve good computer efficiency, and a shift register is ordinarily used to effect the serial to parallel transformations. A shift register consists of a

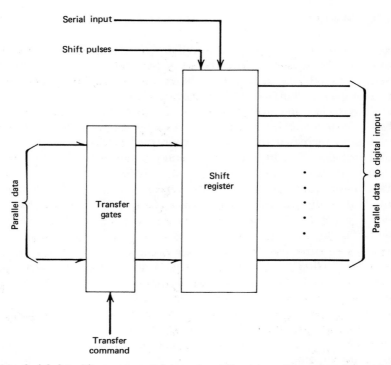

Fig. 14. Serial data bits are accepted into the shift register in synchronism with the shift pulses. The contents of the shift register are shifted along with the shift pulse. Parallel data can be entered onto the shift register via the parallel input transfer gates. The contents of the shift register can be entered into the computer via the computer digital input facility.

clocked serial entry port and buffer transfer stages. The buffer stages may have individual outputs. At any given time the buffer output contain the input in parallel form for the received bits. The buffer also may contain parallel input facilities when a serial output is needed. Thus, depending on the shift register configuration, parallel to serial and serial to serial conversion can also be effected. These uses will be discussed separately. Shift registers of all types are available in bipolar and MOS integrated circuits.

An example of shift register operation will best illustrate its application and utility. Data are presented to the shift register at its first buffer stage, one bit at a time, in serial form. Each bit is accompained by a clock or synchronization pulse. The clock pulse is used to strobe the input data stream and is also applied to the shift register pulse line. The status of the data line is strobed, and the resultant data pulse is entered into the first stage of the shift register. The former contents of the first stage are transferred into the second stage. The data bit of each subsequent stage is transferred to the next element. When the next clock pulse arrives along with a data bit, the input line is again strobed into the first shift register buffer stage and the contents of each subsequent buffer stage are shifted one position. When N clock pulses and data bits been received, N stages of the shift register have data bits stored. If each shift register element has its output brought out, the full parallel contents of the assembled data bits are always available for connection to external devices. When the number of shift pulses exceeds the number of shift register elements, the bits first received are lost. They are merely shifted out of the shift register.

Connection of a serial to parallel shift register to the computer is made directly to the digital input facility. The actual time of data read-in is determined by the shift register control circuits, which indicate that a full word has been assembled. The full word indicator serves to initiate the data read-in, through either a data channel or an interrupt program control.

10 Digital Output

In Chapter 9 digital input was discussed. The techniques used for sensing the environment and entering these data into the computer were examined. It was shown how both digital data and digital status information were input to the computer. In an analogous fashion, the computer output may be in the form of either digital data or digital control information. As was explained when discussing inputs, analog input information must be converted to digital form via an analog to digital converter. Similarly, analog output is derived from the computer digital output facility via digital to analog converters.

DIGITAL OUTPUT BUS

The basic computer digital output facility is via the computer accumulator or the memory data bus, depending on the particular computer. A single computer digital word is transferred for each output command executed. These signal sources are not usable directly in most practical applications. Usually, more outputs than the single output available from either the accumulator or the data bus are needed. The data destination signal requirements and the data format requirements must usually be matched to the computer output.

Additional signal processing and some form of digital multiplexing to form multiple computer addressable outputs is needed. The digital output may be directed to more than one output device. The digital multiplexer, under computer program control, determines the signal flow path of the data on the computer output bus and directs the data word to a particular addressed device. Each device has a unique computer selectable address.

Voltage level shifters and impedance converters must usually be inserted between the computer and the data destination. Many computer manufacturers provide the necessary multiple digital outputs, each individually addressable under program control. Level shifters and line drivers may also be provided as part of this operation.

In spite of the limitations described, data may be taken from the accumulator or output bus in many significant applications. When a single output is needed, there is obviously no reason to multiplex. Also, many special-purpose periperals are interfaced directly to the output bus. The interface circuitry routes the signals appropriately.

OUTPUT REQUIREMENTS

A number of distinct digital output forms are needed to couple the computer effectively to the experiment or process. These include data and control signals. Data lines may be used to transmit digital data to on-line connected digital devices, as well as to other computers and peripherals. Digital data may also be transmitted to data conversion units such as DACs. Digital control signals are identical in form to data but are used to control and address the connected devices. Any number or combination may be needed to connect a computer to a particular experiment or process.

DATA OUTPUT

Data outputs are usually single word registers, each capable of storing a full computer word (Fig. 1). This output consists of a parallel output register. Each data output register connected on line to the computer is individually addressable by the computer program. Data may be transferred to any output register under program control, one word at a time. When the data output is under direct program control, a separate I/O instruction is needed for each word transferred. The output may also be under data channel control. When the initial data channel I/O instruction is issued, data are transferred under data channel control until the number of data words specified by the program has been transferred.

The data transfer rate is limited by the rate at which I/O instructions can be issued when direct program control transfer is used. In addition, time must be allocated for housekeeping functions, such as keeping

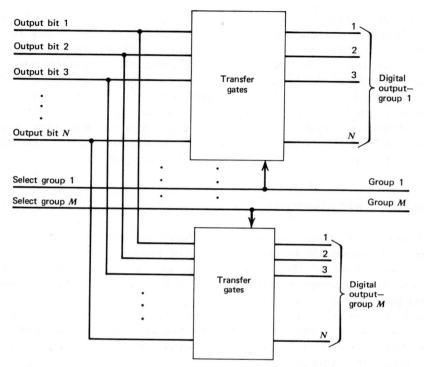

Fig. 1. Computer digital output facility consists of a digital output bus. The number of output bits is usually equal to the word size of the computer. A multiplexer may be used to obtain multiple digital outputs. The computer program selects a particular multiplex path by outputting the address of the desired output. The individual digital output bits may be power drivers or logic level signals, depending on the requirement of the application.

track of the number of words transferred or the current word address, and loading the accumulator as the data transfer through it. The current contents of the accumulator may have to be saved before loading with the word to be transferred. Direct program control data transfers are recommended for situations in which small numbers of data are to be transferred or a relatively slow transfer rate is allowable. Large blocks of high-speed data transfer are most effectively handled under data channel control.

Data transfer synchronization can be controlled either internally by the program procession rate or externally by a clock signal. Each time a clock pulse is received, the data channel cycle begins. If direct program control data transfer is specified, the external clock causes inter-

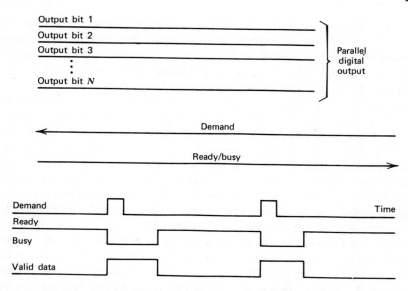

Fig. 2. The digital output signal may be outputted under computer internal clock control. In this case an output word is issued whenever the particular I/O command instruction is reached. The output may also be under external clock control. The external clock can be connected to the computer interrupt facility if relatively low speed data are required or through a data channel if high-speed data are needed. Each external clock pulse is accepted by the computer as a "demand" for service either as an interrupt or a data channel synchronization signal. The computer responds by issuing a "ready" signal for the desired output group.

rupts. The program servicing the interrupt responds by outputting the next data word.

Data output signals (Fig. 2) are generally adequate for most purposes if they are integrated circuit compatible, a feature that makes it convenient to connect data output signals directly to other digital logic systems. Interface problems in regard to impedance level and voltage level matching are minimized. Integrated circuit compatible logic signals are inherently capable of high-speed switching. When data channel operation is specified, data rates equal to the computer memory cycle time are possible.

CONTROL SIGNALS

The distinction between digital data output and digital control signal output is primarily one of application. In general, data can be transmitted at a higher rate than control information, primarily because the rate of transmission of control information is limited by the response capability of the connected device. Data are transferred to other devices that can store or logically transform the data presented to them. Thus data can be entered into another computer or a DAC.

Control signals generally actuate some mechanism or control the operating sequence of a device such as opening or closing valves or relays. Thus addresses are used to select the destination of digital data words. In some cases, as when the address of a multiplexer point is sent, the digital control signal has the same electronic characteristics as digital data. However, in the actuation of a relay the digital control output has quite different characteristics. Its required repetition rate is rather limited because electromechanical devices are involved. Considerable power is needed compared to digital logic. The computer may be required to switch many medium-power circuits on and off. Control power pulses may be needed when certain electromechanical devices are connected. To accomplish these functions, both electronic and electromechanical devices should be available as computer digital control outputs in addition to ordinary logic level circuits. These devices include relays, power transistors, and integrated circuit power drivers and silicon controlled rectifiers (SCRs). In most cases the number of output points is available in increments equal to the computer word size. A large number of groups can be connected to the computer through a digital output multiplex facility, which must be designed by the user if the computer does not provide the options.

RELAYS

Computer controlled power output devices (Fig. 3) may be computer controlled relays or electronically controlled solid state power devices. When the output is relays, each computer output group controls a number of relays equal to the number of bits in the computer word. The user essentially has access to a set of contacts on each relay. His power load is connected to this isolated set of contacts. When the output word needed to control a particular relay group is issued by the computer program, the relays associated with "one" bit positions in the control word are closed. Relays receiving "zeros" are open. One relay is provided for each bit.

Mercury wetted contact relays or hermetically sealed glass reed relays are ordinarily used in these applications because of their high reliability

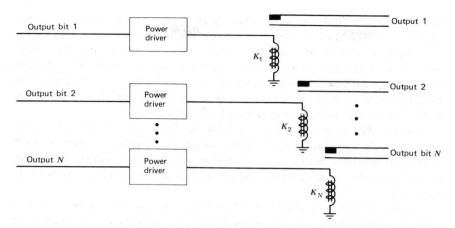

Fig. 3. Relay output-computer digital output actuates relay contact when output bit is in "one" state. The output relay is open when the associated bit is "zero." A separate relay is provided for each output bit. The number of relays is usually equal to the number of bits in the output word. The relay contact rating is a function of the type of relay, required life, and contact material. A register is used to hold the desired status of relays and control power driver stages.

and fast operation times. Relay contacts that are computer controlled may be used in the same way as any other relay contact. The status of the relay is under complete control of the computer program. The designer must be careful not to exceed the contact ratings of the relay. Mercury wetted contacts exhibit very little discernible bounce when making contact, and they break very rapidly without bounce due to mercury surface tension cohesion effects until the breaking point is exceeded.

Relay contacts are completely isolated from electrical ground and act as an almost ideal switch for DC and low-frequency signals. For higher-frequency signals, however, problems of capacitive coupling and electromagnetic interference prevail, as in any other electrical circuit. Because of the relay's excellent switch characteristics, balanced signal circuits can be switched using double-pole relays. Furthermore, relay contacts made with precious metal will switch "dry" circuits, that is, they are capable of reliably switching very low current, low voltage signals. Relay switches have a price advantage for switching low-level balanced signals. In fact, most low-level, low-speed analog multiplexers are made up of banks of relay switches. Solid state low-level switches with comparable superior low-level signal characteristics are much more expensive and are used when high speed, small space, or insensitivity to shock and vibration is an overriding consideration.

Computer relay power output points are useful when complete isolation between the computer and the external device is needed. Although high-voltage (100 V rating) transistors are available for switching, it is usually more economical to use relays for switching higher voltages. Relays can easily switch several hundred volts.

Another advantage in relay switching is the ability of the relay contacts to safely withstand large current surges and voltage overloads. Such adverse conditions, even when occurring as short transients, are likely to destroy silicon transistors unless elaborate protective circuitry is included.

Another factor to consider is that relays switch AC as well as DC voltages. Transistor switches cannot switch AC voltages without resorting to complex circuitry.

Computer driven relay switches have several disadvantages in comparison to solid state switches. Relays are much slower switches, and they are relatively large in size. They operate electromechanically and are sensitive to shock and vibration. Relay coils are inductances, and when a relay operates high-level noise pulses are generated, requiring spike suppression circuitry.

A memory circuit is required between the computer output bus and the relay. The signal on the output bus remains stationary during only part of the time of the actual execution of the I/O instruction. The I/O instruction may select a group of relays for actuation or turn-off. The computer output commanding the relay status is stored in the memory circuit. The contents of the memory circuit are not disturbed until the program issues a command changing the relay status. The memory circuit is connected via a driver to the relay coil. Because of the relatively high power requirements needed to drive the relay coil, a driver buffer is preferable to connecting the relay coil directly to the memory stage. The memory circuit is usually selected to be a flip-flop.

ELECTRONIC CONTACTS

An alternative computer controlled power output switch involves the use of electronic contacts (Fig. 4). A large number of solid state electronic power switching devices are available. Many can conveniently be controlled through a computer digital output. All the devices of interest

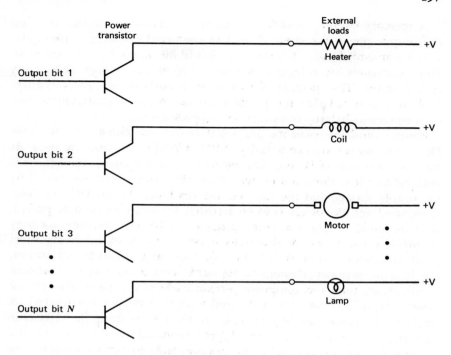

Fig. 4. Electronic contact output group consists of a group of output power transistors, each of which is associated with an output bit. A flip-flop register holds the contents of the output word and in turn controls the conducting/nonconducting state of each power transistor. Power transistors capable of switching several amperes at voltages up to 100 V are readily available. Power transistors may be PNP or NPN types, depending on the polarity of power voltage to be switched. If AC switching is required, Triacs or SCRs can be used as the control element.

are based on silicon semiconductor technology. These devices are controlled from full on to full off by logic voltage level signals. Thus computer compatibility is straightforward. The computer "one" output bit is used to turn on an electronic switch; the "zero" state turns the switch off. A separate electronic switch is associated with each computer output bit.

The major devices used for solid state switching are power transistors, (SCRs), and triacs. Power transistors capable of switching several amperes at up to 100 V are suitable for DC switching. Power transistors switch in a few tenths of a microsecond. Usually PNP transistors are used when negative voltages are to be switched; NPN transistors are preferable for switching positive voltages.

A memory circuit is needed between the computer output bus and the output power transistor. The I/O command selecting a particular power transistor is held in a memory circuit associated with that element. Only commands issued by the computer program can change the memory circuit status. The memory circuit in turn controls the power switch. It should be noted that the power transistor must be protected against high-voltage switching transients by suppression diodes.

Power transistor switches are effective for switching DC voltages. Depending on the voltage polarity, NPN or PNP transistors are used. As long as the transistor is "on," the effective transistor circuit impedance is reduced to a few ohms and current flows. The current is determined by the supply voltage and the total circuit resistance. When DC switching is required and the switch is to be actuated for an indeterminate period, as determined by the computer program, a bistable flip-flop memory circuit is used. In many situations a power pulse of relatively short predetermined duration is desirable. To provide a pulsed power output, the bistable memory element is replaced with a monostable one-shot circuit. Each time the computer program selects the particular pulsed power output, the one-shot associated with that output is triggered. A single output pulse will be generated, which in turn closes the electronic contact for a specific time interval predetermined by the delay of the one-shot circuit. Periods of a few microseconds to several seconds are realized.

Silicon controlled rectifiers switch AC voltages of up to several hundred volts and at currents as high as several tens of amperes. Since a SCR is a rectifying device, it will pass only one polarity of the power input waveform. To provide full wave rectification a full wave bridge arrangement of SCRs may be used.

The SCR average current is determined by controlling the point in the AC cycle where the SCR fires. The firing point is a function of the applied DC control hold-off voltage. This is the computer controlled input to the SCR. When the computer output is "on," the SCR conducts. When a "zero" output is provided, the SCR remains nonconducting. Current control is not possible in this mode. Such control is feasible, however, by driving the SCR through a DAC computer controlled output.

Silicon controlled rectifiers generate high-amplitude noise spikes when they turn on or off. These rectifiers are driven through inductive circuits and are capable of switching very rapidly; thus a very high rate of change of current may be applied to an inductive circuit by a switching SCR. The resultant induced voltage can be of extremely large amplitude, and this noise spike can interfere with associated equipment. A major effort is made in the design of SCR control circuits to eliminate switching transients. To ensure noise-free switching it is desirable to switch the SCR when the zero crossing point of the AC waveform occurs. Current is selected by controlling the number of full SCR conduction cycles and the number of full nonconduction cycles. All firings occur at the zero crossing point. Special circuitry that provides for this function very conveniently is available from a number of vendors. These circuits are designed to be controlled by signals that are typical of computer digital outputs.

Triacs are AC switches controlled by an input DC voltage. They conduct on both halves of the AC waveform. The control signal is DC, as in SCRs. When the DC control signal exceeds the critical level, the triac fires and conducts for the remainder of the cycle. Triacs, like SCRs, should be fired at the zero crossing point to avoid the introduction of excessive noise spikes.

HIGH-SPEED DIGITAL OUTPUT

In many situations the computer is required to communicate with other digital logic level devices such as other computers, interface circuitry, or peripheral devices. These external devices communicate through logic level signals. They usually respond to parallel data I/O formats and can operate at relatively high data rates. A single word output group usually suffices to establish a linkage. Many groups can be provided.

The computer output is divided into word groups, each individually addressable by the program. Each word group is equal in width to the number of bits in the computer word. Because of the high-speed potential of devices that may be connected, data channel cycle stealing capabilities are usually required.

The output is most conveniently provided directly from the collector terminal of the output device. Because integrated circuits are almost universally used, voltage levels between 0 and +3 V are to be expected. A drive capability of about 50 ft over cable or twisted pair is possible. If longer cable lengths are necessary, line drivers are required.

APPLICATIONS

Digital output facilities constitute the computer's communication path to external devices that are not ordinarily part of computer systems.

Through the use of the relay switches and solid state electronic switches described above, the computer can perform required control functions and data output transfers to a large class of external devices. A brief examination of these devices from the viewpoint of computer control shows how the connection is made. The various power output circuits can be used to control relays, solenoids, motors, stepping motors, and various other electromechanical devices. Lamps and other power controlled display devices can also be operated by the power output components. Through the application of these circuits, complete computer determined selection and control are achieved.

A comprehensive list of all instruments and laboratory devices that can be connected to a computer would be well beyond the scope of any book. The components discussed in the following sections are indicative of how the computer interacts with external devices. The computer power output, as exemplified by the relay contact or electronic contact, is used mainly for electromechanical devices that are relatively slow responding, whereas the logic level high-speed output is suited for connection to electronic devices.

MOTORS

A motor may be driven by on-off or proportional control signals. A second input indicating desired direction of rotation is needed for many systems. Digital power output is applicable for on-off control of small motors. When proportional control, that is, control of motor speed as a function of an input control voltage, is required, more elaborate control circuits are needed. A DAC is required to produce the voltage signal to control the motor speed. In most computer applications this type of motor control is avoided when at all possible. Proportional control of small motors requires power amplifiers following the DAC stage.

A small motor can be driven directly by the computer electronic power contact output, provided that the motor's power requirements are within the limits of the computer power output switch rating. If higher-power motors are to be controlled, intermediate relays and contactors can be actuated. Direction may be determined by the polarity of the applied voltage in the case of DC motors. A relay actuated by the computer can perform this function.

In cases where variable speed is needed, prewired discrete speed control signals are prepared. Each speed can be individually actuated by the computer. In this way, a desired speed is set under program control.

When motor control is used, it is usually necessary for some form of feedback to the computer. Position and/or speed are sometimes needed. Position can be provided by shaft encoders, synchros, or potentiometers; speed can be indicated by incremental pulse generators or tachometers.

Safety mechanisms should be designed into moving systems to prevent damage. These include travel end stops, overspeed indicators, and proximity switches when approaching an unsafe condition. These indicators and warnings are entered into the computer via interrupts; thus, as soon as a warning condition occurs, an interrupt is generated.

In many systems involving motors a "zero" point interrupt is needed to indicate to the computer the location of the device being controlled. Each time the motor drives the shaft through the "zero" point an interrupt is issued.

STEPPING MOTORS

Stepping motors (Fig. 5) can be designed on the basis of a number of different techniques. From the system designer's point of view a stepping motor is a device capable of rotating a shaft in steps with a relatively high starting torque. Both rotary and linear stepping motors exist, although the rotary type predominates by far. Each time a stepping motor receives an input pulse it moves one step. All steps of a stepping motor, because of the motor design, are precise in size. Usually a stepping motor is essentially a special case of a multiple-pole motor.

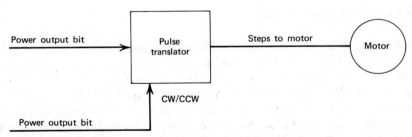

Fig. 5. Stepping motors may be driven directly from the computer electronic power output point. Pulses can drive the stepping motor pulse translation network to form a properly phased pulse sequence, depending on the particular type of motor being used. Multiple computer pulse power outputs may be used to form the proper pulse phase sequence directly from the computer. A second direction indicating signal is usually needed.

Most stepping motors require additional circuitry between the idealized pulse input and the actual windings in the stepping motor. Various types of multiphase translation networks may be needed to power a stepping winding properly. Even in the simplest cases careful pulse shaping is required to transform an input step command pulse into a pulse that will drive the stepping motor. Most important is power amplification of the input step command pulse before application of the pulse to the stepping motor drive. Most stepping motor manufacturers provide the circuitry necessary to accept a pulse train as an input and to deliver proper waveforms and power to drive a connected stepping motor. Every pulse into such a network causes the connected stepping motor to respond by advancing one step. It is recommended that users purchase the translation circuitry with the stepping motor; most users are not equipped to design and fabricate special translation networks. It is also not worthwhile to undertake such an effort unless a large number of drives are required and nothing applicable is available from the stepping motor manufacturer.

Along with the train of step command pulses to the stepping motor controller a direction command signal is required. This signal determines whether clockwise or counterclockwise rotation will occur. In the case of linear motion stepping motors this control signal will also determine the direction of advance.

Steppers capable of responding to step commands at a rate of several hundred per second are readily available. Torque capabilities to tens of pound-feet can be obtained, depending on the physical size of the motor. By appropriate gearing any desired step size can be provided.

RELAYS AND SOLENOIDS

These on-off devices are controlled by computer power output. This class of devices is very broad, covering on-off relays, rotary relays, stepping switches, and solenoids among others. Essentially, these devices all operate on the basis of actuating electromagnets. When current is allowed to pass through the electromagnet, the device operates by attracting a spring-loaded ferrous heel plate. Interrupting the current flow releases the electromagnetic field. The simplest relays make electrical contacts when actuated. Solenoids operate on the same principle as the simple relays except that a linear mechanical displacement is imparted to a plunger or piston type mechanism. Depending on the device attached to the solenoid, various types of translation motion can be carried out, such as valve control.

Rotary motion for shaft angular positioning and contact selection can also be accomplished by electromagnets, using various combinations of linear motion translators, ratchets, and pawls. Usually, each actuation creates a rotary step to the next sequential position. The angular displacement for each step is an equal increment each time the actuating electromagnetic is energized.

One type of rotary switch is the stepping switch which is a multiple-position relay. Each time the stepping switch electromagnet is energized, the switch steps to the next sequential position. Contacts associated with each step are made when the switch stops at a particular position. Stepping switches with 12 to over 50 positions are available. Each position may have from 1 to more than 12 switch levels. One position, the "zero" position, is the reference point, or "home" position. It should be recognized that stepping switches are pulsed devices, and an operation takes place only when power is applied. Power must be switched off and then reapplied to produce the next step. Most switches pull in during the power-on period and move when the power is turned off. In order to provide rapid operation, a large power pulse is usually applied. Care must be taken to apply power for the shortest possible duration (as recommended by the manufacturer) in order to prevent the relay coil from overheating. Rotary solenoids operate in the same fashion as stepping switches, except that mechanical rotation and/or electrical switching are possible on the same shaft.

Latching relays are usually two-coil electromagnets operating on a pole piece having a relatively large latent magnetic field. One coil is the latch coil, whereas the second is the unlatch coil. When the latch coil is actuated, the relay contacts are operated. When power is removed, after the few milliseconds needed to operate the relay, the contacts are held in the operated position by the latent magnetism of the pole piece. To release the contacts, the unlatch coil must be energized. Sufficient flux is applied to counter the latent field and open the contacts. When unlatch power is removed, the relay continues to remain open because the latent field is insufficient to hold the relay in position without re-energization of the latch coil.

Each of the electromagnetically operated devices is energized by applying power to a coil. The computer electronic contact digital output is well suited to such work. Electromagnetic coils may be actuated by either power transistor output or relay contact output. In the case of pulse actuated devices, the computer outputs are turned on for the specific time needed to actuate these devices.

INDICATOR LAMPS

One of the simplest and most useful digital outputs is the indicator lamp (Fig. 6). Its value when used as an interactive device to acknowledge to the user that the computer has accepted his input has already been stressed. Indicator lamps may be of the incandescent, solid state, or ionized gas type. A single bit is needed to drive each lamp. It is also necessary to provide a storage circuit with each bit in order to keep the lamp lit. Incandescent lamp and solid state displays can be driven directly from transistor or integrated circuits. Displays based on ionized gas devices usually have to be driven through high-voltage transistors or integrated circuit drivers to provide a sufficiently high voltage to ionize the gas.

LOGIC DEVICES

Logic devices include most digital systems that accept control and data signals. All computer peripheral devices fall into this category.

Data and control signals emanating from the computer appear identical. It is not possible to distinguish between the two classes of signals except by the way in which the information is used. Generally data are passed on without being operated upon in any way to change their characteristics. The only operations may be logic level matching and amplification. Parity and error correction code generation and testing

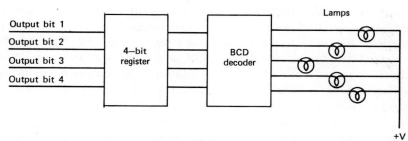

Fig. 6. Indicator lamps may be connected directly to the computer digital output facility. Each lamp is controlled by a single output bit. If the lamps are connected as a numeric display, the proper lamps to form the desired number must be actuated. The numeric code to actuate the display may be decoded in the computer or external to it as part of the display device.

may be performed. Control signals, on the other hand, are used by the external device itself to carry out the required functions.

PRESET COUNTERS

A preset counter (Fig. 7) is a counter that can be set to an initial value from an external device. A typical external device may be the digital output of a computer.

Counters may be preset to a value corresponding to the 2's complement of the desired count. The counter begins counting upward from the preset value and will exceed its maximum value when a number of pulses equal to the desired value is received. A signal indicating this condition is generated.

Alternatively, a backward counting configuration can be used. This counter is loaded with the number to be counted. Each input pulse

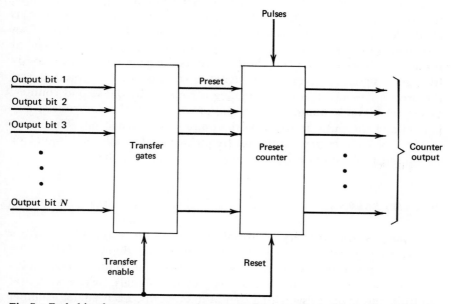

Fig. 7. Each bit of a preset counter is connected to a separate bit on the computer digital output. The computer program sets the desired output word to match the counter preset value. The counter is then set to begin countihg from this preset value. Shown is the preset configuration for a 4-bit counter.

decrements the count until the counter reaches zero, when a signal is generated to indicate that the desired preset count has been reached.

It is also possible to load the desired count into an auxiliary storage register. The contents of the counter are then digitally compared with the value loaded into the auxiliary register. The counter is initially preset to zero, and each incoming pulse adds one to the contents of the counter. A preset count signal is generated when the number in the counter is equal to the number stored in the auxiliary register.

In all these systems pulses for "start" and "stop" counter must be provided. The stop counter signal occurs when the preset count is reached. The start counter signal may come from an external source or from the connected computer. A pulse is generated to open a control gate permitting the pulses to be counted to reach the counter. The start signal may zero or initialize the counter.

The counter can receive its input from the pulse source to be measured. The pulses could come from a precise source, such as a crystal controlled oscillator. Counting a predetermined number of pulses from a crystal controlled oscillator source is equivalent to measuring a precise time interval. By coupling two such preset counters logically, a simple technique for measuring events or pulses received per unit time is available. Such a scheme can be used to measure the frequency of an unknown signal source. A basic FM digital detector can be configured using these basic components. Both counters are actuated simultaneously by a start signal. The unknown signal is counted by one counter, and the precise crystal controlled time base is counted by the second counter. When the second counter reaches the preset count, the control flip-flop is reset and the pulse trains to both counters are turned off. The count in the first counter represents the frequency of the unknown signal or the number of events occurring per unit measured time.

MULTIPLEXERS

Multiplexers are basically multipole electronically controlled switches and can be designed to switch either analog or digital signals. The circuit designs of the two multiplexers are quite different. Analog multiplexers, as the name implies, switch analog signals, whereas digital multiplexing involves switching digital data words. Each analog channel connects one analog signal. A digital multiplexer switches a number of bits at a time. The number of bits is usually equal to the word size of the attached computer. The required multiplexing functions of the two types are the same: sequential scan, random scan, and single point.

Multiplexers are under the control of the computer program. Each device connected to a multiplexer is assigned an address. The computer program specifies to the multiplexer the address of a particular multiplexer input point. When initiated, the multiplexer connects the signal present on the particular input point to the multiplexer common output bus. Disposition of the data on this bus is up to the system. Analog switched signals are forwarded to an ADC. Digital data are forwarded directly to the computer.

The computer program determines the multiplexer mode of operation. In the sequential mode the multiplexer expects to receive from the computer a single address that specifies the first point to be scanned by the computer. Each time the computer issues an instruction, the multiplexer connects the next sequential address to its output. Thus the computer does not have to furnish addresses to the multiplexer once the initial address is delivered. The sequence continues until the program stops requesting additional steps. Some multiplexers are designed to issue an interrupt and to stop themselves when the maximum addressable point or a common maximum group address is reached. Other multiplexers have a wrap-around sequence; the next sequential address after the maximum address is reached is the zero address, and the multiplexer wraps around to this address.

The random scan mode permits the computer program to access multiplexer data in any order whatsoever. The order of accessing input points is determined by commands issued by the program. The sequence can be stored in a data access table in the computer memory, or it can be calculated on the fly by the program. For each scan word the computer must issue first an output command consisting of the address of the next desired multiplexer input.

Single-point scanning permits the computer program to select a particular input for multiple readings. The one selected point is read in continuously until the multiplexer is advanced to another desired point.

DIGITAL TO ANALOG CONVERTERS

A DAC provides an output analog signal that is proportional to its input digital signal (Fig. 8). A digital output signal can be connected directly to the input of a DAC. Digital to analog converters are usually followed by buffer amplifiers to provide drive capability. These converters can follow the digital input applied as their input.

Many practical systems utilize a number of DACs. In the past it was economical to provide analog storage circuits and to multiplex the

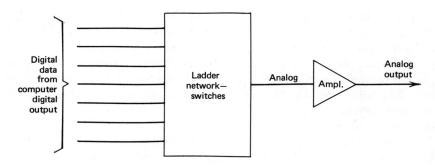

Fig. 8. The computer digital output is connected directly to the input of a ladder network. The ladder network determines the value of the output analog signal.

DAC among a number of analog storage circuits. Integrated circuits and hybrid circuits have brought the cost of DACs so low that it is now more practical to use a separate converter for each output.

In most systems a separate digital output register drives each DAC. Thus the digital multiplexer selects each digital output register in turn. The effect is a time displacement between settings of the DACs associated with the various output registers. In cases where this is a serious problem double buffering is used. The computer program drives a digital multiplexer that transfers data to each primary register in sequence. When all the registers are loaded, a bulk transfer signal is generated. Simultaneously, the data in all the primary registers are transferred to the DAC drive registers. Thus the values of the analog outputs are set simultaneously.

11 Peripheral Devices

Input/output units connected to a computer consist of instruments and other real-time devices and standard computer I/O devices. In laboratory applications the primary emphasis is naturally on the specialized instrumentation that must be connected to the computer. Nevertheless, to provide a viable system most of the standard I/O devices used in normal data processing and scientific computing applications are also required for laboratory automation computers. In this environment these standard computer peripherals are used in smiliar ways and for similar reasons to those prevailing in ordinary computation. Some peripherals, however, are used in special ways in the laboratory environment, especially in experiment-computer interactive modes. Perhaps the major distinction between a peripheral used in laboratory automation and one used in ordinary data processing is cost. It is usually necessary to specify the least expensive cost systems for laboratory automation work, and thus certain peripherals naturally find their way into these systems in preference to higher-cost devices used in standard data processing. In the design process the trade-off analysis must indicate that a lower-cost peripheral is adequate in comparison to a higher-cost, better-performance alternative.

The following is a list of commonly encountered peripheral devices (Fig. 1) that are used extensively in computer aided experimentation systems. What should be evident is that this list includes most of the peripherals that are used in any stand-alone system. As indicated above, what is sought in most peripherals in this situation is lowest cost.

1. Paper tape reader/punch.
2. Card reader/punch.
3. Magnetic tape transports.
4. Disk drives.

5. Line printers and typewriters.
6. Plotters.
7. Cathode ray tube displays.

Selection of these peripheral devices depends on the particular application and on budgetary considerations. When considering the application, certain devices are mandatory in order to do the required job. This is the case if multiprogramming is required, for instance. Disk files, or some other form of rapid access random storage is necessary. If large volumes of data must be stored, magnetic tape is usually selected. Budgetary considerations imply trade-offs in speed and capacity. Another factor that has an important bearing on peripheral selection is the programming effort required to accomplish the desired tasks.

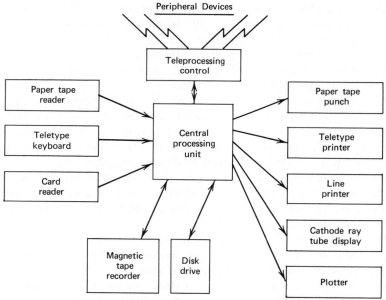

Fig. 1. The central processing unit of the computer, whether a minicomputer or a large scientific machine, must have a variety of peripheral devices connected. These provide a means for inputting and outputting data as well as auxiliary storage media. A typical minicomputer configuration with a number of the more common peripheral devices is shown.

PUNCHED PAPER TAPE

Punched paper tape (Fig. 2) is the most popular medium for small binary computers, primarily because of the relatively low cost of the devices needed to handle punched paper tape and its relative convenience. Paper tape is punched with 5, 6, 7, or 8 information bits per character. Each character is punched across the width of the tape, which depends on the number of bits per character. Eight-level code of 8 bits per character across the width of the tape is punched into 1-in.-wide tape. All tapes are punched with 10 characters per linear inch. Each character is accompanied by a sprocket hole, used to drive the tape and to identify the presence of a character. Sprocket feed holes are punched even when no data are punched. Sprocket holes are smaller than data holes, being 0.04 in. in diameter as compared to 0.06 in. for data bits. The sprocket precedes the data bits by 0.02 in. and is placed between columns 2 and 3 on five-level tape and between columns 3 and 4 on eight-level tape.

Paper tape is available in reels when large numbers of data are to be handled. Another convenient way to handle paper tape utilizes fan folds; the paper is folded every 10 in. Short amounts of paper tape are most easily handled as fan folds or on minireels. Paper tape is available

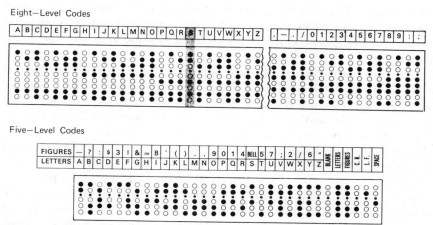

Eight—Level Codes

Five—Level Codes

Fig. 2. Paper tape is the most often used input medium to minicomputers because of the relatively low cost of paper tape readers and punches. A section of paper tape is shown; the hole patterns used to represent various characters are also depicted.

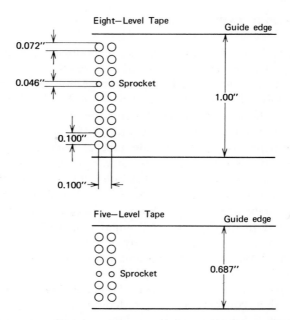

Fig. 3. Paper tape dimensions for five- and eight-level tapes. In both cases the packing density is 10 characters per linear inch.

in a variety of colors. When photosensing detectors are used to detect the holes in the paper tape, a dark color, such as black, is preferable because of the greater contrast between the opaque area and the transparent holes.

The most prevalent paper tape formats (Fig. 3) use either five- or eight-level codes; five-level code is the older of the two formats, and for most new equipment eight-level coded tapes are specified. Five-level code permits 32 code combinations. This number is patently insufficient to represent, at a minimum, all the letters in the alphabet and the digits. To overcome this deficiency, two code combinations have been reserved as Letters and Figures, respectively. A Letters code signifies that all subsequent codes are part of the Letters set. These include the alphabetics and some punctuation marks. The Figures code indicates that all subsequent codes, until the next Letters code, are numerics and special characters. Letters and Figures have the same effect as shifting a typewriter carriage from upper to lower case. With this coding scheme almost 60 code combinations are feasible. This type of code is usually referred to as Baudot code. Telex transmissions use 5-level Baudot code.

This code was developed and is used for transmitting data over communications lines for teleprinter and teletype service. The technology was subsequently adopted by the computer industry in a more expanded form, as described below.

A definite need to communicate and handle data with many more than 50 code combinations has been recognized by the communications industry. In addition, a capability for error detection as a means of more reliable information interchange was required. The Baudot code has no error detection capability except by retransmission. To answer these needs eight-level code has been developed. Each character contains 8 bits; 7 bits are data and the eighth bit contains a parity check bit for error detection. This coding technique permits 128 data combinations to be encoded directly with the 7 data bits. In addition, each data code can be tagged with a parity bit by using the eighth bit. When read, the correctness of information can be immediately checked by examining the validity of the parity check bit. Errors can be readily detected. The United States has adopted the American Standard Code for Information Interchange (ASCII) format as the standard for data transmission and has specified a full alphanumeric code set for eight levels. This widely accepted code format is also used in paper tape codes for computer applications. Other codes are also employed with paper tape. The Extended Binary Coded Decimal Information Code (EBCDIC) is also used as a 8-bit code structure.

Punched paper tape is handled by two distinct devices on the computer: paper tape readers and paper tape punches. Paper tape is usually read by photosensing devices, which recognize the holes in the tape. A light source with a narrow slit to direct the light beam illuminates the width of the paper tape as it moves across the slit opening. Photosensors are arranged in a bank to correspond in alignment with the data and sprocket holes across the width of the tape. When the sprocket photosensor senses a sprocket hole, a signal is directed to the control circuits to alert them for imminent sensing of data; the status of the data sensors is then sampled. Thus the sprocket indicates the presence of a character. Photosensing paper tape readers capable of handling 1000 characters per second are readily available commercially. These units are also capable of stopping the tape motion on a single character from the time the tape stop command is given. Paper tape readers using mechanical sensing devices are used when slower tape reading is permissible. Mechanical paper tape sensing devices operate at speeds of up to about 150 characters per second.

Paper tape punches capable of punching as many as 300 characters

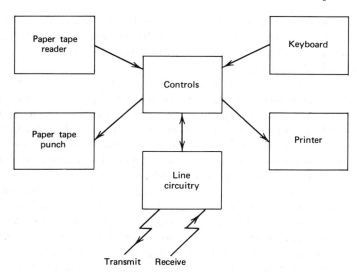

Fig. 4. An ASR-33 teletype. This unit is the most popular I/O device used with the minicomputer. It is also the lowest-cost peripheral available. In addition to a keyboard-printer facility, it has a built-in paper tape reader and a paper tape punch.

per second are commercially available. The units operating at this rate are very sensitive, and great care must be exercised in their use. Paper tape punches that can punch 100 to 150 characters per second are reasonably priced and reliable.

The most common and least expensive paper tape device is the Tele-type (Fig. 4), which is essentially a typewriter mechanism with built-in paper tape reader and punch. The basic models of this instrument are capable of operating at 10 characters per second; print, read, and punch. A Teletype can punch and print from keyboard data entry, or it can read paper tape and print and/or punch what is read. A Teletype can be connected directly to a computer, or it can operate stand-alone. Its original application was operation as transmit/receive terminals on communications networks. When connected to a computer, it can serve as an input device via its keyboard and/or via the paper tape reader facility, or as an output device by printing on its output printer and/or by punching paper tape. When operating in the computer mode, the Teletype is under computer control and responds to instructions issued by the computer.

The Teletype and the computer are connected via a line pair. In-formation is transmitted serially along the cable. (Other, similar devices transmit data over parallel lines, a full character at a time.) It should be noted that the Teletype and its serial I/O data transmission concepts were developed primarily for communications.

A Teletype unit operating in a stand-alone mode may be used to prepare program or data tapes. Previously produced tapes, either manually keyed or computer generated, may be printed. By actuating a single switch on the Teletype, the unit can be placed on line to the computer. The Teletype is then completely under computer control. In the off-line position the Teletype may be employed to prepare program tapes. These tapes are then used to read programs and data into the computer.

Newer Teletype models are capable of typing at rates in excess of 100 characters per second. These devices, in common with the 10 character-per-second Teletypes are serial devices. However, to attain such high speeds electronic printing techniques are used. Also, the paper tape reader and punch functions are separate devices. One technique uses electrostatic deflection of charged ink particles to form printing characters. Another employs multiple styli, resting on a chemically treated conducting paper. By energizing selected styli, desired characters are formed. Current is conducted from these styli through the sensitized paper, leaving a closely spaced pattern of data representing the desired characters.

Paper tape is used as a recording medium for many data acquisition systems. In many cases it is necessary to process this information on the laboratory computer. A paper tape reader is used as the read-in device. In many cases programs for these computers are distributed by the computer manufacturers to users on punched paper tape, which also serves as the main program entry media. Programs are punched onto paper tape using one of the Teletype-like devices described above. Programs may be punched in assembler language or a higher-level language. The computer assembler program and/or compiler programs convert these source language programs to object code. The object code, in core image or relocatable form, may be outputted to a paper tape punch. In many cases an intermediate paper tape is punched by the assembler or compiler; this is particularly necessary when multiple-pass assemblers or compilers are used. An early pass prepares intermediate results on the paper tape, and subsequent passes read these data for additional processing. As indicated above, the final result (the object code), may be punched into paper tape for future use. Paper tape is also used as a back-up store. Critical data tables and programs may be periodically dumped onto paper tape to ensure a reliable check point of the current condition of the system.

PUNCHED CARDS

Punched cards (Fig. 5) are the most convenient media for preparing computer programs for initial entry. Program debugging, modifying, and changing are easiest and most convenient when a unit record form is used. Each statement or line of code can be represented on a single card. Making changes requires insertion and deletion of single cards in the appropriate locations in the card sequence.

A punched card reader is used to read data into the computer. A punched card can contain 960 bits of information arranged in 80 columns of 12 rows each. Cards are $7\frac{3}{8}$ in. (18.7 cm) by $3\frac{1}{4}$ in. (8.2 cm). The card dimensions and tolerances on hole locations are closely specified.

Each column represents one alphanumeric character. A total of 80 characters can be punched into the card, 1 character per column. Each column contains 12 rows, designated as 0 through 9 and A and B. Digits are represented by a hole punched in the row corresponding to the desired digit. Only one hole per column need be punched to represent any digit between 0 and 9. To represent alphabetics and special symbols multiple punches are required. Combinations of the 0, A, or B row and rows 1 to 9 are used to represent all the alphabetic and special characters.

Punched cards may be produced either by a computer card punch mechanism or a keypunch. Punched cards produced by a keypunch

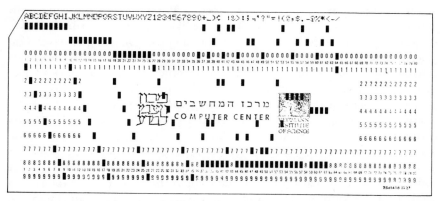

Fig. 5. A standard 80-column punched card. Codes for representing numerics and alphabetics are shown punched into the card. An alphanumeric coded card can hold 80 characters. A binary coded card can store 960 bits.

usually contain an interpreted printed line across the top edge. Computer produced cards must be processed through an "interpreter" in order to print the data punched into the card. In some cases punched cards are produced as the output of a data acquisition system. These cards are punched by a keypunch that has been modified and interfaced to the data acquisition system. Card punches interfaced directly to computers are usually relatively high speed devices, whereas keypunch machines are meant to be manually operated and are therefore comparatively low speed. Keypunches used in data acquisition are basically manual data entry devices that have been modified to be electrically actuated.

Computer card punches and card readers operate on cards, on either a column by column or row by row basis. The highest speeds are obtainable only when the reading or punching is on a row by row basis. In this kind of operation the 9's in all 80 columns are punched or read first, followed by the 8's, and so on. Eighty positions are needed because all 80 columns are handled simultaneously. A slower but less expensive technique is to handle the data on a column by column basis. First the character to be stored in column 1 is processed, followed by column 2, and so. Data handling by the logic is considerably simplified by the column serial technique because the device processes 1 character at a time. The faster technique requires that the logic handle 80 characters at a time since all the 9's, followed by all the 8's, of each character are processed simultaneously for all 80 columns.

The most efficient way for the computer to transmit data to the card read/punch logic is in the natural code inherent in the design of the particular computer. The card read/punch logic converts the more efficient computer code to Hollerith. To reduce hardware costs, the computer may be used to convert the internal character codes to Hollerith code. This considerably reduces the card read/punch logic at the expense of added load on the computer processor.

Card reading is accomplished by photosensing or through mechanical sensing using electrical brushes. When photsensing is used, a light source illuminates the row or column to be read. The card is moved under the light source either column by column or row by row, depending on the type of reader. Either 80 or 12 photodetectors are precisely aligned to the positions where light would pass through the row or column of holes. Detection of light is indicative of a hole; no detection corresponds to no hole. As in the case of the punch, the data can be transmitted to the computer in Hollerith, or they can be converted by the logic to the more compact internal code. Card readers that use mechanical sensors have sets of 12 or 80 brushes that make electrical contact through the punched holes. The brushes are unable to complete circuits where no hole has been punched. Photosensing permits much higher reading rates than mechanical sensing.

Most computers used for laboratory automation do not have card punches attached because of the relatively high price. Card readers are much more prevalent than card punches when card equipment is attached. Most card punches are part of the card read mechanism in these systems. The same card handling and card paths are used for punching and reading. A card read station and card punch station are positioned in the card motion path.

The major uses for card equipment are (1) program entry, (2) data entry, (3) data output, (4) back-up storage, (5) program distribution, and (6) object program store.

As stated previously, by far the most convenient way of preparing programs is on punched cards. A keypunch is used to prepare source program decks. Debugging, adding and deleting, and code changing are simplified by changing individual cards, each of which contains a single instruction or data set. To modify programs appropriate cards are altered. Each card is a unit record that is easily inserted or removed from the program deck without affecting any other cards in the deck. This feature also facilitates the handling of individual unit records in debugging and modifying programs.

Data from various data acquisition and recording systems are collected on punched cards. A card reader on the computer permits reading the data for further processing.

Many situations require transfer of data between computers. Cards are convenient media if the data volume or data rate is not excessive. Cards are particularly useful when computers of different manufacturers are involved, and data code compatibility uncertainties exist with other media.

Most computers with programming systems require back-up storage for the operating system and certain critical parameters. Punch cards provide such a capability. Portions of the disk or magnetic tape containing valuable or critical files may be dumped onto cards for back-up.

Many computer manufacturers distribute programs to customers on punched cards. To handle these programs a facility for reading cards is required on the computer.

Assembled or compiled programs can be stored on punched cards in object code format. Object decks contain programs that have been converted into computer instruction codes. They may be executed without the delay required for assembly or compilation. The object program is read from the cards directly into the computer's storage in machine language; once in the computer memory it is ready to begin execution.

Card readers can be buffered or unbuffered. By buffering the card reader data output, the data read from the punched card are entered into an external buffer that assembles and temporarily stores the contents of the complete card. When the buffer fills with the data from a complete card, the buffer content is transferred at a high-speed burst to the computer. When operation is unbuffered, the card data are transferred one column at a time to the computer. It is evident that buffering offers a more efficient but also more expensive utilization of the computer data channel. A high-speed-burst data transfer is initiated only when a number of data characters have been assembled. Buffered card readers are usually used on more expensive installations where I/O efficiency is paramount. In laboratory automation efficiency of card reading is not a significant design parameter.

Computer controlled card punches can operate over the range of about 10 columns punched per second to several hundred cards per minute. Card punching capacity is usually not required or specified for laboratory automation. It is an expensive feature whose cost is not justified unless cards are the only usable output media. In some cases where data must be interchanged with another computer, the only common devices capable of handling the same data formats are card readers and punches.

MAGNETIC TAPE TRANSPORTS

Data may be recorded on magnetic tape in either analog or digital form. In this chapter digital data recording is considered; analog recording is quite different in almost all respects and is discussed separately in Chapter 7. Digital data can be recorded in IBM compatible format or in a special format compatible only with the computer in question: IBM compatible recorded tapes are preferable because they can be transferred between computers of different manufacturers with ease. Almost every computer, both large and small, has an I/O IBM compatible tape transport capability. In effect, IBM compatible recording has been adopted as the standard format for digital data recording. Lower-cost (and lower-performance) recording can be effected by using special non-IBM devices and formats, as described below. However, these techniques are nonstandard and the resultant tapes are not transferable between computers. When limited numbers of data are recorded at relatively low rates, however, these devices are satisfactory. Generally such tapes can be reproduced only on computers of the same manufacturers that produced the recording.

Digital tapes may be recorded on continuously recording start/stop tape transports or incremental recorders. Computers almost always record on continuously recording, stop/stop transports, whereas data acquisition systems without buffer storage generally use incremental recorders. This is especially true for long-term, low-data-rate applications.

The following topics are covered under the heading "digital recording:"

1. IBM compatible recording.
2. Incremental recorders.
3. Cassette recorders.
4. DEC tape.

IBM COMPATIBLE RECORDING

IBM compatible digital recording techniques use $\frac{1}{2}$-in.-wide magnetic tape as their recording medium. Transports can handle reels up to $10\frac{1}{2}$ in. in diameter and have as much as 2400 ft of magnetic tape. Shorter tape lengths on smaller diameter reels may also be handled.

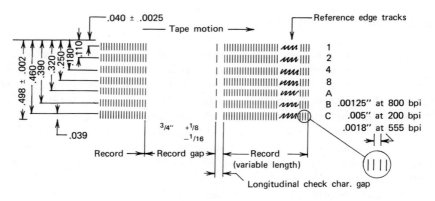

Notes: Oxide side up on diagram, recording head on same side as oxide

Fig. 6. IBM compatible seven-track data format. Six-bit characters are recorded across the tape width. A seventh bit, the parity check bit, is recorded with the 6-bit character. This bit is used for error detection purposes. Groups of characters are recorded as records under computer program control. Records are separated by blank end-of-record gaps. A longitudinal redundancy check character is recorded at the end of each record. Seven-track tapes may be recorded at a density of 200, 556, or 800 characters per linear tape inch.

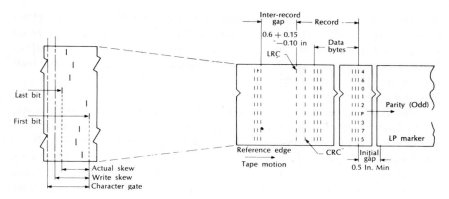

Fig. 7. IBM compatible nine-track magnetic tape format. A single 8-bit character is recorded in parallel across the width of the tape. Depending on the computer program, a number of characters form a physical record. A check bit is recorded with each character. Redundancy check characters are recorded with each record and are used for error detection and error correction. Records are separated by blank end-of-record gaps. Nine-track recording may be at a density of 800 or 1600 characters per inch.

The originally announced standards for IBM magnetic recording called for seven-track (Fig. 6) 200-bits-per-inch (bpi) recording density. In 1964 IBM announced nine-track (Fig. 7) 800-bpi recording density tapes. At present seven-track 200-bpi, 556-bpi, and 800-bpi and nine-track 800-bpi and 1600-bpi magnetic tape recordings may be expected in laboratory environment. 6250 bpi tapes are still too expensive for CAE.

Data are recorded in parallel on the seven- or nine-track standard version. On seven-track recorders, each 7-bit parallel character recorded consists of 6 data bits and a seventh parity check bit. Nine-track recorders record 8-bit data characters, along with a ninth bit that serves as parity check bit for the character. Character streams are recorded serially along the length of the tape. Seven-track recordings are made at a density of 200, 556, or 800 characters per linear inch of tape: nine-track recordings, at 800 or 1600 characters per linear inch. Recording density is determined by the control unit of the computer recording the tape or the type of data acquisition hardware used to make the recording. Regardless of the recording density or number of tracks the tapes are played back on a computer controlled magnetic tape transport. One parameter of the playback program must obviously be the recording density of the tape. Different transports are used to play back (and record) nine- and seven-track tapes. Most computer tape transports can handle all three densities in seven-track tape because the same recording and playback circuits can handle all three. Seven-track recordings are always made using NRZ-1 (nonreturn to zero—change of flux for one recording). Nine-track recordings use NRZ-1 for 800-bpi and phase encoding techniques for 1600-bpi recordings; therefore different electronics must be used for 800- and 1600-bpi nine-track recordings.

Seven-track magnetic tape systems capable of handling all three seven-track densities (200, 556, and 800 bpi) usually allow selection of recording density as a function of the quality of the magnetic tape used. For a particular tape speed, data rates four times as great can be recorded at 800 bpi as at 200 bpi. Thus the selected density must be capable of sustaining the I/O rate needed by the program and data source. Magnetic tape is not inherently designed for a specific packing density but is usually certified by its manufacturer as capable of handling reliably a specified packing density. The certification implies that the manufacturer has recorded test patterns on each reel of tape and has successfully read the tape at or below an allowable error rate. Seven-track and nine-track recordings can be made on the same magnetic tape, that is, on $\frac{1}{2}$-in.-wide tape. However, tapes recorded on seven-track transports cannot be played back on nine-track transports, and vice versa. Once a tape is erased, however, it may be used again on either type of transport. There is nothing inherent in the tape that makes it nine or seven track; the recording heads on the transport determine the number of tracks on a tape.

Digital data are recorded in records. A record may consist of any number of characters. The number of characters in a record usually is specified to be a convenient size buffer for the computer memory. Data on the magnetic tape are read by the computer under program control in records. Therefore the record size must correspond to or be smaller than the buffers specified by the computer program. A record can be quite short (for instance, 80 characters to correspond to a punched card image) or quite long (several thousand characters). In theory a record can be a full tape, but in that event it could not be read. Longer-length records are most advantageous in regard to tape utilization and program efficiency.

A 2400-ft reel of magnetic tape recorded on a seven-track recorder with a packing density of 200 bpi would contain

$$2400 \text{ ft} \times 12 \text{ in./ft} \times 200 \text{ bpi} = 5,760,000 \text{ bits per track}$$

This is equivalent to 5,760,000 7-bit characters. In practice the full tape would not be recorded. The data would be recorded in records, and therefore a figure less than the maximum mentioned above would be recorded. The exact number would depend on the record length used and the number of records. The same tape recorded at 800 bpi could contain 4 times the amount of information on a 200-bpi tape.

Each recorded data record is delineated by leaving a blank gap between records. A $\frac{3}{4}$-in. blank gap separates seven-track records; 0.6-in. interrecord gaps are used for nine-track recordings. Thus an 80-character record recorded at 200 bpi would require 80/200 + 0.75 in. = 1.15 in. of magnetic tape for the record: 0.4 in. for data and 0.75 in. for the interrecord gap. A 1000-character record for the same recording conditions would use 1000/200 + 0.75 in. = 5.75 in. of tape: 5 in. for recording the 1000 characters and the same 0.75 in. interrecord gap. The advantages of longer data records are self-evident.

Recording on magnetic tape is a function of time and geometry. To assure reliable recording and playback, packing density may not vary from the nominal value by more than a few percent. The technique used to record on magnetic tape is to establish a clock generator to provide a clock rate for the data rate that is commensurate with the tape speed and packing density. Thus, if a tape speed of 100 in. per second (ips) is selected and the packing density is to be 800 bpi, the recording data rate is 800 × 100 or 80,000 characters per second. To record under these conditions the clock generator is set to 80,000 pps to obtain the desired rate of 80,000 characters per second. If 200-bpi packing were required at a tape speed of 100 ips, the clock generator would be set to 20,000 pps. To achieve reliable recording, the clock generator must be stable and accurate to within about 1% of the nominal value. The computer and/or data acquisition device must be capable of sustaining data rates equal to the specified clock rate. The data are in synchronism with the clock. As a practical matter, in order to achieve synchronous data rates the computer must have all the data for the tape record available before recording is started. In order to accomplish this, areas in the computer memory are set aside by the program as tape buffers, for reading or writing on magnetic tape. These areas are set up only when needed. The data to be recorded or played back are stored in these contiguous areas and are outputted (or inputted) in response to the clock generator, which is part of the magnetic tape controller or the data acquisition system. The amount of space that may be reasonably set aside for such buffer areas determines the size of the record on the magnetic tape.

Digital magnetic tape is usually in the "stop" condition, that is, the tape is at rest until data are to be recorded or reproduced. Then (and only then) is the tape in motion. The computer program or the data acquisition system starts the read or write operation by issuing a tape start command to the tape transport. This command is usually executed through the tape control unit. Digital magnetic tape transports are designed to accelerate tape to full speed in a very short time. A typical magnetic tape transport can accelerate tape to 100 ips within 2 mslc from the full stop position. It can also decelerate the tape from full speed to full stop in the same amount of time. As indicated previously, recording is at a synchronous rate. Therefore, to ensure that the recorded tape packing density is within the tolerance of the specified nominal density, actual recording cannot begin while the tape is being accelerated or decelerated. The tape is left intentionally blank during acceleration and deceleration times. The blank tape gap permits the tape to be accelerated and decelerated and also serves as the delineator between records. Thus, even if data are to be recorded continuously, blank $\frac{3}{4}$-in. end-of-record gaps must be inserted in the data stream to delineate records. In addition, longitudinal redundancy check bits are recorded at the end of each data record on the tape in order to provide a means for error detection. In addition, more sophisticated error detection and correction codes are recorded on the tape.

Data are recorded by magnetizing tape tracks to one direction of tape flux saturation or the other. Square law magnetic material is used for digital recording tape. Various techniques for representing data are used. A simple technique is to saturate the tape in one direction for binary "one" and in the reverse direction for binary "zero." With this technique, a string of alternating "ones" and "zeros" in a track would be recorded as a succession of tape flux reversals. Each "one" recorded on the tape would result in tape flux saturation in a particular direction, and each "zero" would cause tape flux saturation in the opposite direction. A continuous string of "ones" would begin with the flux saturated in the "one" specified direction. No changes in flux saturation would result until the next "zero" was recorded. Upon playback a flux reversal and resultant output voltage pulse would be detected each time that a "one"/"zero" or "zero"/"one" transition occurred. No signal output would occur for a string of "ones" or "zeros" because no flux changes would result for a string.

The technique used for IBM compatible magnetic tape recording is nonreturn to zero with flux reversal for ones—NRZ-1 (Fig. 8). "Ones" are recorded as a reversal in the flux saturation on the magnetic tape. "Zeros" do not affect the direction of saturation. Thus a string of "ones" in a particular track appears as a succession of flux reversals. "Zeros" are produced by not affecting the direction of flux on the tape.

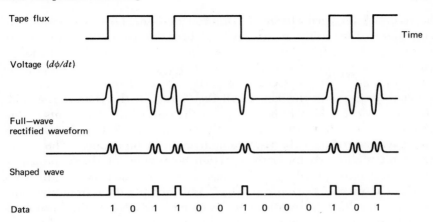

Fig. 8. The waveforms associated with NRZ-1 recording for a single tape channel. Each "one" recorded on the tape causes the direction of the recording current to reverse, thereby reversing the direction of the recorded flux. A "zero" does not affect the flux direction. Upon playback an output voltage is obtained for each flux reversal since only where flux changes have been produced are voltages induced in the record/ playback head $(v = d\phi/dt)$. The induced voltages are full waved rectified, amplified, and suitably shaped.

The same direction of flux saturation as occurred when the previous "one" was recorded is maintained as long as "zeros" are recorded in the track. This techniques simplifies the playback because only flux reversals have to be taken into account. Every flux reversal detected when the tape is played back is a "one," regardless of the change in flux direction. No change in flux direction is interpreted as "zero." At a recording density of 800 bpi, 800 flux reversals per inch will be recorded for a string of all "ones" in a particular track.

Data from both seven- and nine-track tapes are read out in parallel, that is, seven or nine read/record heads are always in contact with the tape. A bit from each track is read or recorded in parallel: one for each bit that makes up a character. It should be evident that if "ones" are recorded in each of the tracks (i.e., an all-"one" character is recorded), flux reversals in each track will take place for that particular character if NRZ-1 recording is used. However, if an all-"zero" character were to be recorded, no flux reversals would take place in any track. On playback there would be no way to recognize the character because no track would respond by a change in flux: To obviate this potential shortcoming, a data coding scheme requiring that at least one "one" must be recorded for each character has been devised. This is most readily accomplished by using an odd parity check bit convention for binary recording. The parity bit associated with each 6- or 8-bit character is computed to produce an odd number of "ones" in the character. In the case of an all-"zero" character, the parity check bit must be a "one" in order to ensure that the sum of all the "ones" in the character is odd. The partity check bit will be a "one" if the sum of the "one" bits in the character is 0, 2, 4, or 6; otherwise it will be "zero." In this way each character recorded on the tape contains at least one "one." The parity check bit is also used for error detection because on playback the parity check bit is recomputed and tested against the recorded parity bit.

The circuitry of the tape playback unit accepts data from the tape playback amplifiers through a seven- or nine-way OR circuit. As soon as a "one" is detected from any track, the clock flag is set, indicating that a character is being received from the tape. After a slight delay to take tape skew into account, the data lines from the playback amplifiers are sampled. Tape skew is the effect of differential tape motion between tracks, tape head alignment differences between heads and transports, and inaccuracies in record/playback amplifier timing. The delay introduced between the time a "one" is detected on any channel and the time all the channels are sampled is sufficient to ensure that, if a valid "one" for any bit of the character is to be detected, it will have been accepted by the playback logic. This technique makes the tape self clocking because the playback data clock is derived from the recorded data. The tape clock is derived from the data itself. Reasonable deviation in the data rate from the nominal value can be effectively handled by this scheme. Nonbinary codes are usually arranged so that each character, even blanks and zeros, are signified by nonzero characters. For these codes, odd or even parity can be used equally well.

Phase encoding is used for nine-track recording at a packing density of 1600 bpi. The practical upper limit for reliable NRZ-1 recording is approximately 800 bpi; dust particles and minor imperfections in the tape drastically affect the reliability of the recording at higher packing densities, and NRZ-1 recording is particularly sensitive to these imperfections. To achieve higher recording densities phase encoding using a system of sine wave flux modulation is used.

Nine-track magnetic tape recording has become the standard for most new computer installations. The advantages over seven-track recording are self evident:

1. Higher data recording density and more data recorded per tape.
2. Higher data transfer rate.

3. Compatibility with 16-bit and byte oriented computers.
4. Greater reliability using phase encoding.

The capability to pack many more data into the same tape space is an effective cost saver. The use of 1600-bpi phase encoding (Fig. 9) is additionally attractive; such a tape can store almost triple the data that a seven-track 800-bpi tape can handle. Double-rate data transfers are also obtained. This is an important consideration in increasing computer performance.

Nine-track tapes record 8-bit data characters. Most modern computers used for data processing are byte oriented, that is, their basic data unit or addressable memory element is the 8-bit type. Thus a byte matches the data format of nine-track magnetic tape exactly. In addition, most real-time laboratory computers use 16-bit words and have 16-bit-wide data paths. One word very naturally matches two 8-bit tape characters. This advantage is important in small binary computers because the cost of interface circuits needed to arrange data words on the tape is minimized. This is obviously a consideration in the practicality of attaching a magnetic tape unit to a small binary computer. Also, the compatibility of magnetic tapes with most other computers is an advantage not to be overlooked.

Digital magnetic tape transports have been developed over a long period of time and are available from a large number of manufacturers in a very wide price-performance range. The most advanced tape transports will drive magnetic tape at over 200 ips and will transfer data at a rate exceeding 320,000 bytes per second. Lower-performance low-cost magnetic transports operate at speeds as low as 10 ips and at transfer rates of 2000 bytes per second. The tape format is, of course, the same

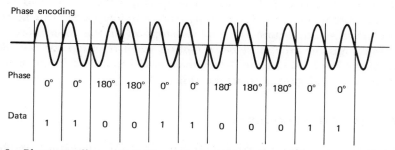

Fig. 9. Phase encoding recording waveforms. Although requiring more complicated circuitry, phase encoding is a more reliable process and permits higher data packing densities.

for all units; the only differences are in tape packing density and number of tracks. However, these are not functions of tape speed only but involves also recording clock rate and physical characteristics of the tape read/write head. Packing densities of 1600 bpi can be handled at 10 to 200 ips; similarly, 200 bpi can operate at 10 to 200 ips. Most digital recording is done above 10 ips because it is difficult to maintain a stable tape speed using conventional digital tape transport techniques very much below this low speed. Incremental recorders can operate at very low speeds; they are discussed in the next section.

In addition to the lateral parity bit associated with each character recorded on the magnetic tape, a second longitudinal redundancy check character (LRCC) is associated with each record on the tape. The LRCC is equal to the logical sum of the bits in each track position in the record. If the sum of the "one" bits in a particular track of the record is odd, the LRCC for the record in that track will be a "one"; an even number of "ones" will generate a "zero" LRCC bit for the track. The LRCC is recorded two character intervals after the last data character in each record. With the aid of the LRCC and parity bits associated with each character 1-bit errors in the record can be detected and corrected.

Most computer controlled magnetic tape recorders are equipped with dual-gap record/playback heads. One set of heads is used to record, while the second set serves for playback. The separation between the two gaps is about 0.3 in. When data are recorded, the playback head and its associated amplifiers are active. The data just recorded pass under the downstream playback head and are detected. The playback amplifier logic is arranged to compute the parity check bit for the detected characters. If a parity error is detected, a signal is issued to the computer to notify it of the recording error. The computer must be programmed to take appropriate remedial actions. The spacing between the two heads must be close so that, when recording, the complete record can be read at full tape speed, before the tape is stopped in the interrecord gap interval. Thus the tape must be in motion when it brings the last character of the record across the downstream read head. The 0.3-in. spacing between the dual gaps is sufficient (Fig. 10).

INCREMENTAL RECORDERS

Incremental recorders record digital data in IBM compatible formats, and tapes made on these recorders can be played back into computers having IBM compatible tape units. Incremental recorders operate at

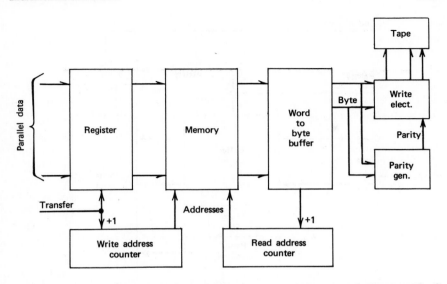

Fig. 10. A block diagram showing the components needed to record on a standard digital recorder. The buffer memory may be part of the computer memory, or an independent buffer memory. Digital recorders record ·and reproduce data at a fixed rate determined by the product of tape speed and data packing densities. Small data rate variations (about ± 1%) may be tolerated.

very slow rates, from essentially 0 to about 1000 characters per second. Most incremental recorders are record only. Some units are capable of playing back also but usually in a synchronous mode rather than incrementally; incremental playback is much more difficult to design than incremental record. However, it is not apparent that playback capability is needed or even useful on most applications for which incremental recorders are employed. Generally, incremental recorders are used for record-only data acquisition systems and are very rarely connected directly to computers. Their tapes are, however, processed on computers using ordinary computer start/stop synchronous digital magnetic tape transports, as described in the preceding section. Incremental recorders use the same $\frac{1}{2}$-in-wide magnetic tape as start/stop synchronous recorders.

Incremental recorders (Fig. 11) with full record electronics and control circuitry are made by many manufacturers. Interfacing to these units from data systems is relatively simple, requiring only data input lines and a data clock pulse. When valid data exist on the input lines, the external control circuitry transmits a clock pulse to the incremental

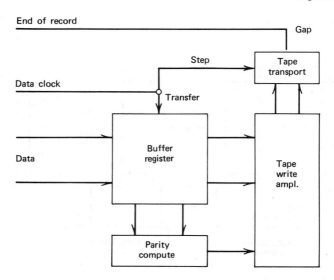

Fig. 11. Block diagrams and timing charts show the operation of an incremental recorder. Each time an output character is received it is recorded. The data rate can be any rate up to the maximum stepping rate of the incremental recorder tape drive motor.

tape electronics. This triggers the parity generator circuitry and the character record amplifiers. The specified parity (odd or even) is generated by the parity computation circuitry for the data character being presented at the data input lines, and the appropriate NRZ-1 code is set up and recorded on the magnetic tape. The recorder is then ready to receive the next character. Depending on the type of recorder, up to 1000 characters per second can be recorded. Each time a character is recorded the tape is advanced one character. Thus if recording is at 200 bpi, the tape will be advanced $\frac{1}{200}$ in. for each recorded character, and recording at 800 bpi require tape advances of $\frac{1}{800}$ in. for each character. Stepping motors or printed motors are used to step the tape. These limit the recording rate to about 200 to 1000 characters per second, depending on the motor used by the transport manufacturer. Recording can be at any character rate from zero to the maximum allowable for the particular recorder—hence the asynchronous characteristic of incremental recorders.

Incremental recorders have end-of-record and end-of-file select lines. An "end of record" is written when this input line is pulsed. The LRCC character is written and the tape advanced the required interrecord gap interval. Similarly, actuation of the end-of-file line causes an appropriate end of file to be written.

Incremental recorders are rarely used as computer I/O devices directly because they are relatively slow in their data rate capability. They serve primarily as data recording devices in data acquisition systems where the data rates are modest and no buffer storage is available or needed. The data acquisition device records on incremental recorders directly asynchronously.

In many aspects incremental tape recorders take the place of paper tape punch devices. The convenience of producing direct computer compatible magnetic tape is a major factor. In most cases paper tape data are converted to some other medium before entry into a computer. This is particularly true for large scientific computers. Paper tape punches are less reliable then magentic tape recorder devices, and paper tape as an input medium to large computers is discouraged by most computer centers.

CASSETTE RECORDERS

A newly developed product that is gaining wide acceptance for recording digital data, especially for small binary computers, is the cassette tape recorder. Such devices use magnetic tape cassettes identical in appearance to the cassettes used for entertainment type tape recorders. The major difference is that the cassettes used for data recording are loaded with high-quality magnetic tape suitable for digital data recording at high density. Cassette tapes are typically between 150 and 200 ft in length, depending on tape thickness.

At present, recording on cassette tape recorders is the least expensive way of recording digital data on magnetic tape and playing them back into a computer. Their relatively low cost, coupled with the convenience of these devices, makes them ideal for input, output, and auxiliary storage for small computers.

Tapes produced on one firm's cassette recorder are not necessarily compatible with those produced on similar devices from other firms. Although the tape cassettes are physically interchangeable, each firm uses its own particular technique for recording. No industry wide standards for producing compatible digital cassette tapes exist as yet, but it is expected that this situation will eventually be resolved. It should be pointed out that cassette tapes are not compatible in any way with the tapes used on most large scientific computers. It is necessary to translate every digital cassette tape format into an IBM compatible tape format for entry into large scale machines. This can be done off line by a special translator or on line if a cassette tape drive and an IBM compatible tape drive are interfaced to a particular computer.

Most cassette recorders use two tracks. On one track a clock signal is prerecorded, and on the other track data are recorded. The data are recorded serially on the data track in synchronism with the clock track prerecorded information. The interface electronics accepts parallel data words (or characters) from the computer or data acquisition system and serializes them for recording on the tape. Upon playback the serially recorded data are arranged into parallel characters or words and transferred to the computer. Parity and other check characters are also generated and recorded. Cassette tape drives can be accelerated or stopped within a few milliseconds. The normal mode of operation is to issue a start command and wait a few milliseconds until the tape is up to speed. At that time the computer controller begins to transfer parallel characters or words to the interface for serialization and recording. The character transfer rate must be a synchronous rate based on the effective word or character transfer rate of the cassette recorder. When all the characters are recorded, the cassette tape is stopped. Playback follows essentially the same sequence as recording except that the data transfer is between the tape and the computer memory or external device

Most cassette tape transports record or play back at about 5 ips. Data are recorded at between 1000 and 1600 bpi, serially. Thus a cassette loaded with 150 ft of magnetic tape can hold 1,800,000 bits, or about 100,000 16-bit words. The exact capacity, of course, depends on record lengths. At 5-ips tape speed, transfer rates of 500 words per second are attained. Fast forward and rewind are usually quite high—about 100 ips, permitting a data record on any part of the tape to be located within 20 secs. Special record counting circuitry must be built into the interface in order to exploit this feature.

Various data recording techniques are used by the different firms manufacturing cassette recorders. The most prevalent recording forms are NRZ (nonreturn to zero) and phase encoding. It is usually necessary to use phase encoding techniques for recording densities over 1000 bpi while NRZ is satisfactory for lower densities.

Ordinarily, the user of cassette recorders will not be concerned with the technical details discussed above. His primary concern will be with the data interface with the computer. Parallel data will be transferred synchronously between the data acquisition system or computer and the cassette tape tansport. The cassette electronics will serialize, add parity and check bits, and detect errors upon playback.

Cassette tape recorders are also available as incremental record devices. In this mode data are recorded one character at a time in an asynchronous manner. Each time a character is presented to the interface, the tape is advanced and the data are recorded. As indicated previously, incremental techniques are most suitable for slow-speed systems that do not have buffer facilities.

DEC TAPE

A large number of small computers use DEC tape as their primary I/O device. This tape, which is used almost exclusively on Digital Equipment Company (DEC) computers, provides a highly reliable and low-cost data recording technique (Fig. 12). Reliability is achieved by redundant recording of all data. The DEC tape serves both as a data storage medium and as a random access device where programs and files are held.

DEC tape utilizes a 10-track read/write head. Redundant recording of each character bit on nonadjacent tracks materially reduces bit dropouts and minimizes the effect of skew. The series connection of corresponding track heads within a channel and the use of Manchester phase recording techniques, rather than amplitude sensing techniques, virtually eliminate dropouts.

The timing and mark channels control the timing of operations within the control unit and establish the format of the data contained on the information channels. The timing and mark channels are recorded before all normal data reading and writing on the information channels. Since the timing of operations performed by the tape drive and some control functions is determined by the information on the timing channel, wide variations in the speed of the tape motion do not affect system performance. Information read from the mark channel is used during the reading and writing of data to indicate the beginning and end of data blocks and to determine the functions performed by the system in each control mode. During normal data reading, the control assembles the data into computer length words from the information channels of the tape. During normal data writing, the control disassembles words and distributes the bits so that they are recorded on successive lines on the information channels. A mark-channel error check circuit ensures that one of the permissible marks is read in every 6 lines on the tape.

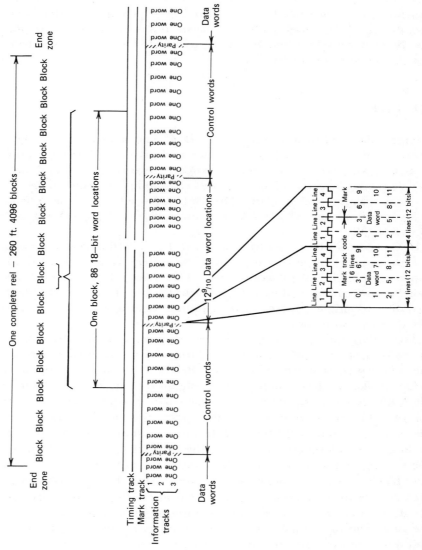

Fig. 12. The data recording format for DEC tape.

This 6-line mark-channel sensing requires that data be recorded in 12-line segments.

A tape contains a series of data blocks that can be of any length which is a multiple of three 12-bit words. Block length is determined by information on the mark channel. Usually a uniform block length is established over the entire length of a reel of tape by a program that writes mark and timing information at specific locations. The ability to write variable length blocks is useful for certain data formats. For example, small blocks containing index or tag information can be alternated with large blocks of data. Most DEC tape, however, is written in fixed block lengths only.

Between the blocks of data are areas called interblock zones, which consist of 30 lines on tape before and after a data block. Each of these 30 lines is divided into five 6-line control words.

DISK DRIVES

Disk drive availability as a peripheral device is a major factor in the capability of a small computer; a program supported disk drive on a small binary computer can increase its effectiveness many fold. The disk drive provides storage area for programs and data files and, disk space can be allocated to swap program segments with main storage. In this way the effective utilization of core is greatly enhanced.

Disk drive storage devices are based on recording data on high-speed rotating disk surfaces coated with magnetic material. Each flat, round disk is rotated on its axis at high speed. More than one disk may be mounted on a spindle. Some disk packs have as many as 12 disks on a single spindle thus providing up to 24 recording surfaces. In most such configurations the outer surfaces, which are more exposed to handling, are not utilized in order to enhance reliability. Disks may be permanently mounted as part of the disk drive, or they may be removable packs. Removable packs are convenient and permit almost unlimited storage, because each disk can be separately loaded onto the drive. Any number of disks can be interchanged. The construction of an interchangeable disk drive mechanism is obviously complicated because packs recorded on any drive must be capable of being interchanged on any other drive with comparable specifications. A permanent disk is attached and is an intergral part of the drive. No provision for manual mounting and dismounting is necessary.

Disk data are organized in cylinders, tracks, and sectors. Data on each disk are recorded in concentric tracks (Fig. 13); a surface may have a

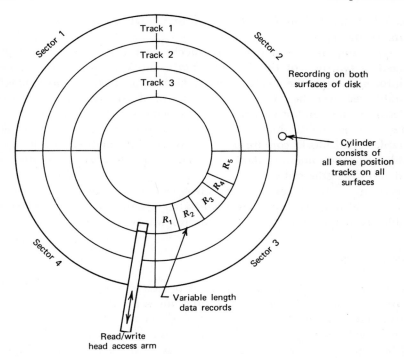

Fig. 13. The physical layout of a disk recording surface. Data are recorded in tracks. When multiple recording surfaces are used, tracks in the same vertical plane are referred to as a cylinder. The arm bearing the record heads accesses all tracks in a given cylinder simultaneously. Data in a track are arranged in sectors and records.

few or several hundred tracks. The corresponding track on all the disk surfaces is called a cylinder. The disk drive mechanism is equipped with a comb-like read/write head structure. One read/write head is provided for each surface. Thus, if 10 data recording surfaces are provided, 10 read/write heads will also be available, one for each surface. The read/write head positioning mechanism positions all the read/write heads simultaneously to the desired cylinder, which corresponds to the same track on each data recording surface. To address a particular cylinder the disk drive read/write head positioning mechanism drives the head to the desired cylinder. Each track in the selected cylinder is under the corresponding read/write head. All the heads for all the surfaces are moved together across the surfaces to the cylinder into which the data are to be transferred. To select data from a particular surface, the read/write head "riding" over the surface is electronically switched and data from that head are selected. Thus, to transfer data to a particular track involves mechanical and electronic actions. The read/write head assembly is driven to the cylinder of interest, and then the read/write head in the appropriate track is switched on electronically.

Data are recorded serially along the length of a track. The minimum element is a computer word. Check bits are recorded with each word in order to verify the validity of every word transferred. The transferable data group between the disk and the computer is a block or sector. To simplify programming and hardware, sectors of fixed word length are usually specified; therefore each sector contains a specified number of computer words. A sector is the basic addressable element on the disk. To add or delete one word in a sector, the complete sector must be read into the computer memory, where appropriate modifications, additions, deletions, or other changes to the data can be made. The data are then written back into the specified sector. To address a particular sector, the cylinder, track, and sector must be specified.

Some disks use fixed heads, one head per track, whereas others use a movable head assembly whereby one read/write head is provided for each surface. Access to data on devices using a single head per track is much faster than on devices that have one read/write head per surface which has to be mechanically driven to the addressed cylinder. In the devices that have fixed heads with one head per track, so that the number of heads is equal to the number of tracks, access time is dependent only on the rotational delay or latency time of the disk drive. In all cases data cannot be transferred until the sector with the addressed data segment rotates under the read/write head. In the best case the request for data can occur at the moment in time when the data are about to move under the read/write head. In the worst case the data will just have passed under the read/write head and a full rotation of the disk surface will be required before the data are again in transferable position. On the average the delay is equal to one half the disk rotation time (Fig. 14).

The total time required to access a particular datum is the read/write head positioning or seek time plus the latency or rotational delay. The read/write head seek time is a function of the speed of the head positioning mechanism and the number of cylinders that the read/write head has to be moved. The time varies from a minimum of tens of milliseconds for a few tracks to a maximum of 100 to 200 msec. A disk driven at 3000 rpm rotates one complete revolution in 20 msecs. The average access time within a cylinder is 10 msec.

Drums are essentially special cases of disk drives with nonmovable

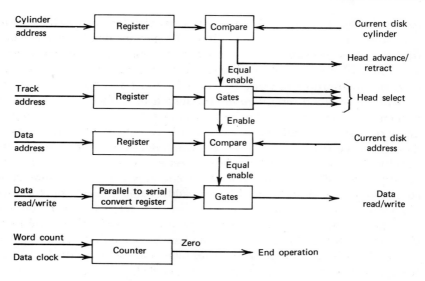

Fig. 14. An interface between the computer and a disk drive. This interface or its equivalent is usually provided, along with the disk drive, by the computer manufacturer.

heads. Drums are cylinders that rotate about the cylinder axis. Heads are positioned along the circumference with one fixed read/write head per track. In functioning as well as addressing, drums perform in the same way as fixed head disks. The only advantage of the drum design is that latency time can be made less than it is for disks because the drum geometry permits higher rotational speeds. In most situations, however, this is not the critical parameter. High-speed drums imply small-diameter cylinders and hence lower storage capacity.

The following factors are used in defining the characteristics of a disk drive:

1. Capacity (bytes or words).
2. Number of cylinders.
3. Number of surfaces.
4. Data packing density.
5. Access time.
6. Latency time.
7. Data transfer.
8. Disk removability.
9. Access methods.

The most commonly used disk drives have removable disk packs and are extremely flexible. This arrangement permits the stored disk data to be removed from the drive and replaced conveniently with another data set. Removable disk packs having capacities of several tens of thousands to a hundred million bytes are available. As would be expected, the lower-capacity units are contained on a single disk (two surfaces), whereas the higher-capacity units consist of multiple disks mounted on a single spindle. Manufacturers have made provision for easy mounting and dismounting. The disk pack case is designed to prevent damage to sensitive disk surfaces by touching or accidental contact.

Disk drive units for removable disk packs have retractable read/write head mechanisms, one head being provided for each surface. The access mechanism positions the head to the program directed cylinder. When power is removed or when the disk pack is to be changed, the read/write head positioning mechanism automatically retracts the read/write head to permit disk pack removal. This feature also prevents the heads from "crashing" into the disk surface when the power is removed. Most modern heads embody an aerodynamic design; the heads effectively "fly" on a thin air cushion at a precisely defined, close clearance above the disk surface. Aberrations and irregularities in the disk surface are followed closely. Automatic head retraction before power off or in the event of a sudden power failure prevents damage to the disk surface through "head crashes."

PRINTERS

Every computer system of any size must have a printer attached to it for outputting information. Printers are used to list programs, give instructions to operators, log data, and print program results, to mention a few of their functions in computer systems. Printers are available in a large range of capabilities with print speeds of thousands of lines per minute or as low as 10 characters per second. Printers may be electromechanical with many moving parts or electrostatic with a minimum of mechanical operations. Some printers can print a full line of 160 characters at one time, whereas others print serially 1 character at a time. Printers for computer output applications may be categorized as follows:

1. Typewriter printers.
2. Character-electronic printers.
3. Line printers.
4. Nonimpact printers.

TYPEWRITER PRINTERS

These are the most common output devices used for computer systems. Almost every small computer is equipped with at least one typewriter-like device for printed output. Most large computers use typewriter-like devices as console printers to give instructions to the computer operations staff and as logging devices for the jobs being run.

Printers classified as typewriter-like devices may be modified office electric typewriters or communications devices. The major differences between an ordinary office typewriter and the computer driven device is that the print mechanism of the latter may be driven by electrical signals that select the characters to be printed; also, nonprinting controls such as carriage return, shifts, and paper feed are electrically controllable. Although the typewriter and communications device have keyboards, these are not connected directly to the print function and depression of a key does not directly actuate the associated print hammer. An electrical signal indicating the code of the particular key depression is sent to the computer (Fig. 15), which may, in turn, under its program control actuate the print hammer. When connected on line to the computer, the keyboard and printer are linked via the computer program. For all intents and purposes the keyboard and print mechanism are separate devices and may even be in different places. As a matter of fact, it is possible to obtain separate independent entities consisting of keyboards and printers. When a keyboard-printer combination exists, as in the case of an electric typewriter or communications device, an off-line link between keyboard and printer is provided. Therefore, when the printer is not connected on line to the computer, it may be used as a conventional typewriter. This mode is usually referred to as "local."

Some printer-keyboard stations are also equipped with punched paper tape facilities. These can print and/or punch paper tape or transmit from either the keyboard or prepunched paper tape. Paper tape facilities were discussed earlier in the chapter. In the off-line or local mode, the keyboard-printer paper tape facility can be used to punch paper tape via keyboard entry. Programs are conveniently prepared in this way without tying up the computer. Program tapes may be read into the computer using the paper tape reader, or they may be reproduced via the punch. This procedure facilitates correcting or updating tapes. Certain portions of the tape are reproduced and the changes are keyed in anew from the keyboard.

A number of firms producing printer-keyboard I/O stations have combined their devices with cassette type magnetic tape recorders. The cas-

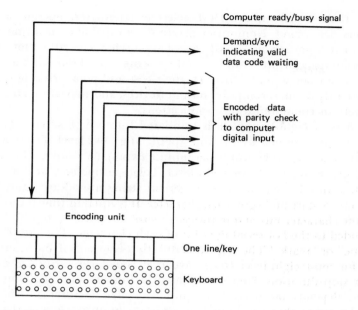

Fig. 15. A block diagram showing the interface between a keyboard-printer and the computer. An encoder is used to convert keyboard key depressions to computer compatible alphanumeric codes.

sette tapes are used instead of paper tape. Data may be keyed in off line with the keyboard and recorded on the magnetic tape; the recorded data may be played back into the computer. Also, computer data may be recorded on the cassette tape for later printing at the stations. These capabilities add to the flexibility of the I/O device. Tapes can be used to store data, source programs, object programs, and files of all types. Access time to any portion of the data can be quite short through the fast forward and rewind controls. Being in the form of cassettes, the tapes can be quickly interchanged without the necessity for rewinding to the beginning.

Depending on the type of keyboard-printer used, a parallel or serial interface between the computer and the printer may exist. In all cases the characters are transferred serially, 1 character at a time. When the character has been printed or the command has been executed, the next character or command is issued. Data are outputted at or below the rate set by the device. Communications devices such as Teletypes operate at 10 characters per second. Electric typewriters used as printer-keyboards, such as those based on the IBM Selectric typewriter, operate at 15.5 characters per second. Nonimpact printers are capable of printing 40 to 400 characters per second, in all cases 1 serial character at a time. Some of the nonimpact printers can even follow a high-speed data link at up to 300 characters per second. However, their cost and poor printing quality do not qualify them as computer output devices, and they are used almost exclusively in communications applications.

Each five- or eight-level code is translated into 5 or 8 serial bits. The data rate is determined by the line speed. Most five-level Teletypes are designed to operate at 60 words per minute (wpm). (A word is assumed to contain five characters.) An eight-level Teletype operates at 100 wpm. To each 5- or 8-bit serialized character bit string are added "start" and "stop" bits. A start bit begins each character. It is equal in time duration to any of the character bits and is always a "zero" or space. A stop bit "zero" is appended to the last serial data bit of each character. The "stop" must be a "one" or "mark." The stop time duration is usually 1 bit interval in length for most eight-level codes; five-level codes ordinarily use a 1.42-bit-long stop duration. Stop durations of 2 bits are also common. The selection depends on what the equipment manufacturer provides. It should be noted that the "stop" may always be made longer than the minimum specification; as a matter of fact, if the line is operating below its rated value the intercharacter time will be the stop or "mark" condition. The "stop" was selected to be the current-on condition to indicate that the line is in use.

As the preceding discussion indicates, eight-level codes become at least 10 bits in length (8 data + 1 start + 1 stop), and five-level codes become 7.42 bits in length (5 data + 1 start + 1.42 stop). Thus 60-wpm five-level code is transmitted at 37 bits per second or 37 baud; 100-wpm eight-level code, at 110 bps or 110 baud (a "baud" is defined as 1 bit per second).

For a computer to transfer data to and from a Teletype printer-keyboard a serializer/deserializer interface must be provided. This is usually part of the computer I/O hardware. Start/stop bits must be added to each character transferred to the printer; the start/stop bits are stripped off in the reverse direction.

A large group of I/O printer-keyboards are based on electric typewriters. These accept data in parallel coded or in fully decoded format, one line for each print character and control line, according to whether the code logic is built into the computer I/O or the electric typewriter I/O interface. Parallel 8-bit character and control codes may be transferred between the computer and the printer-keyboard electric typewriter.

Each key depression actuates a contact associated with the key. Thus, if the keyboard has 44 keys, 44 unique contact closures are provided. In addition, a separate contact indicates whether the carriage is set for upper or lower case. Similarly, print actuators on the typewriter actuate the 44 print keys, and a separate solenoid shifts to upper and lower case.

The 44 unique conditions can be presented over 44 lines to the print mechanism and 44 lines from the keyboard, for instance. Extra lines will be needed for control functions. A second scheme is to code the lines at the computer and do the recoding at the printer-keyboard. Thus 7 parallel lines in each direction could be used to transfer data between the printer-keyboard and the computer. These would carry the appropriately coded characters and control codes. It should be noted that both techniques described here are used on the various commercial devices available.

The most common electric typewriter used for printer-keyboard functions is the IBM Selectric, which is capable of coding and printing 15.5 characters per second. The Selectric mechanism uses 7-bit code. However, this code is not compatible with ordinary communications codes. The code controls the movements of the ball carrying the print characters; the ball is controlled in positive and negative rotation and in upward and downward tilt. The conversion between the communication codes and the typewriter codes is performed by the interface logic. The communications device is not sensitive to or aware of the specialized typewriter coding needed to actuate the typewriter ball.

Another popular computer I/O printer-keyboard is the Flexowriter. This typewriter-like device made by the Friden Company can be equipped with an optional paper tape reader and punch. The Flexowriter accepts electrical signals over parallel data lines. The signals from the data source, the computer, are coded in ASCII format or Flexowriter code, depending on the option ordered. The ASCII code is eight line; Flexowriter, six line.

NONIMPACT PRINTERS

The newest type of device to appear as a character serial printer-keyboard is the nonimpacting printer. Such units accept information at much higher rates than mechanical printer such as Teletypes and typewriters and permit printing rates that can follow high-speed communication lines up to 300 characters per second. The interfacing characteristic for nonimpact printers are similar to those of the mechanical models previously described.

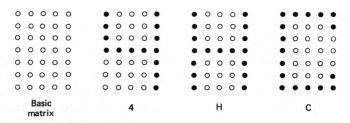

Fig. 16. Matrix printing examples using a 5 × 7 matrix. Higher-quality printers use more dots in forming the matrix.

Nonimpact printers do not use print hammers for letter and ink impressions, as do Teletypes and electric typewriters. The only moving parts in these printers are the paper feed and the print head. As a result, many fewer mechanical parts are needed. Printing is performed using special papers sensitive to electric current flow or heat. Letters and symbols are printed by means of point styli actuated to produce the desired letter. The styli usually consist of 35 points arranged in a 5 × 7 matrix (Fig. 16). Current flows from the selected styli through the paper in a pattern chosen to produce the desired letters. Various types of sensitized paper are used. The electric current affects the paper either by chemical reaction or by burning the sensitized surface layer. Another type of device relies on the use of thermally sensitive paper.

The quality of printing, although quite legible, does not compare to that obtainable with the mechanical printers described previously. The Inktronic printer (next section), however, produces higher-quality text.

INKTRONIC PRINTER

The Inktronic printer prints character by character on ordinary paper with an electronically controlled jet of ink. Print lines contain any desired number of characters, from one to the maximum.

The Inktronic printer operates at 1200 words per minute (120 characters per second) or less. Printing is of the nonimpact type and is quiet. Inktronic equipment is available for use with either five-level or ASCII code. As in other types of nonimpact printers, the only moving parts are the ink-jet character advance and the paper feed. Because of the few moving parts, the need for mechanical maintenance is practically eliminated.

Printing is accomplished by electrostatic deflection of highly charged ink particles fired at the paper from jets. The ink jets trace characters on the page in much the same way that a beam of electrons traces pictures on a TV tube. Characters are sharp and well defined, and each is immediately visible as printed.

LINE PRINTERS

Line printers are capable of high printing rates and produce high-quality results. Line printers that operate at from 100 to 2000 lines per minute are available. These devices are distinguished from character printers in that a full line of data, rather than one character, must be presented to be printed at one time. Line printers are essentially parallel character devices, as compared to the serial nature of typewriters. Line printers are equipped with print hammers for each print position on the line and can be obtained to print 80, 120, 144, or 160 characters per line.

Line printers can be designed as drum (Fig. 17) or as chain printers. Comparable speeds can be obtained with either technique, but chain

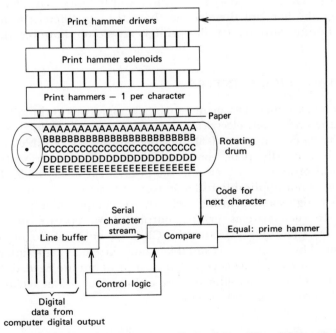

Fig. 17. A block diagram of a drum type line printer. The alphabet is arranged around the circumference of the drum. When a desired character is between the paper and the print hammer, the print hammer for that column is activated.

printers provide the possibility of changing type fonts. Chain printers also produce higher-quality printing than drum printers. Drum printers have type fonts arranged around the circumference of a high-speed rotating drum, on which a complete set of characters is engraved for each print position. The drum signals the printer interface each time a character is ready for printing. The interface logic actuates the print hammers where the upcoming character is to be printed. Once the drum has rotated so that every possible character has passed, the line is completed and the paper is advanced to the next line.

Chain printers use chains that carry the print character sets. The chain is driven across the width of the printed page. A print hammer is provided for each print position on the line, and a signal indicates each time the chain is aligned over a print position. The interface logic must ascertain which character is over each print position and issue print hammer actuation commands to the hammers where printing of the character is desired. Chain printers are designed with continuous chains.

In an alternative design the character set is on an oscillating bar, which carries the character set over the full line width. Since it is relatively easy to change the bar and thereby the character set, different fonts can be provided quite conveniently. Bar printers are slower, however, than chain printers.

NONIMPACT LINE PRINTERS

To provide extremely fast print capability nonimpact techniques, including writing on various electrically sensitized papers, are used. Extremely high print rates of up to 20,000 lines per minute are possible. The print quality is generally poor compared to that obtainable with electromechanical printers, however, and the price is extremely high. This type of printer is not applicable to laboratory automation systems.

Another high-speed printing technique is computer output microfilm (COM). In such systems printer output characters are produced on cathode ray tubes (CRTs), and the CRT screen is photographed onto microfilm. This technique is suitable when extremely large quantities of data are required and many copies of each print-out are needed. Once the computer produces microfilm images, ordinary microfilm techniques are used for reproduction and viewing.

PLOTTERS

A convenient computer output form is the graphic. Graphic data are helpful for visualizing results; they are particularly easy to use and natural for scientists because of their familiarity with graphic representation of results.

Many different plotters may be attached to computers. The most popular is the digital incremental plotter (Fig. 18). Conventional X-Y plotters may also be attached to computers. A pair of digital to analog converters drives the X and Y plotter drives. A new device combining CRT technology and microfilming (COM) techniques is useful for plotting when a large amount of plotting is needed. This device is justified, however, only in large-scale computer sites; its cost and capability are not compatible with most laboratory systems. Rough plot results can be obtained using the computer printer to print graphs with the printer's ordinary character set. The incremental digital plotter is the most common and useful general-purpose plotting device used with computers.

An incremental digital plotter is directly driven by the digital computer. Special sprocketed graph paper (in rolls) is used. Plotters are available for plotting on either 12-in.- or 30-in.-wide paper. The width of the plots on these models is 11 or 29 in., respectively. The length of the plot can be up to the full length of the paper roll.

The incremental digital plotter contains a pen that is driven along a fixed track across the width of the paper. Thus the pen can be positioned, by means of lateral steps, over any desired coordinate across the width of the graph paper. To position the pen along the length of the paper, paper motion rather than pen motion is utilized. The paper, as was men-

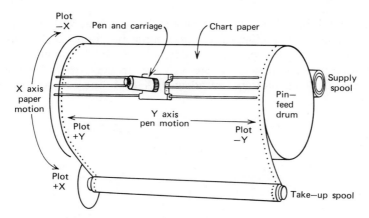

Fig. 18. A schematic diagram showing the operation of a digital incremental plotter. Incremental stepping motors drive the plotter in the X and Y directions. The Y direction drive is via a cable driving the pen across the width of the paper. The X direction drive consists of stepping the drum around which the plotter paper is wrapped.

tioned previously, is wrapped around a drum. Along both edges of the drum's circumference are sprockets that engage sprocket holes in the paper. The drum can be commanded to step clockwise or counterclockwise. The drum's rotary motion causes the paper to be fed from the feed reel to a take-up reel, and vice versa. Any point along the length of the roll of paper can be positioned under the print pen by stepping the drum.

The print pen is positioned across the width of the paper incrementally. The pen drive electronics generates a series of pulses in response to the computer commands, and each pulse steps the head across the paper by one incremental unit (Fig. 19). The unit step is determined by the particular plotter model, with steps of 0.01 in. available. The pulse command must also contain direction information: plus or minus. If the step size is 0.01 in., 120 pulse step commands will be needed to move the print pen 1.20 in. To move from one extremity of the paper to the other (assuming 11 in. width per travel) would entail the issuance of 1100 pulse commands. Various incremental digital recorders operate at from 300 to about 1000 steps per second. The controller or computer program must account for the number of positive and negative step commands issued from the reference or start position in order to keep track of the current position of the print pen.

No limits are imposed on the motion of the paper in the lengthwise direction as long as the length of the reel of paper is not exceeded. The plotter controller issues pulse commands to the drum, which drives the paper in steps in the indicated direction. The step size is the same as for the lateral direction.

Incremental digital plotters receive a series of X and Y step commands from the plotter controller or the computer program. Each command consists of an X-Y pair and a pen order. The X and Y command can be incremental positive or negative steps (X can be negative and Y positive, or vice versa). Some plotters can advance X or Y one or two steps on a

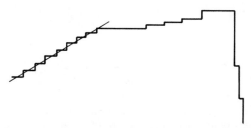

Fig. 19. A typical small section of a plot from an X-Y digital plotter. Note that the lines are made up of small step increments.

single command. In general, for one step at a time, a command can have the following effects (Fig. 20):

X	Y	Pen/Paper
+1	+1	+45°
+1	0	0°
+1	−1	−45°
0	+1	+90°
0	−1	−90°
−1	+1	+135°
−1	0	180°
−1	−1	−135°

The pen command determines whether the pen is up or down. If the pen is up during paper motion, no plotting occurs; if the pen is down, the curve traced by the pen across the paper is plotted. The pen may be commanded down after the paper arrives at the desired location. When the motion is resumed, the pen is raised. This causes a series of dots to be drawn in correspondence to the paper motion.

It should be evident that the function of the computer program is to prepare the series of commands that will trace out the desired curves. Programs are available to print alphanumeric characters, graphs grids, title blocks, and most housekeeping requirements. The quality of computer plots is adequate for inclusion directly in reports for printing. Software is available from the plotter manufacturer or computer manufacturer.

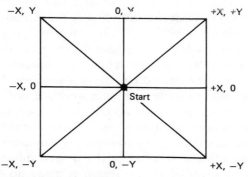

Fig. 20. Various possible motions of the pen. Each command can drive the pen one unit increment. By combining X and Y unit commands, eight directions of pen motion can be effected.

Incremental plotters can plot approximately 300 points per second. To plot a curve on an $8\frac{1}{2} \times 11$ in. size, together with grid lines and a title block, would require several thousand points, even for the simplest graph. Such plots require tens of seconds.

CATHODE RAY TUBE DISPLAYS

Cathode ray tube (CRT) displays are among the most convenient man-machine interactive devices connected to computers. Such displays are useful when information must be received quickly from the computer. Keyboard devices are generally used to enter data. Computer controlled CRT displays are available in a large number of different configurations with widely varying capabilities and over an extremely broad price range.

Cathode ray tube devices can be divided into two categories, those that are purely alphanumeric and those that have graphics capability. Cathode ray tube displays may be designed to have a high refresh rate to produce a flicker-free display, or they may use storage techniques to achieve a steady display. The following topics are covered in this discussion:

1. Cathode ray tube oscilloscopes.
2. Alphanumeric CRT dislays.
3. Graphics CRT displays.
4. Light pens.
5. Scan converters.
6. Storage oscilloscopes.

Any CRT oscilloscope having X and Y deflection amplifiers can be used as a computer output device. The X and Y deflection amplifiers are connected to the computer via DACs. The computer program outputs to the DACs a string of words that represent the sequence of CRT electron beam positions. The DAC output voltages are amplified and deflect the CRT beam to produce the desired pattern on the screen. Since the size of the screen is of no concern to the computer interface, ordinary 5-in. CRT screens or 19-in. CRT display oscilloscopes can be used. Of course, if the resolution is good, more information can be written on the large screen.

In the simplest hardware configurations, the computer must provide the X-Y deflection voltages to produce the desired information pattern. Each character that is traced on the screen is made up of a sufficiently large number of points to produce a legible character; an average character can be produced with 15 to 20 closely spaced dots. To produce a curve or straight line a series of dots representing the desired curve or line must be generated. With this technique any desired character or curve can be written on the CRT screen. A modulation signal to turn on the electron beam is also outputted by the computer when the beam is positioned to the desired screen position. The Z modulation can be a simple on-off signal if all that is needed is to turn the beam full on and off. A DAC can control the beam if gray scale is desired. If a DAC controls the beam intensity, characters of different brightnesses can be generated. By turning the beam on and off periodically, a flashing character can be created. To generate a number of characters and curves or straight lines the computer must output a very large number of points. The number of points increases even further if displays of very high quality are desired.

Most CRT oscilloscopes useful for computer output have screens with phosphors that have relatively short persistence times. To produce a display that is comfortable for viewing, the flicker on the screen must be above the retention level of the eye. It is generally agreed (and has been determined experimentally) that at least 15 to 20 display frames per second must be provided to exceed this threshold. As a practical matter, CRT displays are refreshed about 40 to 60 times per second. It is convenient to synchronize the refresh rate with the power line frequency. These factors contribute to the high output data rate that the computer must sustain in order to maintain a satisfactory display. Most practical displays, therefore, use almost all the available computer memory cycles to maintain a satisfactory display. Early CRT display devices operated in exactly this manner. This simple approach is acceptable if the computer can be dedicated to the task of refreshing and regenerating the display. However, newer technologies permit lower-cost displays by providing character generators and local display memories. When these features are used, the burden on the computer for keeping the display refreshed is drastically reduced.

An alphanumeric CRT display station (Fig. 21) receives data from a computer and displays the information on its integral CRT display. Information is received in character coded form in either EBCDIC or ASCII. The alphanumeric display stations may contain a character generator, a memory unit, a keyboard, and a CRT display. Character information received from the computer is decoded by the character generator, which generates a series of X-Y deflection voltages corresponding to the selected character. These voltages may be a series of dots, line segments, or curvelinear elements, depending on the character generator design. The X-Y deflection voltages, together with Z blanking informa-

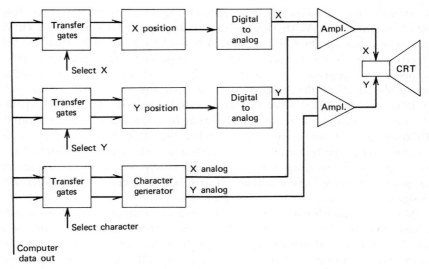

Fig. 21. A block diagram showing an alphanumeric CRT display station.

tion, control the CRT display deflection amplifiers to draw the desired character. By controlling the voltage amplitudes, the character size can be selected. Each coded character received from the computer selects from the character generator the circuitry needed to draw the required character. Character generators in the latest designs are made up of LSI circuitry, thereby greatly reducing the burden on the computer because the character structure is generated in the display station rather than by individual dot or point commands from the computer. However, this scheme still requires that the message be refreshed often to prevent undesirable flicker.

Most display stations have integral character buffers to store the complete message to be displayed. Thus, once the computer transfers a message to the CRT display station, it is stored in the memory there. It is read out about 40 to 60 times per second on a character by character basis to the character generator circuitry.

Until recently, the standard memory device for the CRT display station was a delay line memory. However, advances in LSI technology have enabled designers to use as the memory element LSI/MOS memory devices. Inclusion of LSI character generators and memory devices has permitted drastic reductions in CRT display terminal prices.

The X and Y deflection voltages for the CRT display are generated via two DACs, one connected to the X register and the other to the Y register. The capacity of the X register is equal to the maximum number of characters in a line; Y register capacity, to the number of lines that can be displayed on the CRT face. When entering characters into the display buffer, the X register is incremented by one from each character whenever a line is filled or the carriage return line feed button is actuated.

The CRT display terminal responds like a typewriter or Teletype. The same hardware and software interface may be used for both. The major difference is that the CRT display terminal can handle data at a much higher rate, typically at the maximum rate of the transmission line. The interchangeability between typewriter terminals and CRT displays contributes to the ease of installing the latter devices.

Most CRT display terminals are equipped with keyboards for alphanumeric data entry to the computer. Each time a key is depressed, the corresponding character is displayed on the CRT face and is at the same time also stored in the CRT display terminal memory for continuous refreshing. When a complete message is displayed on the CRT and visually verified by the operator, the end-of-message transmit key is depressed. The message in the memory is then transferred to the computer for further processing.

Cathode ray tube display terminals may be directly connected to the host computer via a hard-wire connection or a telephone data communications network. Operation of the terminal is the same for both types of connection, except that when a direct connection is made the data transfer rate is dependent on the computer channel rate, whereas with a communications connection the data transfer rate is dependent on line condition, modulator-demodulators (modems), and computer communications hardware.

An electronic cursor is usually provided on the CRT display. The cursor points to the position where the next character will be displayed. The fact that the cursor can be positioned anywhere on the CRT screen is particularly useful when making corrections to data displayed on the screen. The operator positions the cursor to point to the character to be changed.

Another technique for interaction between the CRT display operator and the display itself involves the use of a "light pen" (Fig. 22). The light pen responds when it is pointed at a particular location on the CRT screen. When the refresh generator paints the character selected by the light pen, the instantaneous value of the X and Y registers are stored. The information identifies the screen position where the selected character was displayed. Auxiliary function keys on the display terminal serve to indicate what action is to be taken regarding the selected characters.

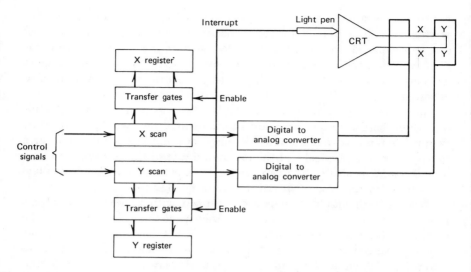

Fig. 22. The light pen, which consists of a photodetector that responds to the light output of the CRT phosphor, is used to point to items of interest on the CRT face. When the light pen detects the CRT light, a signal is issued to the attached computer. The instantaneous CRT beam position is read into the computer, thus identifying the location of the point of interest.

A graphics display terminal is similar to an alphanumeric CRT display terminal except that the former usually has vector generation capability and every point on the screen can be discretely addressed. A vector generator draws straight lines between two coordinate points presented to it. The number of points that may be addressed is usually between 1024 and 2048 in X and Y. A binary power of 2 multiple is usually chosen for data transfer efficiency. The graphics terminal usually contains capability to store the data to be displayed. A refresh rate of 40 to 60 per second is used to provide a flicker-free, steady display. The computer has to address the graphics display station and transfer new information to it only when the program changes the display; at that time transfer of the new picture information takes place. The more expensive graphics terminals have vector generation electronics capable of generating straight lines and curves. The less costly devices rely on addressing individual points to draw the desired graphics.

Alternative schemes for storage of the display information rely on storage screen CRTs. Although these devices do not produce pictures of the same quality as ordinary short-persistence phosphor CRTs, the much lower overall cost of graphics displays using storage screen CRTs makes this approach attractive. Storage screen CRT devices are very useful for computer output devices because character and vector storage, as well as character and vector generation capability, is not required. These functions are implicit in the storage screen CRT itself. The computer program draws the desired picture and characters once. The storage screen CRT device is interfaced to the computer via a pair of digital to analog converters, and instantaneous X and Y coordinate information is entered into the DAC control registers. The DACs are connected to the X and Y deflection amplifiers of the CRT storage display. The program outputs each point on the display to draw the complete picture. If higher-speed operation is mandatory, a character generator and a vector generator are included in the graphics display electronics. A Z input is provided to blank and unblank the beam; while the beam is on, writing takes place. A picture written on a CRT storage device can remain usefully on the screen for several minutes. In many devices of this type it is possible to decrease the beam current so that a picture is displayed but storage does not take place. This facility is used to generate a cursor and to display information temporarily. An erase signal from the computer clears the display completely.

Cathode ray tube storage screen scopes are currently available with useful writing surfaces of up to 9 × 12 in. They are relatively easy to interface to computers via DACs, as described above. They provide the least expensive way to provide graphic capability on a small computer. Much of the program support already available for incremental plotters can be easily adapted, and much faster operation than plotters is achieved. Storage screen graphics place a low burden on the host computer because, once the picture is displayed, the computer connection to the CRT display is suspended.

Scan converters are used to produce large-screen steady state displays from transient information. A scan converter is a dual-purpose I/O CRT-like device with storage capability. An input signal to a scan converter is stored on the storage screen of the device. Entirely independent circuitry is used to read the stored data. Scan converters can serve to convert radar signal PPI format to TV picture video. For information display purposes the computer alphanumeric and graphics data can be outputted slowly and stored on the scan converter storage screen. The picture can be read out as ordinary TV video continuously for a long period, and the video can be distributed and received on any TV receiver. Thus with the aid of a scan converter the computer output can be displayed on an ordinary television set.

12 Input/Output Instructions

The characteristics of a computer's input/output are most important in determining computer suitability for use in a real-time environment. The external device or experiment is connected to the computer via the I/O structure of the machine. The ease of interfacing and the capability of the I/O distinguishes between computer designs. In principal, any computer can be adapted to a real-time environment. The following discussion shows, however, that certain computer features and characteristics can simplify the hardware interface between the computer and the external environment. These features also influence the complexity of the I/O routines needed to carry out data transfers and command sequences.

Computer I/O data and commands may be transferred via the accumulator or the memory data bus; that is, data and commands may be passed to the external device either from the computer accumulator or directly from specified memory locations. Instructions that transfer data by means of the accumulator (Fig. 1) can be executed faster than memory reference instructions. An accumulator I/O instruction does not require a following memory fetch. An input always alters the accumulator contents because the input is entered into the accumulator. A succeeding instruction is needed to store the input word in memory if immediate data manipulation is not feasible or needed. Output accumulator instructions require that the accumulator has previously been loaded with the desired transfer operand. Memory I/O instructions work directly with specified storage locations; data are transferred directly into memory without disturbing the contents of the accumulator. Large volumes or blocks of data can usually be transferred more effectively when transfer to memory is involved. When cost is the overriding consideration, however, and if relatively low-speed or low-volume transfers are required, accumulator directed I/O transfers are most economical in terms of hardware interfacing circuitry.

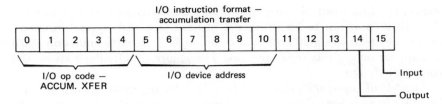

Fig. 1. Input/output instructions that involve accumulator transfer are directly executed.

Input/output data transfer rates may be set either under program control or under the control of the external device. When the data transfer rate is set under program control, transfers occur whenever an I/O instruction is issued by the computer program. This mode of operation assumes that the external device is ready to receive or transmit data whenever the program issues an instruction. Alternatively, the program can halt and test before issuing an I/O instruction and continuously loop until the device responds ready.

Interrupt and data channel techniques are used to handle transfers at rates that are independent of the computer program. Under interrupt and data channel control the data are transferred at the clock rate determined by the external device. These techniques can also provide other efficiencies in operation, as described in further detail elsewhere in this chapter.

COMMANDS AND DATA

The computer program issues control commands and causes the transfer of data to external devices. Insofar as the computer is concerned, commands and data appear the same internally, that is, the two are stored in exactly the same way in memory. Examination of a particular memory location will not indicate whether data or a command is stored. The difference is the interpretation by the external device and the program controlled time of appearance of the words on the I/O bus. Commands are instructions to the connected device to perform certain functions: accept data, rewind, start a motor, and so on. Data, on the other hand, consist of information to be collected or accepted. The external device distinguishes between commands and data by a number of different techniques that may be hardware or software dependent. In some cases the order in which signals appear distinguishes commands from data. For instance, the first word in every group may be designated as a command. The distinction can be implemented in hardware with special auxiliary pulse lines used to signal data and commands. Also, data and commands can appear on entirely separate lines. The choice usually depends on the computer design.

The list of commands that may be issued by the program usually also includes instructions. This class of instruction senses the status or condition of external lines connected to the devices. A control command transfers signals to the device. A reply from the device indicating that it has accepted the command is expected on certain computers. A sense command, on the other hand, always expects a reply from the device. The computer program effectively requests the device to transfer the status of certain flags and indicators to the computer for examination. Through its control and sense facilities, the computer can sense the status of a device and, depending on the results, take necessary programmed actions. Computer programs can, for instance, skip one or more instructions, depending on the sensed status of a device.

Commands and sensing words have different interpretations, depending on the particular device. It is usually convenient, if possible, to assign a separate code to each command and sense condition. However, the code is interpreted by the device to which it was directed.

Just as commands and status words flow bidirectionally between the computer and the external device, data flow is also bidirectional. The computer may output (write) data on a particular device, or it may input (read) data from the device.

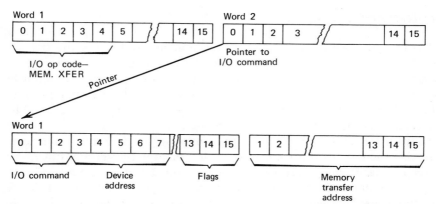

Fig. 2. Typical I/O instruction format, together with command format. Input/output instruction defines address of device that is involved in data transfer. Command table contains commands for data transfer, locations in memory where data are to be transferred, and number of data to be transferred.

INPUT/OUTPUT INSTRUCTIONS

An I/O instruction (Fig. 2) includes an operation code (op code), a command, a device address, and data or command locations. The op code specifies to the computer that an I/O operation will take place. The exact operation is usually not specified by the op code; this is a general class instruction. The exact operation to be performed is specified by the command portion of the I/O instruction. The format of the command is dependent on the computer; it is up to the programmer to format the I/O instruction so as to specify the desired operation. The device address indicates the specific external device attached to the computer to which the command is directed. The last part of the I/O instruction specifies the location to which data or commands are to be fetched or transmitted.

DEVICE ADDRESS

The device address specifies the particular I/O device that has been selected, each device attached to a computer being assigned a unique address. Since the device control unit is wired to recognize its address, a device will respond only to commands bearing its particular address. Some devices, however, may respond to more than one address. This is done in order to assign more functions than can be accommodated if each device has a single address. It is also feasible to assign more than one device to an address. This is usually the case when a number of identical devices are attached to a single control unit. To select a particular device, the address field is usually taken as containing two parts: a control unit address and a subaddress indicating the selected device among the identical units connected to the controller. A device has been selected when the device control unit recognizes its address on the device address signal lines. The device is then able to accept the commands and transfer data, as specified by the computer program.

COMMANDS

Once an I/O device address has been established and the device accepts the address and is selected, commands can be passed to the device and data transferred. The address lines are recognized by the selected device, effectively putting the device into a "listen to command" mode. The selected device (and only that device) accepts the command code outputted along with the device address.

The command can be a coded output word or a sequence of pulses. In the former case, the device must have the necessary hardware to interpret the code. As indicated previously, each device decodes commands in accordance with its particular design. Hence the same command code could be interpreted differently by two different devices.

When commands are passed on to external devices as a sequence of pulses, the program is written so as to output a sequence of pulses when a command is required. Only the addressed device accepts the pulse sequence and interprets it in accordance with its internal circuit design. Again the design of each external device control unit determines how the pulse sequence is interpreted.

OPERANDS

Every I/O instruction must specify the location of the command (sense) and data. Some computer architectures provide specific locations for data and command, whereas others accommodate these in the accumulator and/or various specified memory locations. When single words or small numbers of data are to be transferred, the accumulator can serve effectively as the source/destination of all I/O transfers. In most basic computer configurations data I/O is provided only through the accumulator.

Many computers provide I/O paths from memory to the I/O buses. These computers can transfer information directly from memory locations to the outside buses, an arrangement that has the advantage of not disturbing the contents of the accumulator during I/O transfer. Transfer through the accumulator simples the I/O instruction, however, because the latter does not have to specify the location of the data or command; the accumulator is implied.

PROGRAMMING

Transferring single-word commands or individual data words is relatively simple. A single instruction usually suffices to effect the actual information transfer of command-sense.

The difficulty in programming I/O transfers is normally associated not with the actual data flow but with set-up procedure, housekeeping while the transfer takes place, and ending procedures. These functions usually require considerable programming attention. The program must take into account all possible circumstances and possible error conditions during

I/O. The possibilities of unexpected results are almost unlimited as compared to ordinary program execution. This is evident when one considers that the computer must interact effectively with a relatively unpredictable external device. The restriction is even greater with experiments where the device operation was not specifically designed for computer connection.

STARTING AN INPUT/OUTPUT OPERATION

Starting an I/O operation usually implies a subroutine that will initate information transfer between the external device and the computer. Most standard computer peripherals are handled adequately by the software supplied by the computer manufacturer. However, each special nonstandard device or experiment connected to the computer must be handled separately by the user, whose responsibility it is to prepare the software to test the device attached to the computer and initiate the data transfer operation.

Input/output start instructions set up the device so that it can accept commands, execute them, and then, if commanded, transfer data. The sequence of instructions involves both device status and internal computer logic. The design of the interface between the computer and the experiment must also be taken into account in preparing the program. The general conditions for initiating an I/O start operation are the same for most devices. The following steps are required:

1. Sense status.
2. Initiate (start) device.
3. Sense status/interrupt.
4. Transfer information.
5. Sense status/interrupt.
6. Terminate device.
7. Sense status/interrupt.

The control program must first determine the condition of the selected device. This requires sensing its status and ascertaining whether it is available and in a condition to perform the desired operations. If the device is busy and not available, the program must wait until it is free or perform other functions. If the device is not in a position to execute the operation, the program must initialize it accordingly. If the status is such that the device is available and ready, the program must take appropriate actions. The program should notify the user concerning exceptions.

The initiation procedure itself can be a complicated operation involving a number of sequential or logical steps. One step can follow the preceding one only when the preceding go-ahead conditions are satisfied. While waiting for a particular step to be executed, the program continuously senses, loops, and senses until the desired status is met. It is prudent to provide a time-out interrupt to prevent an endless loop if the device malfunctions and never reaches the required status. The user is then notified that the device is unable to attain the required status.

An alternative technique is to rely on the device itself to signal the computer that it has executed a command. In that situation, the computer does not have to loop while the program waits for the device to complete the command but can proceed to other tasks. After the program has initialized the device and ascertained that the latter is actually in the desired status, the program proceeds in its execution. This procedure runs until the device executes all the conditions specified by the program. A comprehensive procedure is needed to initiate the device the first time it is encountered by the program. On subsequent occasions during the program run, however, an abbreviated initiation sequence will usually suffice.

A sequence similar to the initiation sequence is needed to terminate a device. It is good practice to restore an I/O device to some neutral status after use. The I/O termination subroutines perform this task by means of a sequence of commands, status sensing, or interrupts.

DATA TRANSFER

Data transfer between the computer and an external device may involve a block consisting of one or two words, or a large block made up of many words. It may be required to fill a table of data values in memory or to transfer the data table to the external device.

Single-word transfers require very little program action as compared to large block data transfers. To transfer a single data word, the program issues the appropriate I/O instruction and device address. Depending on the architecture of the computer, the data word may be transferred to the accumulator or a specified memory location. A number of different techniques are used to synchronize the data flow between the computer and the external device. The simplest techniques, which need no synchronization, assume that whenever the computer outputs a word or requests a word from the external device the interface is ready to accept or transmit the information. All that is required is an indication, such as a pulse, that a data transfer is taking place. Some systems do not make use of any indication; the data are simply transferred when the I/O instruction is issued.

In many situations the information is not ready for transfer or is not in an acceptable form when the computer program reaches the I/O instruction. In these situations some form of synchronization, or "handshaking," must be provided between the external device and the computer. One form that may be provided is a ready-proceed signal sequence. The computer program specifies an I/O operation, a device address, and a function: read or write. In the write mode the selected information is placed on the computer output wires, and the CPU enters into a "wait" condition. For a read (input) instruction, the computer immediately enters a wait condition. In both the read and the write mode, the hardware raises a "ready" line that, together with the read/write command, indicates to the external device that the computer is waiting for data, or that data are available on the computer output bus. As soon as the interface accepts the write data, it must signal the computer to this effect. The program can then proceed. In the read mode the interface signals the computer that it has placed valid data on the CPU input bus line. When the computer accepts the data, the program proceeds. The important point is that the program interacts with the I/O data flow and waits until the device can accept or transmit valid data. The external device responds to the acceptance of data from the computer and notifies the latter when it transfers information to the computer.

In order to transfer a number of words, the preceding sequence of instructions must be repeated for each transfer. The program must, of course, perform the necessary bookkeeping to keep track of the information flow. It must continuously calculate the next location in which data will be stored or to which they will be fetched and the number of words that remain in the transfer sequence until completion.

DATA TABLES

In many situations it is necessary to transfer large blocks of data between the computer and the external device. Whether the data flow through the accumulator or directly to memory, a table of data values is formed in memory. Data are transferred between the data source and the computer memory. Data in memory are usually stored in a table of sequential memory locations (Fig. 3). The program must be designed to provide the specified number of sequential memory locations as an I/O data table. As a matter of fact, a number of data tables can be specified in a program. One or more tables can be operated on concurrently or sequentially.

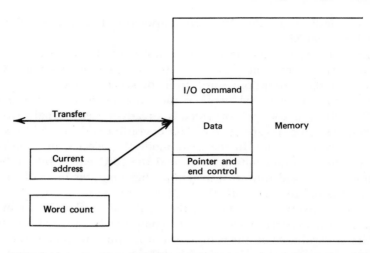

Fig. 3. Data from input (output) is routed directly to location of data table specified by I/O command. When the table is filled (emptied) with the required number of words, the computer program is informed through flags or interrupts.

To understand how a computer transfers data to or from a data table, the program steps needed to carry out a transfer sequence should be examined. The following program steps could be used to transfer a block of N words of data into a particular table in memory:

BEGIN	LD	N	Set-up table length $= N$
	STO	WC	Store $N =$ Word Count (WC)
	LD	ADDR	Starting address of data table
	STO	LOC	Starting location
IO	TIO	DEVICE	Test device if busy
	B	*–1	Loop back if busy
	LD	I LOC	Get address of current location
	SIO		Transfer data to LOC
	TIO		Test for IO complete
	B	*–1	Loop back until complete
	LD	WC	Housekeeping; load word count
	SUB	–1	Subtract one from word count
	BZ	DONE	If word count $=$ zero, then done
	LD	LOC	
	ADD	1	Increment current location by one
	STO	LOC	
	B	IO	Continue
DONE			

The program that carries out and controls the data transfer sequence is composed of several major functions: table set-up, device set-up, transfer, and housekeeping. To set up the table, the program must establish an area in memory for the data transfer to take place. This is done by specifying an address, LOC, that indicates the first location in memory to which data transfer is to take place and the extent of the table WC (word count), that is, the number of words to be transferred. The program then performs various tests to determine readiness and sends control codes and signals to the selected I/O device to ascertain that it is ready to perform the desired I/O operation. The program thereby senses the status of the I/O and issues the necessary set-up commands.

Once the operations described in the preceding paragraphs have been successfully executed, the actual data transfer can commence. It should be noted that the foregoing procedure must be executed for each transfer sequence independently of the number of words transferred. The program issues an SIO (start input output) or equivalent instruction. This instruction performs the actual data transfer. As mentioned previously, the transfer may be directly between an instruction specified memory location and the I/O bus, or from the accumulator to the I/O bus. This is a function of the computer architecture. Before the SIO instruction the accumulator must be loaded with the contents of the memory location (LOC) of the data transfer word. For input, the accumulator is stored in LOC after completion of the SIO.

Some computers are designed with interlocks that prevent the program from proceeding until the computer receives a response from the external device indicating that the I/O instruction has been completed successfully. In other computers the program must test an I/O device flag to ascertain that the I/O command has been fulfilled. To do this, a two-instruction loop can be executed. The program senses the I/O device flag. If the flag is not set, indicating that the device has not yet executed the I/O command, the program branches back one instruction. If the flag is set, the next sequential instruction is accepted and the branch back is not taken. Thus the program loops until the device sets its flag, indicating I/O completion. It is permissible, of course, to assume that each I/O instruction is executed by the external device. In that case the program continues after each I/O instruction without testing for successful execution. This is the usual situation.

Each time a word transfer takes place, the program must perform a number of housekeeping functions in order to keep track of the I/O progress. The first step involves subtracting one from the number stored in location WC. The initial value in WC indicates the total number of words to be transferred into or out of the table. After each SIO instruction, one is subtracted from WC. Thus the value in WC always indicates the number of words remaining to complete filling or emptying the data table. After subtracting one from WC, the value of WC is tested for zero. If it is zero, the table data transfer has been completed and the program branches to DONE, which essentially ends the transfer sequence. If WC is not equal to zero, the housekeeping continues. The value in location LOC, which holds the address of the next word in the table, is increased by one. The program branches back to I/O and continues. The process repeats, and the next sequential word is transferred to the data table in memory. The program loops WC times, until WC = 0.

MULTIPLE BUFFERS

A table area is sometimes referred to as a buffer. It is possible and even desirable in some situations to operate with several buffers. Buffers are not fixed areas in memory, but rather are any convenient areas assigned by the program. Several such areas can be assigned, as needed. One or more areas can be used for inputting data; others are for outputting data. By using interrupt techniques several input and output tables can be handled concurrently (Fig. 4).

A useful technique is a double-buffer scheme; while one buffer is being filled with data, a second buffer that was filled previously is processed. When the second buffer is filled, the data in it are processed. If the processing of data in the first buffer has been completed, the buffer is released and refilled with new data. The same technique can also be used for processing and outputting data.

INPUT/OUTPUT BUS

Most computers provide a single port for information input and a single port for output. This arrangement is sometimes referred to the input/output bus. This group of signal lines consists of data lines, control lines, and timing lines. Signals flow on these lines between the computer and the external devices connected to it. The signals on the timing and control lines are undirectional. The data line signal flow can be either undirectional or bidirectional, depending on the computer design.

The I/O bus is usually specified to have electrical characteristics capable of driving approximately 50 ft of connected cable. In addition, each line can carry about 5 to 10 transistor loads. Each standard computer peripheral and each special-purpose experiment device must be designed

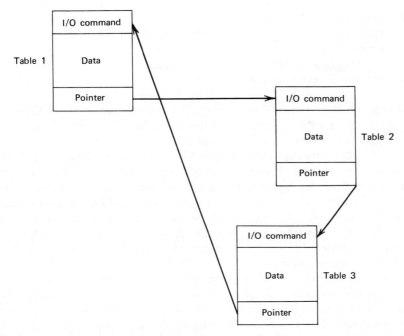

Fig. 4. Data transfer from multiple chained tables. Data are transferred from table 1; when this is completed the transfer from table 2 takes place, followed by a transfer to table 3. Chaining back to table 1 after table 3 is shown. While data are transferred from one table, the computer program can be operating on the data in another table.

to interface to the computer I/O bus; special designs are needed for every computer to be interfaced. The I/O bus cable is usually connected in series to each device to be attached to the computer. The 50-ft cable length and 5 to 10 transistor load limitation is based on the drive characteristics of transistor or I/O drivers. If longer cable lengths or more devices are to be connected, one of the permissible devices is usually specified to be a cable driver. This permits the conection of many more devices.

The following is a list of signal lines that are usually part of an I/O bus. Although the actual number and description vary from computer to computer, these functions must be provided in some manner.

Parallel data input.
Parallel data output.
Device address.

Function code.
Control lines.
Timing pulses.
System condition lines.
System initialization and reset.

When the data channel and external priority interrupt facilities are provided, the I/O bus contains additional lines. They are discussed in connection with these topics mentioned.

The parallel data input and output lines contain one line for each bit. In some cases the same lines are used for input and output; however, the usual situation is for separate input and output lines. The address lines contain the addresses of the external devices specified by the I/O instructions. A unique address is provided for each device attached to the computer, and the function code specifies the command to be executed by the selected device. Each device decodes commands in accordance with its particular characteristics.

Control lines indicate whether data or address/function lines are active. In some cases the same lines are used for data and address/function signals. The control lines indicate how the data lines should be interpreted by the external devices. Timing signals are otuputted on the I/O bus and are used by the external devices for synchronization to the computer. System condition signals, indicating that the computer is on and ready, are sent to all devices. In addition, power-on, initialize, and reset commands are sent out on the I/O bus. These indications are used to initialize and reset the external devices.

CONTROL UNITS

Each external device, whether a standard peripheral or a special instrument, is connected to the computer I/O bus via a control unit, which acts as the interface between the I/O bus and the external device. In some cases one control unit can be connected to several devices. This is usually the situation when a number of identical or similar devices are connected. In other cases a device can have more than one control unit, that is, more than one path to the computer can be established.

Control units connect the I/O bus and the I/O devices. All controls "listen" for their respective addresses to be outputted by the computer. When a control unit recognizes its address, it accepts the information transmitted on the I/O bus. This usually consists of function selections.

The control unit signals the I/O bus that it has accepted the command, and at the same time sets up internal logic paths to the device to execute the command. The device is ready to exchange additional sense and control commands or data with the computer via its control unit.

It should be evident that the control unit plays the dominant role in connecting the external device to the computer. A control unit must be designed to interface between a specific computer I/O bus and a particular device. The number of different control units is large because it is difficult to design general-purpose units.

INPUT/OUTPUT TERMINATION

Every I/O sequence must provide for termination as well as initiation. Initiation was described previously. Termination involves both normal ending procedures and abnormal condition ending procedures. The normal ending procedure assumes that the I/O operation was successfully completed. The program must then restore the I/O device. It may also have to notify the program that the I/O has been successfully completed. When an error condition is detected or some other condition prevents successful I/O execution, the program must also be notified. Various options must be designed into the programs to account for unsuccessful I/O. These procedures can range from ignoring the error indication to suspending the job and shutting the system down. Other techniques can also be implemented. These include provisions to try the I/O a specified number of times and then, if all attempts fail, to shut down and/or notify the operator. As another possibility, an alternative I/O device may be selected. The available procedures are limited only by the ingenuity of the programmer and the system capabilities.

TIMERS

In order to time events and coordinate the computer program with real time (Fig. 5), timers or clocks are designed into the computer hardware. A computer can have one or more timers available to the program. The parameters of interest for a timer are its resolution and capacity. The resolution of a time is determined by it incrementing interval. A pulse train is usually derived from the basic computer clock and/or the power line frequency and is formed from the selected time base. Derivatives of the computer clock can be specified over a much broader range than is

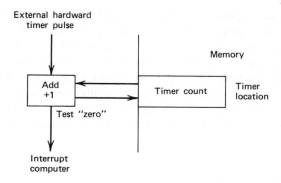

Fig. 5. Operation of timer. Pulse train is actuated by program. Each pulse causes one to be added to a particular memory location. When the number stored in the location reaches zero, a signal indicating that the desired time interval has been timed is issued as an interrupt.

possible with power frequency; resolutions ranging from microseconds to seconds can be specified. The capacity of a timer is equal to the maximum number that the computer word size can present. Timer counts are held in specified memory locations.

The computer program can start each timer selectively. The timers are usually preset to time a desired interval. The program loads a particular timer with a number equal to the complement of the number of time intervals. When the counter overflows, it issues an interrupt, thereby notifying the computer that the desired time interval has elapsed. As an example, if a computer word is 16 bits in length, the timer resolution is 1 msec, and it is desired to time 1 sec, the program will set the number 64,536 into the timer and then start it counting. After accumulating 1000 pulses, the timer will reach 65,536 and overflow. The overflow will interrupt the computer. In this way a 1-sec interval will have been timed.

Timers are usually specified as memory locations. The computer program can always interrogate a specified timer by addressing the appropriate memory location. In this way the program can always determine elapsed time from a particular reference time. To time long intervals, a subroutine is used to accumulate overflows of the high-resolution timers. Once one timer is provided, other time bases can be derived from it through programming. It is convenient to derive a time-of-day clock from the interval timer, so that the program can relate events with respect to their time of occurrence in real clock time.

OPERATIONS MONITOR

An operations monitor (sometimes called a watch-dog timer) is used to alert the system to a program malfunction. The monitor is an external hardware timing device. A time interval of approximately 30 sec may be assigned to this monitor. The computer program must reset the monitor at least once every 30 sec; if the monitor is not reset before it expires, it sounds an alert and also interrupts the computer. The operations monitor ensures that program malfunctions, such as loops, will be detected. This function is particularly useful in a real-time environment.

REAL TIME

With the hardware and software described up to this point, the computer program is limited in the way it can keep track of external events. The programmer must have written instructions that sense the status of external events on a regular basis. Thus, whenever an external event is expected, the program must continuously be searching for its occurrence. If the event of interest does not need quick response service after it occurs, the program may be written to sense for the event on a regular basis. However, if immediate response to an event is necessary, the program must be made to test and loop until the expected event occurs.

In order to control external events, the program must account for time intervals. Knowing time intervals is obviously necessary if several I/O commands must be issued in a precise time controlled sequence. One technique is to count the number of program instructions between I/O commands and to pad the program with a sufficient number of NOP or loop instructions to reach the desired time interval. This procedure assumes that the number of program steps will remain fixed and that the time of execution of each instruction is constant. Since this assumption is not always true, a more practical technique is to refer to the computer timer. The program sets the timer and either waits for it to expire or continuously interrogates it until the required time interval has elapsed.

In the procedures outlined here, it should be apparent that the program can be affected by an external event only if the program itself senses the occurrence of the event. Interrupt facilities must be provided in the computer to furnish a means whereby external events can influence the order of execution of the program. Without an interrupt facility there is no simple way for the external world to affect the program.

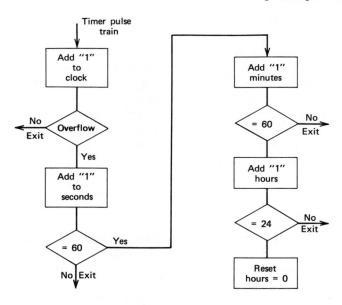

Fig. 6. A time-of-day clock consists of hardware or software that accumulates clock pulses to provide time of day. The hardware or software logic needed to provide time of day to a resolution of 1 msec is shown.

The program must sense the external environment to determine that an event has occurred.

TIME-OF-DAY CLOCKS

To account for time, many computers include time-of-day clocks (Fig. 6) that provide time in hours, minutes, seconds, and fractions of a second. The importance of correlating an event with its time of occurrence is self evident. The problem becomes more acute when collecting data from more than one system. In fact, in some experiments it may be necessary to handle data originating in remote locations and processed by multiple independent computers. The importance of having accurate and identical time-of-day clocks at all sites is critical to the success of the experiment in such an environment. Time-of-day clocks are usually designed as computer options. The current time is sensed by issuing an I/O instruction referencing the time-of-day clock.

Time-of-day clocks can be implemented by hardware as well as software. Hardware time-of-day clocks can be synchronized to radio reference times such as those broadcast by WWV. A hardware time-of-day clock can be separately powered by batteries to ensure accurate time even if a power failure occurs.

13 Interrupts

An experiment or instrument cannot directly affect the operation of the computer program. For the external device to affect the computer operation sequence, the computer program must first interrogate the externally connected device to determine its status. With the computer features discussed previously, there is no way for the external environment to influence computer operation unless the program actively checks the device status or data emanating from the connected device. The program may then execute any number of actions or branches, depending on the interrogated status of the external device. However, regardless of what happens in the external device, no effect on the program sequence can occur unless the program samples the device status. The system should be designed to take into account the likelihood that an external situation at a particular time may induce a program switch.

To respond quickly to the occurrence of an external event of interest, the program must frequently interrogate the indicators for the event. The response time cannot be faster than the frequency with which the program senses for the occurrence of the event. It is quite apparent, therefore, that to provide quick response the program must spend a large proportion of its time in external sensing. This procedure is particularly time consuming if an event occurs very infrequently. A program can thus become extremely inefficient and wasteful of computer resources.

An external interrupt facility (Fig. 1) provides a way to obtain faster response and greater program efficiency. The interrupt facility allows external events of interest to influence the program execution sequence. When an interrupt occurs, the computer program in progress is halted at the current instruction. A branch to the interrupt handling program is automatically forced by the interrupt hardware, with the address of the initial branch fixed by the hardware. Ordinarily, the programmer will have placed the intial interrupt servicing subroutine at the interrupt

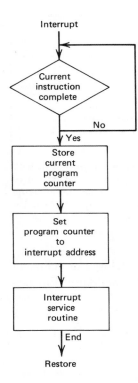

Fig. 1. Interrupt sequence. As soon a current instruction is completed, interrupt servicing begins. Noninterruptable sequential instructions are executed. An automatic branch to a unique location specified by the type of interrupt is taken. The current contents of the instruction counter are stored and replaced by the interrupt branch address. Thus the interrupt servicing begins at the specified location. At the same time the return address to ensure continued processing at the interrupt point is stored. This address is restored in the program counter at the interrupt service routine termination procedure.

branch location. Therefore, as soon as an interrupt occurs, the program sequence control immediately branches to the interrupt servicing program stored at the interrupt branch location. The interrupt initiation logic hardware is usually designed to preserve the current contents of the program counter when the interrupt occurs. This value is usually stored in a particular hardware controlled location. When the interrupt servicing is completed, the interrupt servicing program (Fig. 2) can reset the program counter to the address that it held immediately before the interrupt. Thus the program can resume where it left off when interrupted. Usually machine condition indicators, such as overflow and carry, are also stored and restored.

It is the responsibility of the programmer to store the working registers of the computer before entering the interrupt servicing routine. Before yielding control back to the interrupted program, the interrupt servicing program should restore the stored status of the computer working registers. In that way, when control is restored, the interrupted program be-

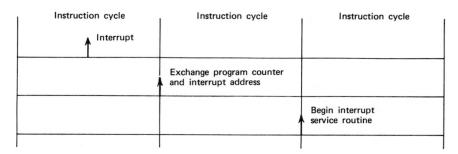

Fig. 2. An interrupt can gain the attention of the computer when the current instruction execution cycle is completed. The current program counter value can be exchanged in a single cycle with the stored interrupt branch starting location. Thus the interrupt service can begin as quickly as one cycle after receipt of an interrupt. In practice, however, this delay is much longer.

gins execution at the instruction immediately following the point of interrupt. Many programming systems provide the interrupt linkages needed to ensure smooth transitions.

RESPONSE TIME

An interrupt signal will gain control of the computer as soon as the instruction in progress when the interrupt occurred is completed. In some computers the interrupt must be received before the final phase of the in-progress instruction. Generally, the longest waiting time for an interrupt signal before recognition by the computer hardware is one instruction time. The start of the interrupt servicing routine is therefore a variable, depending on where in the in-progress instruction cycle the interrupt occurs and the time required to execute the particular instruction. The time for recogntion is no longer than one instruction time, however.

Interrupt signal lines should operate via noise suppression filter circuits wherever possible. The filters prevent spurious noise from triggering the interrupt facility. In such situations, the response time of the computer to the interrupt signal is delayed by the filter delay characteristics.

Most computers are designed to recognize the leading edge of a pulse or DC level shift as the interrupt (Fig. 3). As described above, noise suppression filters are used to the extent that delays in response can be tolerated by the application. In these cases the interrupt occurs after the

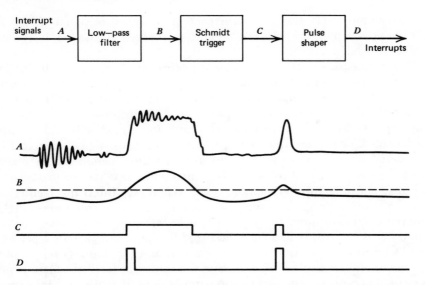

Fig. 3. An interrupt is recognized when a pulse or shift in DC level occurs. To prevent false or spurious interrupts from being triggered due to noise, low-pass filters should be included in the interrupt signal lines. For fastest response the noise suppression filters must be omitted.

signal passes a preset level. It should be stressed that without noise suppression filtering delays the interrupt signal can obtain the attention of the computer as soon as the in-progress instruction is completed.

ENABLED AND PENDING INTERRUPTS

The computer interrupt facility can be actuated and deactuated under program control. Instructions are provided for these functions. Interrupts that occur when the computer interrupt facility is deactuated are ignored. The computer can act on an interrupt only if the interrupt facility is actuated. As a practical matter, the interrupt facility should be deactuated during program load, for example. An interrupt during that time would be intolerable because it would interfere with the program loading and could occur before the subroutines capable of handling the interrupt were loaded. Therefore the interrupt mechanism is disabled until the program ascertains that the computer is prepared to handle interrupts. As another example, it is necessary to deactuate the interrupt facility immediately after the occurrence of an interrupt signal. If this is not done, the program will not be able to proceed if another interrupt occurs immediately.

The interrupt signal sets the interrupt flip-flop (Fig. 4), which can be designed to be settable independently of the status of the interrupt facility. If the interrupt facility is actuated, the interrupt signal is accepted and immediately interrups the program in progress. If the interrupt facility has been deactuated, the interrupt signal will still set the interrupt flip-flop indicator. Thus, when an interrupt signal occurs, it is registered by the interrupt flip-flop and remains "pending." In many cases the status of this flip-flop can be sensed under program control. After sensing, the interrupt flip-flop is reset. When the interrupt facility is actuated under program control, a pending interrupt will immediately interrupt the computer. In many cases it is desirable and necessary to be apprised of interrupts that have occurred during the deactuated period. If this information is of no interest, the interrupt flip-flop register should be sensed and cleared before actuating the interrupt facility. There is no way of determining how many interrupts occurred while the interrupt facility was deactuated except by using an auxiliary counter. If one or more interrupts occurred during the deactuation, the interrupt pending indicator will be set. Sensing will reset the indicator.

As soon as the computer recognizes the interrupt and branches to the interrupt servicing routine, the interrupt facility is automatically deactuated by the computer hardware, and it remains deactuated for at least one instruction interval. In this way the interrupt handling can begin without being reinterrupted if another interrupt signal occurs immediately. The interrupt servicing program usually deactuates the

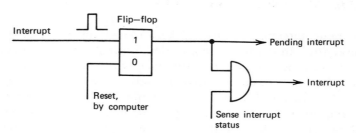

Fig. 4. An interrupt signal sets a flip-flop which signals to the computer the presence of a "pending" or waiting interrupt. The computer recognizes the pending interrupt and begins to service it. As part of the interrupt service the status of the interrupt flip-flop is sensed; at the same time the interrupt flip-flop is set, no further interrupts on the particular input can be sensed. Once the flip-flop is reset, however, the interrupt line is capable of accepting further interrupts.

interrupt facility as its first instruction in order to prevent succeeding interrupts from disturbing the servicing program. Interrupts occurring during this time will remain pending. Before yielding control to the interrupted program, the interrupt servicing program should interrogate for pending interrupts, thereby resetting the interrupt flip-flop register and actuating the interrupt facility.

MULTIPLE INTERRUPTS

In many cases interrupts originate from a number of sources (Fig. 5). A signal from any one of these sources should be able to set the interrupt facility in motion, if it has been actuated by the program. A number of techniques have been developed to handle this situation.

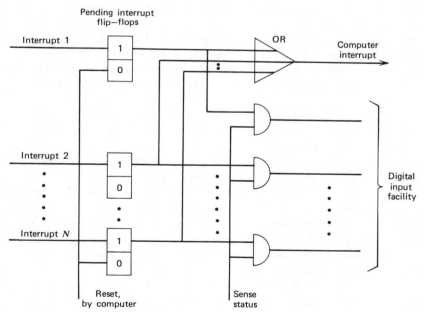

Fig. 5. Multiple interrupts can be sensed by a single interrupt facility when a bank of flip-flops is provided. Each flip-flop is connected to a separate input line. The output of all the flip-flops are ORed together and form a single interrupt input to the computer interrupt facility. Part of the interrupt service routine must sense the ORed flip-flops to determine which of them are set, indicating interrupts on those lines. The flip-flops are connected individually, one flip-flop to one bit, to the computer digital input facility.

The simplest approach is to OR all the interrupting signal sources to the input of the interrupt flip-flop register. As soon as any interrupt source is activated, the interrupt facility is operated. Each interrupt source is directed to a separate flip-flop element in addition to the multiple-input OR. Once the interrupt is recognized and the interrupt servicing program begins execution, the particular interrupt source among all the possible interrupt inputs must be identified. Any one of the interrupts connected to the OR circuit can initiate the interrupt facility. Another function must be added to the interrupt servicing program when handling multiple interrupts ORed together. The interrupt servicing program must sequentially sense the status of each interrupt flip-flop and thus determine the interrupting signal source. Since more than one source can activate the interrupt facility simultaneously, the program must search through each interrupt flip-flop to determine which sources caused the interrupt. Before exiting, the interrupt servicing routine should sense the status of the interrupt flip-flop register. This is the same operation even when a single interrupt source is connected. The processing time for multiple interrupts ORed to a single interrupt point is greater because every possible interrupt must be evaluated each time an interrupt occurs. The delay in determining which interrupt source activated the facility may be unacceptable in some situations. To overcome this deficiency a multiple-interrupt facility can be designed into a computer.

A multiple-interrupt facility permits each interrupt to cause the computer to branch to a unique address. The selected branch is determined by the particular interrupt activated, and a unique address is associated with each interrupt. Each interrupt point is connected directly to the computer via a separate interrupt terminal. An interrupt on any actuated interrupt line suspends the program in progress and causes the hardware to branch to the particular memory location associated with the interrupt. Thus, if 12 interrupts are provided, 12 sets of memory locations are set aside, 1 set for each allowable interrupt. A separate branch is thereby provided for each possible interrupt signal. When a particular interrupt occurs, the flip-flop register indicator is set and a branch is taken to the memory location. As described previously, for every interrupt the current program counter address is stored, together with other vital computer indicators. The interrupt servicing program should store the working registers and deactuate the other interrupt lines. Before restoration of control to the interrupted program, the working registers should be restored and the interrupts actuated.

Each interrupt line can be separately actuated and deactuated. An interrupt that occurs when its flip-flop is program deactuated will remain pending. It can be sensed and reset while deactuated. If the interrupt is pending and then is actuated by the program, the interrupt will be sensed immediately after actuation.

It should be noted that either multiple-interrupt scheme described can be increased in regard to the number of interrupts that can be handled. The number of ORed interrupt groups or multiple individual interrupts can be greatly increased. In the first scheme the program must first sense an interrupt register to determine which of the many possible interrupts caused the one in question. Once the set bit (or bits) is recognized, an additional word (or words) corresponding to the set bit is sensed by the program. In the second scheme a particular external interrupt line is associated with each interrupt. Each interrupt causes a program branch to a unique location associated only with that interrupt.

PRIORITY INTERRUPTS

The interrupt schemes that have been discussed are arranged so that the first interrupt that occurs gains control of the computer. If the interrupt servicing program deactuates the interrupt facility, no other interrupt can be serviced until the present interrupt service program is completed and issues a reactuation to the interrupt facility. While the interrupt facility is actuated, interrupts will be serviced as soon as they occur. If the interrupt facility is actuated while an interrupt is being serviced, subsequent interrupts will be honored, the in-process interrupt servicing program will be interrupted, and chaos will result. If two interrupts occur simultaneously, an indeterminate condition will occur; both will contend for CPU attention. Obviously, in a system that permits more than one interrupt a priority scheme (Fig. 6) is needed to prevent chaos. Hardware and software priority schemes can be used for this purpose.

Hardware interrupt priority levels are assigned at the time the computer is manufactured or installed. When several interrupts occur simultaneously, the priority interrupt hardware recognizes the highest-priority interrupt and begins servicing it; lower-priority interrupts remain pending. When the high-level interrupt service is completed, the pending interrupt of next highest priority is honored. In this way the priority interrupt hardware orders the interrupts and honors them according to their priorities. The highest-level interrupt receives the attention of the CPU. If the system is in the midst of servicing a particular interrupt and a higher-level actuated interrupt occurs, the attention of the system will be immediately directed to the higher-level interrupt. If a lower-level interrupt or a higher-level deactuated interrupt occurs while a particular interrupt is being serviced the system continues servicing the in-process interrupt. However, if a higher-level actuated interrupt occurs while a lower-level interrupt routine is in progress, the attention of the system will be directed to the higher-priority interrupt. Lower-priority interrupts, however, will always remain pending whether actuated or not, if an interrupt of superior level is being serviced.

In summary, the highest-level actuated interrupt always receives CPU attention in a priority interrupt system. High-priority interrupts are recognized and received in preference to lower-priority in-process interrupts. This assures that interrupts designated as important can always be serviced rapidly ahead of all lower-priority interrupts independently of computer status. It should be noted that under program control an interrupt servicing program can selectively actuate or deactuate other priority interrupt levels.

Priority interrupt levels can be assigned numbers, the higher levels being designated by lower numbers. Thus, for instance, interrupt priority level 5 would have a higher priority than interrupt level 8, and interrupt level 1 or 0 would have the highest priority. A simultaneous interrupt

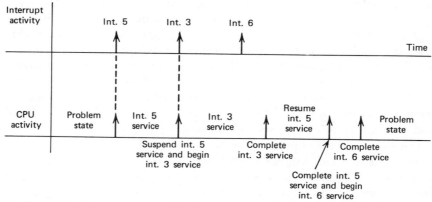

Fig. 6. Priority interrupt provides that, when several interrupts occur simultaneously, the order in which they are serviced is determined in a prescribed manner based on the priority assigned to each interrupt. When a high-priority interrupt occurs while a lower-priority one is being serviced, the latter is suspended. After the higher-priority interrupt servicing is completed, control is returned to lower-priority interrupt. Above is shown a nested interrupt sequence where lower-priority interrupt servicing sequences are interrupted by higher-priority interrupts.

on levels 5 and 8 would automatically give control to interrupt priority level 5. This, of course, assumes that both levels are actuated; if interrupt level 5 were disabled, level 8 would be selected. The interrupt on level 5 would remain pending until cleared by the program. If level 5 were actuated before clearing, however, the pending interrupt would be serviced. If a status word is associated with the interrupt level called, the interrupt servicing program must sense the status word and determine which source (or sources) set the interrupt. The program will then branch appropriately.

If an interrupt occurs on a higher priority level, say level 2, while the servicing program for level 5 is being executed, and interrupt priority level 2 is actuated, an interrupt on level 2 will occur. The regular scheme for handling interrupts is executed by the priority interrupt hardware. The program counter address is stored, and the interrupt entry address is fetched in the locations assigned to the particular interrupt priority level. When the interrupt service program for priority level 2 is completed, the return address is restored and control given to the interrupted program on level 5. It should be reiterated that, while a higher-priority interrupt level is being serviced, all lower-priority interrupts and other interrupts on the same level are deactuated. All actuated higher-priority interrupts, however, can interrupt when they occur. This effectively permits nesting of interrupts.

A software priority interrupt scheme relies on the program to selectively actuate and deactuate the various priority levels. This permits dynamic allocation of priority levels. The program or any subroutine being executed on any priority level may actuate or deactuate all priority levels or any specific one. In this way each program can set up the priority level to suit during execution.

INTERNAL INTERRUPTS

Interrupts can originate from a number of sources. Of prime interest to system designers are external interrupts. These may occur through sensing of voltage level shifts, contact closures, or pulse indications. Control through contact closures implies relay or manual switch actuations. Voltage level shifts and pulses can be either logic or electromechanical in nature. In passing it should be noted that an easy way to create an interrupt and gain the attention of the computer is via an external push button.

Interrupts may also be generated internally to the computer. This class of interrupts may be defined by program actions, peripheral device actions, and equipment malfunctions. Some computers provide the capability for program initiated interrupts. When an interrupt on a high priority level occurs, only initial recognition and servicing are done on that level. The interrupt servicing program calls a lower-priority interrupt level and then terminates the high-priority subroutine. Only preliminary and essential servicing is executed under the high-level interrupt control; subsequent processing is done at a lower-priority interrupt level. In this way intermediate interrupt levels can be serviced before the less essential portions of the first interrupt service are completed.

When a peripheral device completes an assigned task, it may issue an interrupt. The program recognizes that the source of the interrupt was a particular peripheral device and takes appropriate action. Interrupt facilities considerably simplify I/O device programming and also make the computer run more efficiently. The computer program does not have to concern itself with the I/O device until an interrupt is received indicating that the command has been executed or the data transfer has taken place.

A major use of interrupts is to indicate equipment malfunction or possible failure. For instance, when a command to an I/O device is not accepted for some reason, an interrupt may serve to indicate the failure to the computer. When a limit or stop condition is reached, the interrupt can alert the program. Dangerous or potentially damaging situations can be utilized to alarm the computer.

Machine malfunction interrupts are usually assigned to the highest interrupt level. These may be computer failures or external factors, and it is obvious that an equipment failure should be reported to the computer immediately. Parity error detection is an example of a computer malfunction condition. Machine error indicating interrupts cannot be deactuated by the program.

POWER FAILURE INTERRUPTS

Many computers have built-in circuits that sense the AC power mains and the DC power supply voltages. Sensing out-of-tolerance conditions of the AC power network is done within a fraction of a cycle. In all cases the sensing circuits must sense out-of-tolerance AC within a short time interval compared to the DC filter time constants (Fig. 7). The imminent power failure is reported as an interrupt on the highest-priority level. The power failure sensing also initiates an orderly shutdown of the

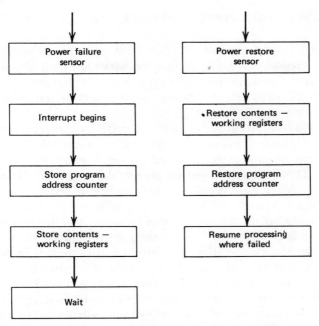

Fig. 7. A power failure interrupt occurs when the power sensing circuits sense that the AC power mains are beginning to fail. Sufficient energy is stored in the computer power supply capacitors to assure several milliseconds of operation between the power loss sensing and the actual stoppage due to power loss. Receipt of the power failure interrupt calls an interrupt servicing sequence, which stores the status of the computer active registers. When power is restored, an automatic restart can be initiated, the contents of the registers can be restored, and processing can commence from where it was interrupted.

system power supplies to ensure that the stored memory information is not lost or altered because of shutdown transients that could occur if the power suddenly failed. A few milliseconds are usually available between the time an imminent power failure (or out-of-tolerance condition) is sensed and shutdown initiation. An interrupt servicing program has sufficient time available (until shutdown of the power supplies begins) to store the contents of the working registers, including the program counters. When the power comes on again, the system can restore the working registers and address circuits and continue where it left off when the power failure was sensed. This feature is especially useful when frequent power failures are anticipated and quick, unattended work resumption is essential.

UNINTERRUPTABLE POWER SUPPLIES

If computer shutdown due to power failure cannot be tolerated, back-up power procedures must be considered, although such alternatives can be quite expensive. Back-up power supplies can be battery powered solid state electronic inverters or rotating motor-generator sets with flywheels and deisel cut-ins.

The all-solid-state approach consists of batteries and an inverter power supply. In addition, transformers and rectifiers are needed to charge the batteries and to power the inverter during normal AC power mains operation. The inverter AC output powers the computer. When the AC power fails, the battery provides power to the inverter. The time the system will run depends on the battery capacity; several hours of back-up can be provided if the budget is large enough. Another factor that can increase the back-up power source costs is a requirement to start the computer on battery operation. A computer will typically require a very large inrush current when turned on. Since the inrush time period is long enough to damage inverter semiconductors, an inverter having several times the rating of the steady state current must be specified.

Another approach is to use a motor mechanically linked to a generator; power for the computer is then derived from the generator. A large flywheel is coupled to the M-G common shaft. The inertia of the flywheel will keep the M-G shaft up to speed for several seconds after power to the motor is removed. For longer periods a diesel can be coupled to the M-G shaft. The flywheel inertia is sufficient to keep the shaft and generator at speed until the diesel can cut in to take over the load.

14 Data Channels

Data channels increase input/output data transfer efficiency on a computer system. In effect, a data channel relieves the central processor from issuing repetitive I/O transfer instructions. By handling these tasks, the data channel allows the central processor to proceed with the main program and initiate data transfers to other external devices.

Data channel capability is available as an option on almost every computer except perhaps the least expensive models. Each manufacturer gives the data channel function its own nomenclature. The following designations are common:

Data channel.
Data break channel.
Direct memory access channel.
Selector channel.
Multiplexer channel.

Data channels are combinations of hardware and software. The techniques for implementing data channels strive to provide a means for moving data into and out of a computer memory at high speed. A data channel may be viewed as essentially a special-purpose processor that supervises data transfer between the computer main memory and peripherals. A separate data channel (Fig. 1) can be provided for each data transfer path. A number of data channels can be implemented on a single computer, each channel controlling an independent data transfer path. In effect, the computer can operate a number of high-speed independent I/O data transfer operations concurrently. Data channels, although effectively special-purpose processors, are initiated by the computer program and are under its control. The computer program must initiate a data

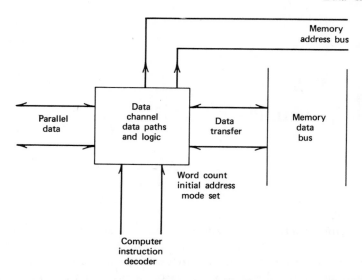

Fig. 1. A data channel is in effect a special-purpose processor that deals with I/O data transfers. A data channel relieves the computer of the task of supervising each data transfer; the data channel handles all of the details required to effect an orderly transfer of information. The data channel begins its operation under computer program control and then proceeds on its own until the required transfer has been completed. It then notifies the CPU.

channel operation. The data channel then performs its data transfer functions and control sequences without need for further intervention by the initiating program. When a data channel completes its instructed operations, it signals the main computer program that initiated it. It is important to realize that a data channel proceeds in its data transfer tasks without disturbing the CPU; thus the latter can continue operating while simultaneous I/O operations proceed. Data channels can be implemented in hardware, software, or a combination of both. Obviously, higher-speed operations can be supported by an all-hardware implementation, but this is usually a more expensive technique.

The program steps required to transfer a block of data into or out of the computer were described in Chapter 12, where it was shown that a relatively large number of instructions are needed to transfer each word. In addition, the same instruction sequence must be repeated for each word transferred. During all the time that a data table is being transferred, the computer is busy servicing the I/O. The work actually performed by the computer during the transfer is highly repetitive and relatively unproductive because the computer is waiting or looping most of the time. A more effective use of the central processor while repetitive I/O data transfer operations take place is highly desirable and is achieved through data channel operations.

INTERRUPT DATA TRANSFER

Two methods are extensively used to effect efficient data transfers. One utilizes the computer interrupt facilities; the second, data channels. The interrupt technique was discussed in detail in Chapter 13, where it was shown that, when the I/O device is ready to transfer a word, it issues an interrupt. The computer suspends execution of the in-progress program at the completion of the current instruction and begins execution of the I/O transfer interrupt subprogram. A sequence of instructions needed to transfer the data word and to update the word count and current address is executed. Upon completion of the interrupt service routines, control is returned to the interrupted in-progress program. In-

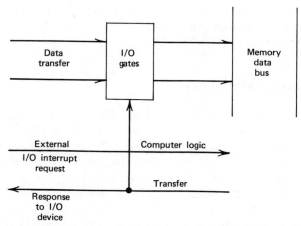

Fig. 2. Data transfer under external interrupt control is effective for transferring small blocks at relatively low rates. Each external interrupt signifies to the computer that a data word is ready for transfer to the computer in input mode or that the external device has accepted the preceding word and is ready for the next output word. The computer I/O program performs all the housekeeping functions needed to keep track of the current address of the word being transferred and the number of words yet to be transferred in the current record.

terference with concurrent computer usage occurs only when an interrupt from the external device signals the computer that data are ready for transfer. No waiting for the peripheral devices to be ready to accept data is required. Also, a number of devices can be connected to the computer. Each device signals the computer via its own unique interrupt line when it is ready to accept data (Fig. 2). The computer can identify the source of the particular interrupt and then execute the necessary I/O data transfer to the requesting device. Housekeeping consists of updating the word count and current address pointer. The I/O operation, like any other such operation, must be initiated by the computer program. The I/O device must be actuated and tested. The data store areas (tables) and the data transfer program must also be initiated by the program. Each data transfer serves to decrement the word count until the latter reaches zero. The interrupt service program must continuously sense for a zero word count, and when it reaches that condition it must branch to a device termination routine.

Interrupt signaled I/O data transfers are very useful when transferring at relatively slow data rates. A practical upper limit where time is left for processing when interrupt controlled I/O transfers occur is about 1000 transfers per second. The actual value is dependent on the number of instructions that must be executed for each transfer. The response time between receipt of the interrupt and actual transfer can be quite short, and a number of housekeeping functions must be performed after each data transfer to keep track of it.

DATA CHANNEL REGISTERS

Regardless of how it is implemented, the data channel (Fig. 3) may be viewed as a special-purpose processor whose function is to supervise the transfer of a specified block of data from the computer memory to an external peripheral or vice versa. The data channel is initiated by the computer program but, once started, proceeds independently of it until the specified transfer has been completed successfully or the data channel encounters an abnormal situation. The data channel is usually designed to signify its termination via an interrupt to the program or by setting a data-channel-complete flag. The program senses the flag to ascertain the data channel status.

A data channel consists of three functional registers:

1. Word count register.
2. Current address register.
3. Command register.

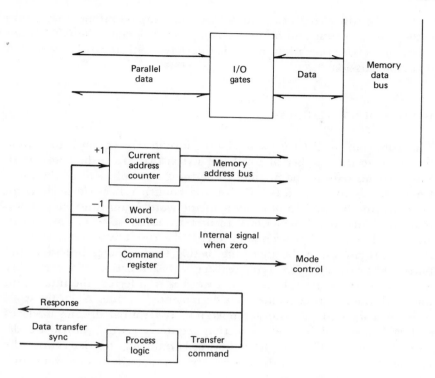

Fig. 3. A block diagram of a basic data channel implemented in hardware. The data channel hardware consists of three main control registers: (1) word count register, (2) current address register, and (3) command register. After each data transfer, the count in the word counter is decremented by one and the count in the current address register is incremented by one. Thus the word count register contains the number of words that remain to be transferred; the content of the current address register is a pointer to the next location in the computer memory for the data transfer operation to interact. The command register holds data concerning the direction of data transfer, ending codes, chaining information, and so on.

The word count, current address, and command registers are initially loaded through the computer program via an appropriate I/O instruction. Once these registers are loaded by the computer program, the data transfer sequence proceeds under channel control. The channel modifies the status of these control registers in accordance with the data flow. Each data word transferred passes through a buffer data register on its way between the external device and memory. The direction of data transfer and other control parameters are specified by the command word register contents.

Once the three registers are loaded, the input/output commences without further intervention by the computer program. The CPU is not aware of the I/O operation, nor is it interfered with until the operation is completed.

WORD COUNT REGISTER

The word count register is loaded by the initiating program with a number equal to the number of words (or bytes) that are to be transferred. Some systems require the number to be the 2's complement of the number of words to be transferred, because counting is performed in an incrementing fashion. In other systems the word count must be one less than the actual number of words to be transferred, so as to assure that, after the last word has been transferred, the count is at zero. What is relevant, regardless of the algorithm, is that the computer program computes and loads the word count register with a function of the number words to be transferred. Each time a word is transferred, the number in the word count register is effectively decremented by one. When the word count reaches zero, the transfer operation is terminated. The mode of ending is specified by the instruction register contents, which are described in detail. The length of the word count register determines the maximum number of words that can be transferred by one command.

CURRENT ADDRESS REGISTRY

The current address register is loaded with the address of the first word in the data table. The contents of this location consist of a computer word that may contain either data or instructions. In order to account for a first instruction word, the initial word count is sometimes greater by one than the actual number of data words to be transferred. In some cases the first word of the table referred to by the current address register is a command. The data channel interprets the word to be the command word and automatically loads the first word into the command register. The contents of the current address register always point to the next location in memory to which data reference is to be made. Each time a word is transferred the contents of the current address register are incremented by one. In this way, the current address is continuously updated. The capacity of this register must allow addressing all memory.

In some computers the word count register is loaded not with the number of words to be transferred, but with the upper address of the table of data words to be transferred. In that case, the contents of the updated current address register are continuously compared with the contents of the limit address. Each time a data word is transferred, the current address register is incremented, as described previously. When the current address and upper limit address are equal, indicating that the requisite data have been transferred, the data channel transfer operation is terminated.

COMMAND REGISTER

The command register (Fig. 4) is loaded by the program with information concerning the direction of the data transfer operation, data rate control specifications, and continuation and termination instructions. The command register specifies whether the data transfer is to take place from memory to the external device or from the external device to memory. In addition, the channel is responsive to clear and reset commands, which are necessary to reset the channel because of error conditions or improper termination. Most channel designs indicate a "busy" status unless the

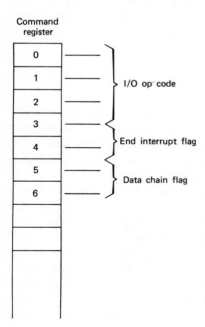

Fig. 4. The construction of the command register contents. Each bit or group of bits represents different instructions to the data channel. The first three bits in this example specify the I/O operation, such as input, output, or test. The successive bits specify termination instructions to be executed by the data channel when the operation is completed, that is, the word count decrements to zero. A flag indicates a program interruption when the data channel reaches its end condition. The flags signify data chaining or command chaining.

word count register is at zero. A "busy" data channel will not accept new commands. Thus a command must be provided to force the data channel to a "ready" status if it does not naturally deinitialize itself.

The command register may indicate whether the data are to be transmitted at a rate determined by the computer or at a rate set by the connected data device. Usually, one bit in the command word is assigned to indicate "external synchronization." When the external device is ready to effect a data word transfer, it raises its demand, or sync, line. The signal initiates the transfer sequence for one data word. Only when the computer is "ready" can a demand or sync signal be accepted. The computer usually responds to the demand or sync signal by indicating that the request is honored. While the computer is in the process of honoring the request, the data channel signals that it is "busy" and unable to honor additional requests. When the data channel operates at the rate determined by the computer, it will transfer data much faster; the rate can be equal to the computer memory cycle speed. Many computers have built-in interlocks that prevent a data channel from taking all available memory cycles. Usually, in these schemes alternate memory cycles are available to the data channels, while the other available cycles are allocated to other computer functions. When operating at the computer specified data transfer rate, it must be ascertained that the external device is capable of handling this rate and of accepting or delivering data whenever they appear on the data transfer bus.

DATA CHANNEL TERMINATION

Several ways of terminating data channels are possible, and many of these techniques have been implemented on various computers. In one method, when the decrementing word count register reaches zero, a flag indicating this condition is set. The computer program must interrogate this flag to determine the status of the data channel. This is the simplest operation and is quite satisfactory as long as the data channel termintes before the concurrent computer program reaches a point where the end of the data channel becomes significant. Flag sensing is also adequate if the program can loop and test the flag until the channel terminates. This approach would be wasteful, however, if the computer could be doing useful work instead of waiting for the channel to terminate. The command word structure is sometimes designed to provide an interrupt option when the data channel terminates. In this way the computer can provide service to the data channel upon termination with the least possible delay. While waiting for the data-channel-end interrupt, the computer can do concurrent processing.

Some form of time-out interrupt should be provided with every data channel operation. A timer should be set to expire after the longest expected data channel operation. Then, if the data channel malfunctions or takes longer than anticipated to complete a particular operation, a timer interrupt will initiate a data channel remedial routine.

DATA CHAINING

Data channels having chaining capability are (Fig. 5) common in more sophisticated systems. Data chaining and command chaining are used. Most large computers have these facilities; they are sometimes found also in

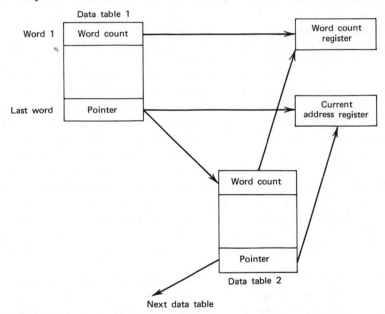

Fig. 5. When the termination flag in the command register word indicates that data chaining is to take place, the contents of the last word in the current buffer are used as a pointer to the beginning of a new data table. The contents of the current address register are replaced with this word. Thus the next data word is accessed from this location. The first word in the new data table is extracted and loaded into the word count register. Data tables are chained together; after the data for one table is completely transferred, automatic chaining to a successive table occurs without central processor intervention. Several successive data tables may be chained. The chain may close on itself.

small computers. Chaining options are indicated in the structure of the command word to the data channel. Bits in the command word denote the various chaining conditions. Data chaining directs the data channel to a new I/O area in memory after data for a particular area, as indicated by a zero word count, have been transferred. The contents of the current address location when the word count is zero constitute the address of the start of the next table. Thus, when data chaining is indicated, the word stored in the last address of the data table is interpreted as the starting address of the next data table. The contents of the last word of the current data table are transferred by the data channel logic to the current address register, which is thereby reinitialized for the next data transfer block.

The data word of the first location in the location pointed to by the address word of the current address register is entered into the word count register. This is taken to be the number of words to be transferred to the table. Hence the contents of the last word of the preceding table are taken as the address of the first word of the next table, and this address is entered into the current address register. Thus the last word of the preceding table and the first word of the present table furnish the contents for the current address register and word count register.

The command register contents are maintained as originally received. The chaining bit may, however, be taken among the high-order bits in the word counter. A bit is sometimes reserved as the chaining control bit. Thus each chained table determines whether chaining is to continue. In this way data chaining can be specified to continue over any number of tables, and any table can specify chaining back to a preceding table—even itself. Thus, once the data channel has been initiated, continuous input/output without further I/O program instructions can be initiated. After each table has been transferred, the program is notified by the end-of-table flag. The flag can be used as an indication to be sensed by the program or as a program interrupt.

When chaining is specified, it is usually necessary to use the data channel end signals as a program interrupt. Thus the program is notified as soon as a table transfer has been completed. In this way, the program that loads or unloads the table and processes the necessary data can be in synchronism with the I/O data transfer.

A common technique is to data-chain three tables continuously. One table is used as an input area, the second as the in-process area, and the third as the output area. As soon as interrupts are received indicating that input and output are completed, the table buffer areas are changed. The first table becomes the in-process area, the third buffer can be used for new inputs, and the second area, which previously was the in-process area, is now the output area. Synchronization of current input, output, and in-process areas is maintained by the program through interrupts.

COMMAND CHAINING

Command chaining is similar to data chaining, except that the latter restricts the operation to be performed in each chained table to the same operation. All operations in a sequence of data chained transfers are the same. Command chaining also transmits a new command word to the command register in the data channel, which must be considerably more complicated to handle this additional flexibility.

DATA CHANNEL PRIORITIES

A data channel is given access to the computer memory as soon as the in-progress memory cycle is completed. Data channels receive the highest priorities in a computer system, because I/O is highly time dependent. Delays in responding to external data demands can result in erroneous data transfer and overruns. An overrun occurs when the data input cannot be accepted by the computer. This condition arises when a word has to be transferred before the preceding word has been handled. An overrun condition can be created even if the basic data transfer rate of the computer greatly exceeds the data channel required transfer rate.

Data channels and CPU vie for memory access cycles. When both request the same cycle, the cycle is allocated to the data channel. If more than one data channel is attached to a computer, priorities are assigned to the data channels. When more than one channel requests the same memory cycle, the computer logic circuits allocate the memory cycle to the highest-priority requesting channel. High-speed synchronous peripheral devices should be assigned to the highest-priority channels. It should be noted that high activity on the data channels will prevent the CPU from receiving its share of memory cycles.

IMPLEMENTATION VIA MEMORY

Data channel registers may be implemented in hardware or in memory. Hardware register implementation is inherently faster because active elements perform the functions of word count register and command register storage, as well as the necessary decrementing and/or increment- ing functions. By being hardware, all the register data are fully accessible and available at all times. The only computer time required is the single memory cycle needed to transfer the data word to memory. The maxi- mum delay between data demand and actual start of data transfer can be as short as the time needed to complete the current memory cycle.

Many computers have their data channel registers implemented in storage. The word count registers and current address registers are held in memory locations. The effective contents of the command register must be held in an active register. When data transfer permission is given to the requesting channel, at least three memory cycles (Fig. 6) are allocated to the data channel. The first memory cycle accesses the in- memory word count register. Depending on the computer construction, the word count can be accessed during the first half of the memory cycle and restored during the second half. This is the fastest way to implement these registers in storage. The computer memory access circuit decrements the retrieved data word by one. The new value of the word count is tested for zero value, or zero remaining word count, before restoration. The second memory cycle performs similar functions on the stored cur- rent address word, which is accessed during the first half of the second memory cycle and restored during the second half. Before restoration, the

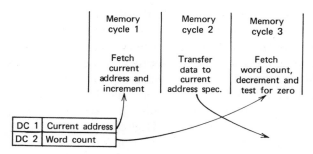

Fig. 6. A three-cycle memory based data channel or data break facility. Two memory locations are assigned to each data channel. Each data transfer requires three additional memory cycles—one cycle to fetch the current address register contents, increment its value, and use its value as the address for the next cycle. Data are transferred to or from the current address on the second cycle. On the third cycle the contents in the word count location are fetched and decremented one and tested for zero. If the resultant value is not zero, the process continues. However, if the word count has decremented to zero, the contents of the command register are used to indicate the type of termination as specified.

current address is incremented. The current address is then used as the address of the operand. Depending on the operation, data are transferred to or from the computer memory location specified by the current address word. The data channel transfer is terminated and control reverts to the CPU or another data channel if an additional data channel request is pending. In some computers the order is reversed and the current address-data transfer operation occurs first.

This type of data channel implementation has a larger interference effect on the CPU than an all-hardware implementation. However, as long as the data rate is less than one third that of the maximum memory transfer rate, this type of implementation is satisfactory and provides a minimum-cost solution. While the three memory access cycles are dedicated to the data channel function, all CPU and other data channel operations cease. Each data channel transfer requires three memory cycles, as compared to a single cycle for a hardware implemented data channel.

The word count and current address are usually stored in two consecutive locations. A unique contiguous pair of locations is reserved for every data channel. Each pair of locations is hardware addressed in accordance with the data channel that is allocated the current memory access cycle.

In some computers normal CPU data processing paths are used to implement the data channel functions. In that case more than the three cycles described here are needed to transfer a word. When the computer arithmetic unit is used, the current contents of the computer when the data channel request is received must be stored. Specific memory locations are reserved to store the CPU status. The word count and current address are then accessed, incremented, tested, and restored. These automatic functions are performed by the CPU arithmetic circuits under microprogram control. The data transfer is then effected. If no additional requests for data transfers are pending, the suspended status of the computer registers is restored and computer processing continues where it left off. Interference with the CPU program can be significant in this minimum hardware approach.

MULTIPLE MEMORY BANKS

Although a data channel is an effective way of moving data into and out of computer memory, it nevertheless interferes with CPU operation. Each cycle taken by the data channel obviously prevents the CPU from accessing memory, fetching or storing operands, and fetching instructions. Except for instructions with long execution times, such as multiply or divide, the CPU can utilize almost every memory cycle.

One way to increase the number of non-CPU-interfering memory accesses is through the use of multiple memory banks. This technique also effectively decreases memory access time when organized in an interleaved fashion. To expedite data transfer, data addresses can be assigned in sequential memory banks. Thus, if two memory banks are provided, the first half of the memory words are stored in bank 1 and the other half in bank 2. If four banks are available, the lowest quarter of the addresses are in bank 1, the second lowest quarter in bank 2, and so on. This is in contrast to interleaving, where the memory words are arranged sequentially in adjacent banks. Thus, if two interleaved banks are available, all the even addresses are in bank 1 and the odd addresses in bank 2.

Organizing memory in multiple sequential order increases CPU efficiency. Computers with multiple memory banks can have independent addressing and buffering registers for each bank. This permits each bank to operate completely independently of the other banks. Thus, if a data channel is accessing addresses in one bank and the computer program is fetching its operands and instruction from the other banks at the same time, no interference will result. Both the input/output and the CPU will operate at maximum efficiency. In very high speed CPU configurations, interleaving permits more rapid access to memory because successive addresses are obtained from different data banks.

CYCLE STEALING

Data channel facilities are referred to by a number of designations by the various computer manufacturers. In addition, many of the facilities are implemented in different ways. The major feature common to all these devices is that, once a data channel is started by the computer program, it operates as a special-purpose processor independently of the calling program. The data channel "steals" cycles from the main CPU program in order to accomplish its functions. Whenever a data word is to be transferred, the data channel "steals" a memory cycle from the CPU. Thus data channels implemented with hardware current address and word count registers need steal only one memory cycle to transfer each data word. These channels are referred to as selector channels or direct memory access channels, depending on the computer manufacturer. Usually, such a channel can service only a single peripheral device at a time. Only after one device has been fully serviced can another begin to receive service from a particular data channel. These services operate in "burst" mode.

The selector channel or direct memory access channel places a low load on the computer. Only one cycle need be "stolen" for each data word transferred. It is necessary in many systems to initiate and operate more than one I/O device concurrently. If each is operated via a single-cycle data channel, as described here, a separate channel must be provided for each device. Thus the hardware must be duplicated for each channel attached. Although a single channel can be connected to a number of I/O devices, at any time only one of the devices attached to a particular channel can be active. One way around this deficiency is to connect each important device to its own channel. Another alternative is to connect each selected device to two channels via a two-channel switch. Thus, if one data channel is busy giving service to a particular I/O attached to it, the device attached via a two-channel switch can be accessed through the alternate data channel. The switch is program controlled.

THREE-CYCLE CHANNELS

A number of computer data channels operate on a three-cycle "steal" principle, as described previously. The external computer hardware is minimized because the registers that would ordinarily be needed to store the current address and word count are kept in specified memory locations. At least three computer memory cycles are "stolen" for each word that is transferred: two in order to access the current address and word count, and the third to transfer the data, In most computer systems three. cycles suffice; however, an extra cycle is sometimes allocated for input.

Each device is connected to the computer via a channel. A number of devices may share a channel, but in that case only one device can be active at the time. Because of the relatively low cost of such arrangements, each device is usually allocated its own exclusive channel. Each channel is permanently associated with a pair of specific memory locations, where the current address and word count for that channel are stored. In some computers the address decoding necessary to translate a channel I/O request into the addresses pertaining to the current address and word count for the channel is part of the computer circuitry. In simpler computers, however, the burden of providing this address is placed on the external equipment. It is obviously much simpler to interface to a computer with built-in address encoding for each channel.

Three-cycle "stealing" channels are referred to as three-cycle data break channels or as multiplexers, depending, of course, on the nomenclature assigned by the computer manufacturer.

FIXED STORED-PROGRAM CHANNELS

Multiplexer channels such as those implemented on the IBM/360-370 series use CPU hardware to perform the channel function. When a multiplexer channel requests service, the multiplexer gains control of the CPU and its memory. A program stored in the computer read-only memory executes the necessary instructions to perform the required data transfer. This procedure uses a relatively large number of cycles to effect the transfer, but the amount of external hardware is minimized.

The multiplexer can handle I/O transfer from a large number of channels concurrently, provided that the aggregate data transfer rate is within specified bounds. The limitation is determined by CPU and memory performance. When a particular channel exceeds its limit, the multiplexer operates in burst mode, that is, the high-data-rate device takes complete control and locks out all other devices. Thus, when a particular high-speed device is activated, all other activity on the multiplexer ceases until that device finishes. If this is an intolerable condition, the device attached to the multiplexer channel should be connected via a higher-speed single-cycle or three-cycle "steal" channel.

WORD ASSEMBLY

Many I/O devices are character or byte oriented. This is particularly true of card equipment, printers, and tape. Computer memories, on the other hand, may be organized with word lengths capable of storing several bytes or characters. A function of the data channel or external hardware is to ensure that the computer word and external device word match. This can be done via hardware or software. One approach is to build special hardware logic to assemble bytes or characters into full computer words (Fig. 7). Only after a full word has been assembled is the channel informed that a transfer to memory is required. Similarly, on output the computer transfers full words to the channel; the channel in turn disassembles each word and transfers one byte or character at a time, upon request, to the external device.

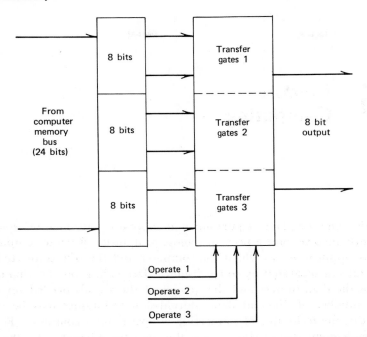

Fig. 7. A word assembly buffer may be provided as part of the data channel I/O structure. This provides a facility for collecting a number of characters or bytes and storing them temporarily in the buffer until a full computer word has been assembled. On output the word disassembler accepts a full computer word from the main memory of the computer. The word disassembly buffer then transfers out one byte or character at a time until the full word or number of bytes has been accounted for.

To conserve on external hardware, transfers to and from memory can be made one byte or character at a time. Either under software or channel control, each byte is ORed into the proper segment of the memory word on input or extracted from the memory word on output. Of course this scheme multiplies the number of memory cycles required, because a data transfer is effected for each byte rather than for each word.

15 Remote Computing

Even the simplest data acquisition and laboratory automation systems inherently involve some aspects of remote computing. Remote computing includes applications in which the computer and the interconnected instruments are separated by some distance. Depending on the characteristics of the data sources and the quality of the signals needed for control, a number of different data transmission techniques may be used. Generally, the technique of connecting a device and a computer (Fig. 1) is dependent on the specific device, the data interchange rate, the distance from the computer, the required accuracy of signal transmission, the nature of the existing facility, the anticipated future system requirements, and cost and budgetary considerations. Close-by, slow-speed, low-

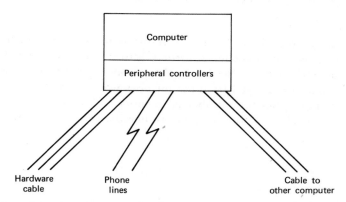

Fig. 1. Overall block diagram showing various types of remote computer connections. These methods include cable, start/stop communications, synchronous communications, and direct computer to computer connection.

accuracy requirements involve the least costly connection, whereas long-distance, high-speed, high-accuracy environments entail the implementation of more expensive configurations.

This chapter deals with digital transmission techniques only. Analog signal sources predominate in most real-time environments; hence the first choice in signal transmission would naturally be an analog technique. In many cases, however, because of accuracy and distance considerations analog transmission is not suitable. Analog signals cannot be entered directly into a computer; some form of analog to digital conversion is necessary. For the purpose of the present discussion it is assumed that the necessary analog to digital conversions have already taken place and the signal is available in digital format. The criteria for selecting and implementing suitable analog to digital conversion were discussed in Chapter 4.

The following techniques for connecting digital signals to a digital computer are considered:

1. Hard wire connection.
2. Driven multiple cable.
3. Start/stop communications.
4. Synchronous communications.
5. Direct computer to computer.

HARD WIRE CONNECTION

The simplest connection to a computer is a direct wire connection (Fig. 2) to the I/O structure. This, of course presupposes that the computer has the necessary input and output lines needed to sustain the desired data link. The specifications of suitable input and output lines are discussed in Chapter 12. For each digital input or digital output bit, a separate signal line must be provided. Read-in and read-out of data are under program control.

Direct hard wire connection usually is limited to instruments and data devices that are relatively close to the computer. As the distance increases, the allowable data rate decreases because of attenuation, cable capacitance, and other long line effects. For most applications, the allowable separation between the computer and device to be hooked up is about 50 ft. No special precautions or techniques are required to effect a connection at this distance. What is needed is the assurance that the voltage logic levels fall within the limits specified by the computer and

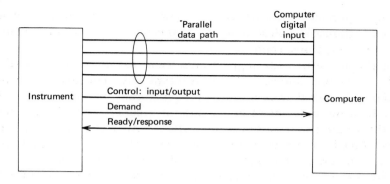

Fig. 2. Remote computing: parallel data link connecting instrument to computer. A wire or cable connects each bit in the parallel data stream to the computer. In addition, separate cables for control and synchronization are provided.

the device to be connected and that the timing sequences are in accordance with the computer and remote device specifications.

For most connctions twisted wire pair cables are sufficient for data signal transfer. Because the distances involved are under 50 ft, this type of simple connection is adequate. The twisted wire pairs consist of two wires, one of which is the signal line and the other the ground line. The ground line is connected to the signal ground. Care should be taken to keep the twisted pair grounds separate from the system ground except through a single point connection. This common point (and only this point) should be connected to system ground. The value of prudent grounds handling cannot be too strongly stressed.

The considerations discussed here are equally valid for connection directly to a computer, or through a data acquisition device that logs data onto a recording medium or to a data acquisition-transmission terminal. In all cases, hard wire connections constitute part of the network, whether the connection is directly to a computer or via data conditioning circuitry for transmission or direct on-the-spot recording.

Direct hard wire connection constitutes connection via parallel wires to the computer or other data acquisition systems. The number of parallel input lines and parallel output lines must equal the number of input bits and output bits, respectively. The actual transfer of data may be under computer program control or under the control of the data acquisition system. As explained previously, data are transmitted under program control at the rate and at the times determined by the program. The external device has no effect on the transmission rate or times. It must be capable, however, of responding to the controller command rate; this rate should be commensurate with the data handling capabilities of the device.

Interrupt control is one way for the external device to affect the timing and rate of data transfer. An interrupt from the device is used to signal the computer that the device is ready to transfer data. A second technique for device data timing transfer control involves external synchronization of the external device with the computer. This type of transfer may be an input or an output, as determined by the program that initiates the operation. The data rates and timing between the interrupt or the external synchronization and the data transfer are dependent on the devices being used. Data channel timing relationships with respect to the synchronization signal that initiates a data transfer cycle are quite stringent because once a transfer sequence begins precise timing must be maintained. Data channel transfer rates are typically faster by one order of magnitude than interrupt controlled transfer rates.

DRIVEN MULTIPLE CABLE

Driven multiple-cable connection to the computer is similar to direct hard wire connection except that longer distances are involved. As was explained in the preceding section, when direct hard wire connection is permissible it represents the easiest method of connection. Distances of 50 ft or less are usually allowable. At these short distances no special efforts at signal transmission are needed for most signals of interest in a digital data environment. Simple twisted pair wire connections are used for all inputs and output. These signal transmission lines can be driven through simple transistor or integrated circuit collectors. Ordinary circuitry is used. The line load is simply the fan-out drive capability of an integrated circuit. These simple circuit techniques are not effective, however, when line lengths exceed 50 to 100 ft. In such situations signal transfer over a transmission line must be considered because of long-line effects characteristic of wide band signal transmission.

Fortunately, a wide variety of transmission line drivers and receivers made up of integrated circuit drivers for transmission lines are available. The availability of these integrated circuit drivers and receivers in quantity and at reasonable prices makes their use in most transmission line driving and line receiving designs highly effective, and their low cost and high performance are attractive. Special circuitry may be necessary when complete isolation of grounds between signal sources and destinations is necessary.

The noise margins of most logic circuits are adequate for the transmission of digital data over a distance of a few feet. The transmission of error-free data over longer lines in noisy environments, however, requires special transmission line drivers and receivers and careful selection of a suitable transmission line. This requirement is especially critical when data must be transmitted between the computer and remotely located peripheral equipment and data acquisition devices. A special group of integrated circuit line drivers and line receivers has been designed to interface between most families of integrated circuits used in digital applications and transmission lines. The universal applicability of these components for data transmission and reception in this kind of environment makes it worthwhile to examine their characteristics in detail.

A study of the problem of data transmission indicates that the use of a terminated transmission line is desirable from a performance standpoint, since signal reflections are minimized while allowing high-speed data transmission. A balanced or two-wire system is desirable because in such a system noise is primarily of the common mode type and can be rejected by a differential input line receiver with adequate common mode rejection properties.

Depending on the length of the transmission line, the costs of the line and of its installation can be influencing factors in line selection. For short transmission lines, relatively expensive shielded coaxial cable may be acceptable. For longer lines, however, less expensive flat or twisted pair cable is desirable. To further decrease the cost of a transmission system, a "party-line" system, in which several lines drivers and receivers share a common transmission line, may be employed.

DIGITAL DATA TRANSMISSION

A high-speed driver/receiver system designed for long transmission lines is almost universally applicable since it can also be used to advantage with shorter lines or lower data transmission speeds. The following characteristics are desirable for such a system:

1. High-speed data transmission ($\sim$ 10 Mbps).
2. Use of popular supply voltages.
3. Compatibility with popular logic (TTL, DTL).
4. High sensitivity ($\sim$ 50 mV) at receiver input.
5. Receiver relatively insensitive to overload.
6. High receiver input impedances.

7. High common mode rejection at the receiver input.
8. Strobe capability for receiver.
9. Driver capable of driving low-impedance terminated lines.
10. Inhibit capability for driver, with high output impedance in inhibit mode.

The system described here using integrated circuit drivers and receivers (Fig. 3) is capable of meeting the design goals stated. A balanced, twisted pair transmission line is terminated at each end in its characteristic impedance. The line terminations also bias both lines at a nominal positive level of a few hundred millivolts. The driver is composed of a stage that converts input logic levels to voltage levels which control a current switch. The current switch unbalances the voltage on the transmission lines, resulting in a voltage difference at the receiver input.

The input stage of the receiver is a differential input stage that exhibits high common mode rejection. An intermediate stage converts the polarity of the line signal to the desired logic levels at the receiver output. It should be noted that the driver output is not affected by the common mode signals induced on the line, thereby ensuring error-free transmission and recovery of data.

An important feature of the system is that provision can be made for removing the driver output current from both lines. In this inhibit mode, another driver can be used to transmit data over the line. A strobe or gate provision on the receivers allows any driver to communicate with any or all actuated receivers while other drivers are inhibited and other receivers are strobed off. Line receivers and drivers may be connected any-

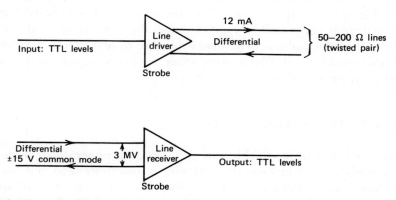

Fig. 3. Example of integrated circuit cable driver and receiver pair.

where along the line. Since line terminations are required only at the extreme ends of the lines, a single transmission line can service several computers and peripherals.

As stated, drivers have been designed to drive balanced terminated transmission line systems. The loading effects of line capacitance are minimized with these circuits. These drivers accept TTL or DTL input levels and convert them into an output current supplied to the lines of two-wire balanced systems. An output current of 12 mA for the driver allows very long balanced lines to be driven at normal line impedances of 50 to 200 Ω. The resulting low-level differential signals minimize power dissipation. The positive level at the bases of the driver output transistors allows at least 3 V of noise to be induced on the line before saturation of the driver output occurs. Because of the high collector-emitter breakdown of the driver output transistors, up to $\pm$ 10 V of induced noise can be tolerated before transistor breakdown occurs. Additional protection can be built in if higher noise is expected in a particular environment.

RECEIVER PERFORMANCE

The receiver circuit has a nominal propagation delay of several tens of nanoseconds, thereby making it ideal for use in high-speed systems. The receiver delay is almost completely insensitive to overdrive voltages of 10 mV or greater. The circuit responds to input signals with repetition rates as high as 20 Mbps.

The input sensitivity is defined as the differential DC voltage required at the inputs to the receiver to force the output above the gate threshold voltage level. The input sensitivity of the receivers is nominally 3 mV. This feature is particularly important when data are transmitted over a long line and the pulse is deteriorated because of line effects. A receiver with this sensitivity also finds many other applications, such as in comparators, sense amplifiers, and level detectors.

TYPES OF TRANSMISSION LINES

Many types of wire and cable can serve to interconnect logic systems. Plain insulated wire or loose shielded wire is sometimes used, but not in long line interconnections because of the indeterminate value of their line impedance. Coaxial cables used are typically of the 50- and 75-Ω

variety, such as RG 58/U and RG 13A/U. There are special types of coaxial cables with lower or higher impedances, but seldom are cables with impedances of over 200 Ω used.

Twisted pair lines have impedances of 100 to 200 Ω; these may vary under special conditions. For any given cable size, a twisted pair line usually has considerably greater impedance than a comparable coaxial line.

The impedance of any unknown line can easily be determined with an RX meter. The impedance, Z, is computed from the measured short-circuit impedance, Z_{sc}, and the open circuit impedance, Z_{oc}, thus: $Z = (Z_{sc}Z_{oc})^{1/2}$.

Normally the line impedance is considerably smaller than the driver output or receiver input impedance. This is very desirable, since connecting several drivers and receivers to one line does not affect the line impedance, and critical mismatch is avoided.

SIGNAL DEGRADATION

In long lines the transmitted signal experiences two type of degradation: frequency insensitive and frequency sensitive. Frequency-insensitive degradation is primarily attenuation due to line resistance. The resistance of the wire is insensitive to frequency except at very high levels where skin effect becomes evident. Since this frequency is beyond the consideration of these units, it is not discussed.

By using a driver ($I_{out} = 6$ mA) and a twisted pair line with an impedance of 100 Ω and an attenuation factor of 0.01 Ω/ft, data can be transmitted over line lengths of several thousand feet before line resistance effects degrade signal amplitude to an unusable level.

The other category of signal degradation, the frequency sensitive type, is related to the capacitive characteristics of the line. RG 55/U coaxial cable has an attenuation of about 1.3 dB/100 ft of length at 10 MHz, for example.

The attenuation of a twisted pair or of flat wires is slightly more difficult to determine because of its sensitivity to different physical characteristics and environmental conditions. As a typical example of the frequency sensitive attenuation of twisted pair lines, RG 58/U coaxial cable has an attenuation of about 1.5 dB/100 ft at 10 MHz. The maximum permissible length of coaxial cable is about 1700 ft for a receiver sensitivity of 25 mV. For operation at 1 MHz, RG 58/U cable has an attenuation of 0.4 dB/100 ft, and the maximum length is about 6500 ft.

When a twisted pair is used, the characteristics of the line must be known. This information may be used to determine the maximum length that could be driven in this particular case.

The unique output circuit of the driver allows terminated transmission lines to be driven at normal line impedances. High-speed operation of the system is ensured since line reflections are virtually eliminated when terminated lines are used. Crosstalk is minimized because of the low signal amplitude and low line impedances, and the total current in a line pair remains constant.

Data are impressed on the twisted pair line by unbalancing the line voltages by means of the driver output current. Line termination resistors, labeled R_T, are required only at the extreme ends of the line. For short lines, termination resistors at only the receiver end may prove adequate.

PARTY-LINE BALANCED SYSTEM

The need to communicate between many receivers and line drivers could require large amounts of wire and consequently increase installation costs. For example, in transmitting and receiving information from the cockpit of an airplane to some remote area in the tail of the plane, the wire required for a multichannel system might well weigh more than all of the equipment involved. For this reason a method for sharing a single transmission line by several drivers and receivers is desirable.

UNBALANCED OR SINGLE-LINE SYSTEMS

When these circuits are used in unbalanced (i.e., single-line) systems, they do not offer the same performance as balanced systems for long lines. They are adequate for short lines, however, when environmental noise is not severe.

In such systems, the receiver threshold level is established by applying a DC reference voltage to one receiver input terminal and supplying the transmission line signal to the remaining input. The reference voltage should be optimized so that signal swing is symmetrical with respect to it for maximum noise margin. The reference voltage should be in the range of -3 to $+3$ V. It can be provided either by a separate voltage source or by a voltage divider from one of the available supplies.

For large signals swings, higher output is needed. Two drivers may be paralleled for even higher current.

TRANSFORMER COUPLING

To connect two digital devices whose ground planes must be kept isolated, transformer coupling techniques may be used. Because digital signals of interest are at logic levels, transformers cannot be used directly. The most common technique is to AND the signals of interest with a high-rate pulse source. Thus an AND gate that controls the passage of the pulse source is incorporated into each line that must be passed between two ground isolated devices. When a particular line is true, the pulse train passes; a false condition inhibits the pulse train. Each pulse train is coupled out via a driver and pulse transformer. The pulse transformers completely isolate the grounds from each other.

At the receiving end the pulse train is again received via a pulse transformer. A one-shot multivibrator arrangement is used to restore the DC level. The one-shot interval is set to be slightly longer than the pulse clock rate. Each time a pulse is received on a particular input line, it is coupled through its pulse transformer to the associated one-shot via an amplifier. The one-shot will reset to the false state if a second pulse is not received before its natural period is over. Thus the one-shot remains in the "one" or true state as long as the condition (at the transmitting end) remains true. It will revert to the false condition within one pulse interval after the primary condition goes to the false state. A line will remain false until its transmitting pair goes true. The maximum delay will be one pulse period.

A number of different techniques can be used to provide digital isolation of circuit grounds. Transformer isolation circuitry is quite useful in a multidevice environment where high ambient noise levels are encountered. This class of circuits is useful when one of the devices must be at a high offset voltage with respect to ground or the other system. Another method for obtaining ground isolation utilizes optical techniques. Each signal to be transmitted modulates a light source; light emitting diodes (LEDs) are ideal devices for this component. Light detectors sensitive to the emitted light respond to the received beam. Ground isolation by such means should be applied only where there is a need to overcome high noise or where high voltage differentials between system elements exist.

INTEGRATED CIRCUITS

Most modern digital systems are designed using some type of integrated circuit logic. This ensures that input and output between system components will match; and voltage logic level matching problems do not exist. The most serious problem is to ensure that the true levels of one device are the same as those of the device to which it is connected. This problem is not too difficult to overcome, however, as long as the data are eventually entered into a computer. An inversion of logic levels can be easily accomplished by a simple program complement instruction sequence.

Most bipolar integrated circuit logic operates at a nominal ground and +3 to +5 V. The assignment of the "one"/"zero" designation varies depending on system definition or, more often, design convenience in the particular circuit. Problems in voltage level do exist when a system intermixes ECL, MOS, and transistor logic. Voltage level shift circuits can be be designed quite easily. However, most shifts can be readily accomplished using MOS/TTL/DTL or TTL-DTL/MOS level shifters; these simple, relatively low-cost integrated circuits perform these functions well over very wide voltage ranges. The MOS/TTL/DTL type will shift negative logic levels to bipolar levels. The TTL-DTL/MOS performs the converse: a shift of positive bipolar levels to negative voltage logic levels.

TELEPHONE COMMUNICATIONS

When the distance between the data acquisition site and the computer exceeds several hundred feet, it becomes expedient to use communications techniques to transmit the information. A large number of different techniques exist for transmitting data between remote locations. High-speed transmission costs more than low-speed transmission, and transmission over long distances obviously is more expensive than transmission over short distances.

The most important considerations in data communications are the data channel bandwidth and path length. These factors determine the rate at which data can be transmitted and the cost of transmission. Data channels (Fig. 4) are full duplex when bidirectional simultaneous transmission is needed; half duplex when bidirectional sequential transmission is required. Simplex lines allow transmission in only one direction. Full duplex lines are always four wires, two in each direction. Simplex lines are two wires. Half duplex lines may be either two or four wires, depending on the terminal arrangement. Four-wire half duplex permits faster line turn-around times when reversing the direction of transmission.

The bandwidths of most communication channels are limited in both upper and low frequency capability. The upper frequency limit is

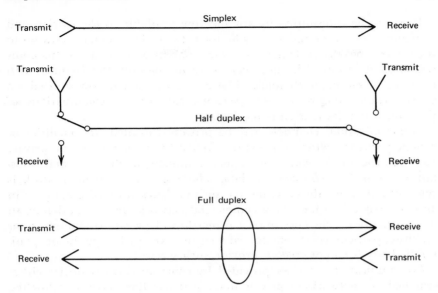

Fig. 4. Telephone lines are available as simplex unidirectional lines, half duplex bidirectional lines capable of operation in one direction at a time, and full duplex lines capable of simultaneous bidirectional transmission.

affected by line impedance and line length. Most useful communications networks have repeaters built in to the data channels. These are amplifiers and filter networks that compensate for upper frequency band limiting factors and line attenuation due to distance. The upper frequency is limited by the amplifier-filter combination. The amplifiers placed in the line also limit its low-frequency characteristics because it is much less expensive to design and build high-quality AC amplifiers. Hence very few communications channels have DC or very low frequency capability. Also entering into communication channel design is the fact that most common carriers multiplex a number of communications channels onto various carrier frequencies. In practice the communications channel does not transmit the data at the base band frequency range in which it originates but at some higher carrier frequency. This is necessary in order to make data transmission of many channels economically feasible. The common carrier network (the telephone company or the post, telephone, and telegraph service) accepts data from one location at the base band frequency and delivers at the receiving terminal the same base band frequency range. However, because of filtering for band limiting, as well as the modulation techniques used, low-frequency cut-off is inherent.

Data can be transmitted by any medium available to the carrier, and in many cases several media may be used. From the customer location to the carrier's nearest exchange, hardware connection is used. At this point carrier modulation techniques can serve to combine the channel with many other customer channels. The data may then be transmitted via coaxial cable, microwave relay stations, satellite, or combinations of these until the destination is reached.

Communications channels may be private dedicated line facilities or common carrier switched networks. When transmission is via private facilities, the user provides the various amplifiers, modulators, and transmitters needed to transfer the data. Therefore this type of network is relevant only when the customer has such facilities at his disposal or is in an inaccessible location where commercial networks are not available. In most situations tariff laws restrict ownership of private communications facilities, particularly if commerical facilities exist or if a public or quasi-public body is empowered to provide such service.

Communications services provided by common carriers utilize either switched line networks or private lines. Switched line networks allow the use of the regular communications network. The user can dial any number on the network and establish communications. A private line provides point-to-point communications only. Several points can be tied into a private hook-up, but the actual method of connection is chosen by the user. Connection between private lines and the switched network is usually not encouraged by the telephone service organization. Noise on a switched network is usually much higher and more unpredictable than on private lines. Signals sent over the switched network must pass through a number of central exchanges, and the signal lines will pick up noise from high-switching transients in the vicinity of switches. The route of line connections between the same two points will vary from time to time, depending on how the switched network sets up the circuit. For this reason the network characteristics and resultant noise are unpredictable. When private lines are ordered, on the other hand, the carrier company is usually able to provide a connection over a specific path. Although the connection path is not guaranteed, it generally will remain constant, and if a change is made the carrier can notify the user. Thus the line quality, line length, and other characteristics are definable. Also, since no switching is involved, less noisy lines are possible.

A private line is available to the user on a full-time basis. The connection is always available for use without any delays in circuit selection or set-up. The dialed switched network, however, is available only after the switched connection is completed. If the network is busy, the user must wait until a circuit becomes available. Of course, he pays only for time actually used on the switched network, whereas he is charged a flat rate for a private line regardless of how much time is used. Thus to a large extent the decision as to whether a private or a switched line should be ordered will be based on the amount of time during which transmission is to take place. Many locations and many countries provide only private lines for data transmission, either because there is insufficient experience with digital data transmission or because the quality of the switched network is not adequate for reliable data transmission.

Another consideration is the terminal equipment. Until recently, only telephone company equipment could be attached to the switched network. A user could select any terminal manufacturer's equipment only for use on private lines. These regulations vary from state to state and country to country. The legal requirements for data transmission and terminal connections must, of course, be considered.

BANDWIDTH

The most common communications channel available anywhere in the world is the voice grade channel (Fig. 5). Depending on the quality of the telephone network, a voice grade channel generally passes signals in the range of 300 to about 3000 Hz. This bandwidth is sufficient to transmit voice with reasonably good fidelity, and most practical data transmission systems attempt to utilize it because of the universal availability of telephone channels. In order to transmit data over a telephone channel their frequency must lie in the 300 to 3000 Hz band range. Digital signals

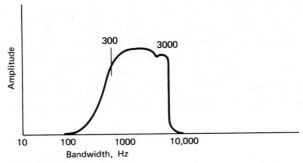

Fig. 5.   Telephone line bandwidth. Telephone lines do not pass low frequency and DC and have high-frequency cut-offs at about 3000 Hz.

encountered in integrated circuit logic systems vary in frequency content from DC to the maximum pulse repetition rate of the signal. As indicated, the ordinary voice communications circuit does not respond at DC. Also, the upper frequency limit is low. The first requirement of the digital network is to limit the data bandwidth to the maximum allowable frequency capability of the communication channel. To handle the low-frequency (DC) requirement of the digital signal, various modulation techniques are used. Although the channel has a nominal bandwidth of 300 to 3000 Hz, this does not imply that the band-pass characteristics of the channel are uniform over the bandwidth. Matching compensation networks must be built into the terminal equipment so as to equalize the frequency amplitude-phase response of the spectrum of the transmitted signals to that of the communications network. Equalization networks are needed to match the spectrum to the communications lines even if special high-grade lines are specified.

As indicated above, the most common communications networks are voice grade lines. Wider band telephone voice grade lines are available; they have guaranteed band passes of 300 to 4000 Hz. Wide band communications channels to 48,000 and 510,000 Hz are also available from some common carriers. Privately owned facilities may have any desired bandwidth. However, if commercially available terminal equipment is to be used (and this is normally the case), the bandwidths of signal transmissions will be determined by the terminal equipment and not necessarily by the communications channel. Obviously the channel bandwidth must be at least great enough to accommodate the terminal signal bandwidth requirements. Most commercially available terminal equipment is designed to match the bandwidth that commercial carriers normally provide.

From the basic theorems of information theory, it is known that the amount of information that a communications channel can convey is dependent on the bandwidth. Wide band channels can pass higher data rates than narrow band channels. Sophisticated modulation techniques can increase the data carrying capacity of a line. Unfortunately, practical channels, as discussed above, are neither noise free nor equalized in response. Thus, to obtain acceptably low error rates and to use reasonably low-cost terminal equipment, data is transmitted at rates below the theoretical maximum or sophisticated signal modulation techniques are employed.

MODEMS

A reasonable data rate for a 3000-Hz-bandwidth channel is usually 1200 or 2400 bits per second. Since communications line costs, especially over long distances, can be quite high, cost considerations cause users to transmit data at the highest feasible rate over a channel. By using more sophisticated terminal equipment, data can be transmitted at 4800 bits per second over such lines. Still more complicated transmission and equalization permits 7200 and 9600 bits per second to be transmitted over high-grade voice quality lines. These techniques include sophisticated modulation methods, high-precision dynamic equalization networks, and error detection and error correction coding.

The most common modulation technique is frequency shift keying (FSK) (Fig. 6). Two separate frequencies are transmitted: one frequency represents "one," and the other "zero." Phase modulation techniques are used for higher data rate transmission over relatively narrow band facilities. Each successive signal is encoded as a phase shift from the previous sine wave cycle. Simple techniques use phase reversal relative to the preceding cycle to indicate "one" and in-phase successive cycles to indicate "zero." Phase shift encoding permits infinite phase relationships between successive cycles. In one system successive phases can vary from the preceding cycle by 0, 90, 180, and 270 degrees. Each successive cycle represents a 2-bit sequence that is 00, 01, 10, or 11 as represented by the relative phase shift: 0, 90, 180, or 270 degrees, respectively.

At this point it is necessary to discuss the terminology used in communications systems. Data are transferred to the terminal device in parallel form. One full computer word or one data acquisition word is transferred. This unit may be a full word, double word, or byte, depending on the particular system that is common to the channel and the computer. In all cases, however, the data transfer between the devices is in parallel. The function of the terminal is to convert the parallel data received from the computer to serial form, compute, and add the necessary check bits for error detection and/or correction. Transmission synchronization signals are introduced in the bit stream. This function is performed by a unit designated as the transmission terminal or by various other labels. The output of this unit is usually required to conform to

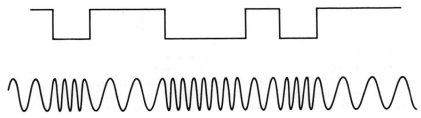

Fig. 6. Frequency shift keying (FSK).

the data transmission standard of the PTT service or carrier system as specified by ASA Document RS-232 or CCITT V-24. The serial signal is then transferred via "modem" (modulator-demodulator) or "data set" to the communications line. The data transmission rate is specified in bits per second or baud (a baud is defined as 1 bit per second; 2400 baud are equivalent to 2400 bits per second). At the receiving end of the communications line a modem or data set amplifies and demodulates the received signal. The serial signal is presented to the communications controller, where the synchronization signal is detected and used to synchronize the data reception. The check bits are verified to ensure that error-free transmission is taking place, and the serial data are converted to parallel form for transfer to the computer.

ASYNCHRONOUS SERIAL

This technique is used by almost all electromechanical serial devices, such as Teletypes. The format for this technique is shown in Fig. 7. This type of transmission is also referred to as start/stop or Baudot code signaling. In the format shown, a fixed amount of time is devoted to sending a binary "one" or a "zero." The number of bits that can be transmitted in 1 sec is the number of baud. A character consists of three parts: a start bit, data bits, and a stop bit.

The start bit is a line state (usually a zero) which lasts for 1-bit time and is used to indicate the beginning of a character. The beginning of a character can be detected through adherence to two basic rules:

1. When data are not being sent on the line, the line is kept in the "one" state.
2. After the last data bit is transmitted, the line will return to the "one" state for at least 1-bit time.

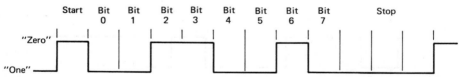

Fig. 7. Start/stop transmission provides full synchronization information in each transmitted character. Codes can be 5-bit Baudot or 8-bit ASCII. In all systems each character is preceded by a 1-bit start code and is followed by 1 or more bits of stop code. Transmission rates from several tens of baud (bits per second) to thousands of baud are possible, depending on terminal equipment used and line characteristics.

By means of these two rules, the interface can detect the start bit when a character is not actively being received, and the line goes from the "one" to the "zero" state. At this time, the receiving interface actuates a clock which strobes the data bits as they are presented on the line. The receiving interface must know how many bits there are to a character in order to determine where the current character ends, and when to start looking for the next start bit.

The data bits represent the actual binary data being transferred. In most applications the characters are 8 bits long, with the least significant bit being sent out or received first; 5 bits are also transmitted. Most European systems use 5-bit code, whereas the ASCII code used in the United States is an 8-bit code.

At the end of the data signal sequences, the line is held in the "one" state for a period which is either 1-, 1.42-, or 2-bit time. The purpose of this is to return the line to the "one" state so that both the transmit and the receive terminals can resynchronize. The lengh of time that the line stops in this state (1-, 1.42, or 2-bit time) depends on the amount of time required for the equipment to resynchronize. Most electromechanical equipment uses a 1.42- or 2-unit stop code; however, newer mechanical equipment such as Teletype Model 37 uses only a 1-bit stop. The line will remain in the "one" state until another character is transmitted. This stop time ensures that a new character will not follow for at least a 1-, 1.42-, or 2-bit time.

The following are the major advantages of this type of transmission:

1. It can easily be generated by electromechanical equipment (keyboard).
2. It can easily be used to drive mechanical equipment (printer).
3. Characters can be sent at an asynchronous rate because each character has its own synchronizing information.

The major disadvantages of start/stop communications are as follows:

1. Separate timing is required for the transmitter and the receiver.
2. Transmission is distortion sensitive because the receiver depends on incoming signal sequences to become synchronized. Any distortion in these sequences will affect the reliability with which the character is assembled.
3. Speed is limited because a reasonable amount of margin must be built in to accommodate distortion.
4. Transmission is inefficient because at least 10-bit times are required

to send 8 data bits. If a 2-unit stop code is used, it takes 11 bit times to transfer 8 bits of data. More than 8 data bits can be transferred to improve efficiency, but this is usually not done.

SYNCHRONOUS SERIAL

In the synchronous serial technique a serial bit stream is sent over the line in the same manner as the asynchronous serial bit stream except that there are no start/stop bits with which to synchronize each character.

The entire block of data is synchronized with a unique code sequence which, when recognized, causes the receiver to lock in and, by use of a counter, to count the incoming bits and assemble characters. As in the asynchronous technique, the receiver must know the number of bits to a character.

Unlike the asynchronous technique, a synchronizing signal must be provided along with the data bit stream. This signal can be generated by the transmitter, or by a separate source which the transmitter uses to transmit timing. In either case, the data must be transmitted and received synchronously with a common clock. The synchronous technique format is shown in Fig. 8.

The advantages of synchronous communications are as follows:

1. A common timing source can be used for both transmitter and receiver.
2. The receiver does not require clock synchronizing logic, as in the asynchronous technique.
3. Transmission is highly efficient because no bit times are wasted with the use of start and stop bits. All bits on the line are data, with the exception of the synchronizing pattern at the beginning of the bit stream.
4. Distortion sensitivity is low because the timing is provided along with the data.
5. Higher speeds are achievable because of the lower distortion sensitivity.

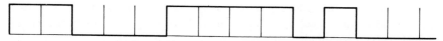

Fig. 8. Synchronous communications are more efficient in bandwidth utilization because, once synchronization between the transmitter and receiver has been established, only data are sent. Most high-speed new designs use synchronous communications techniques.

There are four disadvantages to this scheme:

1. Characters must be sent synchronously, not asynchronously, as they become available, which is undesirable for some real-time and mechanical applications.
2. One bit time added to or missing from the data bit stream can cause the entire message to be faulty.
3. The equipment to accommodate this mode of operation is more expensive than the equipment required for asynchronous operation.
4. Mechanical equipment cannot directly transmit or receive this format.

DIRECT COMPUTER TO COMPUTER

The most effective way to transmit data between two computers is through a direct hook-up between the systems. This can be accomplished by sharing common peripheral devices, by channel to channel connection, or by sharing main memory. The techniques are mentioned here in increasing order of tightness in coupling. Sharing a common peripheral device allows both computers to operate relatively independently of each other, whereas sharing a common main memory implies very close connection. A channel to channel connection implies that the computers appear as I/O devices to each other and are handled by each computer essentially as such. In each case, communications hook-up or parallel data transfers are effectively acting as I/O devices to the other computer. However, a direct channel to channel connection (Fig. 9) permits very rapid data transfers between the two computers, whereas the communications or parallel transfers are limited in speed by the connecting media.

Any I/O peripheral device that is equipped with a two-channel switch can serve to link two computers together; the only requirement is that it be possible to read and write data to the peripheral. Such devices as magnetic tape, disk drives, and drums fit this description very well. The devices most commonly used in such a configuration are disk drives, because it is possible to read and write data and to access a particular area rapidly. One computer writes information on the disk in a particular area. The function of the second computer is to read these data and respond accordingly. A possible problem can arise out of this type of arrangement when the two computers are trying to access the same data simultaneously, with one writing and the other reading. This difficulty is usually overcome by locking out one computer for the whole time that

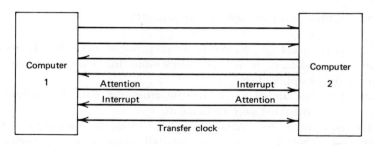

Fig. 9. Computer to computer connection via data channels or I/O facilities. Each computer appears as a peripheral device to the other computer. Highest-speed data transfers can be effected in data channel interconnect mode.

the other computer has any data to transfer. This type of interlock is inherent in the two-channel switch used on most disk drives. Without this, one computer is not aware of the other unless its program happens to interrogate appropriate flags at the specific instant in time. Under most circumstances this arrangement is adequate. When immediate response is needed, interrupts can be used whereby one computer can raise an external flag. This flag is connected to the interrupt on the other computer to signal that a data transfer to disk has taken place.

Channel to channel transfers appear as I/O device data transfers to the two computers. A connection between the two computer channels is made. .When one computer wishes to initiate a data transfer, its program issues an I/O command via the appropriate channel. The second computer channel responds as though it is in a data read-in mode. After the required "handshaking" is completed, the data transfer takes place. For all intents and purposes this is a direct channel to channel transfer. The data transfer can take place at whatever rate the computer I/O structures can accommodate.

A multiprocessing configuration consists of multiple control processors that share a common main memory store. Each CPU has direct access to the same memory, which can, of course, store both programs and data. The computers communicate with each other directly via the shared memory. Care must be taken to avoid accessing the same locations simultaneously from both computers before completion of the transfer by one.

The task of implementing direct computer to computer communications is usually assigned to the computer supplier. If the computers are supplied by one vendor, it is probable that hardware and software support exists for connecting two computers of the same manufacturer. The computer manufacturer is interested in furthering such arrangements.

In many cases linkages such as those described here are provided by the small computer manufacturer as an added inducement to use his system. Hardware and software support for connecting minicomputers is usually available for the more popular large host computer families. Since the problem of setting up this type of connection if it does not already exist or is not available from a computer manufacturer is formidable, every effort should be taken to avoid having to make the hardware connection and provide the software needed to operate the link. If such a connection absolutely must be created, standard communications techniques should be applied.

16   Man-Machine Interactions

Almost every data acquisition and control system requires some form of human interaction in order to proceed satisfactorily. This is the case while a system is being implemented, as well as when an on-going process has been fully debugged and is operational. Human surveillance and interaction with the control computer are usually required. Many well engineered and correctly constructed systems have failed solely because insufficient attention was paid to the man-machine interface. It is important, therefore that the design of a system take into account the human element and make the user fully aware of the progress of the experiment being controlled. Such awareness is necessary to assure the user that the system is functioning correctly; it also makes it practical for the experimenter or other user to intervene if an unexpected or incorrect event occurs. This is particularly important when dealing with a new system and with relatively inexperienced users. Close man-machine coupling gives the user a high degree of confidence in the total system, especially during debugging and run-in.

In this chapter some of the more common devices and techniques for man-machine computer interaction (Fig. 1) are described. The characteristics of these devices and their utility are discussed, although the treatment is in no way exhaustive. The following man-machine interactive devices are of interest:

1. Switches.
2. Push buttons.
3. Multiple-position switches.
4. Thumb wheel switches.
5. Keyboards.
6. Badge and card readers.

7. Potentiometers.
8. Graphic inputs.
9. Indicator lamps.
10. Decimal displays.
11. Cathode ray tube displays.
12. Light pens.
13. Printers.
14. Audio response units.
15. Eye motion sensors.
16. Plotters.

SWITCHES

A large number of man-machine interactive devices are available. As in most system component selections, decisions are based on price-perform-

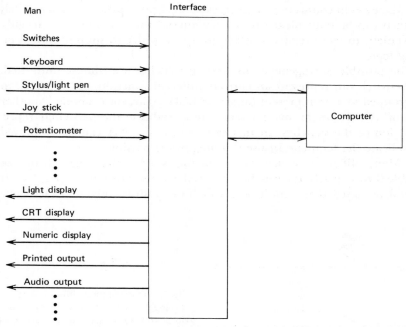

Fig. 1. The man-machine interface determines how well the human operator can be kept aware of the progress and status of the experiment being controlled. The man-machine interface also consists of the techniques used by the operator to effect controls and adjustments to the progress of the real-time process being controlled.

ance considerations within budgetary limitations. The simplest and least expensive man-machine interface consists of switches, push buttons, and indicator lamps. No training is needed to use such an interface. The user communicates with the computer via simple on-off switches and/or push buttons. Results and answers are provided through indicator lamps. The easiest switches to use are single-pole, double-throw toggle switches (Fig. 2). In the "on" position the center arm is connected to a voltage equal to binary "one," and in the alternative position it is connected to a second voltage, usually ground, which corresponds to binary "zero."

Each switch is connected to a bit on a digital input group. The computer, under program control, is instructed to sense the digital input group connected to the swiches. Since the switches are essentially memory elements, in that they remain in the positions in which they were set until changed, the computer can sense their status at any time that the program issues such a sense instruction. This is a particularly important consideration, because it makes interfacing and sensing basic toggle switches a relatively simple operation. By using digital output groups, as was discussed in connection with relay contact multiplexing, many switch contacts can be multiplexed into a few digital input points. It is usually convenient to sense related contact groups in order to simplify programming logic.

The possible arrangements of sensing switches are almost unlimited. Each switch can represent an entirely different function, or switches can be grouped so as to represent binary or BCD digits, for example. Another possibility is to use an overlay template to indicate the particular representation of the switches. In this case several switches can be employed to indicate the template in use if ambiguity is possible.

Many different switch types having single-pole, single-throw or double-throw attributes can be arranged as described here (Fig. 3). It should be noted that a multipole switch can also be used in exactly the

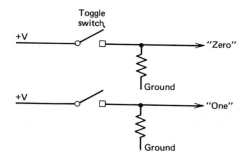

Fig. 2. The simplest input device is the toggle switch, which has two positions controlled by the actuation of its handle. Each toggle switch can be used to represent a single binary bit and can have either a "one" or a "zero" status.

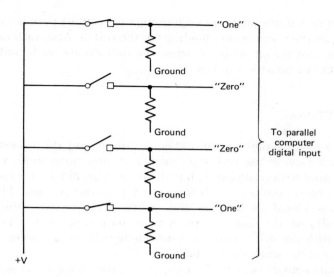

Fig. 3. A number of toggle switches may be grouped together on a panel. The switches may be logically grouped to represent single binary digits and in other groups to represent BCD digits, for example. The outputs of all the switches are connected to the computer digital input facility. Their status may be read periodically under program control or on an externally originated demand interrupt basis.

same way, as long as one pole is devoted to computer sensing. The other circuits on the switch can perform all types of normal switching functions. It is highly desirable to use a separate circuit for computer sensing in order to maintain electrical isolation between the computer and the external equipment. In addition to toggle switches, push-button-operated switches that latch, when actuated, and lever switches can be used.

It is convenient to provide an interrupt to indicate to the computer when to sense the switch status. It is not necessary to sense the status of an external switch again until its status is changed. One way for the computer to determine that the status has changed is to sense the switches on a regular basis under program control and to compare the currently sensed with the previously sensed condition. This technique is satisfactory provided that rapid response to a change of switch status is not required or if the computer program senses the switches on a regular, frequent basis. A separate interrupt push-button or momentary contact switch can be used to create a program interrupt. The interrupt servicing subroutine will then sense the switch status. It should be emphasized that when push-button or momentary contact switches are used, care must be taken to create a single interrupt even though the contact time is variable, depending on the time the user holds down the switch. Also, such switches have contact bounce on actuation when the contacts are made and cause multiple contact actuation pulses.

PUSH BUTTONS

Momentary contact push buttons (Fig. 4) are among the easiest man-machine interfaces to use and implement, and most instruments used in laboratory automation employ such switches in many different ways. Each time a momentary contact switch is actuated, a contact is made. The contact remains closed as long as the switch is depressed. When the switch is released, the contact returns to its normal state. The circuitry associated with the switch ensures that a single push or actuation will be detected for each switch depression.

Momentary contact switches, by their very nature, must be sensed while

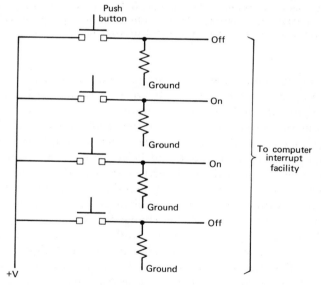

Fig. 4. A push-button switch remains actuated as long as the user keeps his finger on the button. Once he releases his finger, the switch reverts to its nonactuated status. Momentary contact push-button switches are usually connected to the computer interrupt facility, and each time a switch is depressed an interrupt is issued to the in-process program.

they are actuated. If they are sensed after being released, no useful information can be transmitted. Thus, as part of the computer or in external form, a storage element is needed to remember the actuation of the momentary contact. This type of storage element is provided as part of the interrupt structure of most computers. The memory circuit also prevents multiple inputs as a result of contact bounce when the momentary contact is made. Each time a momentary contact switch is actuated, an interrupt is generated or a memory circuit flip-flop is set. The interrupt service routine extinguishes the interrupt signal or resets the memory circuit, so that subsequent interrupts or actuations can be recognized and serviced. When the memory circuit is used, it may be sensed via the computer digital input facility; it is not prudent to sense the momentary contact closure directly because of the transient nature of the actuation signal. Ordinary toggle switches are less expensive and more easily applied if direct sensing is planned.

MULTIPLE-POSITION SWITCHES

Rotary switches and multiple-position, mechanically linked push-button switch assemblies are examples of multiple-position switches (Fig. 5), which usually have three or more fixed positions. The number of positions can be quite large, depending on the switch design; switches with as many as 10 to 12 positions are readily available.

A rotary multiple-position switch is actuated by rotating a knob on the switch. Various knob styles are available, making it easy to see the switch position. A rotary type switch can be set to one unique position at any time. Push-button multiple-position switches are usually mechanically linked so that only one position can remain depressed. Depression of any push button releases the previously actuated position. Push-button switches permit direct selection of a particular position with a one-step action. Rotary switches require stepping through each position intermediate to the current and desired one.

Multiple-position switches are available with one or more independent decks. Any number of decks are available. Each deck with its own wiper arm is a fully independent electrical circuit.

When more decks are needed, electromechanically driven switches are used because of the large force needed to drive the switch and maintain good contact. When multiple deck switches are specified, it is good practice to reserve one deck for use by the computer for sensing the switch position.

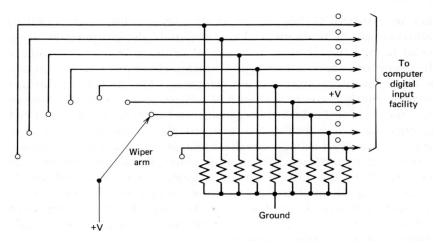

Fig. 5. A multiposition switch has a number of stable positions. Only one position can be active at a time. Each position of a multiposition switch is connected to a separate bit of the digital input facility. By sensing the statuses of all the bits, the computer program can determine the position to which the switch is set. All the bits will have a "zero" value with the exception of the bit associated with the switch set position—that will be "one." The switch status can be sensed periodically under program control or on demand when an external interrupt is issued.

Multiple-position switches are available in either continuous turn configurations or with built-in stops at the extreme positions. The choice is of no special significance insofar as the computer is concerned.

Multiple-position, multideck switches are available from a large number of different vendors in either standard or custom configurations. The switch construction is such that the number of positions can be set by positioning stops on the shaft. The positioning shaft is a long rod notched along its length, with the individual switch decks mounted on the notch points. This technique makes custom switch construction a relatively simple procedure.

Sensing the position of a multiple-position switch is comparatively straightforward. As indicated previously, one deck of the switch should be dedicated to computer sensing. The circuitry of the other decks is of no concern to the computer interface as long as they are electrically isolated from the deck reserved for computer sensing. Each contact on the switch should be connected to a separate digital input point. Thus a 10-position switch would be connected to 10 bits of a digital input group. To sense the switch setting, the computer senses the status of the digital input group associated with the switch. The wiper arm is connected to a

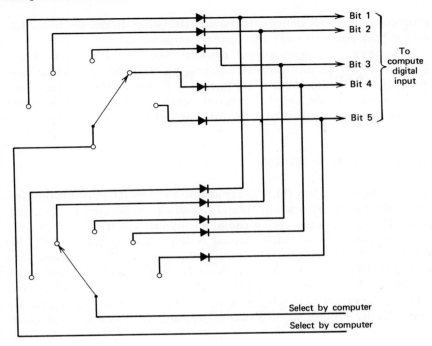

Fig. 6. A simple multiplexing scheme using the digital output facility in conjunction with the digital input facility allows a large number of mutiposition switches to share a single digital input group. A single bit on the digital output is assigned to each multiposition switch or group of toggles. The computer program selects a particular switch by setting the digital output bit associated with that switch to "one." The digital input is then sensed. The sensed input represents only the selected switch information. To select a different switch, the process is repeated with the desired digital output bit activated, followed by a digital input sensing operation.

"one" voltage level so that the selected position shows this voltage on the corresponding digital input bit.

When a number of multiple-position switches are involved, it is economical to use a multiplexing scheme (Fig. 6) so as to economize on the number of digital input points required. This is accomplished by using the wiper arms of the various switches to select the switch being sensed. Under program control a voltage output bit associated with the desired switch is set to the "on" status. All other wiper arms have a "zero" voltage applied to them. The computer then senses the digital input to determine the status of the selected switch. The procedure is repeated by successively actuating each wiper arm and then sensing the digital input group common to all the switch contacts. Isolation diodes are needed to prevent back paths through the "made" contacts.

As in the case of toggle switches, consideration should be given to providing an interrupt push button to alert the computer to read in multiple-position switches. When this facility is provided, the program need be concerned with the switch status only when a change occurs, or when the user specifically wants to enter information into the computer.

THUMB WHEEL SWITCHES

Thumb wheel switches (Fig. 7) are essentially special multiple-position rotary switches. They warrant special consideration because of their usefulness for entering data into a computer manually and because of their wide acceptance. In addition, special coding, such as binary, BCD, or BCD excess 3 codes (Fig. 8), are furnished as potions; these functions can be provided on standard rotary switches by special wiring. Another advantage of thumb wheel switches is the relative ease in reading and verifying the values to which they are set. The current setting is a clearly printed digit. Thumb wheel switches are built in a sideways configura-

Fig. 7. A thumb wheel switch is essentially a multiposition switch turned on its side. Its construction makes visual verification of the switch setting particularly easy. Also the form factor of the switches allows stacking a large number of individual elements on a small panel area.

Ten Position, Binary Coded Decimal					Ten Position, Binary Coded Decimal, with Odd Bit Parity						Ten Position, Complement of Binary Coded Decimal				
Dial	1	2	4	8	Dial	1	2	4	8	P	Dial	$\bar{1}$	$\bar{2}$	$\bar{4}$	$\bar{8}$
0					0					•	0	•	•	•	•
1	•				1	•					1		•	•	•
2		•			2		•				2	•		•	•
3	•	•			3	•	•			•	3	•	•		•
4			•		4			•			4			•	•
5	•		•		5	•		•		•	5	•			•
6		•	•		6		•	•		•	6	•			
7	•	•	•		7	•	•	•			7				•
8				•	8				•	•	8	•	•	•	
9	•			•	9	•			•		9		•	•	

Fig. 8. Thumb wheel switches with a large variety of codes are available. Some of the more popular codes are shown.

tion, thereby using a minimum of front panel space. Rotary switches, on the other hand, are built around a central control shaft, thus requiring that the front panel provide space for the full diameter of the deck. The packing density of thumb wheel switches on a panel is much greater than that of rotary switches.

It is faster to position a rotary switch than a thumb wheel switch. The thumb wheel construction requires one motion for each digit change of the switch position, so that to move from 5 to 8 requires three separate motions. A rotary switch, however, can be turned to the desired position in a single action. Some thumb wheel switch designs have overcome this deficiency by using a long actuator arm that allows for setting in one motion to any digit position.

The same sequence of operations is needed to sense the position of a thumb wheel switch (Fig. 9) as is required with any other type of contact. Each contact position is connected to a separate digital input point. The common or wiper arm is connected to the "one" voltage level. Alternatively, multiplexing can be used; the computer provides the common or wiper arm voltage to select a particular digit. Isolation diodes are needed to prevent back paths, and thumb wheel switches are constructed so that it is convenient to mount the isolation diodes directly on the switch. A standard option on most thumb wheel switches is the availability of isolation diodes as integral parts.

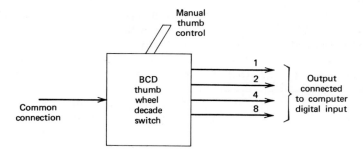

Fig. 9. The physical connection paths of a thub wheel switch.

Thumb wheel switches are used primarily for data entry rather than for general switching. The switching capacity of thumb wheel switch contacts is on the order of a few milliamperes, at most. These switches are made up of printed boards that carry the contact points and optional code diodes, mentioned previously. In addition, logic needed to provide binary or BCD codes can be mounted on the contact carrying cards. The thumb wheel actuating lever controls the motion of the contact arm.

KEYBOARDS

Keyboards (Fig. 10) are arrays of push-button switches that provide a convenient means for entering data to the computer. Each time a key is depressed, a contact associated with that key is made. Keyboards may be arranged in many different configurations and with various numbers of keys. Three common types of arrangements are the 10-key numeric adding machine configuration, the typewriter keyboard providing for full alphanumeric capability, and the multicolumn-multidigit adding machine configuration. The first two keyboards mentioned are momentary contact switches; a switch is actuated as long as the user maintains his finger on the key. The latter is a steady state switch; once set, it remains set until its status is changed by additional data entry.

Ten-key numeric keyboards are arranged in a configuration for adding machine input or for touch-tone telephone dials. Other configurations and additional keys are also possible and are often used. If numeric data are to be entered into the computer, either the adding machine keyboard or the touch-tone push-button configuration is preferred to other possibilities, primarily because users are familiar with these arrangements.

Each time a key is depressed, a set of contacts is made. Most switches

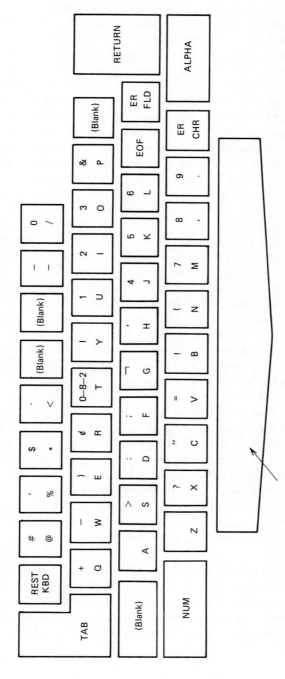

Fig. 10. A numeric and full alphanumeric keyboard. The keyboards contain the circuitry necessary to encode key depressions into computer codes. Each time a key is depressed the corresponding code is presented at the computer digital input facility. An interrupt is also issued for each key depression. The interrupt service program senses the digital input to determine which key was depressed.

are constructed so that only one switch in the set can make contact at a time. A common output from all the switch contacts is provided; this output is usually a 4-bit code representing the BCD equivalent of the depressed key. A fifth parity bit, or check bit, is sometimes available as an option. A pulse or "on" output is also available to indicate that a legitimate stable code appears on the data lines. The computer must sample the data lines while the "on" or "one" state is present. The "on" pulse indicates that the user has depressed a key and that the key is still depressed. If the computer waits too long to sample the input lines, the key can be released and invalid data will be sensed. The sample command pulse or "on" condition serves as an interrupt, indicating that valid data exist on the input lines and a sense command should be issued.

A second, similar keyboard is the typewriter keyboard that provides full alphanumeric input. The operation of this keyboard is the same as that of the numeric-only keyboard except that full 6-, 7-, or 8-bit ASCII or EBCDIC codes are generated. A sample or valid data pulse is generated to indicate that input sensing of the data should be ordered by the program.

The data can be encoded electromechanically or via electronic circuits. If electromechanical encoding is used, the data will remain valid only as long as the key is depressed. With electronic encoding, a memory circuit is sometimes provided; in this case the sampling time is not critical because the data will remain valid even if the key is released.

Key actuation can be accomplished in a number of ways. The conventional method is to close contact sets, as indicated previously. Other techniques can also be used, such as interrupting a light beam with a mask representing the desired code; a key depression will insert a mask representing the key code between a light source and a set of photodetectors.

The numeric or alphanumeric keyboard associated with a computer connected I/O typewriter or a CRT display is connected and operated in the same way as an independent keyboard. Unless specifically connected for local operation, the keyboard and the display on these devices are totally independent. With the typewriter, for instance, the printing of a character always proceeds through the computer. A key depression enters a code representing the character into the computer, and if the program issues a print command, the corresponding character will be printed.

The multicolumn-multidigit keyboard found on some adding machines and on many data entry devices consists of an array of switches. Each column is interlocked to prevent more than one key from being depressed and locked in. Key depression releases the previously depressed key in a particular column. When the user has set up the code set desired by depressing keys in various columns, the "enter" key is depressed. This key has the effect of generating an interrupt, indicating to the computer that the keyboard is to be read. The multiplexing procedure described previously is followed in order to sense the depressed key in each column sequentially.

BADGE AND CARD READERS

Various preprepared media can be used to enter data into a computer from an experiment area. As examples, badge and card readers are considered here; these are similar punched hole sensing devices. Although variations exist, many utilize standard IBM punched card dimensions.

A badge and/or card reader is provided at the experiment station. Cards may be punched on a keypunch. As an alternative to punching holes, mark sensing can be used, in which case the card is marked with a soft lead lead pencil. Badges and cards can be prepared and used when needed. The user selects the badges or cards needed to express desired functions and enters them into the computer by inserting each badge or card in the reader. An "enter" button is usually provided to indicate to the computer that the reader needs service.

Cards and badges may also be magnetically encoded; the data on the media are then read by magnetic code sensitive devices. Such devices are relatively inexpensive and are used extensively for automatic telephone dialers and for programming desk calculators. In some cases their use as laboratory input media is very attractive.

Optical character recognition can be used to sense written numbers as characters. However, it is unlikely that the high cost of such readers can justify their use in a laboratory environment.

POTENTIOMETERS

The devices described to this point are all digital input devices. They all represent discrete position on-off or multiple on-off devices. In many situations, however, it is necessary to enter data with finer resolution. This can be accomplished in many ways. The most common electrical component found in an electronics laboratory is the potentiometer, a device that divides a voltage in proportion to the position of its wiper arm on a resistance element. Thus the voltage on the wiper arm is proportional to the angular displacement of the wiper. Multiturn potentiometers for even higher resolution are also available. In addition, potentiometers capable of generating various mathematical functions can be obtained. These are generated by winding the potentiometer or depositing the film in such a way as to distribute the resistance element in accordance with the desired function. Sine-cosine, log, and other type functions can be provided on potentiometers. Taps at various points along the potentiometer resistance element can be used to insert shunt resistors and thus create many nonlinear functions.

The ready availability of potentiometers makes them important devices for manual data entry. A user can set them conveniently. To digitize the shaft position, the potentiometer output voltage is used as the input to an analog to digital converter (Chapter 4).

GRAPHIC INPUTS

The input devices described previously are basically digital in nature. In many cases, however, it is both convenient and natural to manually describe a variable in analog fashion. A number of devices are available to enable the user to describe input data in purely analog fashion. The most common of these devices are based on the "Rand tablet" design. This class of devices consists of a surface upon which the user can point to a desired value and trace out the behavior of the variable. Devices such as these permit the user to specify his input directly by means of a stylus or some other input device.

Graphic input devices such as those described here are referred to as X-Y digitizers or Rand tablets, depending on the specific application and the manufacturer. The tablet (Fig. 11) consists of a working surface about 12 × 12 in. in size; tablets with larger areas are also available. The user is provided with a stylus with which he enters information by pointing the stylus at a particular point on the work surface of the tablet. The work surface may be overlaid by a paper chart. An image may also be projected on the surface of the tablet. Because of its translucent quality, back projection of images is also possible. The data can be presented as discrete points, curves, alphanumeric symbols, or any other convenient format. The user points the stylus at the desired symbol or discrete point, or he may move the stylus along some path on the work surface. He may follow a curve or trace out a line between points.

The design of the tablet is such that the X-Y coordinates under the stylus are continuously generated. Thus the output of the tablet provides a continuous representation of the curve or points under the stylus. The

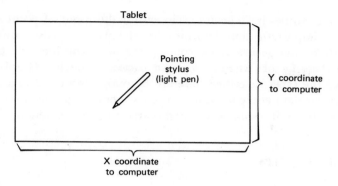

Fig. 11. A "Rand tablet." The user enters coordinate and locus information concerning the sketch or information he has placed on the tablet. Data are entered into the computer by the user placing the stylus over the information or following the path of interest. The output of the tablet is X and Y coordinate information.

X-Y coordinates are read into the computer via the digital input facility. If a curve is being followed, the stylus traces out the path and in effect provides the continuous X-Y coordinate pairs for the curve. For discrete points or symbols, the coordinates of the indicated points are entered.

Various technologies have been adapted to the design of X-Y coordinate digitizers. The simplest rely on mechanical coupling of the stylus to X-Y potentiometers or shaft encoders. A mechanical arrangement similar to a pantograph may be used. Linkages and drive systems like those in digital plotters or X-Y plotters are also used. In these, shaft encoders or potentiometers are the outputs. Other systems rely on magnetic coupling between the stylus and a behind-the-table follower. Direct digitizing devices are also available. One version of the Rand tablet, for instance, relies on two fine grids of orthogonal plated wires. Typically, 4096 × 4096 wires may be deposited on the tablet. Through capacitive coupling, the stylus detects a time-varying-voltage "traveling wave" applied to the grid. Accuracies of 0.1% and resolutions of 1 part in 4000 are attained on a 12 × 12 in. grid. Another technique relies on two sets of orthogonally mounted strip microphones: one set for X, and the other for Y. The stylus emits a sonic spark, and the time of receipt of the sonic pulse by the X and Y microphones is indicative of stylus location. It should be noted that, if a vertically mounted strip microphone were installed (orthogonally to the X and Y microphones), a measure of the stylus location in the Z direction could be obtained by determining the time of receipt of the sonic pulse by this microphone.

Many techniques have been developed for the input of point or curve data. The important considerations for the user are cost, convenience of operation, and accuracy. Of course, one must consider the trade-offs between these factors when selecting a particular device. Graphic input devices of the types described here are becoming more popular and less expensive for data entry because of their general accptance by users and their availability from an increasingly large number of vendors.

INDICATOR LAMPS

The devices considered to this point are all manual devices, employed by the user for manually entering information into the computer. Attention is now turned to computer data output devices. These permit the computer to communicate information to the user; the computer interacts with the user through these data output devices.

An indicator lamp (Fig. 12) is the simplest computer output device. Any number of indicator lamps can be connected to the computer. Each lamp is actuated by a single digital output bit. An indicator lamp can be turned on or off by the computer.

Indicator lamps can be driven directly by the computer digital output facility. A typical incandescent indicator lamp operates at 100 ma at 28 V. Such power is well within the capabilities of medium-power transistors. Indicator lamps based on gas discharge tubes, such as neon lamps, are also useful for computer output. However, because gas discharge devices ionize at about 65 V, their application as computer output devices is limited. Light emitting diodes (LED) are fast capturing a major share of the light indicator market because of their relatively unlimited life, invulnerability to vibration, and low cost. Most important LEDs are low-

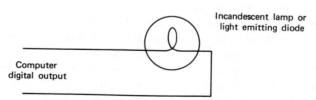

Fig. 12. The simplest digital output activated device is an indicator lamp. A single digital output bit is needed to drive each lamp that is connected to the computer. A medium power transistor output is needed to drive an incandescent bulb. LED lamps can be driven directly from logic outputs.

voltage, medium-current devices well suited to medium-power integrated circuit drivers.

Each indicator lamp to be driven is connected to a separate digital output bit. For convenience and economy the number of output bits in a group should correspond to the word size of the computer. The indicator lamp will remain on as long as the bit associated with the lamp is in the "one" state. One instruction can turn on or off the equivalent of a full word of lamps; a 16-bit-word computer permits actuation of 16 lamps. The "one" bits will turn on lamps or will keep on those lamps that are already turned on. A "zero" bit will inhibit current flow and thereby extinguish the associated lamps.

Although indicator lamps are simple and unsophisticated, they are extremely useful in implementing the man-machine interface. In any system it is essential that the computer acknowledge receipt of commands and data entered by the user. It is highly unsatisfactory to work with a computer in a separate room or with a console not in direct view of the experimenter. The user needs reassuring responses to each action. For instance, when he depresses a button indicating an action of some sort, the computer should respond that the stimulus has been accepted. The minimum (and an adequate) response is for the computer to turn on an indicator lamp, signifying that the computer has accepted the data or command. The user knows that if the appropriate lamp does not light an error condition may exist.

In this connection, it is good practice to provide at the experiment site computer controlled lamps that indicate that the computer is on, is ready and available for service, and will accept commands and/or data. There is nothing as frustrating as attempting to enter commands and data into a nonfunctioning system while being unaware of the malfunction. The simple expedient of providing indicator lamps for computer responses to user actions and commands greatly enhances the user's reliance on the computer and increases his confidence in computer assisted experimentation.

DECIMAL DISPLAYS

A single incandescent lamp or LED can be used to indicate only a single bit. In many situations, however, it becomes necessary to display decimal information (Fig. 13). The light for displaying the information can come from a number of sources, including incandescent lamps, LEDs, gas discharge tubes, liquid crystal devices, electroluminescent panels, and plas-

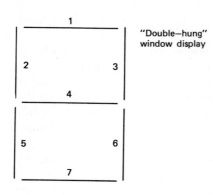

"Double—hung" window display

Fig. 13. A decimal display computer driven output is quite useful. This may be achieved in a number of different ways. One technique is to design a segment display in the form of a double-hung window. Seven segments are provided; each segment is individually controlled by a separate computer output bit. To display the digit 5, for instance, segments 1, 2, 4, 6, and 7 must be activated. The segments themselves can be implemented with LEDs, gas discharge devices, or other devices.

ma devices. Until recently, most numeric displays relied on gas discharge tube technology and incandescent lamps for their light sources. Equipment designers now incorporate LED displays and liquid crystals in their products. These current devices are more reliable, produce high-quality, easily read displays, and, more importantly, are less expensive than the earlier technologies.

Power output transistors can be used to drive projection type lamp display indicators. The devices consist of individual minature projection systems, each containing an incandescent lamp, lens, and mask. The mask image is back-projected on the display face plate. By actuating a particular lamp, the mask, which corresponds to the desired digit or message, is projected for view. Insofar as the computer is concerned, independent incandescent lamps are connected to it. By turning on a particular bit, the desired symbol or message is displayed.

Seven-segment displays are driven in a similar manner. These displays consist of seven segments arranged in the form of a double-hung window. To form a particular digit the segments needed are energized. Each segment is controlled by a separate, independent lamp or LED. Seven-power transistor devices are needed to select a particular character. These devices consume more power because several lamps are usually on to create a digit. Medium scale integrated circuit (MSI) devices containing 4-bit registers, seven-segment decoders, and appropriate power drivers are available.

Since incandescent lamps and LEDs have no memory, a separate memory element must be cascaded with each one to hold the required condition. MSI circuitry is available to perfrom this function in a very effective manner; MSI devices consisting of a 4-bit register, decoding matrix, and driver attached to each decoded output bit are available from a number of vendors. A single MSI device can thus provide all the necessary functions.

Light emitting diode displays consist of a group of LEDs arranged in a dot matrix pattern. The LEDs needed to form a particular digit are selected by the logic and actuated. These diodes can be driven from ordinary integrated circuits. The decoding logic and memory needed for a digit are available on a single MSI chip.

Nixie display tubes were the standard numeric display device until the advent of LED and liquid crystal displays. A Nixie tube is a neon tube with multiple anodes; a separate anode in the shape of each digit is provided. When an ionization path is created to a particular anode, a glow in the shape of the digit anode is created. Nixie displays require relatively high voltages (about 100 V), and special solid state circuits are needed, in turn, for these voltages.

The same technologies can be used for creating full alphanumeric displays. However, in most cases a large number of characters are needed when dealing with alphanumeric data. Hence, CRT displays are almost always used for these data.

CATHODE RAY TUBE DISPLAYS

Cathode ray tube displays use oscilloscope tubes to display alphanumeric and graphics information. Data can be written at very high rates on the faces of CRTs, and a large number of characters (as many as several thousand) can be displayed on a CRT face. The operation of a CRT display is all-electronic and therefore silent.

The simplest CRT displays are of the alphanumeric-only type; only alphanumeric information can be handled. More sophisticated displays permit point plots and offer full graphics capability. If a hierarchy of display types is considered, simple display lamps can be used for several tens of bits, numeric displays for several tens of digits, and CRTs for several tens of lines of numeric and alphanumeric text. Cathode ray tube displays are ideal for situations where moderate amounts of information should be shown rapidly and the operator does not require an on-hand permanent record. The computer can usually be programmed to print the data on a hard copy device also.

Usually CRT displays with graphics capability are much more expensive than alphanumeric-only displays. The circuitry needed to draw vectors can be quite complicated, and a great deal more storage is needed to hold the graphics data.

LIGHT PENS

Light pens are used as input devices in conjunction with CRT displays. They are extremely convenient data entry and interactive devices. A light pen is a photodetector with associated electronics. Light pens are receivers of light; they do not write or emit light.

A user points the light pen at the point of interest on the face of a CRT display. The light pen usually has a built-in lamp to assist the user to pin-point the desired spot on the CRT face. When the CRT display refresh illuminates the point at which the light pen is aimed, the light pen photodetector is excited by the CRT emitted light. The light pen amplifier and associated electronics shape the detected pulse. The instantaneous X-Y position of the CRT beam is continuously transferred to a holding register. The position of the refresh beam on the CRT face represents the coordinates of the beam, and when the refresh beam is detected by the light pen an interrupt to the computer occurs. The held coordinates are then introduced into the computer, and the program determines what is relevant about the point.

PRINTERS

The most common computer output device used to convey information to the user is the printer. A wide variety of printers are available. These operate at rates of several characters per second to several tens of lines per second and range from one-character-at-a-time impact printers, such as typewriters, to very high speed line printers using nonimpact techniques to write on sensitized paper.

Most laboratory applications use typewriters or Teletype type printers. These print one character at a time on ordinary paper or some type of sensitized paper. The print speed varies from about 10 to over 60 characters per second. Almost all computers are equipped with standard interfaces to this type of printer, which constitutes the primary peripheral on most minicomputers. Several such printers can usually be attached to a single computer. A connection distance of several thousand feet between the computer and the printer is permissible.

The printer is a nearly ideal medium of communication with the user. The information printed can be in full text form, facilitating the understanding of messages. The quality of printing is good, and a permanent record of all print-outs can be stored. Printer response is usually sufficiently fast unless large quantities of data are required. The relatively low cost and the great familiarity with printed output tend to make selection of a printer as the primary computer output natural. Most systems are equipped with at least one printer.

AUDIO RESPONSE UNITS

Computer outputs can be arranged to drive audio response units. Such systems will rarely be encountered in a laboratory experiment environment, however, because of their high cost. Audio response units consist of prerecorded key words and phrases, which can be in digital form or in a compact, high-speed analog form. To transmit a message, the selected words are retrieved from the store and arranged in the desired form. The words are reconstituted through digital to analog conversion or slowdown of the high-speed analog. The message is then transmitted over ordinary telephone circuits.

EYE MOTION SENSORS

Eye motion sensors are mounted on the user himself and sense the instantaneous position of the pupils in his eyes. These devices, which are quite complicated and expensive, have come into use for specialized applications, such as sensing the direction in which a pilot is looking. This information is useful in gun aiming. Eye motion sensors would be useful in laboratory experiments with subjects where eye position information is required. The outputs of eye motion sensor devices are the instantaneous pointing angles of the eyes.

PLOTTERS

Plotters are computer output devices that lend themselves to CAE environments. Scientists naturally tend to graphic display of results. Hence, if a computer driven plotter output is available, the work of the scientist and his acclimation to computers in his experimental work are enhanced.

Plotters that provide hard copy and those that furnish only transient displays are available. Transient output plotters imply CRT displays that also have graphics capability. Generally the plot is available as long as the picture is displayed on the face of the CRT. As soon as the CRT is turned off, the picture vanishes. A major advantage of graphics output on a CRT is the relative ease of designing interactive systems. Cursors, light pens, graphical inputs, and keyboard devices can be used to interact with CRT displays. If hard copy is required, the computer can be programmed to plot the results. Hard copy devices capable of immediately printing the picture displayed on a CRT are available from a number of vendors. These involve scanning the CRT display and printing on sensitized paper.

Hard copy output digital plotters designed especially for connection to computers are also available from several vendors. Digital incremental plotters are most convenient when operating in a computer environment. They are relatively fast and provide precise graphics of very high quality. A large amount of software has been deevloped for use with these plotters. The pen on an incremental digital plotter can move one or two increments in the X and Y directors for each computer command. Also, each command has a pen-up (move but no write) and pen-down (move and write) option. Two-step increment plotters have additional options capable of movement in up to two increments in each direction for each command. Incremental plotters capable of steps as small as 0.005 in. and of 500 steps per second are available.

Conventional X-Y analog plotters can be connected to a digital computer via a pair of DACs. Each drive axis on the plotter is driven by one of the converters. Plotters of the X-Y type are slower and less accurate than incremental plotters.

17 Minicomputer Architectures

This chapter discusses the architecture and organization of minicomputers, with particular emphasis on those having characteristics that make them suitable for computer aided experimentation. Although any digital computer can be used in such an environment, certain characteristics are desirable for this kind of application.

The major component, aside from the instrumentation of the experiment itself, is obviously the computer. The computer is usually the most expensive component in the system when all engineering and programming expenses are considered, and its appropriateness determines in large measure the success of the complete project. Selection of a computer is always a difficult task. For real-time applications such as CAE, the selection is even more critical because of the direct connection between the computer and the environment.

SELECTION CRITERIA

Small and medium-size binary, high-speed digital computers are usually used for these applications. Suitable computers are available from well over 50 manufacturers. Complete computers capable of handling these applications range in price from below $1000 to over $500,000; most computers selected for this class of applications are in the $10,000 price range. The market for suitable computers is highly competitive because of the great number of different manufacturers engaged in it. It is significant that computers having approximately the same computing power as these minicomputers but designed for business applications have very much poorer price-performance ratios.

The reader is referred to current periodicals dealing with computing for a comprehensive list of minicomputers currently available from various manufacturers. These listings summarize the performance of each minicomputer and give typical prices for useful configurations. Except for the major manufacturers, the vendors and the models they offer change rapidly between successive listings. The price-performance ratio, which is a measure of the price of a given computer configuration as a function of computer capacity, is continually improving with time. For the user, higher performance is now obtainable at a more attractive price than ever before.

In selecting a minicomputer the user is advised to evaluate the manufacturer's capability for providing support and maintenance. As discussed in Chapter 1, two separate minicomputer markets exist. The first consists of users of computers in experimentation, who are end users. Such a user purchases a computer to perform a specific job and is primarily interested in applying the computer to his application as quickly and expeditiously as possible. He is interested in developing software for the particular application only. Maintenance of hardware from the vendor is usually mandatory because the user is not equipped to maintain the computer system or interested in doing so. In the second market category is the original equipment manufacturer (OEM) customer. The OEM customer purchases a quantity of computers for incorporation into other systems that are meant for resale. The OEM customer typically has engineering capability at his disposal and is interested primarily in price-performance. He can afford to invest in special designs and in software development because his costs are spread over a large number of systems. Since the computer is a component of a system that the OEM customer plans to sell, he usually provides maintenance on the computer as part of the overall system. For these reasons a computer meant for OEM applications, although much less expensive than one meant for the end-user role, will not satisfy the needs of the end user who plans to apply one or two computers. The typical CAE requires a minicomputer from a firm that will provide software and hardware support and maintenance.

GENERAL CHARACTERISTICS

Most current minicomputers are organized around a word structure having 12 or 16 bits, but word lengths of 8 and 18 bits are also used. The relatively short word length is what distinguishes minicomputers from full-size or large-scale computers. More important, it is a major reason why minicomputers can be produced so inexpensively. In most real-time applications, especially in data acquisition, 16 bits are sufficient to maintain data precision and resolution. In situations that require higher resolution, double-word data formats are handled, either by hardware instructions or via subroutines.

The memory cycle time of most commercially available minicomputers ranges between 2 μsec and about 100 nsec. Between 200,000 and 10,000,000 instructions per second can be executed, depending on the memory cycle time selected. Data I/O rates equal to the memory cycle time can be sustained when data channel or direct access memory options are implemented. The speed of a particular minicomputer is almost always a function of the memory cycle time. The integrated circuit logic used for accessing operands and data and for executing instructions is inherently fast, and is usually not the speed limiting factor except when solid state storage is used.

Although most computers used for CAE are small and inexpensive, large computers can also be (and are) used for this application. However, only large, well financed projects can usually justify large systems. Because of budgetary considerations most computers used in CAE are minicomputers, which have sufficient performance capability to provide the compute power needed.

The cost of a minicomputer system is heavily dependent on the amount of memory purchased. Memory is the most expensive component, aside from the central processor unit. Minicomputers performing useful jobs are available with as little as a few hundred words of memory, but the most common minimum memory sizes are 2048 and 4096 words. Minicomputers are usually available with binary increments of memory, or in 2048 or 4096 word increments. Maximum memory on some minicomputers ranges up to 65K words, or even more.

The short word size and limited memory capacity permit economies in the manufacture of minicomputers—hence, the relatively low prices. These features, however, place limitations on the computing capability of minicomputers. The relatively short word size requires that the computer designer utilizes instruction words ingeniously so as to create a powerful instruction set. Some of these techniques are discussed below.

Directly addressing any operand stored in memory with a single-word instruction is not possible with the short word size typical of minicomputers. With 16-bit words, for instance, about half the bits of an instruction would be needed to indicate op code, indexing, and indirect addressing. Only 8 to 10 bits would remain, depending on the computer architecture, for specifying the address of the operand. For this reason various techniques have been developed to address all of memory by using the address portions of short instruction as displacement or relative addresses rather than absolute direct addresses. The displacement may be referenced to various registers in the computer, such as the instruction counter, index registers, or page boundaries. Various methods for address computation are discussed in this chapter.

Another major limitation on the computational capability of a minicomputer is the absence of floating point arithmetic hardware. This is not usually a limitation in data acquisition phases. However, where extensive arithmetic calculations are needed, floating point capability simplifies programming. In many cases (and always where Fortran is available), floating point calculation is accomplished via subroutine, which is a slow process compared to fixed point computation. Although floating point arithmetic options can be designed into a minicomputer, this is expensive and the basic structure of the minicomputer may not justify floating point arithmetic hardware. When extensive floating point computation is necessary, linkage to a larger computer capable of such functions should be considered.

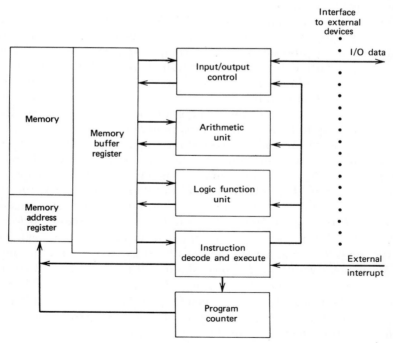

Fig. 1. Computer block diagram, showing major components making up minicomputer.

To fully appreciate what makes a computer more or less useful for laboratory automation and in a real-time environment, some of the basic concepts of computer organization, with particular emphasis on the components and characteristics that facilitate computer applications in laboratory automation and in real-time environments will be described. The actual selection of a computer from among the many available minicomputers necessitates analysis of the specific requirements for the job at hand.

COMPONENTS

Although made up of large numbers of components (Fig. 1), the basic circuits of a computer are few in number. The hardware consists of gate circuits and register elements. Gate circuits permit signals to pass between register elements. Depending on the arrangement of the gates, simple transfers can be affected without altering data, or complicated arithmetic functions can be implemented.

Gate circuits and register elements are made up of integrated circuit devices. Register elements are storage circuits. Each register element stores one data bit, and a register consists of a number of elements. It is usual to design registers that hold full computer words.

BLOCK DIAGRAM

The major hardware blocks of a digital computer are (1) data input section, (2) data output section, (3) arithmetic unit, (4) control unit, and (5) main memory. The data I/O features are most important in evaluating computer applicability to a particular experiment. The data input section of a computer accepts information and instructions from various peripheral devices and instruments in real time and enters them into the computer memory and registers. The data output section fetches data and commands from memory locations and computer registers and presents them to output peripheral devices and various instrument control devices. The data input and output sections may be quite simple, or they may be capable of performing complicated operations. In all cases, their operation is initiated by and is under the control of the program instructions. Connections of an experiment or real-time application to a computer are handled via the I/O sections. Thus these characteristics are most important.

DATA FLOW

Two information transfer paths can be identified in a typical computer system: (1) the data flow path between central memory and the computer working registers and I/O bus, and (2) addresses to store and fetch information from the central memory of the computer. All the major computer working registers and arithmetic and control sections are connected to the data flow path connected to the memory (Fig. 2). This is the central data distribution path for all information. Every register and arithmetic and control section component has two accesses to the data bus: as input and output. To execute instructions, the central logic sets up the data paths between the necessary components. Depending on the design of the particular computer, these data paths may be implemented as bidirectional signal flow paths. Alternatively, two sets of unidirectional buses, one for each direction of data interchange, may be provided.

Data enter or leave the computer main memory through a temporary storage register—the memory buffer register (MBR) This register also plays the central role in regenerating data in main memory. Information fetched from main memory is held in the MBR and is transmitted to the destination register. The contents of the MBR are then written into the memory location that is read from. The read/write memory cycle is thus completed.

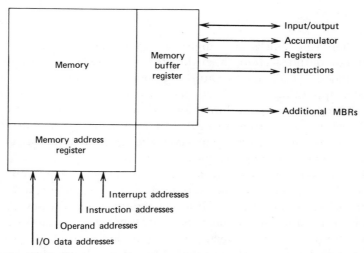

Fig. 2. Block diagram: computer main memory, showing data flow between main memory and various computer components.

An operand may be fetched and held temporarily in the MBR and then added to the contents of register A. The control logic sets up data flow paths between register A and the MBR register via the arithmetic section; these two registers constitute inputs to the arithmetic unit. The control logic primes the arithmetic unit to perform the addition, and the sum is then routed via the data bus to register A.

Input/output information is handled similarly by routing data via the data bus, which is the main highway for interconnecting all data flow paths in a computer system. To speed up computer operations, more than one data bus may be used. In this way more than one data flow path is created, and more than one concurrent data transfer can take place. This feature is particularly useful in overlapping I/O operations with processing. Separate data flow paths can be established for each I/O device.

The second signal flow path in a computer processor is to the memory address register (MAR). Memory addresses may be generated by a number of different system registers. Addresses of instructions, operands, and I/O words are forwarded to the MAR. The information stored at the specified location is fetched or stored, depending on the memory control mode: read or write.

CONTROL LOGIC

All computer data and instructions are stored in the central memory of the computer. A program consists of a sequence of instructions stored in the central memory. Data and instructions may be stored anywhere in the computer memory, and examining the contents of a particular memory location will not indicate whether the data or instructions of interest are stored there. The contents of memory locations are binary numbers. A number may be routed to the arithmetic unit or the control unit. Information routed to the control unit is interpreted by the control logic as an instruction (Fig. 3). The control unit in turn sends signals to all the computer components to execute instructions.

The control logic executes each instruction in accordance with the operations code and operands contained in the word. Instructions may be arithmetic operations, Boolean functions, bit manipulation, branching, or I/O commands. The major components of the control logic unit are the program (or instruction) counter, the operations code register and decoder, and the operand addressing functions. Instructions are normally stored in sequential memory locations and fetched one after another. The

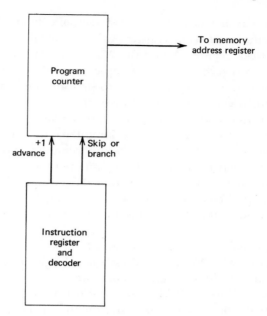

Fig. 3. Control logic block diagram, showing instruction decoding logic and program counter control. All computer operations are controlled by this logic. Program sequences and branches are determined by the program counter, which always is set to point to the address of the next instruction.

program counter points to the address of the next instruction to be fetched.

Instruction cycles are divided into "I" and "E" phases. When an instruction is fetched from memory, the I phase is entered. The instruction is entered into the operations code (op code) register. The op code is interpreted, and execution may begin. In almost all minicomputers, an instruction is contained in a single word of storage. Therefore one I cycle is required to fetch and interpret an instruction. Two I cycles are needed when an instruction fits into two words of storage or when indirect addressing is specified, on computers equipped with this feature.

Many computer instructions do not need a second operand and can be executed without reference to a memory location, that is, they can be executed directly on the contents of an active register. This is the fastest type of instruction to execute because additional memory references are not needed. The control logic can begin the E phase (executing the instruction) immediately after the I phase. Instructions that require a term from memory for execution require also a second memory reference cycle; the E phase cannot be completed until the second memory cycle is taken to fetch or store the specified operand.

Instructions that do not reference operands that are in memory can be executed in a single memory access cycle, which is needed to access the instruction. Instructions that access operands that are in memory require at least two memory access cycles: one to access the instruction, and a second to access the operand. Depending on the addressing mode, additional cycles may be needed. Long instructions, such as multiplying and dividing, usually take several cycles to execute.

INSTRUCTION FORMATS

The format of a possible minicomputer instruction (Fig. 4) may be as follows: OPCODE, IA, X, D, PAGE, ADDRESS. This format contains almost every option found on a minicomputer. Six fields can be identified: (1) operations code (OPCODE), (2) indirect address flag (IA), (3) index (X), (4) double word (D) flag, (5) page, (6) address of operand.

The op code field identifies the instruction to be performed. The op code may be between 3 and 8 bits in length. A 3-bit op code permits the computer to recognize 8 basic codes; a 5-bit op code implies 32 basic codes; and 8-bit code permits 256 codes.

The instruction repertoire is usually grouped into memory reference operand instructions and nonmemory reference operand instructions. Memory reference instructions should use the fewest possible op code bits because a sufficient number of bits must be available in the instruction

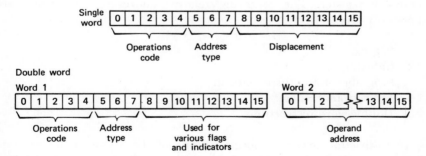

Fig. 4. Instruction word format: each computer program instruction word contains a number of fields that define the operation code and modifying bits. A typical format is shown.

for addressing operands. Nonmemory reference instructions use a two-part op code consisting of one or two basic op code groups, modified by other bits in the instruction. These bits can be used in any manner because they are not needed for addressing. Thus, when a nonmemory reference instruction op code is recognized, the IA, X, D, page, and address fields are interpreted as modifiers to the basic instruction op code by the control logic. In this manner a large number of instructions can be recognized.

ADDRESSING OPERANDS

When an operand is fetched or stored, the control logic must supply the address of the operand to the memory addressing register. An effective address can be computed in a number of ways, depending on the architecture of the computer. The IA, X, D and page fields specify the operand addressing mode for the instruction. An operand may be located anywhere within main memory. If main memory has 4096 locations, an address must be a number of at least 12 bits. Some minicomputers provide for eventual expansion to over 65,536 words. Addresses of at least 16 bits are needed to access any location. An instruction word of even 16 bits cannot hold an op code, index and indirect addressing indicators, and a 16-bit operand address. A number of techniques are available to compute the effective operand address that may be in any permissible memory location and still use single word-length instructions. These techniques involve adding the instruction address field to a base register that is a full word in length. Thus all operand locations are computed to be referenced to a memory location whose address is held in a particular computer register. The following relative addressing techniques are commonly used:

1. Paging.
2. Indexing.
3. Program counter displacement.
4. Indirect addressing.
5. Double-word instructions.

An instruction may use more than one of the above modes in computing the address of an operand. Several methods can be combined in a single instruction. The control logic adds the specified factors together to determine the effective operand address.

PAGING

Memory may be divided into pages (Fig. 5) with each page containing a specified number of words. The size of a page is equal to the binary power of the number of bits in the address field of the instruction. Thus an address field of 7 bits will permit 128-word pages; a 10-bit address field implies 1024-word pages. A 4096-word memory could therefore have 32 128-word pages; it could also be divided into 4 1024-word pages. A page is identified by the address of the first word on the page.

The control logic determines the address of the operand by adding the instruction address field to the current page address. A special register is used to store the current page. The addition is performed by simply ORing the address field to the current page field. The current page field

Memory

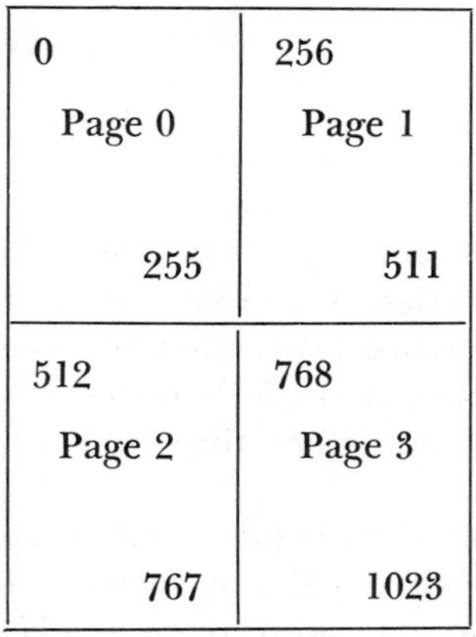

| 0

Page 0

255 | 256

Page 1

511 |
| 512

Page 2

767 | 768

Page 3

1023 |

| P | Displacement |

P = 0
    Address = Displacement
P = 1
    Address = Current Page + Displacement

Fig. 5. A typical minicomputers memory organization technique divides memory into equal-sized pages. Instructions refer to operands, which are displaced with respect to a particular page boundary. In many systems an instruction can refer to page "zero" and the "current" page.

always contains zeros in its least significant bit positions, whereas the instruction address field contains zeros in the most significant bit positions.

The instruction itself will contain a true "P" bit flag, indicating that the address is to be computed by referencing the current page number. This number can be set under program control. If reference is to be made to an address outside the boundaries of the current page, the program must change the current page before issuing instructions referencing a new page. Thus two instructions are needed to reference an operand outside the page boundary.

To provide additional convenience of referencing larger segments of memory without changing the current page number, the instruction "P" bit is set as zero. When the "P" bit is false, the logic assumes that the zero page is being referenced. In this way two full pages are always accessible without altering the current page register. The zero page is effectively exploited by storing common data and communications linkage parameters in the area. Thus instructions in every page can quickly gain access to information in the zero page.

INDEXING,

From the following discussion it will become apparent that indexing is one of the most powerful computer facilities. A computer may have one or more index registers. A memory reference instruction involves index registers if the X bits are not equal to zero. A single X bit permits reference to only one index register; two X bits allow three index registers to be referenced.

Index registers may have additional functions besides address manipulation. They may be designed as integrated circuits or memory location registers. Index registers are full computer word registers. Hardware index registers are preferable because address modification can be performed much more rapidly. If an index register is stored as a memory location, at least one additional memory cycle is needed to access an operand. Some computers do not contain X bits in their instruction formats, but reference index register functions by addressing specific memory locations. The computer hardware can recognize these locations as index formats. In this case a great many index register functions can be implemented.

In the simplest indexed addressing form, the control logic adds the instruction address field to the number stored in the specified index register to obtain the location of the operand. In these index register implementations, the contents of the index register are not changed by referencing.

Index registers are useful for applications other than address modification. It is possible to add or subtract one to the contents of an index register each time it is referenced. This is particularly useful for counting applications and for extracting data sequentially from a table. Most computers use the overflow or zero status of a register to initiate a program switch. When the desired condition occurs, the program may branch to a new area or skip an instruction. When versatile indexing facilities are provided, the uses are limited only to the imagination of the programmer. Index register contents may be stored and loaded under program control.

PROGRAM COUNTER DISPLACEMENT

The operand address may be computed by adding the address field of an instruction to the contents of the program counter. Either the complete program counter or only its most significant bits may be used. It should be noted that the displacement address may be a signed number. In that case the operand address may be in a location either below or above the program counter.

INDIRECT ADDRESSING

To signify an indirect addressing mode the IA bit in the instruction field is set to one. Indirect addressing implies that the operand address is stored in the location referred to by the instruction. The same techniques used to compute the operand address can serve to compute the indirect address. The control logic uses the contents of this location to access the operand. Indirect addressing adds an extra memory access cycle to the execution time of an instruction. Some computers permit several levels of indirect addressing.

DOUBLE-WORD INSTRUCTIONS

Double-word instructions use two sequential memory locations for an instruction. The first word contains the op code, and the second word contains the address of the operand. Double-word instructions are inefficient in the use of memory space because two words are needed to store an instruction but may be required when single-word instructions do not satisfy the programmer's need to access any memory location directly. Computers having double-word instruction capability also have single-word instruction formats. Double-word instruction formats do not preclude indexing and indirect addressing.

INSTRUCTION TYPES

The op code specifies what operation should be executed. Instructions may be grouped into several categories: (1) load and store, (2) arithmetic and logic, (3) register manipulation, (4) program sequence control, and (5) input/output. Register manipulation instructions usually do not need memory reference cycles for operands. Memory reference instructions need an E cycle to fetch or store operands in memory.

LOAD AND STORE

This group of instructions permits data to be stored in the working registers of the computer. Typically the contents of the A, B, and X registers may be loaded or stored in memory. The A and B registers are used for arithmetic and logical operations, and the X registers are index registers. When the contents of a register are stored, they are not altered. Similarly, when data are loaded into a selected register, the contents of the memory location are not changed. Some computers have instructions that load and store both single words and double words. This group of instructions may include the following:

Load.
Store.
Load double word.
Store double word.

Load and store instructions are of the single-word type and refer to register A (the accumulator). When the index flag is set, the referenced index register is loaded or stored. Double-word load and store instructions refer to the A and B registers taken together. Some computers possess multiple working registers. The op code of such a computer contains a field identifying the particular working register to be loaded or stored.

ARITHMETIC AND LOGIC

This group of instructions performs arithmetic and logic operations. The basic add instruction hardware logic must be implemented; from this instruction the other arithmetic operations may be derived. It is more efficient to design a specific circuit for each function. Some computers have the capability of adding and subtracting double-word factors. This group of instructions may include:

Add.
Subtract.
Multiply.
Divide.
AND.
OR.
XOR.
Compare.

Arithmetic and logic instructions are usually memory reference instructions. One operand is in the accumulator (A register), and the other factor is fetched from a memory location. The result remains in the accumulator after the completion of the instruction. Multiply instructions result in double-word products; that is, the product of two N-bit numbers can occupy $2N$ bits. Usually the A and B registers are coupled to hold the product of a multiply instruction. Divide instructions expect to find the dividend as a double word in the A and B registers. The divisor is fetched from memory. The single-word quotient is in one of the two working registers. Hardware implementation of multiply and divide is sometimes not provided on minicomputers. Computers that do not have hardware multiply and divide use subroutines to perform these functions by combinations of successive additions or subtractions and shifting.

Logical operations such as AND, OR, and Exclusive OR (XOR) may be specified. A compare operation is essentially an arithmetic operation because the difference between two factors may be computed. Some computers do not have a subtract function; this can also be done via subroutine by complementing and adding. Similarly, logical functions—AND, OR, XOR—can be done by combinations of steps. Hardware implementation, of course, yields much faster results than multiple instruction subroutines.

Associated with arithmetic instructions is a group of flags and indicators that may be set by the arithmetic operations. These flags, which can be set, reset, and tested under program control, are used to indicate zero results, overflow, and carries, as well as positive, negative, and equal, depending on the operation specified. These flags are particularly useful when performing multiple precision operations or floating point subroutines.

REGISTER MANIPULATION

This group of instructions is not of the memory reference type. The data in the computer general registers are handled without reference to memory operands. Register manipulation instructions include the following:

1. Register zero set.
2. Register one set.
3. Register sense all zeros.
4. Register sense all ones.
5. Register sense negative.
6. Register sense positive.
7. Register sense add.
8. Register sense even.
9. Register complement.
10. Register interchanges.
11. Register arithmetic odd.
12. Register arithmetic subtract.
13. Register logical add.
14. Shift right logical.
15. Shift right long logical.
16. Shift left logical.
17. Shift left long logical.
18. Shift right arithmetic.
19. Shift right arithmetic long.
20. Rotate.
21. Rotate long.

The number of register instructions can be large, and the variety of instructions comprehensive. Most computers use the individual bits in the instruction to microprogram the register manipulation instructions. This category of instruction is the fastest executing because only one memory access cycle time is needed to carry it out.

Shifting instructions involve moving bits in a word a number of positions left or right. Thus a single-bit shift right would convert 100110 to

010011. A three-bit shift left would convert 100110 to 110000. Most computers provide long shift instructions, which have the effect of linking the A and B registers so that the most significant bits (MSBs) of the right register shift into the least significant bit (LSB) positions of the left register on a shift left instruction. On a shift right instruction, bits flow in the reverse direction. Bits shifted out of either end of the linked registers are lost. Some computers use the link or carry register as a one-bit extension to the registers when shifting. Another shift function is the rotate command; that is, the LSB is connected to the MSB position for a rotate right command. A rotate left reverses the flow. A long rotate links the LSB and MSB of the two registers.

Shifts may be classified as arithmetic or logical. In a logical shift the bits are shifted exactly as they are without taking account of sign. For positive numbers this has no effect. For negative numbers represented in 2's complement form, however, a right shift would invalidate the sign. Shifting 1110101 logically right yields 0111010; an arithmetic shift yields 1111010. The sign is preserved.

PROGRAM SEQUENCE CONTROL

Under normal circumstances the program counter fetches instructions in sequential order from memory. The program counter always points to the location of the next instruction to be fetched. When a fetch phase (I) is completed, the program counter is incremented by one. To change the program sequence, it is necessary to change the contents of the program counter. Thus, to skip one instruction, the number in the program counter should be increased by one before the next I phase. To skip two instructions, the program counter should be incremented by two. To branch to an entirely new program area, the program counter should be altered to indicate the new address of the desired program area. The program in the new area will begin execution, and the program counter will be incremented by one from the new location onward for each instruction executed.

The program sequence control logic alters the sequence of program execution by modifying the program counter. The sequence control logic can cause unconditional branches or may make the determination to accept a branch if specified conditions exist. The program counter may thus be altered on the basis of a "true" indication of a number of test conditions. The following are commonly used conditions:

Skip/branch   Register zeros.

Skip/branch Register ones.
Skip/branch Register negative.
Skip/branch Register positive.
Skip/branch Register even.
Skip/branch Register add.
Skip/branch Overflow.
Skip/branch Underflow.
Skip/branch Carry
Skip/branch Indicator set.
Skip/branch Indicator not set.

The next sequential instruction will be taken if the tested condition is "false." Thus the contents of the program instruction counter will not be disturbed. A "true" condtion will cause an additional increment to the program instruction counter, causing the next sequential instruction to be skipped and the following instruction to be executed. The contents of the program instruction counter are replaced by the branch address if a "true" tested condition is detected. If a "false" condition is tested, the next sequential instruction is taken.

INPUT-OUTPUT

Input-output instructions specify the flow of data and commands from the computer to external devices and from external devices to the computer. Data may be transferred between computer registers or memory locations and external devices. In CAE applications, as well as other real-time environments, the I/O facility is paramount. It is through this facility that all communications of data and commands between the computer and the experiment or instrumentation must pass. Because of the importance of I/O function implementation in the selection of computers for real-time application, a full chapter (Chapter 12) is devoted to the topic.

Input/output instructions may be either memory reference or register instructions. When an I/O instruction specifies a transfer to one of the computer registers, the instruction does not need a memory reference cycle. However, the contents of the register are disturbed by an input operation, whereas on output the contents of the selected register are not altered. Input/output instructions involving data transfer from memory locations require an extra memory cycle for each data word transferred.

MEMORY

The main memory storage of a minicomputer may be implemented using core memory or integrated circuit memory elements. For each bit stored in the memory a separate core or circuit is needed. Thus the total number of bits that can be stored is equal to the number of cores or integrated circuit elements. Core memories and integrated circuit memories are organized in words. A specified number of bits make up each word. As indicated, the number of bits per word in most minicomputers ranges between 8 and 18, with 12- and 16-bit words being most common. Computer memory capacities are available in binary steps: 2048 words, 4096 words, and so on. Memories with capacities of 4096 words are a minimum for most applications. Of course, selection of a specified memory size is determined by the particular application. Memories in excess of 32,768 or 65,536 words are rarely used. These sizes are close to the limit of the convenient addressing capabilities of small computers and are also quite expensive. Memories of 16,384 words usually cost more than the basic CPU of a minicomputer.

CORE MEMORIES

A core memory system contains arrays of cores in which information is stored. To access a particular word of information, the computer control logic passes an address to the memory address register (MAR). The address is decoded, and a particular set of sense amplifiers is actuated. This has the effect of selecting a group of cores that contain the word of interest. The memory is organized so that 1 bit for each word is in one plane of cores. For each bit a separate plane is provided; the number of planes is equal to the number of bits in a word. By using coincident current techniques, a particular core in each plane is selected by the address decoding circuit.

The computer control logic must indicate to the memory system if a read or write operation on the address passed to the MAR is desired. If information is to be stored in the memory, the computer must load the word to be written or stored into the memory buffer register (MBR) before starting the memory cycle. If data are to be read from the memory, the requested word will be fetched from the specified word location and read into the MBR by the memory logic control. The memory proceeds through an identical cycle for read or write. The first step is to access the particular location specified by the address in the MAR and fetch the word stored there. If a read cycle has been specified, the accessed word will be loaded into the MBR and is then ready for the computer. The access time is approximately half the total memory cycle. If a write cycle was specified, the data read out of the location are not utilized. However, it is necessary to effectively reset the addressed location to zero so that it can be written into. Sometime during the first half of the read/write cycle, data to be written into the memory are entered into the MBR. The word in the MBR at the start of the second half cycle must be either the word read out during the first half cycle or the word that the computer has requested be stored. The write cycle involves writing the word in the MBR in the location specified by the address in the MAR. If a read cycle was specified, the word previously read out during the read cycle is regenerated and stored in the same location from which it was read. For a write command, the original memory contents are lost and a new word is written.

The memory read and write half cycles are separate and independent. It is entirely possible to organize a memory to read data from a particular location during the read half cycle and write entirely different data into the location during the write phase. This arrangement permits the computer to read a word, modify it, and write it back into memory— all on one memory cycle. Computers generally do not operate in this manner, however, except for very specific applications. It is possible to gain access to the computer MBR and MAR and perform this function using special-purpose interface equipment. In this mode, a pause is inserted between the read and restore cycles, giving the external hardware an opportunity to use the data. An "add one" to the memory hardware option does exactly this. The external device has access to the computer MAR and MBR. Each time the data word corresponding to the address inserted by the external device in the MAR is fetched into the MBR, the external device causes one to be added to the MBR contents, which are then restored in the memory.

BUFFER MEMORIES

Memories can be designed to operate in a read-only or write-only mode. These arrangements, which are especially useful for buffering peripheral data, are essentially half cycle operations. Data are written into locations as specified by the MAR. In the read mode, the data stored in these locations are read into the MBR. To operate in a write-only half cycle mode, the locations to be read into must first have been read out or reset. When working in a half cycle mode, it is convenient to specify the MAR as a counter as well as a register. When using the MAR as a register, the memory functions in a random access mode and any address in any sequence can be accessed. When the MAR is connected as a counter and the memory is set to either read or write, data are transferred in only one direction into or from sequential locations. This half cycle mode is particularly useful for buffer and interface applications.

MAGNETIC CORES

Each bit stored in a core memory is held in a physical core. Cores are made of ferrite ceramic material and are shaped like a doughnut. They typically have outside diameters of 0.020 in. and inside diameters of 0.013 in.

The ferrite core magnetization can be switched electrically and thereby store binary information as clockwise and counterclockwise magnetization. When a current carrying wire is threaded through the core, the core's direction of magnetization can be reversed simply by changing the direction of the current. The magnetic state remains indefinitely after the current is removed, so that switching can be accomplished by bidirectional current pulses. If the magnetizing force is less than the critical value, the state of the core is not affected.

Core memories may be organized in a number of different manners. The most economical arrangement is designated as a 3D structure; the name describes how the address and sense wires are threaded through the cores. The 3D configuration assures a minimum number of external electronics and a minimum-cost system.

The 3D configuration requires that four wires be threaded through each core. Two wires are used for address selection. A core is selected by passing current through it coincidentally in the X and Y directions. A common X wire passes through all the cores in a particular X line. Similarly, a common wire passes through each Y line. A matrix of 4096 cores would be arranged in a square of 64 by 64 cores. There would be 64 sets of X and Y address lines. To select a particular core one X and one Y line are selected. Half the current to set a core is sent down the selected X and Y lines. Only the core at the selected coincidence point of X and Y will receive sufficient current to switch the core. All other cores will receive half current, which is insufficient to change the magnetization of the core.

The function described above is the technique for selecting a particular core in a large array. This selects 1 bit. A separate array of cores is used for each bit of the computer word. Thus, if 16-bit words are to be stored, 16 arrays are needed. The corresponding X and Y lines on each array are selected. In this manner the full computer word is accessed at one time.

Every computer memory cycle passes through two phases, read and write. Reading data from a core memory is a destructive process. To sense the status of a particular core, the memory control circuits attempts to set the core to the zero magnetization state. The X and Y lines for that location are pulsed simultaneously. If a "one" is stored at the location, the state of the core will change magnetization. A pulse will appear on the "sense" line threaded through all the cores of the bit array. The "one" pulse is amplified and presented as the output for the particular bit position. If the selected core stored a "zero," no output will be sensed on the sense line because no change in core magnetization will have occurred. The memory control logic will interpret a sense pulse output as a "one" and a no-pulse output condition as a "zero" bit. A separate sense winding is threaded through each array, one for each bit in the word. This is the third winding through each core in an array.

After each sensing operation the condition of the sensed core is zero. Reading a location causes its contents to be lost. The data are in the MBR. At this point the read-out information may be written back into the same location or new information can be written. To write information, the X, Y, and inhibit windings are used. The inhibit winding is the forth wire that is threaded through all the cores in an array. To write, the directions of current in the X and Y wires of the selected location are reversed from the direction for accessing. The only core that will receive two in-phase half currents will be the one at the intersection of the selected X and Y windings; all other cores receive only half switching currents. To write a "zero," the inhibit winding for the bit array is not inhibited. The selected core will switch to the "zero" state. To write a "one," the inhibit winding is actuated with a half switching current pulse, which will prevent the selected core from switching. Thus it will remain in the "one" state.

INTEGRATED CIRCUIT MEMORIES

An appreciable portion of computer main memory is being implemented with a technology based on large-scale integrated circuits (LSIs). Manufacturers of LSIs have developed several different integrated circuit techniques that permit economical production of memories suitable for the main store of digital computers. The very largest computers, as well as minicomputers, feature main memories that take advantage of this technology.

Both MOS and bipolar LSIs have been perfected for use as main memory components. At present, choice between MOS and bipolar circuits is on speed-cost considerations. Bipolar devices are faster than MOS devices, but the latter are fast enough for most computer memory applications. Single chips with 1024 to 4096 bits are readily available and may be arranged in various word size configurations, such as 1024×1, 512×2, 256×4, or 128×8. Sixty-four 1024×1 integrated circuit elements can be connected to form 4096×16 memory. Each chip contains its own address decoding circuits, as well as read/write control lines.

Insofar as the user is concerned, an integrated circuit main memory appears identical to a core memory. Any word can be fetched or stored randomly from any memory location. Data can be written into any particular location and can be fetched when needed. The overriding advantage of an integrated circuit memory over a core memory is the superior price-performance ratio afforded by the integrated circuit memory. Integrated circuit memories typically have cycle times of about 100 nsec. The highest-performance commercially available core memories have cycle times of about 400 nsec. These are at premium prices, however. Integrated circuit memories rated at 100-nsec cycle time are becoming comparable in cost to standard 1-μsec-cycle-time core memories.

In all respects integrated circuit main memories can be used in the same way as core memories. In fact, some computers are designed with interchangeable core memories and integrated circuit memories. In some cases both types are provided in the same computer.

Core memories are inherently nonvolatile. When power is removed from a nonvolatile storage device, such as a magnetic core memory, the information stored in the memory remains intact. Thus the information stored in a magnetic core memory is preserved when the power is turned off or is suddenly disconnected. Of course, a satisfactory sequence control is needed to prevent transients from disturbing the stored data. On the other hand, integrated circuit memories are volatile storage devices. As soon as power is lost or a power transient occurs, the contents of the memory are lost. Recovery and restart after a power failure require reloading the integrated circuit memory. Computers with core memories may be restarted more easily when power is restored.

READ-ONLY MEMORIES

Many computer applications require the retrieval of fixed information that may be data or instructions. There is no need to change the values or commands. It is obvious that a read-only memory should be less expensive and faster than a full read/write memory system. Read-only memories (ROMs) are convenient for storage of data tables, nonchanging programs, and instructions.

A number of techniques have been developed for implementing ROMs, which are usually rapid access and lower in cost than read/write memories of corresponding capacity. Read-only memories use core arrays, core braids, MOS devices, diode networks, and resistor networks. The data stored in a ROM can sometimes be altered by making physical connection changes. This is the case for most discrete device ROMs such as core arrays and diode or resistor networks.

Some core devices and integrated circuit memories can be designed to be electrically switchable; that is, they are used as ROMs normally, but their contents can be electrically switched. Multiaperature cores or partial switching technique devices lend themselves to ROM-read/write operation. Solid state read-mostly devices are also available. Electrically alterable devices such as these are sometimes referred to as read-mostly memories or programmable read-only memories (PROM).

MICROPROGRAMMING

A computer program is a sequence of instructions. Each instruction in turn consists of a sequence of steps. The number of steps that constitute an instruction is determined by the computer hardware and the function to be performed. The steps are individually quite simple. The sequence of steps to execute an instruction is controlled by the logic of the computer, and these steps represent essentially the execution of commands stored in the way the computer logic is made up. In reality, the individual instructions consist of small sequences of prestored commands. To make up a new instruction the computer designer must put together the necessary logic functions to transfer data between registers and control the various gates using the command logic built-into the computer.

With the advent of high-speed, low-cost ROMs, many computer designs are based on implementation of instructions by executing a micro-program stored in the ROM. Thus each instruction is a sequence of ROM stored commands. The computer logic decodes its instructions and accesses the appropriate command sequence in the ROM. To change or create new instructions sets, the list in the ROM is altered. This type of approach provides great flexibility in tailoring an instruction set to a particular application. Microprogramming using commands stored in the ROM provides an economical way to implement the computer control logic.

FIRMWARE

The advent of economical ROMs has created a new term—firmware. The term implies that a set of programs for a particular application is implemented in the ROM and thus is a permanent part of the computer. To change a program, the ROM must be changed.

There are many advantages to this type of programming approach for both the computer user and the computer manufacturer. The user is assured of the integrity of a critical program because the ROM cannot be erased inadvertently; data and instructions are protected from interference. Execution is faster because access to the ROM takes less time than read/write storage. No loading time is needed to get started. As for the computer manufacturer, he has the advantage that he can protect the programs he sells because they cannot easily be reproduced.

PARITY

To ensure a satisfactory quality of data flow between memory, the computer processor, and the I/O structure, parity check bits (Fig. 6) are used, a separate parity bit being assigned to each word. The number of bits per word is increased by one. The parity bit is computed by the memory write hardware before storing a word. When a word is fetched from storage the parity bit is recomputed, and if it does not agree with the parity bit appended to the word an interrupt is issued to indicate a

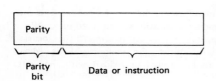

Parity
Parity bit   Data or instruction

Fig. 6. A parity bit can be computed and added to each data word to ensure the integrity of a data transfer. After a data transfer is completed the parity is recomputed, and if the result does not agree with the transmitted parity bit, an error indication is provided.

failure. The same checking process is also implemented for I/O transfers.

The parity bit may be either odd or even. Odd parity is preferred for binary systems because it ensures at least a single "one" bit for each word. Parity is computed by adding the total number of "ones" in a word. If the total is an even number and even parity is desired, the parity bit is stored as a "zero." If odd parity is specified, a "one" bit will be stored for the parity bit when the data word has an even number of "ones." In some cases more than one parity bit may be assigned to a word. For instance, each half of a word or byte can be assigned a separately computed parity bit.

When space is provided for parity bits, the size of a memory system must be increased. Each word is effectively increased in length by one or more non-information-carrying bits. The addition of this bit or bits obviously increases the cost of the system but provides an additional check on the computer hardware. Most small computers provide parity checking as an extra-cost option only.

MEMORY PROTECT

Many small computers provide memory protect features (Fig. 7), which effectively convert certain storage locations under program controlled read-only areas. This can be accomplished in a number of different ways. Memory protection capability is essential in a multiprogramming environment and is extremely useful in a real-time environment. Several programs can be executed concurrently. It is necessary to prevent user programs from interfering with the operating system and with other programs that may be resident in memory at the same time. If an instrument control program were modified or erased by another program, damage to the device operating in real-time could occur. By having a memory protect feature, real-time and control programs can be protected from overwriting each other—an occurrence that is particularly likely when program

Data or instruction

Memory protect bit = 1
　　　　Read/write

Memory protect bit = 0
　　　　Read—only

Fig. 7. A memory protect bit may be provided to convert specific memory locations into read-only. When the memory protect bit is set to "one," the location can be read only. When the memory bit is "zero," the contents can be altered or loaded with new data or instructions.

debugging activities are carried out while a system is functioning. Memory protection prevents one program from interfering with another and also protects areas that are not to be modified.

One technique for achieving memory protection is to provide an extra bit for each word. This bit can be set under program control to the "one" condition so that data can only be fetched from the location in question. The memory protect bit prevents writing into that location as long as it is in the "one" state. An attempt to store data in that location will cause a memory-protect-violation interrupt to occur. To make the location a normal read/write location, the storage protect bit is reset to "zero." Only the control program may issue memory protect status change commands.

Other techniques provide boundaries between the read-only and normal read/write areas in memory. On some computers storage is divided into pages. Each page has a separate key, set under program control. Only if the access program has the same key as the addressed page can the read or write take place to that page.

POWER FAILURE SENSING

In a real-time environment it is essential to be able to recover and begin operating again in the event of a power failure. For this reason it is good practice to design primary power sensing circuitry as an integral part of computers used for real-time applications. A potential power failure may be sensed within a fraction of cycle of the power frequency. This is sufficient time to interrupt the computer. The statuses of the program counter and all the working registers are stored when the power failure interrupt occurs. This process can be completed in a few instruction cycles. Power supplies are sequenced off in an orderly fashion to ensure that transients that may disturb the memory contents will not occur. When power is restored, the system power supplies are again turned on in a prescribed manner. The stored registers are restored, and the program resumes from where the interrupt occurred. Computers with core memories may begin immediately because the core memory contents remains intact whereas integrated circuit memories are volatile and must be reloaded before they can begin operation.

No-break primary power supplies should be used in situations where a power-off condition cannot be tolerated. These supplies are based on the use of circuits that switch over automatically to a battery powered inverter when the regular power main is interrupted.

18 Programming

The most underestimated aspect of any computer project is the programming effort. Program effectiveness determines to a large extent the success of an application. The versatility of a system is a function of the programs available; and, regardless of how good the hardware is, the system itself cannot be better than the software. Without its programs, a system is nothing more than expensive electronics. No useful work can be done without computer programs.

The role of programs and programming systems is discussed in this chapter. The functions and specifications for the component parts of the programming, as well as the overall programming system, are considered. The necessity for providing these functions is demonstrated, and their utility evaluated. The current state of programming is illustrated by citing several examples of existing software systems. These can be used as guides to what can be expected from a software system.

SOFTWARE

Two separate program packages comprise the software for a minicomputer application: systems programs and application programs. The various programs are provided by the computer manufacturer, the user, this instrument and interface manufacturers, and organizations specializing in software. It is necessary to assess the quality and appropriateness of existing programs in each of the categories listed. In one way or another these functions must be provided, and it is up to the application designer to evaluate the utility of software packages already available and to examine the feasibility of modifying existing software that performs a portion of the required tasks. Since the time and the cost of

376

making a system operational are dependent to a large extent on the availability of software, the critical part of almost every computer project is software preparation.

Systems programs and languages are usually the responsibility of the computer manufacturer. As part of the hardware package, most computer manufacturers provide systems programs and languages compilers and assemblers. Some provide these services as part of the overall package at no additional cost: other manufacturers lease or sell software, as separate optional features, in the same way as hardware features. Whether delineated as separate cost items or included in the basic computer package, the systems programs and the language compilers and assemblers are paid for by the customer.

Application programs, on the other hand, may be supplied by the computer manufacturer, the user, the instrument manufacturer, or software houses. For most new systems, the user usually writes his own application programs because programs written at other institutions do not, as a rule, exactly meet his requirements. Preparation of new programs can be accelerated by adapting logic concepts from existing similar systems.

The value of good systems programs is usually underestimated, especially by the novice computer user. Systems programs (also called operating systems, monitors, control programs, etc.) control the operation of the computer. This group of programs performs routine I/O chores, linking of program subroutines, and various utility functions. Taken individually, each of the systems programs may seem trivial and easily written. This indeed may be the case. Taken as a group, however, these programs can form a sophisticated systems package. To a large extent the ease with which the computer can be exploited depends on the comprehensiveness of the systems programs provided. The uninitiated user should be forewarned that he will have the responsibility to make up deficiencies in the operating systems supplied by the computer manufacturer. The functions supplied by a good operating system are needed for every installation. Hence, if some functions are deficient or are not part of the operating system, the user will eventually discover, much to his regret, that he must either provide the functions himself or be severely handicapped in applying the computer system. A good operating system, on the other hand, permits the user to concentrate on the application rather than on the computer.

Computer programs are most conveniently written in high-level languages, such as Fortran. Writing application programs in a high-level language has many advantages over writing them in assembler language.

Most scientists either are already familiar with Fortran or can learn the language in a relatively short time. Many more lines of code can be written and debugged in Fortran than in assembler language, in the same time frame. Also, the nature of the Fortran language makes documentation of the programs much easier. Comprehensive documentation is necessary for program update and maintenance. Almost every program is eventually used or modified by persons other than the original authors; and for a program to be useful to anyone else documentation is mandatory. As a matter of fact, even the program author, regardless of current familiarity, will barely recognize his original program after several months. In short, the value of good documentation cannot be too strongly stressed.

Nevertheless, in spite of the advantages of Fortran programming, most work is written in assembler language. The reasons are mainly economic. By their very nature most real-time experiment control systems use small binary computers, which are almost always short on main memory and do not have floating point hardware. Regardless of how efficient a Fortran compiler may be, the code it produces will almost always occupy more memory than assembler language code. In particular, it must be noted that, even though Fortran compilers have been announced for most minicomputers, the very nature of the minicomputers and the small amount of main memory make their Fortran compilers inefficient and cumbersome. Lack of floating point hardware causes Fortran programs to run much more slowly because floating point operations must be performed via subroutines, and in most Fortran calculations it is necessary to use floating point arithmetic. Assembly language programming, on the other hand, permits doing many of these operations in fixed point because the programmer keeps track of the operation and because he has full control over what is happening in the system at all times. In situations where large amounts of complex computation are required, and where major data manipulations are therefore necessary, it may be advisable to select a faster computer and/or additional memory to permit Fortran programming. Unquestionably, however, experience has demonstrated that programs can be written and debugged in Fortran much more rapidly than in assembler programs. Also, less skill is required by the programmer to obtain adequate results.

Purchase of a computer system with a minimum memory and little or no manufacturer supplied software is justifiable when a large number of systems are contemplated. In this case the user can justify the expense of preparing software for the application because the cost of the software can be allocated to a large number of systems. However, when one system or a relatively small number of systems are required, the availability of good software should be the major criterion in computer selection. Real-time CAE projects almost always involve one unique installation, and every experiment by its very nature is somewhat different. In such cases the cost of preparing software will exceed by many times any savings that might result from selecting a lower-priced computer with minimal software support from the manufacturer.

PROGRAMMING SYSTEMS

The system control or monitor consists of a package of programs that control the operations of the computer and determine the degree of sophistication of the complete system. The effectiveness of these programs determines the ease and flexibility of using the computer. The programming system contains programs that fulfill the following functions:

1. Program scheduling.
2. Program and subroutine linking.
3. Program loading.
4. Data maintenance and management.
5. Input/output scheduling and control.
6. Interrupt servicing.
7. Error handling.
8. Timer control and real-time clock.
9. Debugging aids.
10. Compilers for higher-level languages.
11. Assemblers.
12. Maintenance and diagnostic programs.
13. Foreground/background allocation algorithm.
14. Multiprogramming scheduler.
15. Program library.
16. Utilities.

This list is by no means exhaustive, but it indicates the services and functions that are included in the most comprehensive programming systems. A basic programming system will perform some of these functions. It should be apparent that many of the functions listed above are necessary for almost any real-time environment. If these function are not provided by the computer manufacturer, it will be necessary for the user to supply them.

HARDWARE REQUIREMENTS

The availability of two major hardware factors determines the feasibility of design of a sophisticated and effective operating system: main memory and auxiliary rapid access storage (Fig. 1). The quality of the programming system depends directly on these two components.

The major portion of the programming system routines and data tables resides on the auxiliary rapid access storage device. A small portion of the total system, including communications tables, interrupt handlers, and often used subroutines resides permanently in the main computer memory. Another section of main memory is devoted to transient routines that are brought into main memory from the auxiliary storage device when needed. These are overlaid one upon another as required.

The system resident areas are sometimes referred to as overhead areas. The term overhead usually has the connotation of a function that is necessary but not really productive. It should be understood, however, that all the systems programming functions must be provided in one way or another to perfrom the services needed in a real-time environment. A very efficient technique is to place them in a formal operating system. In this way all user functions can, for instance, share common subroutines and services.

As much main memory as possible should be dedicated as the systems program residence area. This optimizes the programming system functions. However, from an overall systems design consideration it becomes desirable' to minimizes permanently assigned storage areas. The more freely assignable storage available, the more flexible are the types of

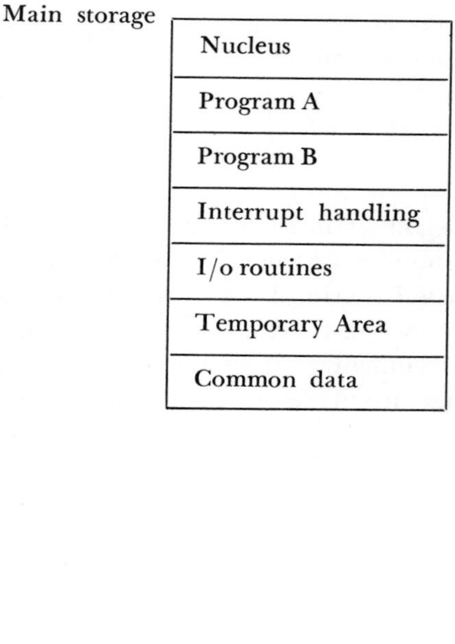

Main storage

Nucleus
Program A
Program B
Interrupt handling
I/o routines
Temporary Area
Common data

Fig. 1. Distribution of programs in main storage and auxiliary storage. Nucleus which links main storage with application programs that must reside in main storage; other programs can be stored in main or auxiliary store, depending on access time and frequency of usage.

programs that can be run. As stated previously, it is good design practice to store in main memory on a permanent basis interprogram communication tables, rapid response routines, such as interrupt servicing programs, and I/O subroutines. Other long-running-time service programs, housekeeping functions, and infrequently used programs, such as compilers, should be brought into main memory as needed. This permits the maximum possible amount of storage to be assigned as required on a transient basis.

The system library and all subroutines and service functions should be stored on a rapid access auxiliary storage device. The preferred devices for this purpose are either disks or drums. Drums are usually faster access devices than disks because they are designed to have one head per track. Disks are also available having fixed heads with one per track. In these cases the disks and drums are functionally and speedwise the same. However, most disks have retracting arms, each holding a set of heads that must be positioned over the desired track. The disk service program seeks the specified track by positioning the arm bearing the read/write head over the desired disk track. Access time on drumlike devices is determined by the latency time of the drum or disk rotation, whereas disk access times must also take into account track seek time. Head positioning times are longer than latency times. Disks cost less than fixed-head devices.

Magnetic tapes can also serve as the programming system 'storage medium. Most systems using magnetic tapes for systems residence employ short reels of tape. This technique permits relatively quick access to all sections of the tape reel. Nevertheless, the access time for tape is still longer by several orders of magnitude than for disk. Tape is inherently a sequential access device, whereas disk or drum is random access.

The prices of the various auxiliary storage devices are functions of capacity and access times. Faster-access, higher-data-capacity units are more costly than slower, limited capacity ones.

An important consideration in the selection of magnetic tape drives or disks as the system residence unit is the ease with which the medium can be changed. Interchanging the system tape or disk pack permits a complete system change, and this feature can be desirable in multiple-use installations.

The components of the control program may also be stored on paper tape or cards. However, in this case the operation is purely manual, with the operator required to handle the cards or paper tape extensively. The operator must repeatedly load data and programs, and automatic operation is not feasible. However, even in such a basic system many of the program components listed above are provided.

SCHEDULING

Program scheduling may be as simple as the initiation of a program already in storage, or it may include a search of a queue to select the highest-priority waiting program, determine if sufficient resources are free to run the program, load the program from its appropriate storage area, and begin its execution. It should be evident that initiating a program already in main memory is trivial compared to performing the alternative set of functions. In the simplest case, program scheduling involves executing a branch instruction to the location where the desired program has been stored. Scheduling the highest-priority waiting program and allocating sufficient computer resources, however, involve considerable program logic. In any system where a great deal of decision making is required or more than one task is to be run, a program scheduling algorithm is needed to select a particular program among several tasks awaiting execution. What is important to recognize is that almost every system, except the very simplest, contains a number of programs and tasks. Some decision making is required in order to select a new task when a current one terminates or runs as far as it can.

PROGRAM AND SUBROUTINE LINKING

Most programs are written as a set of subroutines for two reasons. First, it is usually more efficient to write a program as a number of independent subroutines and debug each individually. Second, it is usually easier to maintain such a system because, when one subroutine is changed or modified, the effects on the complete system can be more easily controlled. If the total job is long or complicated, a number of programmers can be employed, each being responsible for a particular group of subroutines. In many applications it is expedient to use programs and subroutines that have been written previously or have been prepared by users at other installations. On the basis of these considerations, a program is usually a collection of subroutines that have to be linked together to perform desired functions. A major use for the control program is to link a number of subroutines to comprise a full program. The linking function may be performed before program execution, or it may be necessary to do this task a number of times during execution.

Linking before execution indicates that the full program fits into main memory. The storage medium is either tape or disk in main memory image format. In this case preparation of the program from its various subroutine components has to be completed before attempting execution. When the program is called, the complete program is loaded into main memory from disk or tape and execution can begin. If the program is already in main memory, execution can begin immediately with a branch instruction.

In a system with disk or magnetic tape as the data and program storage medium, the programmer is not necessarily limited to programs of the size of main memory. Programs can be segmented and read in from disk or magnetic tape one segment at a time, as needed. As each program segment is read in, it overlays the preceding portion, which is no longer needed. This effectively allows the auxiliary storage to act as an extension of the main storage. The system loads and overlays the various segments as they are called by the segment being executed. Each program segment may in turn consist of subroutines previously linked together into main memory image format. Thus, when a segment is called, it is read into main memory. When read in, it overwrites (overlays) the previously written program or data stored in the specified main memory locations. If the program and data in the overlay locations are needed for subsequent computations, precautions must be taken so as not to destroy these contents. The simplest procedure is not to use the area. If this is not feasible, before new information is written into the area the current information is rolled out onto the auxiliary storage medium. When it is required again, it is rolled in and rewritten into the exact location where it previously resided.

Only a section of the program storage area need be reserved as a root segment that stays in main memory during the whole time that a program is being executed. Segments are brought in as needed, but they overlay a portion of the program storage. It should be noted that program overlaying, that is, writing over an area where information has previously been written, is efficient of computer time. Only one search of information to find the desired sector is required. Roll-out/roll-in procedures use large amounts of time because searches to store and restore the rolled-out information must be interspaced with the new information searches. This is recommended when absolutely necessary, or when multiple access storage devices are on line. Multiprogramming techniques can be implemented to exploit the large access times. While one program is executing, other programs can be waiting for I/O functions to be completed.

RELOCATING PROGRAMS

Programs may be stored in relocatable or nonrelocatable form. Relocatable programs can be executed from any portion of main memory, if properly loaded. Most assemblers and compilers produce object code that is in relocatable form. This means that the program is assembled so that it begins from some fixed location, usually location zero. To relocate the program to some other part of main memory, all that is necessary is to add a fixed constant, equal to the value of the desired starting location, to every address in the program subroutine. Depending on the structure of the computer instruction format, relocating may involve as simple an operation as changing the contents of a base register address, or it may require modifying all the addresses in the program. It is the function of the loading program to relocate a program to a particular region in main memory.

In some operating systems programs are relocated and stored in the desired fixed area format. In other systems programs are stored in relocatable form and are relocated to a desired region before each execution. A program stored in nonrelocatable form, that is, in main storage image format, can begin execution faster because it is stored in executable form. A program stored in relocatable form must be relocated before initiation of execution.

On the other hand, a number of advantages accrue from storing programs in relocatable form that balance the superiority in speed of initiation of main storage image format programs. When a number of main programs call the same segment, it can be advantageous to store the segment in relocatable form. In this way it is not necessary to store on auxiliary storage a separate copy of the subroutine for each main calling program. When a particular program calls a program stored in relocatable form, the system loader must, of course, be invoked to handle the relocation.

RE-ENTRANT CODE

To conserve storage and loading time, subroutines that may be called upon by several main programs can be written in re-entrant form. Each program calling a re-entrant subroutine does not disturb the code. All references and data are held in the calling routine, and access to the subroutine is usually indirect. Thus the code is not changed during any phase of execution. If the execution is suspended before completion, the code remains unchanged; another program may call for execution of the subroutine at its beginning or may resume anywhere within the routine.

Re-entrant coding is very convenient when the environment is such that several programs may be under execution in various stages at the same. This is the case in a real-time experimental situation. Several main storage resident executing programs may reference the same subroutine.

DATA MANAGEMENT

Every real-time laboratory project inevitably generates large data bases and large program libraries. These include data files and tables from previous experiments and program and subroutine libraries. In a simple system each data file or program segment may be stored as a separate strip of punched paper tape.

When rapid access to programs and large data files are required, manual selection of the desired paper tape strip is not a satisfactory solution. The programming system must quickly and automatically locate the desired subroutine or data file and bring it into memory on demand. A satisfactory system requires thorough cataloging and indexing of all the stored information so that retrieval can be direct and fast. It is then practical to obtain desired data files and program expediently.

Facilities to permanently store, delete, and update files are also required. Files and programs are usually identified and called by name or mnemonic, rather than by location. It is the function of the operating system to retrieve the desired data or program.

A difficult function that may be assigned to the data management routines is dynamic allocation of storage. The simplest method for allocating storage for a program is to assign the maximum that may be required, assuming worst case condtions. This method ensures that storage space will be available when and if needed. The technique is adequate when dealing with small files or a dedicated single-use system. When operating in a multiprogramming environment, however, this technique is obviously wasteful of storage because space for every program must be available, even if it is not operating. A more useful arrangement in this case is dynamic allocation of memory space, that is, the assigning of space to programs and data sets as needed. The techniques for relocation apply directly.

INPUT/OUTPUT

A major function of an operating system program set is the supervision of I/O functions. Input/output control involves many tedious and repetitive routines, and I/O control programs can be quite complicated because all conceivable errors and abnormal conditions must be sensed and handled. Before an I/O command is issued, the status of a device should be tested to ascertain that the device is operational and ready to perform the operation; only after successful testing of the device status should the desired I/O begin. Attention must be given to the critical timings inherent in most electromechanical I/O devices.

When an I/O function is completed, procedures for handling normal and abnormal or error conditions must be provided. A large number of details are required to ensure reliable I/O operations. Each device requires a completely different sequence of I/O instructions to initiate an operation, sustain accurate data transmission, and terminate the operation in an orderly fashion.

The subroutines needed to communicate with the standard peripheral devices offered with a computer system are provided with the basic programming package. In more sophisticated systems various techniques permit uniform device-independent calling sequences for all I/O. This capability is very convenient because when a program is prepared no special attention need be given to I/O or device assignment. At program execution time, device assignment is made, and the control program selects the correct I/O subroutines to interact with the selected peripherals. The convenience of prepared I/O subroutines can be appreciated only after one has written these routines for several devices. Even in the most sophisticated program system, I/O routines for special- purpose devices such as those that are connected in a real-time environment are the responsibility of the user. Some general routines to handle this kind of I/O may be part of the system, but the details can be ascertained only by examining the characteristics of the device.

INTERRUPT SERVICING

Most computer systems permit more than one interrupt source on an interrupt level. The advantages of designing interrupts in this manner include system considerations, economy, and convenience. When an interrupt in such a system occurs, the program must determine which device (or devices) on the particular interrupt level involved was the source of the interrupt. If more than one interrupt on the same level occurs, the interrupt service program must recognize the interrupts and provide service to each interrupting source. In the latter situation the interrupt service program must assign priorities to all of the various possible interrupts on each level and initiate programs in the order of these priorities.

The interrupt service routines communicate with the control program and other programs in main memory. The interrupt service system initiates execution of the desired interrupt program. Before initiation of this program, however, the interrupt service program must set up linkages so that an orderly exit from the interrupt program exists after the execution is completed.

Interrupt programs may be stored in main memory or on an auxiliary storage medium. An interrupt program that is already in main memory can be rapidly initiated because it is always ready to run. Interrupts that require rapid response but may occur independently of any particular program should be permanently stored in main memory; interrupts that can occur only when a particular program is executing should have their servicing programs stored along with that program.

An infrequently occurring interrupt or an interrupt that does not require urgent service can be handled on a deferred basis by queueing a program to handle the interrupt. This effectively records the occurrence of the interrupt in question. At some later time a program to handle the interrupt is fetched to main memory and executed.

In some cases interrupt programs much larger than can be stored conveniently in main memory with other programs must be executed. Many programming systems provide facilities to roll out the current program and roll in the interrupt program. It should be evident that this facility provides a great deal of programming power and flexibility. It is time consuming, however, because several searches and data transfers to the auxiliary storage device are required to store the running program, fetch the interrupt program, and finally restore the original program.

From the foregoing discussion it should be evident that a programming system that performs interrupt handling can relieve the programmer of a tedious burden. When maximum response speed to an interrupt is required, it may be necessary for the user to prepare his own interrupt handling routines. Every general-purpose interrupt handler, for example, must assume that the interrupt handling routine called will make use of the general working registers of the computer. The systems program therefore stores all the working registers and creates the return linkage before relinquishing control to the interrupt servicing program. If the user prepares the interrupt handler for a particular interrupt requiring fast response, he is of course familiar with the specific requirements and need preserve only the registers he plans to disturb during the course of the interrupt servicing. Thus, for fastest response to an interrupt, the user can prepare his own interrupt servicing routines.

ERROR HANDLING

Errors inevitably occur in any computer system. In a real-time environment with noncomputer peripheral devices attached, the incidence of errors is even more pronounced. Errors may result from a multitude of different causes, including hardware failures, dust, and transient conditions. It is possible to recover with varying degrees of success from some error conditions, whereas other error causes, such as hardware failure, may force a complete suspension of the computing operations until remedied. The functions of the error handling programs are to detect errors, both in hardware and in software, and to apply prescribed recovery procedures in order to keep the system functioning in spite of error.

The importance of keeping a real-time system functioning in the event of an error should be obvious. It would be wasteful to suspend an experiment or lose data if the error could be remedied. On the other hand, if a serious error, from which recovery was not possible, occurred, the role of the error handling programs would be to shut the system down in an orderly fashion.

An operating system that provides error handling capability allows for subroutine calls that contain abnormal ending parameters. This is especially true of I/O subroutines. When a call to a routine is made, the programmer has the option to specify a particular type of error handling procedure if an abnormal end occurs during the execution of the routine. As indicated previously, an abnormal end can result from a program inconsistency, a hardware problem, or an I/O failure.

TIMER CONTROL

In any real-time situation, it is necessary to account for clock time and to time various functions. Timer control programs can be furnished as part of the programming system to perform these functions. The timer program establishes a real-time clock so that the occurrence of events can be related to clock time. Time can be accounted for in seconds, minutes, and hours. Another function of the timer is to provide convenient timing intervals. Timer references will set up the necessary counters and call sequences to time events to the desired time or cycle rate. These intervals can be timed to a resolution measurable in microseconds, milliseconds, or seconds.

Most real-time computer systems can be obtained with built-in timers; these may be standard features or options. The timer usually provides a continuous source of precise pulses. The pulse rate is derived from a crystal controlled oscillator or the power line frequency. By counting a preset number of pulses a specific time interval can be measured. By measuring time intervals related to real time, clock time can be computed. In this case time in hours, minutes, and seconds, as well as fractions of these units, can be computed. The programming system should provide the software necessary.

A second timer function is to provide preset time intervals or to measure parameters as functions of time. The number of increments of the crystal clock needed to define a desired time interval is computed. Each clock pulse decrements the preset count. When the stored value reaches zero, the desired preset time interval has elapsed. An interrupt can be signalled to initiate a desired sequence at the expiration of the preset time. By counting clock pulses, time can be measured. Each clock pulse is used to increment or decrement a number stored in a particular memory location. By measuring the difference in the accumulated count, elapsed time between two events can be computed.

DEBUGGING AIDS

The most time consuming and tedious task in the design of a computer system is program debugging. The speed with which a program can be prepared is dependent to a large degree on the quality of the debugging aids including conventional program listings and diagnostic messages, provided by the programming system. Messages that exactly pin-point errors or inconsistencies greatly aid in debugging; traces and other on-line techniques are essential in speeding up this task.

COMPILERS

A compiler is a program that accepts as its input a high-level source language and produces as its output machine executable code. Some compilers produce an intermediate assembly langauge, whereas others produce machine language object code directly. Higher-level language programs, such as those written in Fortran, are converted into machine language object code that is executable. Fortran statements are expanded by the compiler program into a larger number of computer instructions. The fact that higher-level languages relieve the programmer of many tedious and error prone tasks constitutes another incentive to use these languages.

Fortran is the prime example of a higher-level language useful for computer aided experiment applications. It is to be expected that in the future PL/I may also be used for this purpose. Programs written in Fortran utilize a notation similar to what scientists have become accustomed to in writing equations. The language is sufficiently powerful to permit coding logical and decision making functions. Anyone interested in CAE can learn Fortran programming techniques, and, if at all possible, CAE programs should be written in Fortran. The reason for using a computer in a laboratory environment is to facilitate data collection and the control of experiments. The faster that an experiment can be implemented with the aid of the computer, the better, and Fortran programs can be written and debugged in a much shorter time than assembly language programs. In addition, it is easier to make changes and modifications to a Fortran program. Because Fortran programs are written in a readily understood form, they are to a large extent self documented. This is an extremely important consideration for future reference.

On the other hand, Fortran object programs usually are not as efficient as assembly language programming and consequently may require longer execution times or more main memory space. These limitations are especially pronounced in small binary computers that do not have floating point hardware. However, in many cases the savings in programming effort using Fortran will balance the inefficiencies of hardware utilization. Higher-level-language programming is particularly recommended when the problem program is not time limited.

When Fortran is used in a CAE environment, an additional requirement is placed on the language or the system. The Fortran language provides I/O subroutines for standard computer peripheral devices. Normal scientific Fortran programs are run on stand-alone computer systems that do not have to react to events occurring in real time outside the computer. Hence these events are not under the control of the computer. In a CAE environment, however, nonstandard I/O devices must necessarily be connected to the computer. Furthermore, these devices operate in real time and require actuation and attention at times that have no relation to the particular program phase the computer may be executing. The computer must pass data and commands at precise times, or devices may be damaged or data irretrievably lost. To satisfy the demands of this kind of environment, the standard Fortran language should be augmented with facilities that make it relatively easy to call nonstandard devices and to relate operations and events to real time. It should be possible to write interrupt servicing subroutines in Fortran.

It is possible to utilize other high-level languages besides Fortran. One such language, as mentioned earlier, is PL/I. Other languages specifically designed for data acquisition and control have been produced for special applications. Although languages with statements and formats that provide for data gathering and data reduction are useful, they are usually limited to the specific kind of job for which they were intended. It has proved difficult to produce a general-purpose data acquisition language.

ASSEMBLER LANGUAGE

In spite of the advantages of Fortran, most programs for CAE are written in assembler language. Each line of assembler language code produces one computer instruction. Hence, by writing in assembler language, the programmer has direct control over each instruction that the computer executes. It is generally possible to write more efficient programs in assembler language than in Fortran or any other higher-level language. This is particularly true in regard to minicomputers, where Fortran compilers are inherently inefficient because of storage and instruction limitations. Higher-level languages must of necessity be general purpose and must be able to handle any possible sequence of legal compiler statements. Hence the compiled object code must examine all conceivable conditions and sequences. When writing in assembler langauge, on the other hand, the programmer need consider only conditions that he considers reasonable and that may occur in the connected devices. The programmer's understanding of the problem and the environment ensures more efficient coding and computer resource utilization. It should not be forgotten, however, that Fortran programs can be written and debugged faster than programs written in assembler language.

As mentioned above, each line of assembler language code is assembled into a computer instruction. Instruction codes are interpreted by the computer hardware. The only direct machine language programming requirements are for initial loading of programs or debugging at the computer console. It is sometimes expedient to alter a few instructions by direct entry on the console switches. Assembler programs are written in a symbolic form and are translated by the assembler programs into computer recognizable codes.

Every assembler language line of code may include four definable functions: label, operation code, operand, and comments. These functions consist of mnemonics that refer to memory locations or computer instructions. The fact that the programmer can refer to a particular binary number instruction or memory location by a group of alphanumeric symbols greatly simplifies his task. Similarly, the programmer specifies instructions by alphabetic mnemonics instead of their binary equivalents. The assembler language program translates these into actual machine language codes that are in turn executable by the computer. The label, operation code, and operand of each instruction are usually referred to as "fields." The fourth field that an instruction may carry is the comment field, which contains comments that the programmer may insert in order to document the program. The assembler program ignores this field.

Most programming systems permit the programmer to use subroutine libraries with assembler language in approximately the same way as with Fortran. Sophisticated programming systems permit subroutines in different languages from that of the calling program. Assembler language main line programs may call both Fortran and assembler language subroutines, for instance. The requirement is that the program system have linking programs that can handle this job. Conventions for subroutine calls and exchange parameters must be fixed if reliable communications between programs are to be maintained.

Macros are specific commonly called functions that may be used by assembler language programs. A macro is a pseudo instruction made up of a number of instructions. It is written into assembler programs in exactly the same manner as ordinary instructions. Macros may be defined by the programmer as he prepares application and/or system programs. Macro capability speeds up program preparation by providing a convenient means for the programmer to handle frequently needed functions. It should be noted that each time a macro is specified in the program the complete sequence of instructions defining the macro is inserted by the macro assembler into the object program. A subroutine, on the other hand, is written once into the program. Every time it is referenced, an automatic transfer to the subroutine is made from the calling statement.

COMMON AREAS

Common areas provide communications between programs and subroutines. When programs are exchanged or subroutines are linked, it is necessary to pass data between programs, and common areas are specified in the memory for this purpose. An executing program may enter or alter data in the common areas assigned to it, or in those it is permitted to work with. When the program exits or calls a subroutine, the data in the common area are not altered or overwritten. Other programs are never written or overlaid into the common areas. In this way a communications link between programs segments, or even between unrelated programs, is created. All programs may have access to a common data base.

MAINTENANCE AND DIAGNOSTIC PROGRAMS

Diagnostic programs are used to exercise a computer and peripheral devices in order to ascertain correct operation and, in case of mulfunction, to locate faults. These programs are provided by the computer manufacturer. Some maintenance programs are designed to localize a fault to one of several components on a particular card. For CAE environments it is convenient and sometimes mandatory to use maintenance programs that do not require taking all experiments off line. This is particularly important for experiments that must be uninterrupted for long periods of time.

PROGRAM LIBRARY

A program library consists of all the programs and subroutines provided by the computer manufacturer, the user, and other sources. These programs may be stored on disk or magnetic tape for automatic fetching under the programming system control, or they may be entered manually by the computer operator as needed. When the program library is stored on disk or tape, a table of contents is required. The programming system prepares and maintains this table of contents, which contains the name, location, and identifying features of each stored program. All data files, system functions, and tables are also locatable via the table of contents. When a program calls a subroutine or data file, the control program enters the table of contents to locate the required item. It then initiates the transfer of the desired file to storage, or its transfer from memory to the specified sector of the auxiliary storage.

UTILITY PROGRAMS

Utility programs are a set of programs usually provided by the computer manufacturer. These programs facilitate data and file transfer between various peripheral devices and between central storage and peripheral devices.

FOREGROUND/BACKGROUND SCHEDULER

Many experiments utilize only a small percentage of the total available computer time. A major requirement is that the computer always be ready to exchange data and commands with the experiment. The computer must also reduce the data, as specified by the program. When the computer is actually collecting or reducing data from the real-time devices connected, the computer is in a wait state. On some types of experiments this condtion may exist for a high percentage of the total available time.

Many techniques have been devised to exploit the computer wait time. This time can be used to reduce the data collected from the experiment in question or from other experiments. It becomes expedient to create programming systems that can utilize the wait time to do ordinary non-real-time data reduction and processing. Fortran or assembler language programs can be compiled and debugged during these times. This feature is especially useful because it allows program preparation while actual work is being done in real time. Thus it is possible to write and debug new data acquisition programs without requiring the control computer to be shut down or disconnected from the experiment. For long running or continuous experiments this feature is extremely important. Effectively, the real-time experiment runs at the highest priority level in the foreground. The background, low-priority tasks are the non-real-time data processing or compiling jobs. It should be noted that the computer is effectively time shared between the foreground and background jobs.

Background/foreground control programs may be implemented in a number of different ways, depending on the computer. The two most common techniques utilize main memory partitioning and roll-out/roll-in. In the first case transition between foreground and background is faster, whereas in the second case main memory resources are optimized but speed of response is sacrificed. Partitioning implies that the main memory is divided into segments, with one segment devoted to foreground processing and another to background processing. Although both programs may be in main memory simultaneously, transitions are slightly more complicated than the issuance of a branch instruction. The complications involve bookkeeping functions to ensure orderly switching.

Roll-out/roll-in foreground/background switching requires more time to switch tasks but makes the overall system much more powerful. More memory is available for both tasks, and program limitations are greatly eased. When the foreground jobs are completed or when a particular job encounters a long wait or no-data period, the background program is called. When a foreground program suspends itself, it is rolled out of main memory and stored on disk. The background job is rolled in from the disk to the area where it was previously located. If no job was in progress, the next job may be started. The background job will run until a preset time expires or until an interrupt occurs. Background jobs are usually set by the control program to run for a specified time. At the end of the time the background job is suspended and a search of the real-time job queue is made. If a real-time job has been queued, it is given control; if not, control is returned to the background. An interrupt always stops a background job in order to service the interrupt. The interrupt service program may initiate a real-time job immediately, or it may queue a real-time job to be executed later. When the background job is suspended, it is rolled out of main memory and saved on a special area of disk. When it is rolled back into main memory, execution is resumed at the point of suspension. The foreground job is then rolled in from disk and its execution begins.

Foreground/background programming is an efficient way to time-share computer resources. The switching algorithm is set to always give priority to the foreground job. During wait time, however, the computer is not unproductive; background jobs are executed.

MULTIPROGRAMMING

Multiprogramming systems (Fig. 2) permit a computer to actively handle several unrelated programs. Extremely efficient computer utilization can be achieved because there is almost no wait time. Any time a running program has to wait for an event or a resource, that program's execution is suspended and control is given to another program that is ready to run. In most multiprogramming systems main memory is divided into several partitions. The number of partitions and their boundaries can be fixed, or the partitions can be dynamically allocated as needed. The result is that several programs can reside in main memory simultaneously.

A variety of algorithms have been inplemented for multiprogramming a computer with CAE capability. The philosophy of operation determines what type of algorithm is appropriate for determining central processor allocations. One approach is to assign an equal priority to all

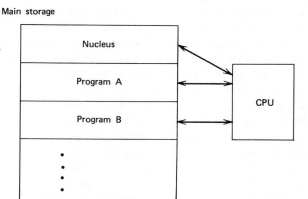

Fig. 2. In a multiprogramming environment a number of programs can reside in main storage simultaneously. Each program receives control of the central processor and executes until a higher-priority program requests service or until the program in progress cannot proceed any further.

programs; another is to assign priorities based on precedence, running time, or some other criterion. An equal-priority scheme is suited to an environment in which each user is independent and considers the central computer a general-purpose CAE service facility. Assigning priorities on the basis of overall facility considerations has the advantage of making the computer operation more efficient and more responsive because the system is subject to rational discretionary management. The computer is programmed so that service requests are handled in an optium manner for the particular installation. For instance, short service requirements may be given higher priority than long running subroutines that can wait for service. An equal-priority scheme usually implies time slicing, whereby each active program is given a specified time period on the CPU. When the preselected time slice expires, the next sequential active job receives its service turn.

Systems having several levels of priority have been written. In those situations, equal time slices can be given to high-priority jobs. These slices are usually reserved for real-time data acquisition and control program phases, which ordinarily are short subroutines. Processing and reduction of the acquired data are run as lower-priority jobs. Several different algorithms can be designed to apportion computer resources among the various priority elevels. When time remains, background batch type processing jobs can be executed.

SYSTEM GENERATION

It would be impossible to write a programming system that would fit every computer configuration. Hence it is necessary to tailor the programming system to the particular computer configuration and installation environment. System generation consists of a group of programs that select subroutines from the full program set and build a software system suited to the particular environment. Device names and priorities are assigned at this time. System generation for a sophisticated programming system can become an involved and lengthy process.

Along with the system generation program, a system update program is needed to make the inevitable additions and alternations to the system after the basic system generation has been completed. It is desirable to update rather than rebuild the system for each change.

19 CAMAC Interfaces

No standard, generally accepted technique for interfacing to computers exists. Many special-purpose designs have been implemented for specific applications by some companies and research organizations. However, no standard interface that permits direct interfacing between a variety of instruments and devices and the more popular minicomputers is available. Generally, to interface a particular instrument to a computer requires that a special design be undertaken. The user can implement the interface in several ways: (1) design and build the interface himself, (2) contract for the interface through an electronics firm, (3) buy the interface from the instrument manufacturer with the instrumentation, or (4) buy the interface from the computer manufacturer with the computer. It would be highly desirable if a standard set of components existed which permitted rapid configuration of interfaces between an experiment and a computer without the need for special designs. CAMAC is one of the techniques developed to answer this requirement.

INTERFACE PROCUREMENT

Design of interfaces by the user requires either that he become intimately familiar with digital electronics or that he have access to a staff that includes electronics specialists. If the experimenter does the interface work, his research will be delayed because he must master a new technology. Unless absolutely necessary, an experimenter should devote his attention to his research specialty and leave interface design to experienced digital engineers. Since it is certain that computer assisted experimentation will become even more important in the design of experiments, research departments should consider including experienced digital engineers or their staff. Groups with experienced digital technologists at their service will be in the best position to exploit this powerful tool effectively.

Contracting through an external group or company can be an acceptable way to handle interface design and execution. When a one-time computer interface design is necessary, this approach eliminates the need to hire staff and purchase test instruments and supplies necessary for design and fabrication of interfaces. However, this approach does not relieve the experimenter of the responsibility of carefully specifying the interface needed. For this reason the user must have a basic understanding of the computer and its interaction with the instruments that are to be connected to it. When dealing with an external organization through a contractual arrangement, the experimenter's responsibility to define the nature of the interface exactly is even greater than when an in-house effort is undertaken because his interactions with the executors of the interface are limited by time and distance. When dealing with local engineering groups, proximity and familiarity can account for many details that would otherwise have to be specified. For these reasons, although contracting is expedient if no alternative is available, in-house interface design capability is preferable.

Many modern instruments are available with interfaces that the instrument manufacturer has developed and made available. Usually the interface is designed for use with a particular computer that does the desired tasks. This approach is ideal when the package consisting of the instrument, the interface, the computer, and the software performs the desired job. Unfortunately, in many cases the prepared package is not quite what the experimenter requires, and changes are necessary. The packaged configuration may not exactly fit the needs of the experimenter, or the software may not be appropriate. The user may already have a minicomputer different from the one for which the instrument manufacturer designed the interface. In short, for a variety of reasons—all of which should be examined by the user—the instrument manufacturer's interface package may be inappropriate. If the differences are not excessive, the user can make the needed modifications through his own staff. In some cases the instrument manufacturer will do the necessary tailoring; however, this is the exception. In this connection it should be recognized that the instrument manufacturer is primarily interested in selling instruments—his product, and he has added instruments interfaced to computers to his product line in order to enable him to meet the general market requirement for computer controlled instruments. Also, a higher-quality instrument system results when the computer and the instrument are offered as an integrated hardware-software package.

Many computer manufacturers offer packages consisting of instruments interfaced to their computers. If a particular package meets the experimenter's needs, this is a viable solution. The computer manufacturer has designed these packages as a means of encouraging the sale of computers. Most computer manufacturers, however, are reluctant to commit their engineering resources to the design of special interfaces. They prefer to use their engineers to design computers and peripherals—their primary business activity. Special interface design is of interest only when a large number of computer sales are involved. When the volume is sufficient, it is worthwhile to devote engineering resources to special interface design.

CAMAC STANDARDS

A definite need exists for rapidly implementing a wide variety of instrument-computer interfaces using standard, readily available modules. Such a system should make the design of even one or two special interfaces a simple, straightforward task. A great amount of effort has been invested in developing such a system of modules. Many laboratories and companies have developed such systems for their own internal use. The problem with all private standards is that, since each group or organization is independent, changes and modifications can be made at any time without prior notice or consultation. Hence future compatibility is never assured. No generally recognized reproducible standard has been acceptable until very recently. The CAMAC system, whereby a wide variety of compatible interface modules from a number of manufacturers can be used to interface many different devices to a wide variety of computers, is such a system. In principle it should be possible to put together complete interfaces using standard CAMAC modules. No special wiring is needed to implement a CAMAC interface; one need only plug the modules into a CAMAC crate.

CAMAC standards for modular interfaces were developed by the European Standard of Nuclear Electronics (ESONE) Committee and have been adopted by many American and European nuclear laboratories. The outstanding characteristic of these standards is a highway for the transfer of digital data and control information. Any CAMAC compatible module may be plugged into the highway, and it will operate without additional design or wiring.

The need for a new instrumentation standard, with a data transfer scheme independent of computer type as its central feature, was brought to the notice of the ESONE Committee in 1966. As a result, a collaborative study was instituted and working groups were established to develop mechanical and electrical standards for a system directed toward instrumentation for data acquisition and control. CAMAC is constructed with closely packed integrated circuit devices mounted on printed circuit boards, and with few manually operated controls.

The CAMAC specification defines construction standards for crates and plug-in units, and electrical and logical standards for digital signals. The mandatory sections of these standards are presented in sufficient detail to ensure mechanical and electrical compatibility between equipment from different sources. Further detail is given in the form of recommendations which allow some freedom of interpretation.

The CAMAC specifications may be used without license or charge by any organization or manufacturer. There is widespread interest by laboratories and manufacturers in Europe and the United States. Crates and a rapidly expanding range of plug-in units are available from several commercial sources. The standards simplify the task of designing and commissioning instrumentation systems for measurement and control,and also permit manufacturers to sell their products to a wider market than has hitherto been possible. Although developed by representatives of nuclear laboratories, CAMAC was designed for use in any field of digital instrumentation.

MECHANICAL FEATURES

CAMAC specifies the mechanical features of the CAMAC crate and CAMAC module. When these specifications are met, mechanical interchangeability among CAMAC units of different types and different manufacturers is assured.

THE CRATE

The crate (Fig. 1) has up to 25 mounting positions or stations, each having upper and lower guides for the runners of a plug-in unit, and an 86-way socket giving access to a multiwire highway called the CAMAC Dataway. The crate is defined as a 19-in. rack mounting unit with a minimum height of 5U ($8\frac{3}{4}$ in.), but this height may be increased as necessary (for example, to include a ventilation aperture). The guides

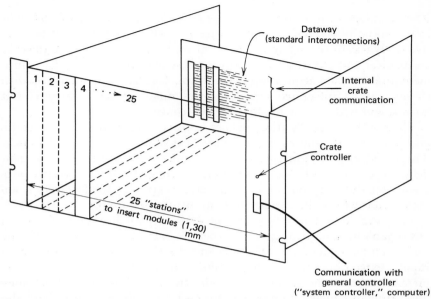

Fig. 1. A diagram of a CAMAC standard crate. The crate contains sufficient slots for 25 CAMAC modules and also has a built-in power supply and ventilators for cooling.

are on a pitch of 17.2 mm, which defines the minimum width of the plug-in unit.

PLUG-IN UNITS

A plug-in unit consists basically of a vertical card with offset runners, an 86-way plug to suit the Dataway connector (Fig. 2), and a front panel. A typical unit has a printed circuit card which includes 86 printed plug contacts.

Units may occupy as many stations as they require, although they normally need access to the Dataway at only one station. CAMAC modules are 306 mm in depth and 200 mm in width.

DATAWAY

The CAMAC Dataway is the interconnection path for CAMAC logic and control signals. CAMAC compatible modules (Fig. 3) may be plugged

Title	Designation	Pins	Use at a Module
Command			
Station number	N	1	Selects the module (individual line from control station).
Subaddress	A1, 2, 4, 8	4	Selects a section of the module.
Function	F1, 2, 4, 8, 16	5	Defines the function to be performed in the module.
Timing			
Strobe 1	S1	1	Controls first phase of operation (Dataway signals must not change).
Strobe 2	S2	1	Controls second phase (Dataway signals may change).
Data			
Write	W1–W24	24	Bring information to the module.
Read	R1–R24	24	Take information from the module.
Status			
Look-at-me	L	4	Indicates request for service (individual line to control station).
Response	Q	1	Indicates status of feature selected by command.
Busy	B	1	Indicates that a Dataway operation is in progress.
Common Controls			Operate on all features connected to them, no command required.
Initialize	Z	1	Sets module to a defined state (accompanied by S2 and B).
Inhibit	I	1	Disables features for duration of signal.
Clear	C	1	Clears registers (accompanied by S2 and B).
Reserved			
Reserved bus	X	1	Reserved for future allocation.
Private wiring			
Patch points	P1–P5	5	Free for unspecified interconnections. No Dataway lines.
Power		14	±24 V, ±6 V, ±12 V, $+200$ V, AC, 0 V
Total		86	

Fig. 2. The allocation of CAMAC connector pins.

into any position of the CAMAC crate. Adherence to the CAMAC Dataway specification ensures that a CAMAC module can be connected anywhere within the crate, as are other electrically compatible CAMAC modules.

The Dataway (Fig. 4) is a standardized highway which links the 86-way sockets at all stations within the crate. The right hand station has a special function as the "control station," but the remaining "normal stations" are identical. The Dataway consists mainly of bus lines joining corresponding pins of the sockets at all stations, on all normal stations, together with two individual lines between the socket of each normal station and that of the control station. These lines are used to identify the station and to permit the station to call attention to itself when necessary.

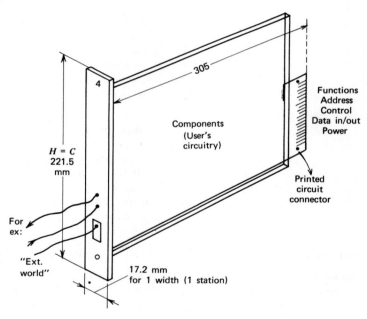

Fig. 3. A mechanical schematic of a CAMAC module. A CAMAC module may fit into one or more CAMAC crate slots, depending on its thickness and the number of connector pins needed.

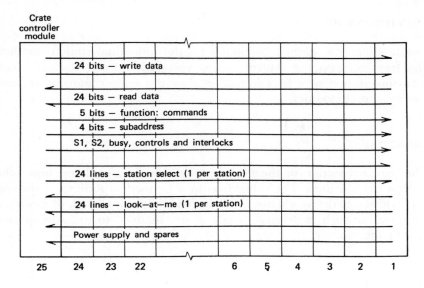

Fig. 4. CAMAC data highway connections. All lines except stations select and look-at-me are connected in parallel to all stations positions. A unique station select and look-at-me pair is connected between each stations and the crate controller module.

MODULES AND CONTROLLERS

A data transfer takes place as a defined sequence of events constituting a Dataway operation and involves at least two plug-in units, one of which acts as a "controller" and the other as a "controlled module."

USE OF DATAWAY LINES

Each line in the Dataway has a defined use. There are 24 read data lines for transfers from modules to the controller, 24 write data lines for transfers from the controller to modules, command lines for selecting the required data transfer or other operation, and lines to distribute power supplies. The Dataway includes power lines for mandatory supplies at +24, +6, −6, and −24 V. Pins are reserved for additional power supplies as needed.

STATION NUMBER

The modules are selected by signals on the individual station number (N) lines between the control station and each normal station. More than one station may be selected, so that the same command can be sent to several modules.

SUBADDRESS

The required section of the module is selected by signals on four subaddress (A) bus lines. The subaddress may be used to indicate a specific data register, to define a status condition which is to be tested, or to direct an operation such as "clear," "enable," or "disable" to the appropriate part of the module.

FUNCTION

The operation is defined by signals on five function (F) lines. Sixteen of the possible 32 functions are fully specified (4 for read operations, 4 for write operations, and 8 for operations that do not use the read or write line). The functions are grouped so that simple decoding in the controller can determine, if necessary, the required direction of data transfer. Of the remaining functions, 8 are reserved for future extensions of the standard operations, and 8 are available to meet the special needs of units or of local practice.

DATAWAY OPERATION

During a Dataway operation (Fig. 5) the controller generates command signals on the subaddress and function bus lines and on one or more individual station number lines. The command signals are accompanied by a signal on the busy (B) bus line, which is available at all stations to indicate that a Dataway operation is in progress.

If the addressed module recognizes a read command calling for a data transfer to the controller, it establishes data signals on the read bus lines. If the controller recognizes a write command calling for a data transfer to a module, it establishes data signals on the write bus lines. In addition, the module may transmit one bit of status information on the response (Q) bus line.

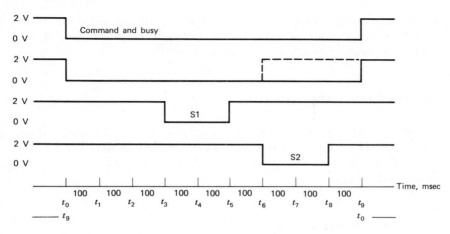

Fig. 5. The sequence of operation pulses on the CAMAC bus.

After allowing time for the data signals to become established, the controller generates two timing signals, strobes S1 and S2, in sequence on separate bus lines. The first strobe, S1, is used by the addressed module to take data from the Dataway in a write operation, or by the controller to take from the Dataway in a read operation and to accept the status information from the Q line. The two strobes may also initiate other actions in the controller and modules, but only S2 can initiate actions that change the status of signals on the Dataway.

The minimum time for a complete Dataway operation is 1 μsec. During an initial period of at least 400 nsec, the command signals are established, the module responds to the command, and data signals are established. Then, during a period of at least 300 nsec, the S1 strobe signal is generated, maintained for at least 100 nsec, and removed. Similarly, the S2 strobe signal is generated during a second period of at least 300 nsec. Although controllers are permitted to extend this cycle or any part of it, the Dataway and modules must be capable of operating with the minimum time periods corresponding to the 1-μsec cycle.

LOOK-AT-ME SIGNALS

Each station has an individual look-at-me (L) line to the control station. Whenever the busy signal is absent, any module may generate a signal on its L line to demand attention. The controller has access to all the

L lines at the control station and may typically initiate a demand to the computer for a program interrupt or a direct access transfer, or may start a hardware controlled sequence of operations.

COMMON CONTROL SIGNALS

Three common control signals are available at all stations, without requiring addressing by a command. They are used to initialize all units (Z) after switch-on, to clear data registers (C), and to inhibit features such as data taking (I).

DATAWAY SIGNAL LEVELS

The signal levels specified are compatible with commonly available DTL and TTL integrated circuit devices. All signals are generated from intrinsic OR outputs, typically free collectors, and are specified with negative logic to facilitate this. Hence the low-level, near-ground potential represents logic "one," and the high-level potential, near +3.5 V, represents logic "zero." Each Dataway line is returned to the "zero" state by a source of current from a positive potential. This "pull-up current" source is generally located in the controller.

The loading and drive capability of most Dataway lines corresponds to one of two main classes. Lines similar to the read lines may be driven by any module but are loaded only by the input gates of the controller. To allow the features of the controller to be divided between several plug-in units, the maximum signal loading is defined as four input gates. The drive capability demanded for signal outputs from modules can thus be achieved by inexpensive integrated circuit devices. Lines similar to write lines may be driven by a few outputs from the controller but can be loaded by signal inputs into every module. Only the controller needs this greater signal driving capability.

EXTERNAL DIGITAL SIGNALS

Two types of signals are recommended for use on coaxial or multiway connectors mounted on the front panel of plug-in units or on the rear of units above the Dataway connector. The first type is similar to Dataway signals, so that it can be derived from, and accepted by, DTL and

TTL integrated circuits. Since it is transmitted over unterminated cables, it is not suitable for fast signals. The second type is similar to the NIM 50-Ω terminated signals, and is intended for more demanding situations and for interconnections with many existing equipments that use the "16 mA into 50 Ω" signal standard.

AVAILABILITY

A large number of electronics instrument manufacturers produce and market a wide variety of CAMAC modules. A partial listing of the available modules appears below. Additional types are continuously being announced.

Controller for Hewlett Packard 2114/2115/2116 computers.
Controller for DEC PDP-8, PDP-11, PDP-15 computers.
Controller for Varian 620 computers.
Controller for Honeywell PDP-516 computer.
Controller for manual operation and test.
Controller for NOVA computer.
Controller for start-stop communications.
Controller for additional crates.
Parallel input registers.
Parallel input gates.
Manual data input.
Data storage modules.
Parallel output modules.
Display modules.
Peripheral input/output.
Multiplexers.
Code converters.
Analog to digital converters.
Digital to analog converters.
Time to digital converters.
Pulse generators and clocks.
Logic function modules.
Delay and attentuator modules.

CAMAC SUMMARIZED

Although CAMAC was developed to answer the specific problems involved in interfacing instruments used in nuclear experiments to computers, there is no question of the applicability of CAMAC concepts and hardware to experimental work in other fields where computer-instrument connections are to be made. CAMAC is an effective way to rapidly interface experiments to computers. When CAMAC is appropriate for a particular application, the user can concentrate on the experiment and need not be concerned with the details of interface design; a large amount of ordinary work can be avoided because standard, available modules are used. CAMAC compatible modules from any manufacturer are usable in a CAMAC system. Hence the user is free to select all modules from one vendor, or to mix in a single system the most appropriate modules from a number of vendors.

CAMAC hardware is more expensive than comparable hardware using ordinary functional logic modules. The reason is apparent after inspecting the CAMAC specifications, which are comprehensive. CAMAC has many built-in features that may not be needed by most users. This is the price one must pay for using a set of components that were designed with a general-purpose interface in mind. However, in most cases the savings in design time and debugging effort more than compensate for the increased hardware costs.

A wide variety of CAMAC compatible modules are available from a number of different manufacturers. In some cases different vendors act as second sources for one another. In other cases specific vendors make unique CAMAC modules. In spite of the relatively high price of CAMAC components, the actual cost to the user may not be more (indeed, is probably less) than the cost of a comparable special design of the interface because substantial savings in design time and calendar time are achieved through the use of CAMAC modules. As stated above, the time savings can more than compensate for the costs of any extra components. Moreover, it is to be expected that CAMAC components will become less expensive as competition between the growing number of suppliers increases and as CAMAC gains acceptance in fields other than nuclear physics.

20   Further Reading

The amount of information available on computer aided experimentation and closely related subjects is immense. However, there are no concentrated sources that deal with these topics exclusively. The information is widely scattered among many professional journals and trade magazines. Another relevant factor is the product technology orientation of the field; laboratories and manufacturers are continuously improving their designs and hence frequently introduce new or updated versions of their equipment.

Gaining further familiarity and insight into minicomputers and the real-time devices that are connected to them is a task that involves consulting a great many different journals and publications. A major source of information is the manufacturers of computer systems, instrumentation, and peripheral devices. They are prolific producers of literature describing new applications for their products, as well as manuals and specifications concerning these products. One of the most effective ways to market highly technical equipment is by reference to successful installations.

Listed below are a number of sources of information. The reader is referred to professional journals and trade magazines that publish articles in this field. Not included are journals that are highly theoretical or are directed to electronics and component designers. Some manufacturers of equipment and instrumentation who publish large quantities of quality technical literature are also listed. Following some of the publications on a regular basis is one of the most effective ways of keeping abreast of what is available and how it is being practically applied.

A. PERIODICALS: BROAD COVERAGE

1. *CAMAC Bulletin*
   ESONE Committee
   JRC Euratom
   I-21020 Ispra, Italy
2. *Computer*
   Magazine of IEEE Computer Society
   9017 Reseda Blvd. No. 212
   Northridge, Calif. 91324
3. *Computer Design*
   221 Baker Ave.
   Concord, Mass. 01742
4. *Electronic Design*
   Hayden Publishing Co.
   850 Third Ave.
   New York, N.Y. 10022
5. *Electronics*
   McGraw-Hill Bldg.
   330 W. 42 St.
   New York, N.Y. 10036
6. *Industrial Research*
   Beverly Shores, Ind. 46301
7. *Information Display*
   825 S. Barrington Ave.
   Los Angeles, Calif. 90049
8. *Instruments & Control Systems*
   56 Chestnut St.
   Philadelphia, Pa. 19139
9. *Instrumentation Technology*
   Instrument Society of America
   400 Stanwix Ave.
   Pittsburgh, Pa. 15222
10. *National Computer Conference Proceedings*
    AFIPS Press
    210 Summit Ave.
    Montvale, N.J. 07645

B. LIFE SCIENCES APPLICATIONS

1. *Bio-Medical Computing*
   Applied Science Publishers, Inc.

Ripple Road
Barking Essex, England
2. *Biomedical Engineering*
United Trade Press
42/43 Gerrard St.
London WIV 7LP, England
3. *Computers & Biomedical Research*
Academic Press, Inc.
111 Fifth Ave.
New York, N.Y. 10003
4. *Computers in Biology & Medicine*
Pergamon Press
Headington Hill Hall
Oxford OX3 OBW, England
5. *IEEE Transactions on Biomedical Engineering*
Institute of Electrical & Electronics Engineers
345 E. 47 St.
New York, N.Y. 10017
6. *Medical & Biological Engineering*
Peter Peregrinus Ltd.
P.O. Box 8, Southgate House
Stevenage, Herts SG1 1HQ, England
7. *Medical Research Engineering*
Woods Road
Great Notch, N.J. 07424

C. CHEMISTRY SCIENCES APPLICATIONS

1. *Analytic Chemistry*
American Chemical Society
1155 16 St., N.W.
Washington, D.C. 20036
2. *Chemical Engineering*
McGraw-Hill Bldg.
330 W. 42 St.
New York, N.Y. 10036
3. *Chemical Instrumentation*
Marcel Dekker, Inc.
95 Madison Ave.
New York, N.Y. 10016

4. *Industrial & Engineering Chemistry*
   American Chemical Society
   1155 16 St., NW.
   Washington, D.C. 20036
5. *International Chemical Engineering*
   American Institute of Chemical Engineers
   345 E. 47 St.
   New York, N.Y. 10017
6. *Journal of Applied Crystallography*
   Minksgaard International Booksellers
   35 Norre Sogade
   DK 1370 Copenhagen, Denmark
7. *Nuclear Instrumentation and Methods*
   North Holland Publishing Co.
   P.O. Box 3489
   Amsterdam-C, Netherlands

D. COMMERCIAL LITERATURE: BROAD COVERAGE

1. Control Data Corp.
   8100 34 Ave. S.
   Minneapolis, Minn. 55440
2. Data General Corp.
   Route 9
   Southboro, Mass. 01772
3. Digital Equipment Corp.
   146 Main St.
   Maynard, Mass. 90733
4. Fairchild Semiconductor
   464 Ellis St.
   Mountain View, Calif. 94040
5. Hewlett-Packard
   1501 Page Mill Road
   Palo Alto, Calif. 94304
6. Honeywell Information Systems
   60 Walnut St.
   Wellesley Hills, Mass. 02181
7. Intel Corp.
   3065 Bowers Road
   Santa Clara, Calif. 95051

8. Interdata
   2 Crescent Place
   Oceanport, N.J. 07757
9. IBM
   1133 Westchester Ave.
   White Plains, N.Y. 10604
10. Motorola Semiconductor
    5005 E. McDowell Road
    Phoenix, Ariz. 85008
11. National Semiconductor
    2900 Semicon Drive
    Santa Clara, Calif. 95051
12. Raytheon Computer
    2700 S. Fairview St.
    Santa Ana, Calif. 92704
13. Varian Data Machines
    2722 Mickelson Drive
    Irvine, Calif. 92664
14. Xerox Data Systems
    701 S. Aviation
    El Segundo, Calif. 90245

E. COMMERCIAL LITERATURE: ANALOG FRONT END DEVICES

1. Analog Devices
   221 Fifth St.
   Cambridge, Mass. 02142
2. Analogic Corp.
   Audubon Road
   Wakefield, Mass. 01880
3. Burr Brown Research Corp.
   6730 S. Tucson Blvd.
   Tucson, Ariz. 85706
4. Cohu Electronics
   P.O. Box 623
   San Diego, Calif 92112
5. John Fluke Co.
   P.O. Box 7428
   Seattle, Wash. 98133

6. Non-Linear Systems
   P.O. Box N
   Del Mar, Calif. 92014

7. Preston Scientific
   805 E. Cerritos Ave.
   Anaheim, Calif. 92805

8. Teledyne Philbrick Nexus
   Allied Drive at Route 128
   Dedham, Mass. 02026

9. Vidar Corp.
   77 Ortega Ave.
   Mountain View, Calif. 94040

10. Zeltex
    1000 Chalonar Road
    Concord, Calif. 94520

F. COMMERCIAL LITERATURE: COMMUNICATIONS

1. Anderson Jacobson
   1065 Morse Ave.
   Sunnyvale, Calif. 94086

2. Codex Corp.
   15 Riverdale Ave.
   Newton, Mass. 02195

3. Collins Radio
   19700 Jamboree Blvd.
   Newport Beach, Calif. 92663

4. Lenkurt Electric
   1105 County Road
   San Carlos, Calif. 94070

5. Milgo Electronic Corp.
   7620 NW. 36 St.
   Miami, Florida 33147

6. Penril Data Communications
   960 Thomas Ave.
   Rockville, Md. 20852

7. Singer Tele Signal Corp.
   250 Crossway Drive
   Woodbury, N.Y. 11797

8. Quindar
   60 Fadem Road
   Springfield, N.J. 07081

G. COMMERCIAL LITERATURE: TERMINALS

1. Adage
   1079 Commonwealth Ave.
   Boston, Mass. 02109
2. Bunker Ramo Corp.
   445 Fairfield Ave.
   Stamford, Conn. 06904
3. Cognitronics
   333 Bedford Road
   Mt. Kisco, N.Y. 10549
4. Computek
   143 Albany St.
   Cambridge, Mass. 02139
5. Computer Display
   223 Crescent St.
   Waltham, Mass. 02154
6. Computer Terminal
   9725 Datapoint Drive
   San Antonio, Tex. 78229
7. Conrac
   330 Madison Ave.
   New York, N.Y. 10017
8. Imlac
   296 Newton St.
   Waltham, Mass. 02154
9. Information Display
   333 N. Bedford Road
   Mt. Kisco, N.Y. 10549
10. Photophysics
    1601 Stierlin Road
    Mountain View, Calif. 94040
11. Teletype Corp.
    5555 W. Touhy Ave.
    Skokie, Ill. 60076

12. Tektronix
    P.O. Box 500
    Beaverton, Ore. 97005

H. COMMERCIAL LITERATURE: DATA ACQUISITION SYSTEMS

1. Biomation
   10411 Bubb Road
   Cupertine, Calif. 95014
2. Computer Products
   P.O. Box 23849
   Fort Lauderdale, Fla. 33307
3. Computer Labs
   1109 S. Chapman
   Greensboro, N.C. 27403
4. Datacom
   40 Lincoln Drive
   Fort Walton Beach, Fla. 32548
5. Data Control Systems
   Commerce Drive
   Danbury, Conn. 06810
6. EMR Telemetry
   Box 3041
   Sarasota, Fla. 33578
7. Metric Systems
   736 N. Beal St.
   Fort Walton Beach, Fla. 32548
8. Vidar
   77 Ortega Ave.
   Mountain View, Calif. 94040

Index